Arab Spring

Reflections on Political Changes in the Arab World and its Future

Arab Spring

Reflections on Political Changes in the Arab World and its Future

Edited by

Anwar Alam
Professor, Department of International Relations,
Zirve University, Gaziantep, Turkey

New Century Publications
New Delhi, India

NEW CENTURY PUBLICATIONS
4800/24, Bharat Ram Road,
Ansari Road, Daryaganj,
New Delhi - 110 002 (India)

Tel.: 011-2324 7798, 4358 7398, 6539 6605
Fax: 011-4101 7798
E-mail: indiatax@vsnl.com • info@newcenturypublications.com
www.newcenturypublications.com

Editorial office:
LG–7, Aakarshan Bhawan,
4754-57/23, Ansari Road, Daryaganj,
New Delhi – 110 002

Tel.: 011-4356 0919

First Published: **July 2014**

ISBN: **978-81-7708-395-8**

Published by New Century Publications and printed at Salasar Imaging Systems, New Delhi.

Designs: Patch Creative Unit, New Delhi.

PRINTED IN INDIA

About the Book

The book, containing 19 scholarly papers grouped into five theme parts, broadly deals with social-political forces, ideas, discourses and events that have shaped the emergence of Arab Spring and attempts to delineate its broad meanings and contours. It examines the contentious issue of relationship between Islamism, nation-state and democracy in the context of Arab world and discusses the strengths, weaknesses, limitations and prospects of Arab Spring for democratic transformation of Arab societies. In addition, the book also analyzes the role of major international powers as well as regional implications of Arab Spring.

About the Editor

Anwar Alam is presently Professor, Department of International Relations, Zirve University, Gaziantep, Turkey. He has served as a Lecturer in the Department of Political Science, Aligarh Muslim University (AMU), and Assistant and Associate Professor at the Centre for West Asian and African Studies, School of International Studies, Jawaharlal Nehru University (JNU), New Delhi. He was awarded the ICSSR Doctoral Fellowship (1991), International Visitor Programme (Islamic) Scholarship, USA, (2002), Indo-French Social Scientist Exchange Programme Fellowship (2003, 2010) and Alexandor Von Humboldt Post-Doctoral Fellowship (2004-06).

He was visiting fellow at Maison des Sciences de l'Homme (MSH), Paris, France, (March-April, 2005), Centre for Citizenship and Ethnicity, Department of Sociology, University of Bristol, Bristol, UK, (May-June, 2005) and International Institute for the Study of Islam in the Modern World (ISIM), Leiden, Netherlands, (July-August, 2005). He was a visiting professor at Fatih University, Istanbul, Turkey (2010-2011).

He has authored/edited 5 books: *Religion and State: A Comparative Study of Contemporary Egypt, Iran and Saudi Arabia* (1998); *India and West Asia in the Era of Globalisation* (2008); *Iran and Post-9/11 World Order* (2009); *Contemporary West Asia* (2010) and *India, Global Powers and West Asia* (2011). Besides, he has contributed several articles in national and international referred journals and chapters in edited books. His areas of research interest include international politics, political theory, religion and politics, political Islam, globalization and Muslim society.

Contents

Part III: Social Media and Arab Spring

Part IV: Islam and Arab Spring

Part V: Arab Spring: Global Responses and Regional Implications

Contributors

Abdulkhalek Al-Zamli holds a Ph.D. degree in West Asian Studies from Jamia Millia University, New Delhi. He was First Secretary, Embassy of the State of Palestine, New Delhi (2003-09). He is currently Financial Security Advisor, Industrial Alliance Company, Montreal.

Ahmad Mohamed Ahmad Abdel Rahman is currently Professor and Head, Department of Urdu, Faculty of Languages and Translation, Al-Azhar University, Cairo, Egypt. He spent 7 years in India from 1987 to 1994 where he earned his M.A, M.Phil. and Ph.D. degrees in Urdu from Delhi University. In 2010, he earned the Career Certificate in Teaching Arabic as a Foreign Language from the American University in Cairo. Since then he has also been teaching Arabic as a foreign language at Al-Azhar's Faculty of Islamic Studies for Overseas Students. He is the general secretary of the Egypt-India Friendship Association.

A.K. Pasha is a Professor at Centre for West Asian Studies, School of International Studies, Jawaharlal Nehru University (JNU), New Delhi where he has served as Chairman and Director Gulf Studies Programme. He has served as Director, Maulana Azad Centre for Indian Culture, Cairo Egypt. He holds MA degrees in Middle Eastern Studies and Political Science from Mysore University, Karnataka; M.Phil. and Ph.D. in international studies from JNU. He has taught at Aligarh Muslim University and has been Research Fellow at Faculty of Economics and Political Science, Cairo University, Egypt. He is associated with the Gulf Research Centre, UAE. He was a Fulbright Scholar at St. Cloud State University, Minnesoto, USA. He has large number of publications to his credit.

Azzedine Layachi is Professor of Government and Politics at St. John's University, New York, US. He holds a Master's Degree and a Ph.D. in International Relations from New York University. He is member of the Executive Board of the American Institute of Maghribi Studies (AIMS) and of the Advisory Board of the Maghreb Center (Washington, D.C.). He is former President of the

Northeastern Political Science Association and of the New York State Political Science Association. He is the author of several books, journal articles and book chapters. His research interests include economic development, political change, political Islam, Middle Eastern and African politics.

Chintamani Mahapatra is Professor of American Studies and is currently Chairperson of Centre for Canadian, US and Latin American Studies at School of International Studies, Jawaharlal Nehru University (JNU), New Delhi. Recently, he was Tagore Chair Professor at the Yunnan University, China. He has undertaken research at American National Archives, Truman Library, Eisenhower Library, Kennedy Library, and LBJ Library of the USA; and various depositories in the UK, such as London School of Economics, School of Oriental and African Studies, and British National Public Record Office. Prof. Mahapatra was a Fulbright Fellow at University of Delaware; Salzburg Seminar Fellow, Austria; Visiting Fellow at Australian Defence Studies Center, Canberra; Foreign Policy Fellow at School of Public Affairs, University of Maryland; and Commonwealth Scholar at School of Oriental and African Studies, University of London.

Fazzur Rahman has done his M.Phil. and Ph.D. in West Asian Studies from School of International Studies, Jawaharlal Nehru University (JNU), New Delhi. Presently, he is associated with Indian Council of World Affairs (ICWA) as a Research Fellow. He is the author of the book titled "Concept of Islamic State: From the Caliphate to Twentieth Century: Pre-Ikhwan and Post-Ikhwan Phase", published by Darul-Kitab-Ilmi, Beirut, Lebanon, 2010.

Gulshan Dietl is currently an ICSSR Senior Fellow affiliated to the Institute for Defence Studies and Analyses (IDSA), New Delhi. She retired as a Professor at the School of International Studies, Jawaharlal Nehru University (JNU), New Delhi, where she also served as the Director of the Gulf Studies Programme. She was a Fulbright Scholar-in-Residence at the Mount Saint Mary College, Newburgh, New York (1993-94), a Guest Research Fellow at the Copenhagen Peace Research Institute (1998-99), a Visiting Professor at the University of Kashmir (2004), a Visiting Professor at the Foundation de la Maison des Sciences de l'Homme, Paris

(2008), a Visiting Professor at the University of Southern Denmark (2010) and a Visiting Professor at Jamia Millia Islamia, New Delhi (2012-13).

Ihsan Yilmaz is Associate Professor of Political Science at Fatih University, Istanbul, Turkey where he is also the Director of the Ph.D. Programme in Political Science and International Relations at the University's Institute of Social Sciences. He completed his Ph.D. at the Faculty of Law and Social Sciences, School of Oriental and African Studies (SOAS), University of London in 1999. He then worked at the University of Oxford as a Fellow between 1999 and 2001. He was the Deputy Chair of the Centre for Ethnic Minority Studies at SOAS (2003-2008) and the Director of the London Centre for Social Studies (2003-2008). He is a regular columnist of Today's Zaman, an English language daily published in Turkey.

Larbi Sadiki works on Arab democratic transitions and is editor of the Routledge Studies in Middle Eastern Democratization and Government. He is currently Associate Professor of Arab democratisation at the Department of International Affairs, Qatar University, Qatar. He obtained his Ph.D. from the Australian National University where he began his academic career before joining Exeter University's Politics Department where he directed the Middle East Politics Programme, 1999-2012.

M. Mahtab Alam Rizvi is Associate Fellow at Institute for Defence Studies and Analyses (IDSA), New Delhi. His areas of research include political developments, economic and trade issues in Iran and the Gulf Region. He has written a number of articles in various reputed national and international journals, books and news papers.

M.H. Ilias is Associate Professor at the India-Arab Cultural Centre, Jamia Millia Islamia, New Delhi. He completed his doctoral research in West Asian Studies from the School of International Studies, Jawaharlal Nehru University (JNU), New Delhi. He has been the recipient of Ford Foundation Fellowship for post-doctoral Research (2007) at Oxford University and post-doctoral Visiting Research Fellowship (2008) at the Centre for Modern Orient, Berlin.

M.K. Bhadrakumar served in the Indian Foreign Service for three decades and was ambassador to Uzbekistan and Turkey. Apart from two postings in the former Soviet Union, his assignments abroad included South Korea, Sri Lanka, West Germany, Kuwait, Pakistan and Afghanistan.

Mohammed Moussa has a doctorate from the University of Exeter in the United Kingdom. His research was principally concerned with the dynamic nature of the Islamic tradition on the one hand and contemporary Muslim political thought on the other hand. He has an M.A. in International Studies from Goldsmiths College, University of London, United Kingdom. His current research interests range from globalisation to the classical Islamic tradition.

Monish Tourangbam is currently Assistant Professor at the Department of Geopolitics and International Relations, Manipal University, Manipal, Karnataka. Previously, he was Associate Fellow at the Centre for International Relations, Observer Research Foundation, New Delhi and also Guest Faculty at the Ansal Institute of Technology, Gurgaon, Haryana. He has a Ph.D. from the US Studies Division, Centre for Canadian, US and Latin American Studies, School of International Studies, Jawaharlal Nehru University (JNU), New Delhi.

Mushtaq Hussain is a Doctoral Candidate at the Centre for West Asian Studies, School of International Studies of the Jawaharlal Nehru University (JNU), New Delhi. He won the Israel Government Scholarship, 2012-13 and conducted research under the aegis of the Bar-Ilan University, Israel as a part of his Ph.D. field work.

Obja Borah Hazarika is Assistant Professor, Department of Political Science, Dibrugarh University, Assam. He completed M.Phil. in American Studies from Jawaharlal Nehru University (JNU), New Delhi in 2012. He taught as Guest Faculty for the Masters Programme offered by Indian Society of International Law and worked as a Research Assistant in the Foundation for National Security, New Delhi.

Pallav Kumar obtained his Ph.D. Degree from Centre for West

Asian Studies, Jamia Millia Islamia, New Delhi in the year 2012. He has a Master Degree in Sociology from Jawaharlal Nehru University (JNU), New Delhi. Presently, he is working as Research Associate-cum-Co-ordination Officer in "High Level Committee on the Status of Women in India" under the Ministry of Women and Child Development, Government of India.

Prasanta Kumar Pradhan is an Associate Fellow at the Institute for Defence Studies and Analyses (IDSA), New Delhi. He holds a doctorate degree from the School of International Studies, Jawaharlal Nehru University, New Delhi. His areas of research interests include foreign policy and security issues in the Gulf Region and the wider Arab world. He has also done extensive research on various aspects of India's relationship with the Gulf and West Asian region and has published articles in several reputed journals.

Sashi Kumar is the founder and Chairman of the Media Development Foundation and Asian College of Journalism, Chennai. He was among the earliest Newscasters in English on national television, *Doordarshan*, Middle East Correspondent of *The Hindu* and news anchor on Radio Bahrain in the mid-eighties. He received the Vijayaraghavan Memorial Award in 2007 and the Swadeshabhimani-Kesari Puraskaram from the Government of Kerala in 2011 for his contribution to media. He writes a regular fortnightly column titled 'Unmediated' in *Frontline.*

Shajahan Madampat is a multi-lingual writer, cultural critic and commentator who currently lives and works in Abu Dhabi, UAE. He has to his credit three widely acclaimed books in Malayalam, in addition to numerous essays and articles, published in leading newspapers, journals and other periodicals in English and Malayalam. He holds M.A. and M.Phil. degrees from Jawaharlal Nehru University (JNU), New Delhi.

Srikanth Kondapalli is Professor in Chinese Studies at Jawaharlal Nehru University (JNU), New Delhi. He was Chairman of the Centre for East Asian Studies, School of International Studies, JNU twice from 2008 to 2010 and 2012 to 2014. He was a Visiting Professor at

National Chengchi University, Taipei in 2004, a Visiting Fellow at China Institute of Contemporary International Relations, Beijing in May 2007, an Honorary Professor at Shandong University, Jinan in 2009, 2011 and 2013 and a Fellow at Salzburg Global Seminar in 2010. He received the *K. Subramanyam Award* in 2010 for *Excellence in Research in Strategic and Security Studies.*

Youcef Bouandel is Associate Professor and Head of the Department of International Affairs, at Qatar University, Qatar. Prior to joining Qatar University in 2009, he was Lecturer/Senior Lecturer in Politics at the University of Lincoln, England and was visiting professor at several universities in Scotland, Bulgaria, Sweden, Latvia and the United States of America.

Introduction: Making Sense of Arab Spring

By Anwar Alam

The unexpected arrival of Arab Spring has unsettled many of the conventional presumptions and assumptions about the Arab world. It is now more than three years since the first occurrence of Arab Spring in Tunis in December 2010—however its moorings and trajectories are still far from clear. Though it succeeded in toppling four longest serving authoritarian Presidents of the Arab world: Zine El Abidine Ben Ali of Tunisia, Muhammad Hosni El Sayed Mubarak of Egypt, Ali Abdullah Saleh of Yemen, and Colonel Muammar al-Gaddafi of Libya, who was killed—its domino effect is yet to be translated into the democratic transformation of Arab polities.

On the contrary, the events and political developments in Arab world during the last two years represent a setback for the democratic potential of the Arab Spring. This includes the assassination of prominent leftist opposition figure, Chokri Belaid in Tunisia that led to the resignation of the Hamadi Jebali government, the political mayhem in Egypt that saw the resurrection of military institution under former Army Chief and now President of Egypt, General Abdel Fattah el-Sisi, who overthrew the first freely elected government of Mohammad Morsi, put him behind the bars and declared Muslim Brotherhood as the terrorist organisation, leading to illegal killing and arrest of thousands of Muslim Brothers and the degeneration of Libya and Syria into militias, regional rivalries and bloody sectarian conflicts.

Elsewhere in the Arab world, there is hardly any substantial democratic changes that have taken place, beyond a few token measures of political liberalization and change of guard at the helm of political affairs. The international and regional powers and other stakeholders also gravitated towards preference for the predictable old order, stability and security of the region than chalking out an unknown democratic transition full of chaos and anarchy which they would find it difficult to communicate and control—direct as well as to understand each other's concerns.

Given this emerging political scenario in the Arab world the Spring has raised more questions about its origin, character and scope. Some of these are: how to make sense of Arab Spring?; What makes the Arab Spring possible?; Was the Arab Spring a mere collective response to progressive erosion of social character of Arab states under globalization and neo-liberal economy?; Or does it reflect a collective desire for a fundamental change in their life situations that conform to universal human aspiration of freedom, equality and dignity?; Was the Spring a spontaneous event or an organized one?; What are the strengths, weaknesses, limitations and prospects of Arab Spring for democratic transformation of the Arab societies?

The collection of articles in this volume addresses some of these questions and to an extent contribute to the ongoing debate about the precise meanings and discourses of Arab Spring. Though the volume is spread over five theme headings from the point of view of organisation of chapters, however in totality, these address the three fundamental themes raised in the context of Arab Spring. The first three theme parts broadly deal with social forces, ideas and events that shaped the emergence of Arab Spring in Maghreb, Mashreq and Gulf and attempts to delineate its broad meanings and contours. In addition they also reflect upon the possibility and nature of democratic transformation of Arab polities in post-Arab Spring setting, particularly in North African countries. The fourth part deals with the contentious issue of relationship between Islamism, nation-state and democracy and examines in what ways Islam can play a role in the democratic transformation of Arab polities. The last part discusses the regional implications of Arab Spring as well responses of some of major international powers to the Arab Spring.

The volume opens with M.K. Bhadrakumar's '*Arab Spring is in Great Distress*' that narrates the journey of Arab Spring from its high moments of 'freedom' and 'progress' to its increasing moments of despair and fatigue with its fate being dependent on the outcome of Syrian crisis owing to its inherent multiple contradictions. Any serious observer of West Asian affairs would agree with Bhadrakumar's keen insight and a sorts of prediction that how Arab Spring is reaching its dead-end in Syria .The paper, which was a key note address, touches almost all vital aspects of Arab Spring ranging from contending role of regional and global powers, its implications for Israeli-Palestinian process, rise of Islamist parties and its uncertain future, the issue of democratic transformation of Arab societies and the resilience of Arab monarchies. Many of these themes of Arab Spring have been explored in great detail by the individual authors in this volume.

An aggregate reading of this volume locates the phenomenon of Arab Spring in a larger historical perspective within which appears many sub-texts of Arab Spring that has been highlighted by the individual authors. The larger historical trajectory here refers to political, social and economic transformation in the Arab world since 1916 'Arab Revolt' [1] and its attended consequences that have alienated a large number of common Arabs from existing state system, its narratives and discourses. From this perspective, the phenomenon of Arab Spring expresses the historical alienation and represent a collective desire to overcome this alienation by retrieving the 'politics of self-determination' as was first encapsulated in the 1916 Arab Revolt.

Ironically, the Revolt that took place in the name of 'Arab independence' from 'Ottoman Turkish Empire' with the support of European powers, soon relapsed into suzerainty of British and French powers in the form of Mandated System of League of Nation in early 1920s. The Arabs felt betrayed by the Europeans and 'Muslim Arabs' felt a more deep sense of betrayal and injustice with the creation of State of Israel in

Arab land—which they primarily saw a political entity deliberately planted by 'Christian European Powers' to humiliate Arabs and Islam.

Soon the Arabs embarked upon the political struggle against the European powers in order to achieve freedom and independence in the name of 'Pan Arabism'—a collectivist nationalist trend that later became the official creed of Egyptian state during the Presidency of Gamal Abdul Nasser. Paradoxically, the outcome of independence struggle in the name of Pan Arabism/Arab nationalism was a fragmented, individual Arab nation state that sought to develop a localised-Islamic version of Arab nationalism, specific to Islamic history of individual Arab countries [2]—a trend that was further consolidated and institutionalised with the demise of Pan Arabism following the Arab debacle in 1967 War against Israel. [3]

Under the spell of modernity, the post-colonial nation building process in the Arab countries gravitated towards building a centralised, authoritarian state system—personified by strong individual leadership and dominance of military institutions—the most modernising sector of post-colonial societies—in order to address the internal challenges of social and economic reforms as well as the external challenges of imperialism and the state of Israel. Though the authoritarian Arab nation state came into existence on the promise of freedom, justice, development and democracy but it preferred to govern the country on the combination of politics of patron-client relationship and threat of coercion.

To an extent, the emerging post-colonial Arab states were addressing the issue of equity and social justice during 1950s, 1960s and 1970s by providing subsidised food commodity, public health, housing, free education, guaranteed employment, infrastructure development, redistribution of national economic wealth, improvement of status of women and other developmental activities as well as mobilising the national public opinion against Western imperialism and the state of Israel and in favour of the liberation of Palestine—the Arab governments were championing the democratic aspiration of the people. Political authoritarianism thrived and continues to thrive in many parts of the Arab world on such populism and succeeded in securing the *active* consent and support of a large number of people.

As Arab regimes itself championed the social agenda of democracy, the issue of political democracy in terms of effective representative institutions was not deeply felt by people at large, except a few critical intellectuals and liberals. In a way and speaking from South Asian perspective, the Arab regimes took care of agenda of social democracy, if not political democracy. Several scholars have called this political arrangement between populace and the regime as 'unwritten social contract' whereby the regime bought the political voice of the people in exchange of social rewards—an arrangement which is not specific to the Arab world alone. [4] Many commentators have pointed out the breakdown of this unwritten social contract in the Arab world in the first decade of 21st century as the *principle reason* for the emergence of Arab Spring.

The 'modern' developmental Arab state was modern only in terms of structure and process (president, parliament, trade union, court, constitution, political party, bureaucratic department and organisations, and so on); in terms of value and functioning, it was practicing the old, customary political traditions in which the state appeared as a 'paternalistic father and guardian' that would take care of each and every section of the society. Hisham Sharabi had called such discrepancy in terms of structure, function and value of Arab states and society as 'Neo-Patriarchy'. [5]

The only difference that lies with the old form of paternalism is at the level of violence. The modern paternalistic Arab state—whether republic or monarchial—has developed enormous capacity to organise everyday physical violence that is deployed not only against its political opponents, but is embedded in the high degree of policing and securitization over its people. Modern concepts and discourses such as secularism, nationalism, Islamism and party-system have at best served as nothing but an instrument of control, disciplining and mobilisation of people in the hands of various regimes of the Arab world.

The reason for high level of violence that is found in the behaviour of Arab state institutions partly lies in the very political project of modern nation-state and is partly derived from the insecure, unstable personalised rule that lacks sufficient legitimacy which in turn propels the individual Arab rulers to rely more upon the coercive instruments of state power—military, intelligence, security apparatus and policing. Examples of such violence are abound in the Arab world; the most recent case of which is state's brutal crackdown against Muslim Brotherhood in Egypt and the ongoing brutality of Alvi dominated Bathiest Syrian regime against its majoritarian Sunni Muslim citizens.

Roger Owen, the distinguished Middle East historian in his recent work, *'The Rise and Fall of Arab Presidents for Life'*, has vividly demonstrated how the structures and processes of political rule retained a particular authoritarian continuity between the colonial and post-colonial Arab state that over time has generated a deep resentment and observes: "Domestically, the response of the new independent regimes was to try to augment their hold over their own populations using institutions and techniques, notably an increasing emphasis on policing, security, and the management of elections, borrowed directly from the practices of their former colonial masters". [6]

Syrian writer Rana Kabbani describes the authoritarian rule of post-colonial elites in the Arab world as 'internal colonialism' and with respect to Syria she observed: "forty-two years of one-family rule was much like an external colonialism of the past, [it] has robbed them and bombed them and impeded them from joining the free peoples of the world".

[7] For common Arabs, it is *Mukhabarat* (the intelligence agency)—a dreaded word that defines a state in the Arab world. As a Syrian Professor told me, *without mukhabarat there is no life of Arab states*. [8] These sentiments are widely felt and applied to all regimes: Zine El Abidine Ben Ali in Tunisia, Muammar al-Gaddafi in Libya, Hosni Mubarak in Egypt, and others.

What enabled and continue to enable the post-colonial Arab states, to escape the successive global waves of democracy [9] is the combination of factors. This includes rentier nature of Arab economies, [10] thrust on development during 1950s, 1960s and 1970s and a general maintenance of social character of Arab states throughout the five decades, the interplay of hard (strengthening the coercive apparatus of state) and soft power (relaxation of civil liberty, media freedom and election), the bipolar Cold War international structure that provided space for diplomatic autonomy and support of Western powers to Arab rulers either in the name of prevention of Soviet communism and later Russian influence or Islamic terrorism/fundamentalism or honouring the international treatise such as Camp David Treaty (1978) that guaranteed the existence of the state of Israel.

These factors even allowed the Arab rulers to sail through the 'difficult years of 1980s and 1990s' during which the financial autonomy, manoeuvring and institutional capacity of the Arab States were significantly eroded on account of falling oil prices, the rapid escalation of the Islamist challenges, the strangulated economic reforms under the IMF-World Bank led Structural Adjustment Programme (SAP), the Washington Consensus, the demise of the Soviet Union and the US invasion of Iraq. Under this context, modern scholarship invented a term called 'Arab Exceptionalism' (which minimally included such components as Arab Islamic formation, its culture, history and civilization, tribalism, oil, level of external intervention in the region, rentier nature of economy and absence of civil society) to describe the non-democratic face of the Arab world in perpetuity or conversely to explain the 'persistence of authoritarianism' in the Arab world. [11]

The unfolding event of Arab Spring that began with self immolation of Tunisian fruit vendor Mohamed Bouazizi on 17th December 2010 represents an attempt to end the above *historical process* of formation and character of Arab nation state—secular or Islamic—that was periodically emasculating the democratic aspiration of the people since the Arab revolt of 1916. The democratic aspiration includes a right to dignified livelihood, freedom from everyday harassment and humiliation by state agencies, participation in public opportunity structure and decision-making process of the government of the day, a rejection of national subjugation and indignation vis-à-vis state of Israel and Western powers, a desire for collective Arab fraternity/brotherhood and a rejection of international and regional order that is insensitive to Palestinian plight and its right to nationhood.

In this sense, the Arab Spring certainly represents an 'End to Post-Colonialism', as observed by Hamid Dabashi. What Dabashi means here is an end to the 'regime of knowledge production', which was fundamentally euro-centric in terms of its categories, terminologies and intellectual frame of reference—a by-product of a colonial mindset, which was totally disconnected with life worlds of common Arabs and sustained an authoritarian political order that was oppressive, abusive, arrogant and insensitive to dignity and aspiration of its own people. [12] In a similar way, historian Ilan Pappé has referred to the Arab Spring as the 'second phase of decolonization' and a 'collective assertion of self-dignity in the Arab world' after decades of humiliation, despotism, and despair. [13]

According to Abdulkhaleq Abdullah, the Arab Spring symbolizes a 'rupture' that was "total, comprehensive, and, perhaps, final. The events of 2011 will enter history as the foundational events, not only for Tunisia, Egypt, Libya, Syria, Yemen, and Bahrain, but also for the entire Arab region. What has been confirmed is that the era of Arab stasis, surrender, frustration, and misery, which lasted too long, extending over more than four decades, has finally reached its end". [14] The Arabic term *karama* (dignity)—the core theme of Arab Spring reflects this 'felt sentiment'—which is at once personal and collective and should not be construed to mere 'struggle for democracy', as is popularly understood in the West. *It is an individualized state of being itself and a collective Arab consciousness that arises in the form of Arab Spring to rekindle the historical moments in the present and move the history forward.* This partly explains Arab's collective identification with personal indignity, humiliation and suffering of Mohamed Bouazizi [15] in Tunisia or Khaled Said [16] in Egypt.

Broadly speaking, Arab Spring was the first Pan Arab people's mass movement in modern history of Arab world that was hardly even witnessed during their struggle for independence from the European powers, except in Egypt and Algeria. Its strength lies in its being largely non-violent, predominantly youth-based that cuts across religious—sectarian and ideological, if not regional—division of the society at least in the initial days of the uprising. Even in the context of Bahrain where opposition has particularly been noted for its Shia sectarian mobilization, the initial people mobilisation against the regime was non-sectarian. Tariq Ramadan, while commenting upon the nature of protest movement in Bahrain, has noted its non-sectarian nature: 'The demonstrators demanded reform of the ruling regime and an end to inequality in the application of the laws governing naturalization. Slogans called for Sunni-Shiite Unity". [17]

It was only at a later stage that the Arab Spring increasingly acquired a distinctly sectarian, tribal and confessional identity in different Arab countries depending upon the location of marginalised groups in the power structure of the country concerned and regime's policy of labelling the opposition with a particular sectarian identity or tag of 'terrorism' in order to weaken and delegitimise the opposition movement. Within this trajectory of Arab Spring the nature, resilience and intensity of people's mobilisation varies from one country to another country of the Arab world.

Thus, whereas Tunisia and Egypt witnessed the long, sustained, relatively peaceful, large scale people's mobilisation at national level against the regime, the oppositional mobilisation in Bahrain and Syria was/is principally sectarian (*Shia* and *Sunni* respectively); whereas in Libya and Yemen it was tribal and regional in character. However, notwithstanding the increasing fragmentation of Arab Spring along sectarian, (*Sunni* vs. *Shia*), tribal, ideological (secular vs. Islamic) and religious (Islam vs. Christian) lines, it did not take away the generalised felt collective sentiment against the misrule of the regimes in the region and hence will continue to haunt the regimes for long time to come unless the regimes seriously address the multiple concerns of their people.

What has made the Arab Spring possible? In other words, what are the causes of the origin of this phenomenon? Was it spontaneous or organised? What makes the Arab Spring to be successful in terms of fall of regimes in some parts of the Arab world (Tunisia, Egypt, Libya and Yemen) and not so successful in other parts of the Arab world, especially the Arab Gulf monarchies? Some of the dominant explanations and factors that have been accounted for regarding the development of Arab Spring, which have also been referred in several pieces of this volume, are: change in the demographic structure of the Arab world, uneven process of modernisation, the pitfalls of truncated neo-liberal economic reforms, economic and social discontents, breakdown of authoritarian social contract, political repression, high degree of unemployment, particularly among youth, rising costs of living, deteriorating food security, high level of corruption and the role of social media.

These factors are certainly important and have their own merits in the explanation of development of Arab Spring.

However most of these factors, except the social media, have also figured in the discussion over the rise of Islamic movements and Islamic militancy *but* without having any serious implications for the survivability of the regime.

In fact, an isolated reading of these factors would not be of much help in explaining the phenomenon of Arab Spring. The fact that the economic, social and political condition of many Arab nations was not bad in terms of macro indicators, calls into question the reliance over socio-economic grievances as the principle cause for the development of Arab Spring. Annual growth rates in Egypt, Jordan, Lebanon, Oman, and Sudan averaged more than 6 percent between 2005 and 2010; and Syria, Tunisia, and Libya grew at about 5 percent on average during the same period, which were around or above the world average over the past few years before the development of Arab Spring. [18] Official poverty rates in most Arab countries are lower than in many Asian and Latin American countries [19] and unemployment in the region had modestly declined from high levels by the end of 2010. [20] Further, the total fertility rate (expected number of births per woman) in the region dropped 'from 7 children per woman in the1950s to 4.8 in 1990 and declined further to about 3.6 in 2001; in 2010 it was down to 2.8'. [21]

Moreover, the fall in oil prices since 1980s has not led to a corresponding or drastic decline in the social expenditure of the governments. While examining the issue of linkage between material distribution and persistence of authoritarianism in Morocco, Tunisia, Egypt and Jordan, Thomas Richter concluded: 'Using annual data from states' budgets between 1970 and the early 21st century, I find that over these three decades, distribution of material resources measured by state expenditures for: (i) defence and public order, (ii) public wages and salaries, and (iii) subsidies have been surprisingly stable. They were even growing on a nominal per capita level measured in local currencies. However, using the real per capita values in US$, which tries to estimate a power purchasing parity, increments are more modest. Most interestingly, with the partial exception of subsidies, I do not find an overarching trend of booms or busts in state expenditure on public wages and pensions as well as defence and public order which might co-vary with natural resources revenues or world oil prices'. [22]

Surveying the economic trend and pattern of government spending in 2010 Magdi Amin and Others [23] has also reached more or less similar, if not identical, conclusion:

It is a mistake to think however that the overall picture in 2010 was one of growing instability or greater political oppression. The trends of quantitative indicators of instability in Arab economies were actually improving between 2003 and 2010. Several governments embarked on a series of tactical political openings, and their polity score—a measure of democracy—got better, but in all cases, the reforms relied on organizations closely tied to incumbents (political parties, the military and security apparatus) to ensure that rival political forces were restrained and co-opted. At the same time, government consumption was able to sustain relatively high levels of welfare payments and public sector jobs. While still highly autocratic and characterized by immense levels of executive discretion, the Arab polities in December 2010 were more "open" than those of the previous generations.

Further, the Arab states have perfected a strategy of political rule that combines an 'expansion and contraction' of politics of repression, democratic space and social spending depending upon the political context—a strategy that has worked well during last 50 years in managing the 'periodic crisis' arising out of student protests, food riots, Islamic militancy, peasant rebellion, terrorism etc. and ensuring the survival of the regime.

Hence, what went wrong in 2010-2011 that triggered the Arab Spring, particularly in the secular republican countries of the Arab world? In this context, one issue that has attracted the scholar's attention most as a factor in the development of Arab spring leading to the downfall of a few authoritarian regimes is the *deteriorating food security* in the Arab world. It has been argued that the tremendous increase in global prices of food commodities between 2005 and 2008 led to an increase in the prices of basic food commodities that adversely affected the financial health of Arab states, particularly non-oil Arab states. As the Arab world accounts for the largest importer of food products in the world, the rising global prices of food commodities cost the state exchequer dearly, particularly the non-oil Arab economy and adversely affected their capacity to control the rising prices of the basic consumer products. Certainly, these factors deteriorated the food security regime in the Arab world, however there is hardly any analysis that indicates *a drastic* erosion in the capacity of the Arab states to effectively address this issue.

The fact that for common Arabs food is not merely an economic commodity but also a social and political commodity, [24] no Arab government would like to appear to be failing on this account—as any 'food crisis or riots' would set in motion, the destabilising process for the government. The governments in the past have withered and survived the impact of many food riots (Egypt: January 1977, 1984, 1986, 1989; Morocco: 1981, January 1984, 1996; Sudan: March 1985; Algeria: October 1988, 1997; Tunisia: 1984, 1986; Jordan: April 1989; and Yemen: 1985, 1988, 1995) by a combination of repression, enhancing the salary of public employees, borrowing from outside to increase the supply of food commodities at normal prices, subsidizing the basic food commodities and extending the subsidy net to hitherto uncovered social groups. Why this same set of public policy will not work under similar conditions, as happened in Egypt, Tunisia, Yemen and many others, if Arab Spring is the result of 'food crisis'?

An investigation into the complex issue of Arab Spring requires an 'inter-generational perspective' that analyses the various factors as listed in preceding pages in an integrated and aggregated manner, not in isolation, within the specific context of Arab World, where 'access to state patronage has defined the shape of the public sphere and economic opportunities, group loyalties and social and political identities have all been shaped and reshaped, based upon where a specific individual stands in relation to the state-sponsored patronage networks that prevailed in the region'. [25] In a public culture where *state is the life,* the inter-generational perspective produces a meaning and narratives in which Arab Spring appears to be the result of 'crisis of rising expectation and diminishing opportunities'. [26] This paradoxical situation is evident from the fact that the Arab world has had the fastest growth of employment between 1998 and 2008 of any region in the world (3.3 percent annually) but still has the second-highest level of unemployment in the world (9.7 percent). [27]

The full implication of this paradoxical development becomes clear when it is situated in the context of public culture that places a very high premium on the employment opportunity in the government sector than in the private sector or self-employment. There is hardly any Arab country where youth prefer private sector employment over the public sector. [28] On average, informal employment (self-employment and working for family without pay) accounted for about 60 percent of total employment in poor Arab countries.

The post-1980 Arab generation found himself/herself stuck up in a public culture that measures status, dignity and matrimonial prospects of an individual from their location in state pyramid. This societal scenario propels an Arab youth to wait long and struggle to secure a position in the government on the one hand and the context of neo-liberal economy that enhances the consumerist appetite of lifestyles, without any corresponding increase in the material prospects of large number of educated Arab youths on the other to realise the same, which they found it blocked on account of high level of corruption and nepotism at the upper layer of pyramid of Arab state structure. It was this chasm between the traditional expectation of Arab youth from the state to guarantee a dignified access to basic provisions which the state had been delivering to their parent generation and exclusion of large number of them from the emerging opportunity structure of neo-liberal economy in the midst of consumerist desire and life styles, that directed the collective anger and frustration against the regime.

Hence, the discontent thus seems to be more closely related to a growing disillusionment with economic prospects. It is not that the people in the Arab world were mostly unhappy and dissatisfied from their livings as the case has been made [29] for explaining the collective outbursts but rather expected happiness in the future is lower in the Arab Spring countries than in the rest of the world. [30] The volcano was not against the system of neo-liberal economy but against the failure of the regime to redistribute the fruits of neo-liberal economy at the national level which was/is believed to be being siphoned by families, friends and cronies of the regime in the most vulgar manner.

Further, the growing inequality between a few superrich and the rest of society became very visible that was resented by underpaid and unemployed consumerist-oriented educated middle and upper middle class who were already exposed to 'good life' of other societies through medium of internet sources and travel abroad. Though the protest across the Arab world, particularly in the Egypt—the very centre of Arab Spring—rent the air in the name of justice (*Aladdin*), freedom (*hurriya*), dignity (*karmah*) and respect (*ihtiram*), the primary demand put forward by the movement was primarily social and economic in nature: (i) a life of dignity rather than one defined by humiliating condescension and oppression by the security forces and public authorities; (ii) equality in access to resources and opportunities instead of clientelistic rewards for compliance; and (iii) the right to participate in the global trend toward prosperity, progress, education and democratic participation.

The Arab tsunami from below took place in a context where authoritarian Arab states, principally the secular-republican, exhausted all four ingredients—ideology, repression, payoffs, and elite solidarity—as expounded by William Quandt [31]—for survival of authoritarian regime. The combination of this factor along with the position of the West and the strength of internal mobilisation sealed the fate of long serving dictators.

Thus, if the end of bipolarity, the increased power of the IMF and the World Bank and the collapse of oil prices throughout mid-1980s and 1990s, severe financial limitations to payoff in an ever increasing 'coalition of dispossessed' on account of demographic changes and pitfalls of neo-liberal economy as well as eroded the capacity for autonomous policymaking, the contrast between political rhetoric of freedom, development, imperialism and Arab nationalism and everyday reality of unfreedom, non-development, subjugation, national humiliation and capitulation robbed the state of its ideological appeal—particularly to the post-1980 generation who had either weak or no memory of Nasser and Borguiba—moral authority and capacity to exercise repression—all combined leading to the collapse of the elite solidarity as evident from refusal of military in Egypt, Tunisia, Libya and Yemen to intervene on the side of state and fire upon the agitating mob.

Moreover, faced with such unprecedented, peaceful, non-violent mass mobilisation the authoritarian state in Tunisia, Egypt and Yemen found themselves unprepared, clueless and without any strategy and capacity to deal with 'politics of peaceful mass mobilization' as the state machinery was accustomed and trained either to co-opt the particular opposition individual leaders or subject them to force if the former strategy does not work. Finally, the Western intervention proved crucial in securing the ouster of Ben Ali in Tunisia, Mubarak in Egypt, exit of Saleh in Yemen through political negotiation and the assassination of Gaddafi in Libya.

The Assad regime in Syria continues to manage to survive on account of sectarian-elite solidarity, the support of resurgent Russia and China, the fragmented nature of Islamist opposition and hands-off approach of the West due to fear of instability. In Bahrain, the regime was secured through combination of West backed GCC intervention and its paying off capacity to buy opposition.

In this context, the present volume contains three significant articles: one each on Libya, Syria and Bahrain. A.K. Pasha's '*Turmoil in Libya: Internal Dynamics and External Linkages*' largely focuses on West's troubled history with Colonel Gaddafi and finally succeeded in overthrowing Gaddafi regime and killing him—taking the advantage of Arab Spring, notwithstanding the fact that Gaddafi accepted and carried out all Western demands including the acceptance of responsibility of 1988 Pan Am Lockerbie bombing and compensation to the relatives of all victims and the dismantling of stockpiling of WMD and long range missiles. Following Gaddafi's assassination, the author concludes that the country has plunged into chaos and anarchy due to infighting among numerous militant Islamic radical groups and tribal militias as well as TNC's (Transitional National Council) inability to provide leadership and restore authority.

Prasanta Kumar Pradhan's *Syrian Uprising: March Towards further Instability* provides a comprehensive analysis of ongoing sectarian civil war inside Syria and demonstrates how an opposition to the misrule of Assad regime increasingly degenerated in a bitter sectarian Shia-Sunni conflicts, fuelled by Iranian-Hizbullah-Shia support to Assad regime and Saudi-Qatari Sunni support to the opposition and Islamic salafist groups. According to him, Syria has become a battle ground for (Shia) Iran and (Sunni) Saudi Arabia to increase their respective spheres of influence and maximise their political gains in the region. The author also highlights the humanitarian crisis of Syrian civil war and explores the role of opposition such as Syrian Nation Council (SNC), Syrian

National Coalition (SNC), Free Syrian Army (FSA) as well as the Islamic resistance groups such as Al Nusra and Islamic State in Iraq and Levant (ISIL). He concludes that while elite solidarity of Alwis and Bathists—that dominate the military and other branches of the state—is helping the Assad government to survive, the sectarian conflicts and infightings within the opposition is pushing Syria towards further instability.

M. Mahtab Alam Rizvi's *Bhrain Crisis and Iran-Saudi Arabia Contestation* discusses the nature of opposition, predominantly Shia, to Al Sabha ruling family and the role of Saudi-led GCC (Gulf Cooperation Council) forces in crushing the 'Shia opposition'. It then outlines the emerging Saudi-Iranian contestation on Bahrain where Saudis consider the political stability of Bahrain as essential for the stability of its own regime as well as to maintain its regional leadership, while Iran is considered to have a significant political and religious clout over Shia community of Bahrain and even considers her as a political entity to be under her zone of influence.

In the context of Arab Spring, much has been discussed about the resilience of Arab monarchial and Sheikhdom countries [32] particularly the GCC countries Kingdom of Saudi Arabia, Kuwait, Qatar, United Arab Emirates (UAE), Bahrain and Oman. Except Bahrain, none of these GCC countries was seriously affected by the wave of Arab Spring, though low scale protest did occur in all these countries with exception of Qatar and UAE. Most of the analysts have either highlighted the economic and repressive capacity (measured in terms of steep hike in the salary of public employees, increase in the food security, employment generation, support to unemployed, strengthening of security services and providing aid to other countries) of Gulf countries or the counter-revolutionary role of Saudi Arabia [33] as a factor to explain the resilience of the conservative Gulf monarchial and Sheikhdom countries to successfully ward-off the disruptive impacts of the Arab Spring.

Gulshan Dietl in her piece on *'Arab Spring: Saudi Exceptionalism?'* investigates the 'exceptionality' of Saudi Arabia and found that 'Saudi Arabia is no exception' to the trend of Arab Spring. In her analysis she first identifies the *sites* of Arab Spring that revolved around three main axes: regional Shia mobilization, urban youth protest and women assertion and then goes on to demonstrate how the Saudi regime responded to the threat of Arab Spring by combining the strategy of political repression (related to arrest of more than five thousand charged with terrorism-related crimes immediately after the 'failed' day of rage on 5th March 2011), limited democratic initiative (related to grant of rights to women to vote and run as candidates in municipal elections and be appointed to the Shura Council) and massive economic inducement [34] to its citizens on the one hand and strengthening the military role of GCC as evident from its role in crushing the Shia protest in Bahrain, offering the membership of GCC to monarchial kingdom of Jordan and Oman and providing economic aids to Egypt, Bahrain and Oman and supporting the Salfists Syrian opposition to Assad regime on the other. The Saudi response to Arab Spring, according to her, is also primarily intended to contain the Iran's (Shia) regional influence, particularly its increasing strategic depth in Iraq, Bahrain, Lebanon, and among the Saudi Shias in long run.

Though economic and security measures are significant factors but they alone do not explain the resilience of the Gulf counties. The underlying assumption here is deeply flawed as it reduces the political survivability of the Arab regimes to its economic and repressive capacity and indirectly argues that with better economic and repressive capacity, the republican authoritarian Arab states would have survived in sailing through Arab tsunami. This hypothesis runs contrary to empirical facts: despite relatively having good economic condition and higher repressive capacity, Egypt and Tunisia witnessed the most intense form of people's mobilisation than that of Jordan and Morocco. [35] Bahrain, a relatively rich Gulf country, faced a very severe challenge of Arab Spring.

What is required is an integrated approach that combines Quandt's four ingredients—ideology, repression, payoffs and elite solidarity along with the position of West/USA in order to make sense of resilience of Arab monarchs and Sheikhdoms. If the legitimacy in terms of Quandt's four ingredients was to be found, it totally collapsed in the case of Arab republican regimes—it remained, along with the support of the West, to a large extent, intact for the Arab monarchies and Sheikhdoms. It may be noted that slogan of Arab Spring "*al-Sha'b yurid isqat al-nizam*' ('the people want to bring down the regime') that rented the air in Egypt, Tunisia, Yemen, Syria and Libya was totally absent in the Arab monarchies and Sheikhdoms, including Morocco and Jordan.

While modern Arab republican state never developed the culture of dialogue and negotiation as a principle to govern the country, the traditional monarchial institution continues to prefer to rule through consultation, which they inherited in tradition, either within the ruling families or with the chief of major tribes of the country; thereby at least providing a modicum of democratic participation, which partly explains why Arab Spring did not visit in the same intensity and form to monarchial Arab Gulf countries as was witnessed in 'modern' Arab republican regimes.

The issue of whether Arab Spring is spontaneous or organised has also been widely discussed in the academia and in public domain, partly due to widely held perception that given the entrenched interest of the West in the region, particularly the United States, political changes is not possible without the latter's blessing. The fact that Arab Spring in the West Asia and North Africa (WANA) coincided with George Bush's 'Greater Middle East' project that focussed on the democratisation of WANA lends credence to this perspective. Ahmad Mohamed Ahmad Abdel's Rahman's *Arab Spring in*

Egypt: Causes and Implications indirectly touches this aspect of the Arab Spring. The article provides a comprehensive background of the development of Arab Spring and examines the roles of various protests groups such as the Youth Movement for Change, the April 6 Youth Movement, the National Association for Change, the Khaled Said Group and the Kefaya (enough) Movement in raising democratic awareness, and mobilising the people's opinion against the misdeeds and corruption of Mubarak regime in a peaceful, non-democratic manner and highlights its regional and global implications.

Rahman's paper sufficiently gives an impression that Arab Spring was not a spontaneous act but a result of an organised work prepared by these protest groups over the last 5-6 years before the fall of Mubarak. Though he does not explore the role of West in organising or supporting the above mentioned groups, a recent work by Tariq Ramadan highlights the linkage between the West and social media in organising and managing the protest peacefully against the Mubarak regime and concludes that the movement cannot be described as spontaneous. [36]

This brings us to the issue of role of social and new media in shaping the development of Arab Spring in the region. Much discussion has taken place on the role of internet and social media such as Twitter, Facebook, YouTube etc. in bringing social and political changes in the Arab society. [37] The debates on the role of social media have mostly revolved around a central question: whether internet and social media have inherent democratic potential to democratise the society without the material social, economic and political context?

The volume contains two significant pieces that have addressed this question in the context of Arab world. Pallav Kumar's *New Media and Arab Spring* provides a detailed description of the development of new media in the Arab world and argues like many, what is called 'cyberutopians', that how internet and new media being non-ideological, youth friendly, horizontal, online, provides a public sphere to debate refute, criticize, mobilize and create solidarity network. In conjunction with its faster communication and exchange of information as well as the capacity to circumvent the authoritarian surveillance, it retains the transformative capacity to convert the 'virtual mobilisation' into the 'real time' mobilisation against the authoritarian system. He provides an example of how the new media spearheaded the movement in the name of '*We are all Khalid Sayed*' and succeeded in mobilising a large number of Egyptian youth in the Tahrir Square against the Mubarak regime.

On the other hand, Sashi Kumar, in his analytical piece *Social Media and Arab Spring,* cast a serious doubt on the inherent democratic potential' of social media and argues much like, what is called 'cybersceptics' such as Malcolm Gladwell, that '*revolution is not tweeted*'. For him, internet and social media are tools of dissemination of information and communication without any inherent capacity of mobilisation because they are not a subject with independent characteristics but an object shaped by the social environment in which it is embedded. With this proposition, he does not find the effective role of internet and social media in the Arab Spring beyond Egypt and Tunisia which could become possible, according to him, partly due to support of the West.

According to him, more than social media it is Al Jazzera —an electronic mainstream media based in Doha that helped in the mobilisation of the people. Sashi's finding on the limited role of social media has also been corroborated by a recent well documented study: 'Egyptian activists had been trying to ignite a revolution using blogs and social media for a decade, with little sustained success. The hundreds of thousands of people who made the Egyptian revolution by coming into the streets on January 25, 2011, did not learn about it through Twitter or Facebook. They saw it on Al Jazeera, or out their windows. Internet penetration in Yemen, which has had one of the most sustained and resilient protest movements, is roughly

2 percent, while the Gulf countries, with the highest regional rates of internet penetration, have experienced little protest. Many of the activists themselves now complain about the focus on new media, and bristle at questions about the role of Twitter or Facebook'. [38]

The fact the author has rightly underlined that the Muslim Brotherhood—a reluctant and late participant—in 'Egyptian Revolution' managed to come to power with a support base that had the least access to internet, Facebook, Twitter, YouTube etc., certainly testifies the limit of the mobilisational role of social media. In this context, he raises a very pertinent question: are the assorted social media manufacturing a public sphere or people-hood which cuts across the traditional categories of the *ummah* (or Islamic nationhood) or the *millet* (for the minorities), or which challenges the *assabiyah* (tribal or clan affiliation) factor, even while upholding the *sharia* as the ultimate arbiter? Needless to say, internet and social media within its liberal framework has very limited role to play—cutting across these sites of identities along which people's mobilisation on the ground takes place.

What role did Islam play in making of Arab Spring? It appears from the several accounts that Islam had hardly any role in the making of the Arab Spring and Islamic groups and organisations were initially reluctant even to participate in organising people's movement against the regime. Islamic movements like Muslim Brotherhood in Egypt and Ehnanda in Tunisia joined the protest movement at a later stage at the organisation level, though members associated with these organisations or other Islamic groups might have participated in the Arab Spring on their own individual level. The non-Islamic character of Arab Spring was also evident from absence of any 'Islamic slogan' or 'Islamic demands' till the overthrow of the regime.

To a large extent, Arab Spring was initially an inclusive secular mobilisation focussed on removing the incumbent regime (at least in Egypt, Tunisia, Libya, Syria, Yemen,) and reforming the governing structure. It is only in post-Spring period, when Spring succeeded in removing some of these Pharaohs, that Islam as an ideological element began to surface in the public discussion and asserted its role in the construction of post-Pharaoh Arab nation-state and society. In fact, Islam began to increasingly surface in the public sphere of Arab world in post-1967 Arab-Israeli War that had jolted the legitimacy of secular authoritarian discourse of Arab nation-state. Along with Islamic Revolution of Iran (1979), which though failed to establish a democratic state but kept the imagery of Islamic democratic opposition alive vis-à-vis secular-authoritarian-imperial order, it was the mainstream Islamic oppositional forces and movement that championed the discourse of democracy and human rights against the authoritarian secular Arab states since the mid-1980s.

This partly explains that even though mainstream Islamists did not have any role in the initiation of Arab Spring, they succeeded in achieving electoral victory in Egypt, Tunisia, Morocco, Palestine, Kuwait, Jordan and Libya in the aftermath of Arab Spring on account of their organisational strength, welfare works, imagery of pro-poor and 'illegitimate victim' of secular order and promises of Islamic democratic order against ruthless, secular-authoritarian political order that would ensure justice, freedom and dignity. On consequence of this process was/is the 'normalisation' of the discourse centred on linkage between Islam, democracy and development in the Arab public sphere. The electoral victory of mainstream Islamists further consolidated this discourse and the claim of public role of Islam in Arab societies.

It is under this context that Arab intellectuals heavily debated the Turkish model centred on the discourse and political ascendancy of AKP (Justice and Development Party) rule since 2002, led by Rayyip Tayab Erdogan, the popular and longest serving head of the government after Kemal Ataturk in modern Turkey. What made the Turkish model attractive to the larger Arab intelligentsia—across secular and Islamic spectrum—when the model is not even fully democratic?

Three factors underlined the growing acceptance of modern Turkey in the Arab world. First, the process of globalisation 'opened' both Turkey and Arab World to each other through exchange of intellectual and cultural products, tourism and intensification of economic engagement [39] as well as political, if not economic, distancing of Turkey from Israel helped in reducing the 'historical chasm' between the two and making the Arabs receptive towards Turkey. Second, as Turkey's democratic transition under AKP coincided with all round development of Turkey, it 'helped to build up perceptions and expectations that the authoritarian regimes in the Arab world were increasingly unable to accommodate the growing social and economic demands of their own citizens'. [40] Third, perhaps most important, the AKP discourses and political rule symbolises the harmony of Islam, secularism, democracy and development.

It is in the above context that Ihsan Yilmaz's *Turkish Faith-Based Civil Society's Transformative Influence on Islamism as an Inspiration to the Middle East* explores 'how' and 'which' aspect of 'Turkish model' is relevant to Arab society. In other words, *in which respect* Turkey can be a source of inspiration for Arab people, intelligentsia and policy makers while reconstructing their society and state in post-Arab Spring phase? While reflecting on this subject matter, Yilmaz rejects state-centered Turkish model that continue to exhibit the traits of exclusivist secular authoritarianism sustained by combination of undemocratic military-bureucratic-oligrach alliance against majority common Turkish's desire of living a life of dignity, freedom and security.

The Turkish model in this form is bound to run against the spirit of Arab Spring and could prove to be counter-productive. Instead he drew attention towards society-centred Turkish model that exhibits tolerance of plurality of discourses and viewpoints as well as democratisation of social, economic and political process. Within this larger framework, Yilmaz highlights the role of Gulen's humanistic discourses and Gulen movement, the largest non-political Islamic movement in Turkey, in the transformation of Mili Gorous-Erbekan (the Islamists) into AKP-Erdogan (non-Islamist Muslim democracy) that espouses an inclusive approach which combines respect and belief in the *secularity* of state, tolerance of religious subjectivity in the public sphere and upholds the conception of democratic space that ensures religious minorities and other ideological minorities including the atheists, the right to full and equal citizenship.

Though he enlists other factors such as moderate character of Turkish Islam, role of Anatolian business houses etc. in shaping the emergence of democratic Turkey, in particular he explores the impact of Gulen discourses in building up a 'culture of normative tolerance' in public domain as well as its transformative impact on the mental outlook of erstwhile Islamists who are currently ruling Turkey. It is in the field of this larger *civic-social process and experience of Islam* that has helped in the emergence of democratic Turkey—that Turkey can play the role of 'Turkish model' or act as inspiration for million of Arabs who dream for a democratic Arab world.

Notwithstanding the merits of Ihsan Yilmaz's analysis, any observer of current Turkish affairs would notice the growing authoritarian tendency, intolerance, disrespect for law and anti-minority posturing on the part of ruling AKP led by Prime Minister Erdogan. More than anybody else, it is the Erdogan himself who is aggressively exhibiting these tendencies. [41] In view of this development, Yilmaz himself has become critical of the democratizing role of AKP. [42] This raises an important question: Can an Islamist be a democrat? Can Islamism be transformed into a 'non-Islamist Muslim democracy' as Yilmaz argues? Can Islamism and democracy co-exist together? Can Islamist party be transformed into Christian Democratic Party of West European countries?

Shajahan Madampat looks into this set of questions in the light of emergence of Islamists as political forces in the post-Arab Spring West Asia. He goes into details of the genealogy of political Islam or Islamism, its history, its internal contestation, and interrogates the fictitious division of radical and moderate Islamism, espouses two kinds of notion of Islamic state—one based on people's consent and other deriving legitimacy from God and highlights various examples such as Nasr Abu Zayed and taken together arrives at the conclusion: while Islam as faith, cultural marker and social process can live with democracy or any form of political order, Islamism as an ideological construction and democracy cannot co-habit together. He powerfully argues in the light of empirical examples how Islamism, in principle, negates the idea of equal citizenship and how the notion of Islamic state is based on the idea of majoritarianism and thus contradicts the essential elements of democracy. According to him, for Islamists, democracy remained an instrument to come to power, not a value to be internalised which makes them suffer from a bundle of contradiction arising out of the conflict between their inherent doctrinal inflexibility and compulsion to maintain the tactical pragmatism.

A few examples testify the insight and hypothesis of the author. The Islamists in Iran during their more than 30 years of uninterrupted political rule failed to create a democratic state, notwithstanding its rhetoric of freedom and democracy. The AKP, a moderate variant of Islamism in Turkey that respects the secularity of state and does not believe in the notion of Islamic state, within 12 years of its political rule, has moved from its once advocacy of civil and political liberty to the increasing display of authoritarianism after consolidating its position, which prompted the Freedom House to designate Turkey in 2014 as 'Not Free' country. [43]

The Muslim Brotherhood in Egypt after coming to power in 2010 displayed authoritarian attitude, refused to share power with major stake holders and remained committed to the conservative vision of Islam that sends misgivings to secular constituency of Egypt who rally behind the popular military under General Sisi to depose Morsi and banned the organisation. Similarly, Shajahan provides an example of experiment of Jammat-Islami-Hind (JİH) (the Indian wing of Jammat-e-Islami founded by Maulana Mawdidi), which though has adopted the democratic and secular framework of Indian constitution and currently at the forefront of championing the cause of democracy and secularism in India on the one hand, but simultaneously it wishes and cherishes the idea of Islamic rule in Muslim majority nations on the other, to illustrate the bundle of contradictions from which political Islam suffers. All these examples certainly point out the democratic limits of political Islam. Hence, it is not without reason that the victory of Islamists in many parts of the Arab world in post-Spring phase raises concern and fear among some quarters of citizenry.

Does this mean that Islam is inherently anti-democratic as consistently argued by the Orientalists since eternity and which continues to find favours with many in the present? Shajahan rightly dismisses such formulation and argues that there is enough conceptual resources in Islam that is easily compatible with the concept of democracy—it is the ideological construction of Islam or Islamism that is problematic and inherently anti-democratic. However, is it the ideological construction of Islam or the *very act of ideological construction itself* which is undemocratic? I think it is the latter, as it entails the process of selection and elimination according to fixed priorities and principles. This applies to every phenomenon and hence Islam is not unique in this regard.

Another contentious issue that has been raised in the volume from the point of view of examination of relationship between Islamism and democracy is the issue of evolution of Islamists/Islamist party into a Christian Democrats

(CD)/Christian Democratic Party (CDP) of Europe, as raised by Shajahan and Ishan Yilmaz, in order to visualise the public role of Islam in a democratic setting. Until this happens, Islamist party will not be recognised as sufficiently democratic. But is the comparison justifiable? A CD or CDP is a product of thorough going specific historical process of democratisation and secularisation of West European countries, which is yet to take place in non-western societies including the Muslim societies. One consequence of this process is that a large number of Christian groups and denominations themselves internalised the secular-functional discourse of religion, which is not the case with the Muslim world. Moreover, following Talal Assad, Islam, Christianity or any other religious traditions are *discursive practices* with their own specific normativity, rules and habitués. From this point of view, a comparison between the two is uncalled for.

However, beyond the issue of comparison, an important question that arises here is that *in what way* CD or CDP represents a democratic Europe? In this context, it may be recalled that a modern, democratic and secular Europe came into existence *only* at the cost of brutal marginalisation and exclusion of religion and religious groups from power-structure. The religious groups were granted religious liberty in the mid-20th century when they lost the political influence and capacity to challenge the secular nation state. [44] Thus, the existence of religious groups and parties in western societies is premised on the acceptance of secular authority of a state. A CDP is expected to use Christianity as 'cultural marker' but not as a political tool to challenge the secular legitimacy of state.

Thus, it can participate in state power structure only by adhering to secular principle and rules of political games. This begets an important question: Should the state be considered democratic only in its 'secular form'? Is religious state inherently undemocratic? Does religious state necessary mean a theocratic state? Does secularism has sole monopoly over state power? M.H. Ilias in his paper on '*Political Theology of Morsi's State (2012-2013) in Egypt*' has partly dealt with these two questions that will be discussed at later stage. Suffice would be here to state that this political arrangement that has come to stay in the European societies and enjoy broad national consensus consists of *supremacy of secular over religious, not the equality between secular and religious.* Should we consider such a political order democratic one that has historically marginalised and excluded religion and necessarily entails the supremacy of secular over religion in perpetuity, as European experiences point out, then most of the post-colonial political order including the Arab world is perfectly democratic in this sense of the term! No wonder the Arab authoritarian states long enjoyed and continue to enjoy the uninterrupted support from the West in their fight against Islamist movements.

As the modernity travels from Centre (Europe) to periphery (post-colonial societies) it transplanted its own conception of 'nation-building process'(based on secular-religious divide) on the (disempowered) post-colonial societies that has altogether different conceptions of 'secular' and 'religious' and interaction between the two (mostly having a fuzzy understanding in which each includes each other without a sharp distinction) with a consequence that nation-state project in post-colonial societies continues to be subjected to intense contestation along secular-religious divide. In no other societies of the world than the Muslim societies, particularly the Arab Muslim societies, this internal contestation between Islam and nationalism about the project of nation state is deeper. [45] As Islam refuses to get secularised and nationalised, as happened with Christianity, it continues to impinge upon the autonomy of nation-state. Both Islam and nationalism lay claim on nation-state as an instrument of organisation of life. Islam has returned to public life in today's Turkey—a nation that witnessed the most thoroughgoing process of secularisation and nationalism under the leadership of Kemal Ataturk with an intent to expunge Islam from any role in public life.

Attempt to synthesise Islam and nationalism has not been very successful. This has resulted either in the use of Islam as a legitimising tool of nation-state (this applies to all republican nation states in the Muslim world) or utilising the nation-state structure for conservative Islamic rule (such as the Kingdom of Saudi Arabia, Iran, and short-lived Taliban in Afghanistan). The synthesis, which apparently exists in almost all Muslim nations, is not based on the idea of equal recognition of each other with respect of each-other's sphere of role and function. Whosoever is in greater proportionality in the power structure expects other to serve as subordinate, though it is mostly Islam that has served the nation-state in modern times either through the process of co-optation or increasing bureaucratisation.

The chasm between the two also results from the fact that notwithstanding five hundred years of engagement with modernity that has deeply affected the functioning and normative structure of state in the Muslim world, the micro structure of Muslim society—the everyday life—for vast Muslim majority remains Islamic in content. The post-colonial nation-building process remained a hybrid one in which attempts were/are made by the political elites—whether nationalists or Islamists—to retain both the elements of modernity (idea of republicanism, nationalism, secularism and democracy) and tradition (cultural and religious traditions), primarily to use them as an instrument of control, disciplining, regulation and source of legitimacy for the purpose of consolidating their rule and without having any desire to internalise and promote the ethical and democratic side of each values, notwithstanding the rhetorical commitment to the same.

Within the above context and frame, Mohammed Moussa examined the issue of interplay of Islam and nationalism vis-à-vis the idea of nation state in the case of modern Egypt. Taking a historical perspective he succinctly demonstrates how the present crisis of power struggle between the military institution and the first elected Islamist government under Muhammad Morsi, who has been ousted in a military coup led by General Sisi, has roots in the historical contestation between the nationalists and Islamists about the constitution and representation of nation-state in Egypt. In other words, the contestation is about the identity and constituent element of 'imagined Egyptian nationhood'. Moussa traces this historical contestation since the late 18th century and beginning of 19th century when Egypt was first exposed to modernity during the brief political rule of Napoleon Bonaparte (1798-1801) and later consolidated under the rule of Muhammad Ali Pasha (1805-1849).

He explores the complex process through which the military institution came to be first identified and perceived as the 'modern' institution and given the successive military rule after 23rd July revolution in Egypt, the military institution axiomatically came to represent the nation and nationalism and even assuming the role of custodian of Egyptian nation-state. The fact that since the bulk of modernisation programme has historically been military-centred in Egypt; it must have contributed in building this image of military in Egypt. On the other hand, the author explores how the Islamic contestation to 'the' secular basis of Egyptian nation and nationalism remained alive either in the form of role and status of Al-Azhar, or reliance of secular military rulers on Islam for legitimacy, or the intellectual discourses of prominent Islamic intellectuals, or the emergence of Islamic mass movements such as Muslim Brotherhood.

The conflicting vision of the two was sharply manifested during the process of Arab Spring. Fearing the Islamist takeover in post-Mubarak period that might tamper with the secular character of Egyptian nation and nationalism, the interim government of Essam Sharif under the auspices of Supreme Council of the Armed Forces prepared a constitutional document (Article 9 and 10) in 2011 that virtually gave army the role of the guarantor of *al-shariyah al-dustouriyya* (the constitutional legitimacy), thereby formally codifying the idea of the Egyptian army as the custodian of the nation-state. On the other hand, the Morsi-led Islamist government scrapped Article 9, diluted the scope of Article 10 and enhanced the scope of Islam in governance of the country which among others included the jurist-consult status of Al-Azhar in the matter of Islamic legislation and Sharia as the source of legislation—which in turn generated a good fear among the secular constituency to rally behind General Sisi to save 'Egyptian nation' from Islamists. In the process, General Sisi, now the elected president of Egypt, came to embody the Egyptian nationhood.

The volume contains two more pieces on Egypt: Fazzur Rahman's *Arab Spring and the Changing Dynamics of Political Islam in Egypt* and M.H. Ilias's *Political Theology of Morsi's State (2012-2013) in Egypt.* These two articles supplement Moussa's larger perspective on the interplay of Islam and nationalism by focussing on the recent events in Egypt. Rahman provides, apart from touching the meaning and reason for the development of Arab Spring, a general background of the development of Muslim Brotherhood and its gradual transformation into a constitutional, mainstream political formation in modern Egyptian context. Whereas Ilias dwelt upon the notion of emerging concept of 'Civil State' (*dawla madaneyya*), also referred in Sahajhan and Moussa's articles, and highlights its basic conceptual elements.

The notion of *dawla madaneyya*, is an interesting one as it attempts to move from modernist as well as the Islamists' frame of binary thinking of religious vs. secular and offers a vision of 'non-Islamic Muslim state', as referred in Ihsan Yilmaz's piece, that differentiates from 'secular conception of governance' on the one hand and from the past model of Caliphate, the present day Iranian-style 'theocracy' and the hegemonic discourse of 'Islamic state' on the other. *The* notion *of dawla madaneyya* while recognising Islam/Muslim as 'cultural frame' and *Sharia* as ethical and moral precepts, attempts to provide a non-discriminatory natural governance based on the principle of democracy, constitutionalism and equality of citizens before the law.

Though governance on the principle of neutrality is indeed a desirable goal, it has so far remained an illusive principle. Even modernity and secularism has poor record in ensuring this principle in matter of governance, notwithstanding their claim of achieving the same through the principle of equal citizenship. In fact, modern conception of nation is inherently a majoritarian concept and hence limits the claim of minority over the nation-state in practice, if not in theory. On the other hand, in the light of modern experience of Islamic rule, wherever it has existed and irrespective of its form, it is difficult to imagine whether Islamism through the notion of *dawla madaneyya* can achieve the same. Further, though all three articles have explored the 'political development' in Egypt in terms of interplay and contestation of ideas, which is indeed important, however beneath these contestations of ideas about the nation state, also lies hard material interest.

Thus, behind the Islamic mobilisation and contestation against the secular, authoritarian nation state lies a desire for social, economic and political empowerment of vast majority of poor, lower middle class, disempowered people, whereas the bulk of educated middle, upper middle class, national bourgeoisie, rallies behind the secular nation-state to defend their state-centred privilege and material interest. This partly explains why majority of middle and upper middler class secular Egyptians preferred the military coup of el-Sisi than a democratically elected Islamist Morsi government because the later endangers their 'entrenched privilege' in the secular state system which was only jolted recently under Mubarak's crony capitalism which they hope would be rectified under the government of el-Sisi.

Similarly, the Arabaphone (majority religious poor) vs. Francaphone (minority, urban secular middle and upper middle class) in the context of Algeria during much of 1980s and 1990s or currently ongoing invisible conflict between what is called 'White Turks' (liciest, secular, state centred middle and upper middle class) and 'black Turks' (the religious, Antaolian majority Turks) within Turkey reflects the similar contestation over redistribution of national resources beneath the contestation of ideas about nation and nation-state.

The most visible, dominant dimension of the Arab Spring was/is its presumed connectivity with democracy. The critical public, policymakers, statesmen and intellectuals across the globe debated the transformative democratic capacity of Arab Spring. Many liberals across the world saw the confirmation of universal democratic sprit of modernity in the Arab Spring. For a large number of Arabs, it signifies the arrival of 'real democracy' in the Arab world. For many liberal Muslims—men and women—it confirms their deeply held view that Islam is not against democracy and modernity; that modernity is not the monopoly of the West; that they are also civilised and are very much like them. For many intellectuals, particularly the liberal Muslims, it signifies the end of discourse of 'Arab Exceptionalism'.

On the other hand, critics and sceptics, mostly coming from orientalist background, outright rejected any 'democracy meaning' in the Arab Spring. Thus, Bernard Lewis, the late distinguished historian, calls Arab Spring as an expression of collective anger and sexual frustration of Arab youth, which has nothing to do with democracy: "in the Muslim world, casual sex, Western-style, doesn't exist. If a young man wants sex, there are only two possibilities—marriage and the brothel. You have these vast numbers of young men growing up without money—either for the brothel or the bride price—with raging sexual desire. On the one hand, it can lead to the suicide bomber, who is attracted by the virgins of paradise—the only ones available to him. On the other hand, sheer frustration'. [46] Israeli Prime Minister Benjamin Netanyahu famously described the Arab Spring as an "Islamic, anti-Western, anti-liberal, anti-Israeli, and anti-democratic wave". [47] Nobel Laureate V.S. Naipaul dubbed the Arab Spring as 'nothing' and remarked, 'it would come and go, and we'll be back where we started...chaos, one-man rule, which is how these things usually end in the Muslim world'. [48] The return of authoritarianism in the form of el-Sisi in Egypt—the very nerve centre of Arab Spring—after three years of Arab Spring might appear to many, as confirmation of these views.

A substantial part of the volume has also contributed to this debate and has attempted to examine a set of inter-related questions arising out of Arab Spring: what are the prospects of democracy in West and North Africa? Whether the Arab world could reverse to the pre-Spring authoritarian political order? If yes, what would be the nature of post-Arab Spring authoritarian accommodation? The issue of prospect of democracy, relationship between Islam and democracy and the shifting pattern of authoritarianism or what is called the notion of 'upgrading authoritarianism' are old ones that have been debated, discussed and analysed in the context of West Asian and North African region for the last three decades. They have assumed new significance and propensity due to a new context of mass assertion from below, in the form of Arab Spring with democratic aspiration and demands for fundamental change in the governing structure of the country concerned.

The new context visualises 'democratic changes' in 'bottom-top format structure' that could ensure the democratic participation and representation of people in all decision-making bodies of the governance, unlike the old 'top-bottom format structure' in which political and economic changes were visualised and initiated in accordance with the principle of survivability of political regime; in order to deal with popular discontents and enhance and strengthen the legitimacy of the regime. Thus, it was the regimes that used to set the agenda, retain the initiative, decide, control and direct the nature and pace of measured political and economic reforms keeping in view its principle of its own survivability.

Precisely for this reason, the scholars have mostly debated the issue of democracy in WANA region throughout 1980s and 1990s within the dominant framework of 'political liberalisation' or 'political reform' or 'controlled political liberalisation' or 'upgrading authoritarianism' in order to gauge the prospects of 'political democracy' in the Arab world. Finding that the two decades of political reforms in WANA not only failed to meet even the minimum criterion of political democracy (independent judiciary, independent election commission, political and civil liberty and freedom of press), the space of 'political openings' has further shrunk by the end of 1990s in the name of containing Islamic militancy and terrorism and which gets a new credence in view of US's War on Terror following the 9/11. A large number of scholars on WANA abandoned the framework of 'political liberalisation' and moved to the discourse of 'Arab Exceptionalism' with a view to examine the question of 'persistence of authoritarianism' in Arab world.

It is in this larger setting and sharing the predicament of scholars on the substantial issue of democracy in the Arab world as indicated above, the volume contains two significant articles which deal with the issue of post-Arab Spring democratic transformation of West Asia and North Africa, mostly with reference to North African countries (Tunisia, Algeria, Morocco and Libya)—the region that has been the centre of Arab Spring. These are Azzedine Layachi's *Popular Uprising in North Africa: Radical Change, Gradual Adaptation and the Challenge to Authoritarianism* and Larbi Sadiki and Youcef Bouandel's *Three Versions of the Arab Spring in North Africa: Protest and Reform in Algeria, Morocco and Tunisia.*

Both pieces, while exhibiting great amount of caution and avoiding rush generalisation, examined the nature of political forces and processes thrown out of the Arab Spring and its potentials for democratic transformation of Arab polities. While Layachi's paper primarily deals with Algeria, Tunisia,

Libya and Morocco, while also touching other West Asian Arab countries, Sadiki and Bouandel's paper is confined to Algeria, Tunisia and Morocco. Though there is not much divergence in terms of approach and method of analysis, both share one definite conclusion: *Tunisia holds brighter prospects for genuine democratic transition than any other North African country or even West Asian Muslim nation.* For Layachi, the factors that favour such prospect for Tunisia includes the extent of economic development, social and political cohesion, and a political military establishment, whereas Sadiki and Bouandel emphasises the transparent process of making constitution which is 'rooted in universal democratic principles, not only championing values of equal opportunity, civil and political freedoms, equal citizenship, pluralism and the rule of law', the free and fair parliamentary election as well as the 'consensus-legal-institutional building path' adopted by Tunisian political leadership.

On the other hand Libya, according to Layachi, holds the least prospect of democratic transition on account of its failure of building of state institutions. Without proper state building, democratic rule cannot be visualised. The post-Arab Spring Libya continues to suffer from deep tribal, sectarian and ideological fault lines without any consensus on state building and respect for law. Arguing mostly within the framework of 'political liberalisation', both Layachi and Sadiki and Bouandel (though the latter does not use this expression directly in the paper) examined recent political initiatives of ailing President Boutlifika in Algeria and young King Mohammed VI in Morocco and demonstrates how these political measures were primarily intended to 'ward-off' the impact of Arab Spring and to ensure the political survival of the regime without diminishing their authority and hold over their respective country affairs.

In the case of Algeria, this includes scrapping of emergency law, promises of new constitution, quota for women in the parliament, enhanced subsidy on food commodities, hike in the salary of public employees, enhanced security, flexible government loans to unemployed youth, legalisation of more political parties along with fear of 'disorder' that Algeria had suffered two decades ago, and the '*le-pouvior*' nature of political regime that helped in concealing the regime as the 'fountainhead of corruption'. In the case of Morocco, it ranges from monarch's policy of dumping the loyal ruling Istiqlal Party in favour of Islamic opposition Justice and Development Party keeping in consideration the 'Islamist wave' in the region, helping the latter to win the parliamentary election, bringing a constitutional amendment that makes government accountable to parliament and investing in the Prime Minister, a power to dissolve the parliament—a prerogative that traditionally belongs to the King, enhancing the subsidy on food commodities, allocating the quota for youth in Parliament and the very nature of '*makhezn*'—the royal network of informal relationship with bureaucrats, army chief, judicial chief, police chief and other important state functionaries where policy decision emerges and is later presented to the Prime Minister.

Developments in Algeria, Morocco and Tunisia represent a case of continuity of politics of 'authoritarian accommodation' [49] according to these papers. However, given the fact that 'people' has emerged as 'active source' of legitimacy in the context of Arab Spring and has set the agenda of political and economic justice with an expectation that the 'people in authority' would implement this agenda in due course of time, it would be interesting to observe whether this 'authoritarian accommodation' would gradually pave the way for democratic transition or revert the democratic gains achieved as a result of the Arab Spring. However, recent events such election of General el-Sisi as President of Egypt in June 2014 and re-election of ailing Bouteflika in May 2014 as the President of Algeria along with setback to oppositions in Syria and in Bahrain do not promise a democratic transition of the region in the near future.

The last section of the volume deals with the global and regional reactions to Arab Spring. In terms of global powers, the volume focuses on the reaction of United States, China and India to this momentous event. This includes Chintamani Mahapatra and Obja Borah Hazarika's *American Response to the 'Arab Spring': Foreign Policy in Quandary,* Srikanth Kondapalli's *China and the Arab Spring: Perception and Policy Responses and* Monish Tourangbam's *Persian Gulf and the Arab Spring: Implications for India.*

The reading of these pieces makes clear that it is the preference for 'stability, security and order' than the 'democratic chaos and element of unpredictability' in the region, which is considered to be vital for global prosperity, security and stability, that has conditioned the cautious, vacillating and contradictory approach of these countries towards Arab Spring. It is pertinent to note that the US administration dithered from supporting the Arab Spring and debunked its own 'democracy promotion agenda' that was launched by the Bush administration in the Middle East, at a time when it is needed most. Chintamani and Hazarika's article demonstrates the vacilatory, ad hoc, and situation-specific responses of Obama administration that varies from one country to another in the Middle East.

This ranges from supporting the ouster of Ben Ali in Tunisia to reluctantly supporting the ouster of Hosni Mubarak and not calling the military's overthrow of first democratically elected President of Egypt, Muhammad Morsi as 'coup' so as to escape the mandatory, automatic invocation of US clause of economic sanction—the application of which would have further deepened the crisis in Egypt; to openly supporting the Saudi-led GCC operation to crush the opposition and secure the thrown of Al Sabha family in Bahrain; to imposing UN's 'no flying zone' on Libya and then fully backing the French-led NATO operations against Gaddafi regime leading to assassination of Gaddafi; while refusing to impose a no fly zone and intervening in Syria despite the catastrophic loss of human life.

Similarly, Srikanth highlights several inconsistencies and contradictions, or even opportunistic postures in China's response towards the Arab states that results from its concern to protect its ever growing trade and investment in the Arab world on the one hand and to secure peace at home by almost imposing media censorship on the news related to Arab Spring within China. Thus, along with Russia, it has consistently supported the Assad regime including the vetoing of the recent Security Council resolution (May 2014) pertaining to trial of Assad regime in the International Criminal Court. Monish Tourangbam's piece highlights how Indian concern was primarily limited to the stability of Persian Gulf countries, which is vital for the India's economy from the point of view of uninterrupted supply of hydrocarbon products, the growing trade and investment, vital markets for the Indian products and finally for the estimated six million Indian expatriates that significantly contribute to the Indian economy.

Though the regional responses and implications of Arab Spring have been broadly touched upon by M. K. Bhadrakumar, Azzedine Layachi, Larbi Sadiki and Youcef Bouandel, Ahmad Mohamed Ahmad Abdel Rahman, Gulshan Dietl, Prasanta Kumar Pradhan, M. Mahtab Alam Rizvi and Monish Tourangbam in their respective papers, the issue has generated much concern and debates about its long-term implications for 'stability and security' of Israel and the creation of Palestinian nationhood.

The volume consists of two pieces that deal with these aspects of Arab Spring. These are Mushtaq Hussain's *The Israeli Dilemma: Winds of Change or More of the Same* and Abdulkhalek Alzamli's *Reading of The Arab Spring: Implications on Palestine.* In his paper, Mushtaq points out the long-term implications for Israeli security arising out of the Arab Spring: it has unsettled the secure border that Israel has come to achieve during last forty years with Egypt, Syria, Lebanon and Jordan. The spectrum of Islamists coming to power has further introduced the element of uncertainty and unpredictability as the Israeli government had become accustomed to deal with secular authoritarian regimes as per mutually expected rules of game. However, there are two other significant implications for state of Israel. First, if Arab Spring succeeds in bringing the democratic transformation of Arab world, the Israelis would lose the strategic appeal and soft value that it has enjoyed so far in the West in the name of 'only democratic country' in the region. This would reduce the Israeli capability to push off the agenda for Palestinian statehood for too long. Ian Pappe, the Jewish revisionist historian, considers this element as the biggest worry for Israeli government. [50]

Second, the Arab Spring has unleashed the process of unity between Hamas and Al-Fatah leading to the formation of National Unity government a week ago. The Israeli government, aware of such an outcome, has refused to accept the Unity government and imposed the travel ban on Hamas leaders to travel to Ramallah. A fragmented, weak Palestinian movement suits the Israeli government most, than a strong, united Palestinian movement. Abdulkhalek in his paper stressed this 'unity' between Hamas and Al-Fatah as one concrete outcome of the Arab Spring, in addition to the fact that this event also prompted the Palestinian Authority to seek UN's recognition of full statehood. However, he also points out that as Spring continues and the fact that Israel settlement expansion in the West Bank has made the creation of an independent Palestinian state impossible, more and more Palestinians are expanding their vision beyond the search for statehood and finding ways to re-establish core principles of the struggle such as self-determination, the right of return, freedom and equality with a hope to live in a federal single state in which all citizens have equal rights and duties loom larger than ever.

This volume is a collection of papers that were presented in an international seminar titled, 'Arab Spring: Region and

India', held on February 15-17, 2012 in the premises of Jamia Milia Islamia (JMI), New Delhi. The Conference was organised by the Centre for West Asian Studies under the then directorship of Editor of this volume. Though there were many papers that were presented in the three-day international conference, however, unfortunately, not all of them could find place in this volume, notwithstanding their respective merits. Papers for this volume were selected in accordance with the structure and theme of this volume. Some of the papers were also invited, which were not originally a part of the seminar proceedings, in order to fill the gap of this volume. It is also tragic that while the focus of the seminar was to dwell upon and understand the various implications of Arab Spring for Indian foreign policy, we could not succeed in getting much response from scholars on this aspect in the seminar. Nonetheless, the volume in totality, provides a comprehensive analysis of Arab Spring whose long-term implications are still to be unfolded and hence serves the purpose of inputs for Indian policy makers to deal with the ramifications of Arab Spring in the future.

I take this opportunity to thank all the participants, students, faculty members and staff of Centre for West Asian Studies, Jamia Millia Islamia (JMI), New Delhi, and many others who helped in organising this conference. Special thanks to all the contributors to this volume, as without their cooperation, this work would not have been possible. I am also thankful to the Ministry of External Affairs, Government of India, Indian Council of Historical Research, New Delhi, Indian Council of Social Science Research, New Delhi, Jamia Millia Islamia, New Delhi, and Indialogue Foundation, New Delhi for providing the financial support for organising this event.

Thanks are also due to Zirve University, Gaziantep, Turkey for providing a congenial atmosphere that helped me to complete this project. A very special thanks to my wife, Zuby, and daughter, Sanober, for being with me under odd circumstances and becoming *the* source of strength, without which this work would have not possible. Last but not the least, thanks to Sandeep Sury, the CEO of New Century Publications, New Delhi for taking personal interest and bringing this volume in public domain.

June 5, 2014 **Anwar Alam**

Endnotes

1. The 'Arab revolt', a rebellion of small-scale nature without mass participation, was organised by a group of dominant Arab tribes against the Ottoman Empire. It was the outcome of a combination of factors: a feeble sense of idea of nationalism and democracy, the process of Turkification of Ottoman Empire, personal ambition of a section of serving Arab elite within the Ottoman administration to carve out their independent Arab space, the political mechanication of European Powers and the perception of declining authority of Ottomans. The Revolt was mostly confined to historically constituted Arab land (modern day nation of Saudi Arabia, Syria, Iraq, Jordan, Lebanon, Palestine and Israel). See an excellent work on the related theme, Ernest C Dawn, *From Ottamnism to Arabism: Essays on the Origin of Arab Nationalism,* University of Illinois, Pr.; first edition, January 1973.
2. See, Youssef M. Chouerie (2003), *Modern Arab Historiography: Historical Discourses and the Nation State*, Routledge: London.
3. Fouad Ajami (1978), 'The End of Pan-Arabism', *Foreign Affairs*, 57/2, Winter, pp. 355-373.
4. Raj M. Desai, Andes Olofsghd, and Tarik M. Yousef, (2009), 'The Logic of the Authoritarian Bargain', *Economics and Politics*, 21 (I): 93-125.
5. Hisham Sharabi (1992), *Neo-Patriarchy: A Theory of Distorted Change in Arab Societies*, Oxford University Press, Oxford.
6. Roger Owen (2012), *The Rise and Fall of Arab Presidents for Life*, Cambridge, Mass.: Harvard University Press, p. 15.
7. Rana Kabbani, "From the Turks to Assad: to us Syrians it is all brutal colonialism", The Guardian, March 30, 2011, available at, http://www.theguardian.com/commentisfree/2011/mar/30/turks-

assad-colonialism-family-mafia, accessed on May 20, 2014.

8. Personal conversation with a Syrian Professor at Zirve University, Gaziantep, Turkey, May 16, 2014.
9. Samuel P. Huntington (1993), *The Third Wave: Democratization in the Late Twentieth Century*, University of Oklahoma Press.
10. Richter has identified five classes of rent: (i) raw-material rents –income from selling natural resources and/or raw materials on international, (ii) location rents–income from the ownership of necessary and important transport routs or infrastructural facilities, like oil-pipelines or the Suez Cannel, (iii) strategic rents–income from geo-political or strategic geographic and/or political positions and behaviour, like the (non-)alignment with international or regional powers or just the (non-)support of specific political or ideological positions of other states, (iv) political rents–income from the acquisition of foreign aid given by the OECD and the Arab oil-states according to solid developmental and moral orientations, (v) migration rents–income from the participation of labour forces on OECD's and Arab oil-states' labour markets. Thomas Richter, *Contending Aspects of Authoritarian Survival in the Middle East and North Africa: The Durability of Material Distributions in Morocco, Tunisia, Egypt and Jordan*, available at, http://www.eisa-net.org/be-bruga/eisa/files/events/turin/Richter-Richter_Turin.pdf , accessed : May 27, 2014, pp. 10-11, 15.
11. Raymond Hinnebusch (2007), 'Authoritarian Persistence, Democratization Theory and the Middle East: An Overview and Critique', in Frederic Volpi and Francesco Cavtorta (ed.), *Democratization in the Muslim World*, Routledge: London and New York, pp. 1-33.
12. Hamid Dabashi (2012), *The Arab Spring: The End of Postcolonialism*,(London: Zed Books, 2012.
13. lan Pappé, interview by Frank Barat, "Reframing the Israel-Palestine Conflict", New Internationalist, April 1, 2011, available at, http://newint.org/features/web-exclusive/2011/04/01/palestine-israel-interview-pappe/, accessed on May 20, 2014.
14. Dr. Abdulkhaleq Abdullah, *Repercussions of the Arab Spring on GCC States,* Arab Centre for Research and Policy Studies, Doha, Qatar, May 2012, pp. 1-30, available at, http://english.dohainstitute.org/file/get/5b1fafdb-19d4-4946-

a18e-f3115c6fd0aa.pdf, accessed at May 25, 2014.

15. Mohamed Bouazizi was a 25 year old young vegetable street vendor in the Sidi Bouzid city of Tunisia. Apparently harassed by Municipal inspector and without any means to get his work done he publicly committed self immolation in the front of local municipal building.
16. Khaled Said was a young man from Alexandria who was brutally tortured and killed by the police for exposing their atrocities.
17. Tariq Ramdhan (2012), *Islam and the Arab Awakening*: Oxford University Press, Oxford, p. 40.
18. The world economy grew at 5.1 percent between 2005 and 2010, according to the IMF (International Monetary Fund), "World Economic Outlook", available at, http://www.imf.org/external/ns/cs.aspx?id=28, accessed on May 20, 2014.
19. World Bank, "World Development Indicators", available at, http://data.worldbank.org, accessed in February 2011.
20. Magdi Amin and Others (2012), *Economic Transitions in the Arab World,* Oxford University Press, Oxford, p. 1.
21. Valentine M. Moghadam and Tabitha Decker (2014), 'Social Change in the Middle East' in Ellen Lust (ed.), *The Middle East,* thirteenth edition. Los Angles, Sage, pp. 73-106.
22. Richter, *op.cit.*, p. 15.
23. Magdi Amin and Others, *op.cit.*, pp. 40-41.
24. On the linkage between food crisis and political liberalisation, Larbi Sadiki, 'Popular Uprising and Arab Democratisations', *International Journal of Middle East Studies,* Vol. 32, 2000, pp. 71-95.
25. Toby Dodge, "From the 'Arab Awakening' to the Arab Spring: The Post-Colonial State in The Middle East", available at, http://www.lse.ac.uk/IDEAS/publications/reports/pdf/SR011/FINAL_LSE_IDEAS__fromTheArabAwakeningToTheArabSpring_Dodge.pdf, p. 7, accessed on February 12, 2014.
26. Navtej Dhillon and Tarik Yousef (2009) (ed.), *Generation in Waiting*, Brookings Institution Press, Washington, DC.
27. Magdi Amin and Others, *op.cit.*, p. 55.
28. See Silatech and the Gallup Organization, (2009), T11e Silatech Index: Voices of Young Arabs, available at, http://efe.org/downloads/Silatech_Gallup_Wave2_Report.pdf .

29. See, Clemens, Breisinger, Olivier Ecker and Perihan Al-Riffai (2011), *Economics of the Arab Awakening: From Revolution to Transformation and Food Security*, IFPRI, Policy Brief 18, May.
30. Magdi Amin and Others, *op.cit.*, pp. 50-51.
31. William B. Quandt (1998), *Between Ballots and Bullets: Algeria's Transition from Authoritarianism,* The Brookings Institution, Washington, pp. 30-34.
32. See, F. Gregory Gause III, *Kings for All Seasons: How the Middle East's Monarchies Survived The Arab Spring.* Brookings Doha Centre Analysis Paper, Number 8, September 2013, The Brookings Institution, USA, pp. 1-30.
33. Mehran Kamrava, The Arab Spring and the Saudi-Led Counterrevolution, available at, http://www18.georgetown.edu/data/people/mk556/publication-61403.pdf , pp 96-104, accessed May 29, 2014.
34. Thus the Royal grants announced by the Office of the King of Saudi Arabia on February 18, 2011, amounting to USD 130 billion, including: (i) an increase in pay in the public sector, (ii) a grant equalling two months of salary for all state employees, civil and military, (iii) a two-month salary bonus for all students in public education, (iv) a monthly salary disbursement for the unemployed, (v) the establishment of a minimum wage for Saudis working in the government sector, (vi) the creation of 60,000 new military positions in the Ministry of Interior, (vii) 500,000 housing units throughout Saudi Arabia, and (viii) an increase in the upper limit of housing loans to USD 133,000. See, Abdulkhaleq Abdullah, '*Repercussions of the Arab Spring on GCC States'*, Arab Centre for Research and Policy Studies, Doha, Qatar, 2012, p. 12; pp. 1-30, available at, http://www18.georgetown.edu/data/people/mk556/publication-61403.pdf, accessed on May 27, 2014.
35. Per capita income based on purchasing power parity in Jordan (& 5, 400 in 2010) and Morocco (& 4, 800 in 2010) was less than that in Egypt (& 6, 200 in 2010) and Tunisia (& 9, 400 in 2010) on the eve of revolts in 2011. See, F. Gregory Gause III, *op.cit.*, p. 12.
36. Tariq Ramadan (2012), *Islam and the Arab Awakening*, Oxford: Oxford University Press, pp. 10-12, and chapter 2, 'Cautious Optimism', pp. 23-63.
37. See, Aouragh, M. (2011), Between cyber-cide and cyber

intifada: Technologic (dis)empowerment in the Palestinian political public sphere. In L. Jayyushi (ed.), *New Media in the Middle East*. Muwatin Press., BBC Monitoring (January 19, 2011). Tunisia: Events show social media not enough to lead to change. Translation of article in *Al-Arab al-Yawm*. Malcolm Gladwell, "Small Change: Why the Revolutions Will Not Be Tweeted," *New Yorker*, October 4, 2010, available at, www.newyorker.com/reporting/2010/10/04/101004fa_fact_gladwell) Philip N. Howard and Muzammil M. Hussain, "The Role of Digital Media", *Journal of Democracy*, 22, No. 3 (2011): 35-36). Miriyam Aouragh and Anne Alexander, The Egyptian Experience: Sense and Nonsense of the Internet Revolution, *International Journal of Communication*, 5 (2011), Feature 1344-1358.

38. Sean Aday, Henry Farrell, March Lynch, John Sides and Deen Freelon (2012), *Blogs and Bullets II: New Media and Conflict After the Arab Spring, United States* Institute of Peace, Washington, p. 4.
39. Turkey's total trade with Middle Eastern countries increased from 4.4 billion dollars in 2002 to almost 26 billion dollars in 2010. Turkey's out-ward foreign direct investment stock, apart from construction investments, also improved in the same period. Accordingly between 2002 and 2009, it reached 11.2 billion dollars, 3.1 of which is directed to Asia, including Near and Middle Eastern countries. See, Ziya Onis, Turkey and the Arab Spring: Between Ethics and Self Interest, *Insight Turkey*, Vol. 14, No. 3, 2012, pp. 45-63.
40. Ibid.
41. See, Anwar Alam, *The Limits of Political Islam: The Other Face of AKP,* Part 1 and II, Todays Zaman, December 22 and 23, 2013, available at, http://www.todayszaman.com/news-334722-limits-of-political-islam-the-other-face-of-akp-by-anwar-alam-.html.
42. In this regard Yilmaz has contributed series of articles in Todays Zaman and other newspapers.
43. 'Freedom House Report Categorizes Turkey among 'NO Free' Country, Todays Zaman, May 1, 2014, available at, https://www.todayszaman.com/news-346618-turkish-press-not-free-freedom-house.html .
44. Gurpreet Mahajan (1998), *Identities and Rights: Aspects of*

Liberal Democracy in India, Oxford University Press, p. 26.

45. James P. Piscatori (1986), *Islam in a World of Nation-States*, Cambridge: Cambridge University Press.
46. David Horovitz, "A mass expression of outrage against injustice," Jerusalem Post, February, available at, www.jpost.com/Opinion/Columnists/Article.aspx?id,February 25, 2011.
47. Barak Ravid, "Netanyahu: Arab Spring pushing Mideast East backward, not forward", Hearted, November 24, 2011.
48. Isaac Chotiner, "V. S. Naipaul on the Arab Spring, Authors He Loathes, and the Books He will Never Write", The New Republic, December 7, 2012, available at, www.newrepublic.com/article/1100946/vs-naipaul-the-arab-spring-authors-he-loathes-and-the-books-he-will-never-write.
49. See for the comprehensive treatment of politics of authoritative accommodation in the region, Rex Bryman, Pete W. Moore, Basel F. Salloukh and Marie-Joelle Zahar (2013), *Beyond the Arab Spring: Authoritariansm and Democratisation in the Arab World*, Lynne Rienner Publishers, USA.
50. lan Pappé, *op.cit.*

Arab Spring is in Great Distress

By M.K. Bhadrakumar

It gives me great pleasure to be invited to deliver the keynote address at such an important conference dwelling on a topic of profound significance to contemporary world politics. I intend to restrict myself to placing the phenomenon of the Arab Spring in a global context. This may seem a futile exercise because when the Arab Spring was nominated for the Nobel Peace Prize last year or when it actually received the Sakharov Prize for Freedom of Thought from the European Parliament, the accent was on its inner world. In the overwhelming bulk of western literature on the Arab Spring, the accent continues to be on the march of the indomitable human spirit in its quest for freedom. The leading human rights organization in Washington, Freedom House, underscored the quintessence of the Arab Spring as of "captive people seeking freedom after decades of oppression".

But then, arguably, Nobel too is imbued with world politics, as we have long suspected; Sakharov legacy certainly occupies the high ground of Cold War politics and indeed Freedom House hinted that the Arab Spring is "very much the same" as the downfall of the Soviet Union in 1991, which of course reset the chessboard of world politics.

Suffice to say, what lends enchantment to the view is that the Arab Spring stands at cross-roads today. It did topple regimes in four countries—Tunisia, Egypt, Libya and Yemen—although what follows remains unclear. Equally, it reinvigorated political Islam, just when the belief was gaining prevalence that political Islam was moribund; and Arab Spring intensified dormant rivalries among regional powers and even rekindled the ambitions of extra-regional powers.

On a broader plane, it has brought to the centre stage the issues that first surfaced alongside the 'colour revolutions' which erupted on the territory of the former Soviet Union—the genesis of popular uprisings and the forces at work behind them, hidden and open; 'democratization' as a means to resolving problems and contradictions in countries with their own unique modes of social formation; indeed, the meaning of 'democracy' itself in the modern world. Economic factors alone cannot be regarded as the motivating factor in the Arab Spring. The upheavals that have surfaced are not even in the poorest or least developed parts of West Asia—with the exception of Yemen. Clearly, the old models of governance have been found anachronistic by the masses that today have easy access to international experiences thanks to the revolution in the media. Indeed, the media provide social networking for a broad enough swathe of society to provoke change.

The key issue is of legitimacy. Yet, curiously, the tremors of popular discontent have somewhat bypassed the conservative monarchies where power is inherited and have instead visited autocratic republics under 'elected' presidents. Why and how this happened needs probing.

Again, Islamist parties have come to the lead on the political spectrum in Tunisia and Egypt, the two countries that went through democratic elections, and across the board their surge is apparent. To my mind, this is primarily due to a combination of two circumstances. One, Islamist forces have long operated clandestinely as neighbourhood groups and over time gained legitimacy and popular acceptance in a political environment characterized by repression and unresponsive regimes. They, therefore, enjoy an early lead as vehicles of popular aspirations. Two, in the stifling environment of autocratic rule, efforts toward building new political systems of representative character were non-existent and secular forces languished in the bargain.

The dialectics involving the robust forces of political Islam and the nascent secular elements in the building of modern institutions becomes an absorbing template of the West Asian politics in the coming period. I do not see a particular version of Islamic democracy—Arab or non-Arab—as offering a model here.

It helps to weigh in, though, that the ascendancy of the Islamist parties is taking place in the shadow of a globalized economy. The big question is how the Islamist revolutionaries are going to acquit themselves in power. History shows that revolutionaries are not above constituting the counter-revolution. This is one thing. Second, the Islamists in power face a hard struggle to reform the deteriorating economic situation and this may prompt them to adhere to the Washington Consensus so that international financial institutions will loosen their purse strings. This is already happening with the Muslim Brotherhood in Egypt and the al-Nahda party in Tunisia, which are inclined to view the Washington Consensus as a pragmatic choice that combines political liberation and democracy with economic freedom, apart from gaining acceptance by the western powers. The White House announced in February 2012 to help Arab Spring countries with more than 800 million dollars in economic aid. It is difficult to tell how much of the proposal is actually new money but the political message is self-evident. In sum, the revolutionary spirit in the current upheaval should not be mistaken as directed against capitalism or anything like that, although corruption and injustice and inequities were causes that triggered the upheaval.

The point is, these processes are not taking place in a vacuum. The regional backdrop has transformed. Gulf Cooperation Council, comprising countries not many of whom are known for democratic rule, is nonetheless acting as the guide and guardian angel of reform in Bahrain and Yemen. The Arab League, which was long derided as a club of dictators, is on a lead role in Syria and within that organization two oil monarchies are at the barricades as the flag carriers of democracy in Syria alongside non-Arab countries belonging to the North Atlantic Treaty Organisation [NATO], while at least four Arab states that could today claim to have some form of representative rule—including two of Syria's immediate neighbours—have dissented. The Arab League may have damaged its credibility in the Syrian crisis. It appears to be unable to have to act without the West and may be displaying its over-dependence on an outmoded paradigm in which Washington always prevails.

The latest Arab League stance to "provide all kinds of political and material support" to the Syrian opposition opens a new chapter in intra-Arab relations. "All options" is diplomatic language associated so far with the US and Israeli threats to Iran and for the first time it is entering the lexicon of intra-Arab politics. Again, the United States' standoff with Iran has been brought forward to replace or to digress attention from the Arab-Israeli conflict and the Palestinian problem. There is also a deliberate attempt to portray Sunni-Shi'ite sectarian confrontation as the dominant regional narrative. Woven into this is the angst over Iran's nuclear programme and that country's dramatic rise as a regional power, which challenges Israel's traditional regional dominance.

A congruence of interests has developed between the 'pro-West' Arab oligarchies and Israel. Over and above comes the canopy of the West's historical hegemony over the oil-rich region, which it is reluctant to relinquish in the era of globalization. China's rise and Russia's return to the world stage impart urgency to the drive to perpetuate the western hegemony. West Asia always remained a pivotal region for world politics through modern history ever since Napoleon set foot in Egypt.

In the Syrian crisis, the interplay of these processes has become more visible than in Libya, which the West used to test a model for regime change under the garb of reform and democratization. Yet, the NATO's military intervention in Libya achieved only contradictory results and the saga turned out to be a cynical parody of the Arab Spring, largely discrediting the concepts of reform and change.

In the Libyan sands, the fine flower of Arab Spring began wilting. True, like in Libya, there is a popular yearning for reform and change in Syria too. But the spectre that haunts Syria is also that taking advantage of the popular yearning, outside powers have jumped into the fray to push an agenda of regime change. Syria's neighbouring countries have become staging ground for inciting civil war conditions, which could at some point be seized as justification for direct, armed intervention. If oil was the leitmotif for the NATO intervention in Libya, much more is at stake in the geopolitics over Syria.

At the very least, Syria's weakening as a state in the forefront of regional politics, coming on top of Iraq's devastation and Egypt's transition would mean the collapse of Arabism for the foreseeable future, which in turn mitigates Israel's acute isolation today. Syria is Iran's strongest ally in the region, and Damascus left a strong imprint on politics in Lebanon as well as on the Palestinian resistance. Once again, we come back to the security of Israel. Quite obviously, in the regime-change bandwagon in the US, we can easily spot many well-known friends of Israel, who espouse that a weakened Syria, marooned in protracted civil war, will weaken Arabism and militant Palestinian resistance.

The West has successfully frustrated repeated Russian efforts to bring the Syrian authorities and opposition on to the negotiating table. On the other hand, bereft of the fig-leaf of a UN mandate, the West and its regional allies are reluctant to plunge into direct military intervention in Syria. Meanwhile, the Syrian regime continues to enjoy substantial support of the people and of the armed forces. The Al-Qaeda chief Ayman al-Zawahiri's latest statement, affirming support for the so-called Syrian opposition—and for regime change—underscores that the beast of anarchic violence is slouching toward Damascus.

I chose to speak at some length on Syria because what happens in Syria is going to seal the fate of the Arab Spring. The spiralling violence inside Syria and the continued ambivalence on the part of the West and its local allies toward the idea of dialogue and peaceful reform are feeding on each other. According to the UN, 10,00,000 lives have been lost in the conflict so far. The entry of Al-Qaeda takes the situation a critical step forward toward the eruption of sectarian violence of a kind that tore Iraq apart in the recent years. Syria is a melting pot of so many ethnic groups and polarization and religious intolerance can plunge the country into civil war. The Arab Spring will never recover if it turns out to be that the West and its local allies have entered into a marriage of convenience with Al-Qaeda, as they once did in Afghanistan.

Iraq's Deputy Interior Minister Adnan al-Assadi stated in February 2012 that jihadists are flocking to Syria from Iraq and weaponry is being sent across the border to support anti-Assad movement in the country. Apparently, outflow of weapons into Syria has assumed such proportions that the price of a Kalashnikov assault rifle has risen in recent weeks from 100-200 dollars up to 1,500 dollars in Mosul. In a historical sense, whoever is paying for this trans-border gun-running operation is rubbishing the reputation of the Arab Spring.

To be sure, the Arab Spring is in great distress already. It is threatened with outright seizure by the West in cohort with local partners to serve as an instrument of geopolitical agenda. But what gets overlooked is that the genie of self-determination once let loose from the bottle in Syria cannot easily be put back and the plain truth is that self-determination has application in one form or another for many countries ranging from the Mediterranean to the Arabian Peninsula that emerged after the collapse of the Ottoman Empire. In short, the induced Arab Spring in Syria could produce results as unexpected as the contrived 'Arab revolt' one hundred years ago. Undoubtedly, a contestation for regional influence has begun, which prompts one to recall Kemal Ataturk's famous words—'Peace at home Peace abroad' as a highly relevant maxim for all.

This is not to deny the authenticity of the natural desire of the Arab peoples to express their political views but I am only drawing attention to the paradox that attempts to impose democracy or choreograph the narrative to suit geopolitical agenda by suppressing that natural desire risks a polarization of allegiances holding the potential for escalation of violence. In sum, the western expectation is to finesse the regional upheaval and guide them as democratic movements that allow space for pro-West democratic liberals to grow and mature and eventually seize the opportunity to build new pro-Western governments overthrowing the old ones it has been long unhappy about. However, although at times it may appear the West has stolen the Arab Spring in Libya and Syria, the interpenetration of revolutionary circumstances is never quite that simple to predict, leave alone calibrate.

Besides, the current wave of social and political upheavals stem from multiple causes and multiple aims. While the upheavals in Tunisia and Egypt wore revolutionary characteristics, those in Bahrain and Libya have been different, rooted in religious or tribal conflicts. In Yemen, the upheaval stems from a variety of factors such as tribal conflict, political separatism and the intervention of Al-Qaeda affiliates. Syria's is also a complicated mix of social, political, religious and ethnic conflicts, which could extend beyond its borders.

The single biggest outcome of the Arab Spring so far has been the marginalization of peace talks between the Palestinians and Israel, which nonetheless remains the dominant question in the region. The West has contrived to push Syria and Iran to the forefront as factors that decide the future of West Asia. However, this will only complicate solutions to the Arab-Israeli conflict and the Palestinian problem. In a long-term perspective, it is small comfort that the Hamas leadership has been forced to relocate from Damascus and it is too dangerous a fallacy to hope that Islamism can be 'Americanised'.

It is apparent that the bilateral ties between Egypt and Israel have radically transformed. This trend is likely to repeat elsewhere too as a series of regimes more responsive to popular attitudes appear on the regional landscape in a political environment where popular attitudes are quite critical of American foreign policy—and especially so in regard of the Israeli-Palestinian issue. As the former US national security advisor Zbgniew Brzezinski noted, "we underestimate the extent to which Arab public opinion on the popular level is truly preoccupied—and in some respects even impassioned—regarding the Israeli-Palestinian issue...the issue is at the base of a lot of anti-American or anti-Western Arab sentiments". Therefore, while Israel might seem to benefit in the short-term, thanks largely on the basis of short-sighted expediency—namely, taking cover behind a seemingly good argument that this is not an opportune moment for negotiations—in the longer run, Israel may be ruling itself out as a viable, creative and influential participant in a more accommodated and peaceful Middle East and the implications of that for Israel's future could be ominous.

Equally, a dichotomy exists as regards the Arab attitudes. Very little is still being posed even after the upheavals appeared as to what truly motivates the Arab masses. The West—and much of the world community, including India—continue to ask themselves what motivates the *Arab elites*. We find it convenient to do so as the Arab elites are more inclined to accommodate our wishes because of the overlapping interests, which are essentially financial interests. But we tend to overlook that this is not the case with the Arab masses. The Arab Spring highlights that we have to pay attention to the Arab masses, given the strong likelihood that a variety of domestic political forces with different political aspirations competing against each other can be expected to emerge out of the debris of the collapse of the authoritarian regimes. Egypt is already showing the way.

The Arab Spring has exposed a great variety of contradictions in the countries of West Asia, which have accumulated through the past century or more since the collapse of the Ottoman Empire. The best hope is that Arab elites themselves explore the ways to resolve the contradictions and work for a historic revival of the Arab people. But that is too much to hope for. Whereas, the probability is that great upheavals such as the Arab Spring and the transformations they engineer play out over a long period of time. Although almost uniformly the people expect that a new Arab world of prosperity, strength, progress, independence and civilizational flowering will emerge in the aftermath of the upheavals, quite obviously, such dreams are seldom if ever fulfilled. I can only repeat the thoughtful observation by a Chinese scholar that I came across recently: While real revolutions may take place in some countries of West Asia, “the signs of revolutionary institutional transformations are yet to emerge” in any of the four countries that the Arab Spring visited.

Part I: Arab Spring in Maghreb

1

Popular Uprising in North Africa: Radical Change, Gradual Adaptation and the Challenge to Authoritarianism

Azzedine Layachi

Even though a lot has been—and continues to be—written about what is termed the "Arab Spring" and "Arab Revolutions", much of the writing has at times been too simplistic or more of a wishful thinking than the complex analysis these historical events that started in December 2010 warrant. This chapter, which tries to relay such complexity, focuses on the mass revolts that led to the overthrow of regimes in Tunisia and Libya in 2011 and the gradual reform processes enacted in Algeria and Morocco during and right after 2011 for the purpose of avoiding unsettling revolts. While the focus is limited to the Maghreb—the North African countries of Algeria, Libya, Morocco and Tunisia—several elements of the discussion pertain to the Middle East as well.

At the outset, it is important to define the subject of this analysis, i.e., what has been called the "Arab Spring." Very few people have taken a moment to define "Arab Spring" beyond simply equating it with "popular revolt against authoritarian rulers." In this chapter, the use of this expression is purposefully limited because the phenomenon it seems to refer to has been misconstrued, misunderstood and, at times, manipulated in academic and media publications. The expressions preferred here are "popular revolts," "mass protests," and "social upheavals". Furthermore, the word "Arab" in the expression "Arab Spring" tends to exclude those who have rebelled but who do not necessarily share the Arab identity, such as the Berbers of North Africa. The popular upheavals discussed here—called "Arab

Spring" by others—is defined as a mass protest (peaceful or violent) against existing political and economic systems, rulers and policies in the Arab region; such protests are persistent, vocal, peaceful or violent, and they either just challenge the status quo or end it.

The mass revolts that began in December 2010 in Tunisia, spread across the Arab world in 2011, and culminated in the overthrow of the leaders of Tunisia, Egypt, Libya and Yemen, aimed at ending three conditions:

1. The political systems that failed their people and crushed their ambitions, wishes and dignity for decades.
2. The social and economic conditions that left many people deprived while a few predatory individuals, with privileged connections to the state, thrived in wealth, prestige and contempt for the rest.
3. The post-colonial order that was maintained in the Arab world many decades after the end of formal colonialism. This post-colonial order was characterized by the rule of local autocrats whose political survival depended on being compliant and subservient to the wishes and interests of former colonial masters (mainly France and the United Kingdom) and the United States.

The revolts were more about this triple rejection than solely a clash between authoritarian states and unemployed youth. The cries of the revolting masses clearly relayed this triple rejection. In the Maghreb, developments in post-Ben Ali Tunisia and post-Gaddafi Libya accentuated this even further when sharp disputes developed between the secular left, the secular right, religious moderates and religious radicals, over social and economic policies, institutions and foreign policy. The issues raised included not only the new order to be established in the various countries, but also the question of where national identity resides on the liberal to religious/conservative ideological spectrum.

Given the fact that genuine and revolutionary change involves more than the overthrow of a leader, two questions beg for answers today, almost two years since all this began in

December 2010 in Tunisia; they are:

1. Did what happened in 2011 in some countries usher in the end of "Arab Exceptionalism" and the start of a genuine regime change—be it paced and gradual or swift and radical?, or
2. Are we witnessing, yet, another adaptation of the authoritarian rule to the circumstances of the day?

To answer these questions, it is necessary to tackle first the notion of "Arab Exceptionalism" and the many ways authoritarian rulers in North Africa and the Middle East shunned real change in the past by subterfuge, superficial reforms, manipulations and plain repression.

Arab Exceptionalism

For a long period of time, many people have commented that the Middle East and North Africa (MENA) in general, and the Arab world in particular, have missed the three historic waves of democratization outlined by Samuel Huntington in his 1993 book, *The Third Wave: Democratization in the Late Twentieth Century*. [1] The first wave started in the 19th century in Western Europe and North America; the second began after World War II in Europe and swept away dictatorships that sprang out before and during the war; and the third wave started in the mid 1970s and affected Latin America, Spain, Portugal, and, more recently, Eastern Europe. [2]

It was often been said that the Arab and Muslim countries of the MENA have missed all waves and were not likely to democratize due to several reasons. This condition became known as the Arab or Middle East Exceptionalism. Some scholars and commentators used the controversial cultural explanation to aver that the local cultures, due to their nature, cannot produce proponents of the democratic creed; they argued that these cultures promoted anti-democratic attitudes among generally submissive populations.

It has also been said that Islam constituted an obstacle to

democratic change because, among other things, this religion is about "submission," not political opposition and accountability. In his 1993 essay in Foreign Affairs titled, "The Clash of Civilizations?", Samuel Huntington argued that "Western ideas of individualism, liberalism, constitutionalism, human rights, equality, liberty, the rule of law, democracy, free markets...often have little resonance in Islamic, Confucian, Japanese, Hindu, Buddhist or Orthodox cultures". [3] In his book, *The Third Wave*, Huntington suggested the same thing and pointed to the case of Lebanon, which, according to him was a democratic state before the Muslim population substantially increased at the expense of the Christian one. "Once Muslims became a majority in Lebanon and began to assert themselves, Lebanese democracy collapsed". [4] Of course, he did not acknowledge (or did not see) that what he called Lebanese democracy, under Christian dominance, was sectarian and flawed.

Beyond the views that attribute endogenous causes (e.g., culture and religion) to the Arab, Muslim or Middle Eastern Exceptionalism, there are those that favour exogenous reasons such as the active Western support to the region's authoritarian rulers. This view, which is usually claimed by local opposition forces, became quite popular, especially in light of the close relationship developed by Western powers with the rulers of Saudi Arabia, Egypt, and Tunisia among others. Regardless of which explanation one espouses—and all have been debated extensively in the past—it is undeniable that the MENA region—with a few exceptions—was not substantially affected by the spread of liberal democracy in the West and beyond, that is, until now.

According to the 2011 Freedom House Report, only four countries in the Arab/Islamic MENA were "partly free" (some restrictions on political rights and civil liberties); these were Morocco, Lebanon, Kuwait and Turkey. The rest were rated as "not free" (i.e., they lacked basic political rights and basic civil liberties). According to most accounts, the whole region fared far worse in democratization than all the regions of the world, including sub-Sahara Africa where recent progress has drastically increased the number of both "free" and "partly free" countries.

For many people, the MENA region seemed so persistently resistant to any serious change, in spite of the occasional utterances of a small but defiant opposition, that the events of the first months of 2011 in North Africa came as shock to everyone, including the protestors who brought down the rulers of Tunisia and Egypt after just a few days of street mobilization. It took much longer and much more violence in Libya, but seeing Colonel Gaddafi on the run for much of 2011 was even surprising to the Libyans themselves.

However, from a different vantage point, it can be said that in the last three decades the region from Morocco to Iran has known some slow but important changes; starting with the Iranian revolution of 1979, these changes included political openings in Kuwait after 1991, in Jordan and Algeria in the late 1980, in Morocco since the late 1990s, and even in Bahrain. These were not gigantic steps toward democracy, but they constituted an important dent in several authoritarian systems of the region.

In spite of the fact that the 2011 region-wide upheavals were difficult to predict, signs of the impending social explosions were visible for many years before 2011. What is certain now is that the remarkable events that are still unfolding may finally put to rest the thesis of Arab and Middle Eastern exceptionally as they exhibit the prowess of the "Arab Street".

Context and Causes of the Upheaval

Since their independence from colonialism, the countries of the Maghreb region achieved important progress in economic and human development. The 2010 Human Development Report places Algeria, Morocco and Tunisia among ten countries designated as "top movers", i.e., countries that achieved the greatest improvements in human development when compared to their respective levels in 1970. [5] However, this does not dismiss the fact that these countries still lag behind in social and economic development. In fact, the limits of the progress achieved became apparent in the last two decades. In spite a relatively positive human development index (HDI) across the region, most countries lagged in social and economic development and could not keep up with their growing populations.

Furthermore, the external pressure for economic liberalization and the effect of global economic shocks and other factors made it difficult for the states to maintain welfare systems and distributive policies dictated by explicit or tacit post-independence social contracts. These factors, in combination with the promotion of neo-liberal policies by international institutions, pushed the states to diminish their role in the economy by privatizing public companies, limiting subsidies and lifting price controls.

While oil and gas exporters, such as Algeria and Libya, remained highly dependent on the export of those commodities whose price fluctuations they do not control, the non-hydrocarbon countries with diversified economies, such as Morocco and Tunisia, became substantially vulnerable to rising international competition and demand fluctuations for their products, including agro-products, clothing and tourism.

Drastic structural adjustment reforms sponsored by the IMF and the World Bank in Algeria, Morocco and Tunisia had some success at the aggregate level, but they did not improve the living conditions and unemployment situation of large segments of society. What made—and still makes—the inadequate social and economic conditions of many people untenable are rampant corruption, cronyism, nepotism, limited outlets for the expression of grievances, and limited possibility for a grassroots impact on public policy.

Furthermore, the coercive capacity of all North African states was perfected over the past decades and its effectiveness and pervasiveness increased in recent years, especially under the effect of the wholehearted willingness of many governments to partake in the "Global War on Terror" (GWT) initiated by the United States after the 9/11 terrorist attack. This policy helped limit political dissent even more.

In the contexts outlined above, the 2011 social upheavals were just waiting to happen. However, no one predicted what would trigger them and when. As they started unfolding, the popular upheavals—commonly known as the "Arab Spring", pointed to a series of common denominators across the region (the general social, economic and political conditions), but also to distinct triggering events.

Common Conditions but Unique Triggers

After the self-immolation of the fruit cart vendor Mohamed Bouazizi in the Tunisian town of Sidi Bouzid on December 17, 2010, people in Tunisia and elsewhere in the region suddenly shed their fear of the state and its repressive apparatus; they abandoned their seeming political apathy and decided to confront their ruling regimes head on and without possibility of retreat. While in Tunisia the upheaval was triggered by the self-immolation act, every subsequent revolt in the region had also its unique triggers. However, all upheavals shared some common elements; this may explain the speed of the contagious effect. The common underlying conditions that stimulated serious and long-standing political and economic grievances include ruling systems which:

1. Were inherently authoritarian over a long period of time,
2. Abused power openly and with impunity,
3. Limited extensively individual liberties,
4. Dealt with citizen with disdain and condescendence,
5. Swallowed up opposition figures and parties via co-optation if they did not neutralize them by other means, including banishment and/or repression,
6. Limited the means of free expression,
7. Inhibited the accountability of institutions and individual power holders,

8. Reduced the judicial branch to both, a system that serves the powerful, and a means to abuse of the non-powerful,
9. Made elections and the institutions of representation a sham,
10. Used oil or other source of rent to quiet occasional social unrest without reforming and to neutralize potential forces of challenge such as the army, and
11. Appeared more subservient to the neo-colonial and imperialist forces than to their own people.

The prevailing social and economic conditions on the eve of the upheavals were characterized by:

1. The lack of employment opportunities for the educated and uneducated youth which make up the overwhelming majority of the region's population (the "Youth Bulge")—over 50 percent are under 30 years old, more in some countries. With a national unemployment rate of 10 percent to 15 percent, the youth often represent 40 percent at least of the unemployed; [6]
2. Failing educational system and their disconnection from the job market and from the changing requirements for employment due to the advent of globalization and the information technology revolution;
3. Very low wages, even unrealistic, which make people in some countries devote almost half of their salaries to basic food purchases;
4. Corruption and the shameless exhibition of wealth by the few people who were connected to the state and its leaders;
5. Nepotism and cronyism which are not only quite obvious, but also parasitic—billions of dollars in the hand of very few well-connected people, often relatives of the ruling leader or his wife;
6. In the oil exporting countries, such as Algeria and Libya, the unexplained paradox that exists between rising national export earning and increasing depravation and poverty among large segments of society;
7. Regional and urban-rural disparities in economic

development and in the provision of public services. (regional disparities are widely apparent throughout the region).

The conditions for upheaval and rebellion have thus been there for a long time, but somehow, this highly combustible situation needed a trigger event to explode. That initial trigger happened, totally unexpectedly, in Tunisia where riots, which had started on December 17 in the town of Sidi Bouzid, spread to the capital city of Tunis within a few days and deposed the president. In neighbouring Algeria, youth took to the streets in early January 2011 with a series of riots in many cities and towns. The triggers included both a sudden rise in the price of basic food and the events in Tunisia. [7] However, these riots, which had no political demands, ended within a few days after the government acted to maintain the pre-existing price levels and promised reforms. In mid-February, it was the turn of Libyan protests to start in the eastern city of Benghazi after the arrest of a human rights lawyer; this quickly turned bloody when government forces started shooting at the protesters. The unrest quickly spread to other parts of the country, starting thereby a protracted war that ended with the killing of the leader Muammar al-Gaddafi in October 2011.

Libya became the first country where an international coalition decided to intervene militarily to help the rebels in the name of protecting protesters from the onslaught that was taking place. [8] On Sunday, February 20, Morocco witnessed a massive, but peaceful, demonstrations calling for economic reforms and constitutional change. Known as the "February 20th Movement", the protest was triggered by the winds of social upheaval that were blowing in the region and by growing discontent among the Moroccan youth. The demonstrations prompted King Mohammed VI to announce reforms, including constitutional amendments. [9]

Contagion Effect and Empowerment of the Masses

This series of events, which are historic and still unfolding, may be unique to each country, but they are connected by a common malaise that has finally produced an unrelenting and massive movement for change. What helped spread the winds of change across the Middle East and North Africa so fast were the contagion effect, the shedding of fear by the masses, the belief held by many people that now is the most opportune time to demand and bring about genuine change, and the role internet social networks and the cell phone? The events in Tunisia, Libya and other Arab countries reflected a new empowerment of the citizens who discovered that that peaceful and persistent collective action can bring about change. Their grievances are real and their voices have become louder than the state propaganda they have learned to ignore.

The new communication technologies (internet—including social networks, YouTube—and mobile phone) facilitated mobilization and, more importantly, empowered everyone to spread the news, the slogans and the calls for action using text, images and video clips. Even though the extent of internet connectivity in the region remains low and closely monitored by the state, there is enough of it to be of some help. These social media helped spread the winds of popular revolt by both presenting events that can be emulated, starting with the Tunisia riots, and by facilitating mass mobilization.

The state leaders in these countries underestimated the strength of their peoples' desire for an immediate, substantial and meaningful change; future leaders will probably never do so again. The rulers who have not been thrown out yet, or have not been themselves directly challenged, have quickly enacted—or announced—reforms and cuts in the prices of basic food items, and promised more jobs, more freedom and constitutional reforms. [10]

The Algerian government finally lifted on February 22, the 19 year old state of emergency. It also promised economic reforms aiming at creating more jobs and low income housing, as well as political reforms, including constitutional changes and new laws on political parties and the media. The

Moroccan state gave permission for the February 20 demonstration and King Mohammed VI announced on March 9, the plan for important constitutional changes that would include allowing parliament to choose government members on the basis of electoral results rather keeping such choice in the sole hands of the king as it has always been done. As for Libya, a few promises by Muammar al-Gaddafi came too late for a society that was muzzled, controlled, and deprived for too long. By mid-2011, a popular rebellion was set on overthrowing him. Aided by NATO military intervention under a United Nation mandate to protect the population from the onslaught of state repression, the Libyan rebellion overthrew the mighty leader in less than a year.

Protests Outcomes and the Paths Pursued

As indicated above, each of the 2011 popular protests in the Maghreb region has had its own trigger(s), style and outcome. The differences in the way each upheaval proceeded and ended can be accounted by a complex series of factors, including:

1. The extent of the grievances and the demands they generated.
2. The number of deprived and disenchanted people across social classes and sectarian strata.
3. The configuration of the economic and political power structure in the country.
4. The place and role of the security services in the governing system, i.e., whether: (a) there is sizeable, coherent and well structured military and police establishments that either have or do not have a major stake in the status-quo, (b) the military establishment is a politicized or not, and to what extent, and (c) the military and police forces are substantially corrupt.
5. The existence of a sizeable middle class that is either generally satisfied with (and well served by) the existing system or unhappy because it is restrained by a predatory

state and its elites.

6. The extent of governmental and social cohesion (less in Libya and more in Tunisia, Algeria and Morocco). [11]
7. The extent of corruption and abject nepotism and cronyism. [12]
8. The existence or absence of labour unions and associations and their level of organizational and mobilization strength.
9. The existence or absence of a key leader against whom the social upheaval focuses.
10. The nature and extent of foreign meddling or intervention.

A detailed study of each case may establish some correlations between the above factors and the extent of each revolt, the way it evolved and its outcome. As a result of these region-wide revolts, are the North African countries today moving away from the authoritarian pattern of governance, or are they just going through an adaptation of the authoritarian rule to the circumstances of the day? This question is often asked, especially when the radical change people expected overnight did not happened. It will be addressed here in the discussion of each of the four Maghrebi cases.

End of Exceptionalism or Adaptation of Authoritarianism?

The literature on authoritarianism is old and rich and yet that are many questions that still elude its scholars, especially in light of the recent rapid collapse of "robust" authoritarian systems in the Arab world, to everyone's surprise. [13] Among such questions are: what makes authoritarianism survive for a long time in one country or region and not in others? What makes authoritarianism able to resist internal and external challenges and how? What factors help bring an end to such system and when? Answers to these and other relevant questions can be helped by the study of the recent wave of revolts that unseated four long-time authoritarian rulers in four Arab countries within a year. The previously held view on the "robustness" of Arab regimes unravelled as fast as these regimes themselves.

For many years, and in the face of resilient authoritarianism in some parts of the world, including the MENA region, some scholars and keen political observers created conceptual shades of authoritarianism to explain the longevity of this phenomenon. [14] These conceptual shades have been used to characterize authoritarian regimes which, under domestic and external pressure, enacted some political liberalization without necessarily changing fundamentally.

The conceptual shades include "illiberal democracy" and "liberalized autocracy," among many others. These concepts may have been helpful in describing shades of authoritarianism but they did not explain much. They were meant more as concepts that inform Western foreign policy than elements of explanation and theory-building endeavours. By all accounts, there was not a single democratic regime in the Arab world on the eve of the 2011 upheavals. The different characterizations of the regimes in place did not change their authoritarian nature.

Tunisia and Libya the Day After: Political Liberalization or Democracy?

The overthrow of the rulers of Tunisia and Libya may be an important step in realizing people's yearning for jobs, freedom, democracy and dignity, but this alone and in itself does not constitute regime change or an automatic end of authoritarianism. Both are long and arduous endeavours; they are also reversible. For this reason, it is too early to say whether Tunisia and Libya are on their way to achieving such substantial change. What was achieved by the fall of 2012 may be best termed political liberalization or political opening; it may lead to democracy after it reaches its peak or it may not.

Political liberalization, as I defined it elsewhere, is "a process that gradually allows political freedoms and establishes some safeguards against the arbitrary action of the state". [15] It is a preliminary set of conditions of democracy. The intermediary stage between political liberalization to democracy is termed democratization, which is "a higher level of political opening, a process through which state control over society is slowly diminished to a point where the state becomes less arbitrary and more prone to bargaining with key groups representing differentiated social, economic, and cultural interest. At this stage, the state tends to progressively resort less to command governance and more to negotiated public policies". [16] Democratization can strengthen the state's legitimacy and give it a new basis as society acquires greater autonomy and is allowed, through independent representation, access to policy-making. However, it is a long and arduous process that may lead either to democracy or to a reverse movement toward authoritarianism, chaos, or a lasting internal conflict within a polarized society.

Democracy is "a set of institutions, a process, and a political culture, which allow individuals and groups to have a regular input in the policy-making process. The authoritarian reflexes of those who rule are restrained by participatory politics characterized by the elite's regular turnover and accountability, and by the transparency of political and economic transactions. Political culture at this stage is characterized by free debates, a tolerance of differences, transparency and accountability in governance, and bargaining-produced public policies. Democracy is also about allowing and enabling citizen 'to pursue their happiness' within the confines of what society, through its representative institutions, decides freely to be in the interest of all". [17]

Based on the above definitions of these distinct processes and conditions, it can be said that what was achieved so far by the upheavals in Tunisia and Libya is, or approximates, political liberalization. Tunisia may have a better chance than the rest in a successful transition away from autocracy and the factors in favour of such prospect include the extent of economic development, social and political cohesion, and a political military establishment. However, the success of the transition will depend also on many other factors, including, a consensus among the religious and secular forces on the economic development strategy and on the political system and its guiding value system. Tunisia is also far more advanced in this transition process than Libya notably because it has had some level of political institutionalization and a functioning state.

In contrast, the post-Gaddafi Libya is starting with almost no state structures and institutions which have to be built from scratch. In Libya today, there is no institution with the monopoly of force and with enough legitimacy to command unity. Instead, there are weak parliament and government whose authority is not yet established, and several, independent, armed groups.

Because social and political cohesion lacks and national unity and security are still fragile, one cannot assert whether a transition has started and towards what end. The new government and parliament may constitute a clear break from pseudo-secular order of the last 40 years, but the strong presence of Islamist forces, both in parliament and as independent armed factions, point to a likely important role of religion in the control over Libya's destiny.

In both cases, Tunisia and Libya, the fundamental elements of authoritarian governance may have been eliminated for now, but the serious challenges facing the new transition governments in Tunisia and Libya (Egypt also) may tip the balance back toward autocracy, especially if the current weakness of the new central institution and the numerous armed groups seriously undermine security and stability.

Tunisia: The Tunisians are quite aware of this and have been trying to avert such a negative scenario. A constitutive legislature was elected on October 23, 2011 and is now working on drafting a new constitution, while a caretaker government (unity government of Islamists and secular leftists) tries to manage the best way it can the transition and the most urgent tasks of the day.

Today's power contenders, who came to occupy positions of high political authority, are the product of the old regime.

They were its nemesis who were persecuted, jailed and pushed into overseas exile. Among them are the Ennahda party and its leader Rached al-Ghannouchi and Moncef Marzoui a former human rights activist and leader of the Congress for the Republic party (CPR). Following the 2011 Parliamentary elections, the Ennahda party became the dominant political formation, with a control of 41 percents of the 217 seats of the Constitutive Assembly. Marzouki was elected interim president of Tunisia by parliament, while Hamadi Jebali, the secretary general of Ennahda and a former opposition figure, was appointed prime minister. The office of the Speaker of Parliament was given to Mustapha Ben Jafar, leader of the third party in the governing coalition, Ettakatol.

Political Islam, which has been in place in Tunisia for quite some time, has now come to the fore, but not necessarily as a united force of political action. It is rather fragmented mostly along the lines of "modern" or moderate on one hand (Ennahda), and radical and uncompromising, on the other (Salafi party Hizb Ettahrir, or Party of Liberation, not legalized yet).

The bulk of Tunisian Islamism has been trying to present itself as a mainstream political force that is driven more by the desire to solve daily material problems rather than bring about the rule of Allah. This might be the reason why Ennahda formed a coalition government with two secular parties rather than impose its will based on electoral legitimacy.

A smaller but quite vocal and active (disruptive) Salafi party *Hizb Ettahrir*, which is supported by a variety of religious associations, has been demanding the establishment of an Islamic regime while trying, on a daily basis, to impose conservative religious values and behaviours on the Tunisians. It is believed that this group was behind the attack on the US embassy in Tunis on September 11, 2012 in protest against the American film, "Innocence of Muslims", which depicts Prophet Muhammad in a very negative fashion. In the current debate in Tunisia on the role of religion in politics in Tunisia, the seculars are suspicious of the true intentions of Ennahda and fear that the highly active and vocal Salafi group would push it to espouse its views in order to benefit from the support of its constituency.

Beyond the tensions between secular and ultra-religious tendencies, post-Ben Ali Tunisia is suffering from a variety of social and economic difficulties in need of urgent remedies. These difficulties include economic problems, the rise of insecurity, crime and even intercommunity strife. The challenge for Tunisia now is to stay the course in building new political institutions, especially once a new constitution is approved and general elections are held and followed by the appointment of a new government by 2014. The biggest tasks ahead are economic, including the creation of enough jobs for the large number of unemployed youth, [18] and the curtailment of regional disparity in social and economic progress. The current interim leadership is reminded daily by protests and strikes that it has to live up to the promises of the "Jasmine Revolution". People are becoming growingly impatient with what they consider the very slow governmental response to its pressing problems.

Libya: Now that the autocrat leader of Libya was removed from power and his governing system and security apparatus were destroyed, the most difficult tasks lie ahead. The easiest part was getting rid of the Gaddafi regime even though it was a very violent episode that caused thousands of deaths and led a huge number of migrant workers to flee the country or fall victim to the raging violence.

Once an interim government was in place, headed by Prime Minister Abdel Rahim al-Kib, the National Transition Council (TNC) faced the daunting tasks of disarming the rebel groups, maintaining national unity, creating governing state institutions, organizing elections, and restarting the economy. Beyond resuming the production and export of hydrocarbons and organizing parliamentary elections, not much was accomplished in the other areas by fall 2012.

On July 7, 2012, a 200 member General National Congress was elected to replace the TNC and set the country on the transition course. The liberal and moderately Islamic tendency represented by the National Forces Alliance (NFA, a political alliance of 58 political organizations and hundreds of independents and NGOs) won the largest number of party-list seats (39 of the 80), well ahead of the Justice and Construction Party (Muslim Brotherhood). The NFA's key figure, Mahmoud Jibril, is former leader of the National Transition Council. Unlike what happened in Tunisia, Morocco and Egypt, Libya's Islamists did not do well in these first free elections. They will try to do better in the forthcoming election of a Constituent Assembly which will write Libya's new constitution.

Of all countries in the region which have thrown out a long-time autocratic leader, Libya has the most uncertain road ahead. "Libya, lack the basic institutional infrastructure of a solid state—a unified and professional military, civil service and judiciary. It is difficult to build a democracy without a state foundation". [19] Libya has achieved a certain degree of political liberalization, but that it is fairly limited due to the fact that the central government does not control much beyond the capital city. There are dozens of armed tribal militia and Islamist groups, which refuse to surrender their weapons and help build national unity. If this uncertain and unstable situation lasts for a while, it is possible for authoritarian governance to return and, as a result, the political gains of the spring of upheavals may be lost. A testimony of this possible development was reflected in the armed attack on the US Consulate in Benghazi which was said to be a reaction to the anti Islamic film, "Innocence of Muslims". That attack killed US ambassador Christopher Stevens and 3 other diplomats. The Islamist group *Ansar al-Sharia* was suspected of being behind the attack. The government forces were incapable to fending off this and other attacks such as those on several Sufi shrines that were desecrated and destroyed in summer 2012 by ultraconservative Islamists who believe them to be heretic and un-Islamic places of veneration and worship.

Algeria and Morocco: Algeria and Morocco did not experience upheavals of the kind witnessed in Libya and Tunisia. There were limited riots in Algeria in early January 2011 and demonstration in Morocco in February. Both countries' leadership reacted swiftly with proactive policies meant to appease people ahead of an almost certain storm. One of the many reasons why the region's winds of upheavals did not quite reach these two countries was that both had been engaged in gradual political reforms for more than a decade. These reforms did not affect the authoritarian nature of the two regimes, but they set them apart from the much harsher autocratic rule that existed in Libya and Tunisia before 2011. Algerians and Moroccan enjoyed relatively more political freedom, but high youth unemployment and wide-scale corruption made them disillusioned and resentful.

Once social upheaval was under way in several countries, it inspired similar protest movements in the two Morocco and Algeria but they were short-lived and limited in their scope. The two countries' leaders quickly acted to limit the contagion effects on their population by enacting some reforms and promising others, preventing the rise of basic food prices, and maintaining subsidies on essential products and services. They also pointed to insecurity problems and disruptions caused by social unrest in Tunisia, Libya, Egypt, Syria and Yemen as things they did not wish to see happen in their respective countries. In short, the revolts in the region did not cause major changes in Algeria and Morocco; the two authoritarian systems—one a republic and the other a monarchy—continued to give the impression of being engaged in a constant and full-fledged political liberalization.

Morocco: The death of King Hassan II in 1999 ushered in gradual reforms by his son, Mohammed VI. The latest concession of the monarchy to social and political rumbling was a constitutional reform enacted in July 2011 in response to street protests that started on February. However, the constitutional amendments did not diminish the political, religious and economic powers of the monarch; after they were approved by referendum, protesters continued to demand much needed economic reforms and a plan to tackle an endemic corruption. The constitutional amendments made the government accountable to parliament rather than to the king, and gave more say to parliament on who becomes prime minister—instead of the traditional prerogative of the monarch to appoint him.

However, they left untouched the oversized authority of the monarchy. New parliamentary elections held November 25, 2011 produced a government led by the Islamist party Justice and Development in alliance with three other parties, Istiqlal (PI), the Popular Movement (MP) and the Party of Progress and Socialism (PPS). The PJD which won the most seats in parliament (107 of the 395) became *de facto* the number one party in Morocco.

The limited popular protests in Morocco in 2011 did not contest the monarch himself; it was mostly aimed at the overall unsatisfactory political and economic conditions. Because the traditional opposition (nationalists and the left) was weakened over the years by repression, wide-scale co-optation and internal division, the PJD became the only hope for much needed changes However, this Islamist party finds itself today in a bind as it heads the coalition government—under the supervision of the monarch: to maintain its popular support and legitimacy in the eyes of its constituency, it must challenge not only the policies but also the institutional setting; this may entail taking on the *Makhzen* [20] and maybe the king himself. Upon becoming prime minister, the pro-monarchy leader of the PJD, Abdelilah Benkirane, decided to focus the efforts of his group on social and economic issues and corruption, two major points of contention raised by the February 20 movement. However, for now, Benkirane avoided questioning the institutional order or take on the *Makhzen* and the big private sector bosses which are perceived as major obstacles to change.

In short, the wave of upheavals across the region has pushed the Moroccan monarchy to accommodate somewhat the vocal protest movement through mild constitutional changes, a promise of economic reforms and more co-optation. While political liberalization has gone a long way since the late 1990s, the essential character of Morocco's governing system remains authoritarian, albeit with a monarch who is popular and seemingly benign.

Algeria: In a region deeply affected by change or the fear of it, Algeria, in a seemingly stubborn way, used its substantial oil and gas income to satisfy immediate social demands, promised political reforms and pointed to instability in Libya, Tunisia, Egypt, Syria and Yemen as a strong reason for not falling "victim" to the "Arab Spring" which was presented as a ploy by foreigners to cause instability in the Arab world. Algeria has thus remained the odd man out in this spring of upheavals and has not engaged yet in any substantial reform.

Like Morocco, Algeria had already enacted some reforms long before the upheavals of 2011. The reform process started in the late 1980s immediately after a major popular upheaval in October 1988; major riots shook the country (500 youth were killed within a few days by military repression) and were followed by a decade-long armed Islamist rebellion that cost 200,000 deaths. The rebellion—the first of its kind in the region—pushed the authoritarian regime to open the public sphere to mass political participation through changes to laws on associations, parties and the media. However, the initial political opening was slowly recanted in the name of security due to the raging Islamist rebellion that lasted from 1992 to early 2000s. The political opposition was either dispersed by intimidation, repression and judicial action or co-opted. Today, Algeria has a full-fledged multiparty political scene and a lively independent press, but no democracy. Political liberalization stalled somewhere along but that was not enough of a reason to get people to challenge the system again, so soon after the bloody decade.

The riots of early January 2011 in Algeria were triggered by rumoured impending price hikes for basic food items and were inspired by the unfolding Tunisian mass protests. However, in contrast with the Tunisian protest, the Algerian rioting youth were not supported by labour unions, political parties, or civic associations; the events lasted a week only and the protestors did not present political demands. The riots ended as soon as the government announced a low price ceiling on basic food, tabled impending market regulations and provided "temporary and exceptional exemptions on import duties, value-added tax and corporate tax for everyday commodities". [21]

On February 12, 2011 began a series of peaceful protests by a newly created National Coordination for Change and Democracy (CNCD), an organization made up of small parties, the National League for the Defence of Human Rights, and other civic associations. However, the protesters, which were prevented by the police from assembling in the centre of the capital, Algiers, demanded democracy, an end to the 19 year old state of emergency, the liberalization of the political and media fields, and the release of people arrested during the January 2011 riots. The protesters focused their attacks on what is known in Algeria as *le pouvoir*, an elusive and ambiguous notion that refers to the real, unelected power holders in Algeria, such as the military and security services and individuals controlling de facto business monopolies.

Reacting to both domestic and regional pressures, the government lifted a 19-year-old state of emergency law, promised more political freedom and announced multi-billion Dollar public investments in the economy aimed primarily at creating jobs and low-income housing. These and other announced measures were received with cynicism by an incredulous audience. If realized, these measures would constitute merely stopgap measures that do not address the fundamental problems embedded in the entire political and economic systems. These problems were clearly reflected in the results (and the very low voter turnout) of the May 2012 parliamentary elections. According to the government, the participation rate was 43%, but other sources place it at 30 percent. In these elections, the long-time sole legal party (1962-1989), the National Liberation Front won 208 seats out of 462 and another pro-establishment party, the Democratic National Rally (RND) came in second with 68 Seats. The Islamists, which had formed a "Green Alliance" and hoped to emulate the successes of their brethrens in Tunisia, Morocco and Egypt, fared badly by loosing even some of the seats they held in the previous parliament.

The political reforms enacted by the end of 2011 included the legalization of more parties and the increase in the female quota in parliamentary elections. As a result, 21 new parties were legalized, diluting further both, the overall political opposition and the Islamist formations—and a new gender quota system for electoral lists and parliament seats helped elect 145 women to parliament in May 2012, i.e., 31 percent of the 462 deputies of the National Assembly, up from a mere 7 percent.

With a pro-government coalition made up mainly of two conservative parties (FLN and RND) that qualified the "Arab Spring" as a foreign ploy, a parliament that is still a rubber-stamping machine for the president and his government, and a president himself who is ill, regularly absent from public view, and a military establishment that is still a key holder of political power, Algeria does not seem to be heading toward substantial reforms. The governing system remains authoritarian, albeit softened a bit by the 10 year war, and concerned about the possible impact of popular upheavals in neighbouring Tunisia and Libya and in Egypt.

Prospects of Change in the Maghreb

Of the four cases examined above, Tunisia seems to offer the most hope for a transition away from authoritarianism within a few years. However, this outcome will depend on how things are played out among the key actors in this post-Ben Ali era. In Libya, the trajectory of the transition is still hard to gage, but the potential for a failed move away from authoritarianism is real. For Algeria and Morocco, the gradual change approach pursued has its limitations and it may be tested in the coming years by protest and upheaval if things do not improve. In these last two cases, since January 2011, there have been clear policies of authoritarian adaptation, as has been the case of Jordan and Egypt under the post-Mubarak military rule.

All four countries have the potential to move toward a governing system functioning according to basic principles of rationality, accountability, compromise, tolerance of divergent views, justice for all, and human dignity. To remedy important problems in these areas requires these countries to take serious and lasting actions on several fronts. They would have to prevent rent (from hydrocarbons, remittances, foreign aid or other) from being used as instrument of state dominance over society, personal power, and select group privileges; there is also the need for professionalization of all security forces so as to prevent from being abusive and based on—and functioning according to—patrimonialism and sectarianism. Of equal importance will be need for blind and equal justice for all, a strong system of accountability of all office holders, even monarchs. To avoid the perennial tenure of office holders, free and multi-candidate elections must be held on a regular basis and monitored by independent institutions.

It is a fact that most of these conditions are not yet established or consolidated in the four countries and the rest of the MENA region; it will take time and persistent efforts to make them a reality. For this reason, Barbara Geddes, in her 1999 article, "What Do We Know About Democratization After 20 Years?", warmed that the fall or breakdown of authoritarianism does not automatically lead to democracy. Several factors determine whether that will happen or not, including the type of authoritarianism in place before the upheaval, the level of economic development and the extent of social mobilization for democratic change. [22] It would thus be unreasonable to expect democracy to flourish overnight in the Arab countries where people have recently overthrown autocrats or have pressured resilient rulers to enact meaningful reforms. Even if the current power holders are intent on moving away from authoritarianism and wish to establish the essential base for transition to democracy, the process is likely to be arduous and full of hurdles, including disagreements between the new governing elite:

"In general, after the post-revolutionary honeymoon period ends, divisions within the opposition start to surface. Although holding new elections is a straightforward step, election campaigns and then decisions taken by new legislatures will open debates over taxation and state spending, corruption, foreign policy, the role of the military, the powers of the president, official policy on religious law and practice, minority rights, and so on. As conservatives, populists, Islamists, and modernizing reformers fiercely vie for power in Tunisia, Egypt, and Libya, those countries will likely face lengthy periods of abrupt government turnovers and policy reversals similar to what occurred in the Philippines and many Eastern European countries after their revolutions". [23]

Commenting on the killing of Ambassador Chris Stevens in Benghazi, Libya, on September 11, 2012, Benjamin Barber, in an article titled, "The West Must Be Honest About Its Role In Libya's Violent Chaos", indicated that what is to blame in that tragedy are "the west's impatience, its belief that democracy can be imposed in a hurry from the outside, and its insistence that resistance to democracy must be the consequence of a few aberrant actors and isolated terrorists". [24] Barber also reminded us the most important lesson to be drawn is from the history of revolutions: overthrowing tyranny does not in itself establish democracy, but more often yields anarchy. And from anarchy and disorder comes renewed tyranny. The French revolution led to Napoleon and the restoration of the monarchy; the Russian revolution ended with elimination of their rivals by the Bolsheviks—call them the secular Salafists of their time. The Iranian overthrow of the shah resulted in the rule of the mullahs. [25]

Besides endogenous factors, there are also exogenous ones that will affect the evolution of the North African countries that overthrew their authoritarian leaders (Tunisia and Libya) and those that opted for piecemeal changes under domestic and international pressures (Algeria and Morocco). The external factors include the regional dynamics and contingencies, as well as extra-regional one such as the actions and roles of great powers in the current turmoil in the Maghreb and the Middle East. Because future developments in the MENA region will be affected by a myriad of internal, regional and international factors and dynamics, it is not easy to predict what will happen in any specific country as it muddles through the effects of the spring of Arab upheavals. However, some broad categories of future developments and outcomes may be tentatively identified. [26]

If the popular revolts that began in December 2011 in Tunisia are thought of as revolutions, they can then only be at their early stages. They will be long, arduous and painful, especially due to the lack of democratic structures, institutions and political culture. Instability may last for a while in countries where incumbent rulers were overthrown and those where they are teetering.

The revolts are likely to continue to have a contagion effect as more people lose fear of bad government, decide to take advantage of the current widespread grievances against them, and catch the wind of change while it is still blowing—this has been happening not just in the MENA region but across the globe, the latest popular mobilizations being those in Russia and the Maldives, and Spain.

Concerns about Islamist take over may be exaggerated in an era that is different from that of the 1980s and 1990s when

Islamist forces tended to be uncompromising, dogmatic and even violent. There is now a strong strand of political Islam that espouses moderation and accommodation, accepts basic democratic principles and respects the constitutional rules. This strand is represented by Egypt's Muslim Brothers, Tunisia's Ennahda, Algeria's Movement of Society for Peace (MSP), and Morocco's Party of Justice and Development. They seem intent on pursuing the political liberalization that brought them to power in the first place and find it their best interest to do so.

Just as stringent, essential, and necessary economic reforms are needed in order to maintain the momentum of change, so are political reforms. These reforms are essential for relative stability in the transition period. The success of transition will rest on starting work on these reforms as soon as possible.

Endnotes

1. Samuel P. Huntington, "The Third Wave: Democratization in the Late Twentieth Century", University of Oklahoma Press, 1993, p. 19.
2. It has been suggested that the 1990s collapse of the USRR and East European socialist systems constituted a 4th Wave.
3. Samuel P. Huntington, "The Clash of Civilizations?", *Foreign Affairs*, Vol. 72, No. 3, Summer *1993*, p. 40.
4. David Brooks, "Huntington's Clash Revisited," March 3, 2011, online at, www.NYTimes.com.
5. UNDP, The 2010 Human Development Report (The Real Wealth of Nations: Pathways to Human Development), November 2010, online at, http://hdr.undp.org/en/humandev/lets-talk-hd/2010-11b.
6. Beyond North Africa, there has been a systematic lack of employment and other opportunities for shi'a populations in the Gulf countries with either a majority or substantial minority of Shiites, as in the cases of Bahrain, Kuwait and Saudi Arabia.
7. On January 25, Egyptian youth started a movement that overthrew President Mubarek on February 11. The triggers included both the beating to death of Khaled Saeed, a rights activist and blogger, by the police in Alexandria and the events in Tunisia, mainly the quick toppling of Ben Ali.

8. UN Security Council Resolution 1973 authorized the use of "any means" to stop the attacks by government force. Ten out of 15 Security Council members voted in favour of the resolution, while Russia, Brazil, China, Germany and India abstained from the vote. See the media account of the vote at in "UN allows 'all necessary means' to be taken in Libya, online at, http://rt.com/news/un-military-intervention-libya.
9. Beyond North Africa, Bahrain, Yemen and Syria also became embroiled in violent protests. While in Yemeni President Abdullah Saleh finally abdicated power and left the country in January 2012, the rulers of Bahrain and Syria decided to repress rather than give in to the protesters' demands. Bahrain became the first country to be assisted by a neighbouring state, Saudi Arabia, in the quelling of the protest under the banner of the Gulf Cooperation Council (GCC).
10. The Saudi monarch handed out billions of dollars; the Jordanian monarch cancelled price hikes, revamped the government and on June 12 announced that from then on governments will be formed by parliament on the basis of election results rather than appointment by him. In Yemen, President Abdullah Saleh promised new parliamentary elections and that he will not run for office again but refused to leave office. In spite of these promises, Saleh became the fourth Arab leader to be unseated by popular protest.
11. There is more governmental and social cohesion in Egypt, but less Yemen, Syria and Mauritania.
12. According to WikiLeaks, a 2006 message from the U.S. ambassador to Tunisia indicated that more than half of Tunisia's commercial elites were relatives of Ben Ali's three adult children, seven siblings, and second wife's ten brothers and sisters). See Mila Sanina, "WikiLeaks Cables Help Uncover What Made Tunisians Revolt", PBS News Hour, January 25, 2011, online at, http://www.pbs.org/newshour/rundown/2011/01/wikileaks-reveal-what-made-tunisians-revolt.html; and "Wikileaks Cable: Tunisian Corruption and President Zine el-Abidine Ben Ali," About.com, URL: http://middleeast.about.com/od/tunisia/a/tunisia-corruption-wikileaks.htm.
13. On the resilience of authoritarianism in MENA, see Eva Bellin,

"The Robustness of Authoritarianism in the Middle East: Exceptionalism in Comparative Perspective", *Comparative Politics*, Vol. 36, No. 2, January 2004, pp. 139-157.

14. See Daniel Brumberg, "The Trap of Liberalized Autocracy," Journal of Democracy, 13 (October, 2002), pp. 56-68. Lisa Anderson, "Absolutism and the Resilience of Monarchy in the Middle East," *Political Science Quarterly*, 106 (Spring 1991), pp. 1-15; Oliver Schlumberger, (ed.), "Debating Arab Authoritarianism" (Stanford: Stanford University Press, 2007); Russell E. Lucas, "Monarchical Authoritarianism: Survival and Political Liberalization in a Middle Eastern Regime Type", *International Journal of Middle East Studies*, 36 (February 2004), pp. 103-119; Eva Wegner, "Islamist Inclusion and Regime Persistence: The Moroccan Win-Win Situation", in Schlumberger (ed.), pp. 75-93; and Holger Albrecht, "Authoritarian Opposition and the Politics of Challenge in Egypt," in Schlumberger (ed.), pp. 59-74.
15. Azzedine Layachi, "Political Liberalization and the Islamists in Algeria," in Michael Bonner, Megan Reif and Mark Tessler (eds.), *Islam, Democracy and the State in Algeria*, (New York: Routledge, 2005), p. 47.
16. Ibid.
17. Ibid. The definitions of the three processes are for ideal-types rather than actual categories and there is no agreed upon model of their sequencing and timing. As we have learned from the demise of the political modernization school, countries cannot be expected to go through similar experiences and follow pre-set stages or chronology of political development. Even though scholars have built theoretical models and identified general patterns, it is necessary to adjust expectations for each particular experience being studied.
18. The general unemployment rate is over 18 percent; however, it is 30.7 percent for young people (15-24 years old), and 44 percent for young university graduates (15-29 years old), and is rising. See, "Tunisia Overview", World Bank, June 12, 2012.
19. Eva Bellin, "Beyond the Arab Spring", *Brandeis Magazine* (Fall 2011. Online at www.brandeis.edu/magazine/2011/fall/featured-stories/arab.html.
20. In Morocco, the *Makhzen* refers to the informal network of power holders revolving around the monarch. They

include royal notables, big businessmen and landowners, tribal leaders, top-ranking security officers, and high-level non-elected bureaucrats. Many important decisions originate in the Makhzen which acts through patronage networks and formal political structures, including political parties and the administration. In a word, it is an informal centre of power that stands behind the façade of the modern state but is more powerful and feared.

21. "BTI 2012 Algeria Country Report", Bertelsmann Stiftung's Transformation Index (BTI) Gütersloh: Bertelsmann Stiftung, 2012, p. 23. Available online at, http://www.b-project.de/fileadmin/ports/2012/pdf/BTAlgeria.pdf.
22. Barbara Geddes, "What Do We Know About Democratization After 20 Years?", *Annual Review of Political Science*, 2 (June 1999), pp. 115-144.
23. Jack A. Goldstone, "Understanding the Revolutions of 2011 Subtitle: Weakness and Resilience in Middle Eastern Autocracies", *Foreign Affairs*, May-June 2011.
24. Benjamin Barber, "The West Must Be Honest about its Role in Libya's Violent Chaos", *The Guardian,* September 16, 2012, online at guardian.co.uk.
25. Ibid.
26. For possible scenarios for the future, see Michael Emerson, "The Arab Revolt 2011", Centre for European Policy Studies (CEPS), Brussels, April 13, 2011, online at, http://www.cewp.fudan.edu.cn/attachments/article/56/Arab%20 Revolt%202011.pdf.

2

Three Versions of the Arab Spring in North Africa: Protest and Reform in Algeria, Morocco and Tunisia

Larbi Sadiki and Youcef Bouandel

Introduction

How has the Arab Spring impacted on the direction and content of political reform in Algeria, Morocco and Tunisia? The gist of the comparative analysis below supports the chapter's main assumption: the three Maghreb countries—Tunisia, Algeria and Morocco—exhibit three distinct sets of political reforms. The direction and actual content of each of the three sets of reform are examined as case basis, cautioning against the rush to 'generalise' about the Arab Spring as being a uniform process. Specifically, since December 2010, the start of the Arab Spring, the Maghrebi countries, Algeria, Tunisia and Morocco, have experienced, to varying degrees, some developments that were unthinkable even a month earlier. The events of Tunisia are certainly the most far reaching, whereas both Morocco and Algeria were compelled to embark on a series of reforms as precautionary measures to pre-empt any potential uprising-whether Tunisian, Libyan, Egyptian and/or Yemeni style. It must be stated, however, that such a scenario was never a serious challenge to both Algerian and Moroccan regimes. Despite the similarities between the three countries—authoritarian regimes, corruption, acute economic and social problems—it is indeed the differences that explain the outcomes of the paths that these events had taken place.

In Morocco, there is a general consensus among the population at large on the 'holy trinity': God, King and Country. The King, referred to as the 'Commander of the faithful' because of the claim that he is a direct descendent from the Prophet of Islam. This gives him legitimacy, a religious one, which his counterparts in the Maghreb lack. Hence, the King occupies a distinctive position within the Moroccan political system and any dissent or questioning of the King's authority is by implication a rejection of Islam and may be considered as treason. The monarchy, which has continued to rule Morocco for four centuries is perceived to be a unifying factor or all Moroccans.

Hence, unlike their counterparts in the Arab Spring countries, demonstrators in Morocco, as well as those in Jordan for that matter, never called for regime change. In Algeria, one of the richest country in North Africa, the regime is perceived to be more open and 'democratic' by comparison. This has brought the regime a level of legitimacy both inside and outside the country. This perception is the result of the democratization process that was started in the late 1980s. Furthermore, the Algerian political system, referred to locally as *le pouvoir*, can best be described as an octopus.

The head of this *pouvoir* is not really known and the military is one of the strongest pillars, heads, of this regime. Calls to bring down the regime, timidly murmured in Algeria, seemed to be an impossibility as since the regime itself is hard to define. Furthermore, Algerians were traumatized by the atrocities of the 1990s and they cherish the return of peace. The Tunisian system, by comparison, lacks any popular legitimacy. President Ben Ali, removed former president Bourguiba in a palace coup in November 1987 and has been ruling the country with an iron fist ever since. The system as well as corruption were closely linked with the Ben Ali, his wife and their respective families and close entourage.

This chapter looks at Arab Spring in North Africa. The Arab Spring will be discussed in some details in Algeria, Tunisia and Morocco respectively. The chapter concludes with an overall assessment of the reforms in these countries, the lessons that can be learnt and the prospect for the region.

Algeria's Transition to Democracy

Until the launch of the 'Arab Spring' in Tunisia in 2011, Algeria has been the only country that had made significant steps towards ending its authoritarian regime that has been in place since independence from France in 1962. The reforms in Algeria began after the riots of October 1988 which paved the way to a number of political reforms starting with the adoption of the February 1989 Constitution. However, over 25 years later, progress towards democracy has been, to say the least, frustrating. Over this period of time, Algeria experienced multiparty elections, the rise of an Islamist party, a coup d'état, a near state of lawlessness, and other attempts at reforming its political system. Thus the Algerian experience is not only worthy of analysis, but might provide valuable lessons for the 'Arab Spring' countries to learn from.

Algeria: Historical Settings: It would be a mistake to assume that transition to democracy in the Middle East and North Africa (MENA) countries, started with the launch of the 'Arab Spring' in Tunisia. It was in October 1988 when Algerians took on to the streets in the same manner that their counterparts in the MENA regions have done over two decades ago. The events in Algeria did not receive the attention they clearly deserve on account of the absence of the social media and TV space channels and most importantly, due to the events that were taking place in the former Communist counties of Easter and Central Europe. While these protests did not result in the downfall of the incumbent regime, it led to a series of incremental reforms that would lead to the establishment of democracy. Dillman argues that 'Algeria to date is the only Arab or Muslim country that has significantly democratized its political system and the only country within an oil-based economy that has abandoned its authoritarianism'. (1992:31) There was much optimism that Algeria would pave the way to the transition in democracy in the region and several serious observers on Algerian affairs predicted a successful transition to democracy. Quandt, for instance, concluded that it would 'not be surprising if Algeria reache[d] the goal of accountable, representative government in advance of many others in the region'. (1998:164)

In the mid-1980s, Algeria's economy faced acute problems as a result of the fall in oil prices on the international market. The state which had, until then was in a position to meet peoples economic and social needs, was finding it difficult to cope. Algeria, then, was sharing many characteristics with pre-'Arab Spring' countries: severe economic and social crisis coupled with high levels of corruption and the near absence of civil rights and political liberties. Algerians were also subjected to what they call *El Hogra* (the absence of dignity). On the face of it, these conditions ignited the popular uprising in October 1988, which paved the way to a process of democratization. (Boukhobza, 1991)

The similarities with Tunisia and indeed with other MENA countries, however, end here. In Algeria, it must be stressed, the October riots were not, as it is popularly believed, a spontaneous reaction and a 'revolution' against the status quo. In an interview with Youcef Bouandel, Abdelhamid Brahimi, Algeria former Prime Minister (1984-88), Brahimi confirmed that the riots should be understood within the internal dynamics of the regime; a struggle within its the highest echelons. Internal divisions characterized the leadership of the former ruling party, the National Liberation Front (FLN). On the one hand, there was a reformist wing, associated with the then president Chadli Bendjedid (1979-1992) that wanted to liberalize the economy and open up the political space.

On the other hand, there was a conservative wing, associated with the former head of the parry Mohamed Cherif Messaadia, who was, at best, reluctant about the direction the country is embarking upon. It was Chadli's wing that orchestrated the riots to force the liberalization programme. [1] Consequently, the President's wing embarked on a series of roles distribution; conservative elements, perceived to be unpopular and responsible for some of Algeria's problems were sacrificed and new figures, who shared the President's vision were brought in. These changes resulted in the beginning of a process of liberalization that opened the political space. In February 1989, a new constitution that put an end to one party system and socialism as the ideological basis of the state was adopted.

Consequently, political parties were legalized, independently-owned newspapers emerged, hundreds of civil society organizations started their activities and multiparty elections were held. (Bouandel, 2003; Tahi, 1994; Roberts, 1992) It is precisely these developments that Algeria experienced between February 1989 and December 1991, which led to those optimistic views, outlined above, about Algeria being the first Arab country to break away from its authoritarian rule in favour of a democratic form of government.

It should be pointed out at this juncture that it would be a mistake to assume that the reforms were intended for the establishment of a democratic government. The liberalization process came, at a time of severe economic and social crisis. The system's legitimacy that, until then, rested on, among others, the provision of welfare rights was seriously questioned and the country's revenues dropped by about a half. Hence, the system was looking for another source of legitimacy through the civil and political rights. Kramer rightly points out that the reforms served to broaden the system's 'support [and] enhance its legitimacy'. (Kramer, 2001, 202) These top-down reforms resulted in the emergence of the Islamic Salvation Front (FIS), perceived to be the anathema of democracy by the several political forces in the country. This party, it must be stressed, represented a serious threat to the regime in place.

Not only did the FIS win the majority of assemblies at the local and regional elections of June 1990, (Tahi and Iratni, 1991) its success in the first round of the legislative elections in December 1991 led the end of the transition to democracy in Algeria. (Bouandel, 1993-94) In January 1992, military nullified the results, declared a state of emergency and banned the FIS. This action led to unprecedented levels of violence that lasted for almost a decade and claimed the lives of about 200,000 people. Nevertheless, whilst the violence was going on, the Algerian authorities did embark on a program of reforms with the plural legislative and presidential elections in 1995, a new constitution adopted in 1996 and legislative elections in 1997. The violence that ripped the country apart was largely overcome and the majority of the so-called terrorists were either eliminated or benefited from the Amnesty laws that were introduced. (Bouandel, 2010)

Consequently, Algerians not only claim, at least in theory, that they are about two decades ahead of the rest of the Arab world in the quest for democracy. As it will be demonstrated later, this quest for democracy has been nothing but short of maintaining the status quo. Nevertheless, 'Arab Spring' countries can learn valuable lessons from Algeria's experience to ensure a smoother and more peaceful transition to democracy.

Arab Spring and Reforms in Algeria

With more than two decades of experience, the Algerian authorities seem to have mastered the art of political survival. They do that with a rare skill that even most of their political opponents would find difficult to argue against. The several processes of reforms since 1988 had two things in common: on the one hand, it introduced a facade democracy in order to increase the regime's legitimacy inside and abroad and on the other ensuring that the status quo remained and the interests of the ruling elite is never threatened. These reforms, usually incremental and cosmetic, just mirror the popular discontent and aim at silencing any critics. It is with this strategy that the Algerian authorities were able to avoid the radical changes that have been taking place in many of the Arab Spring countries.

When protests in Tunisia began in December 2010, following Bouazizi's act of desperation, several observers felt that the winds of change would soon move to Algeria. This is particularly true given the long history of protests in the country. These protests were encouraged not only by the continuous deteriorating economic and social conditions Algerians find themselves in despite the country's wealth but also as a consequence of the level of corruption and *El Hogra* —a term Algerians use to describe the contemptuous treatment that they are subjected to by office holders. Indeed, in early January 2011, demonstrations erupted in the streets of the capital Algiers and other cities, with several young men setting themselves on fire, sent a strong warning to the authorities in Algiers that their tenure was in danger. (Roberts, 2011)

The demonstrators, while demonstrating against the increase in prices of the basic food stuff, such as cooking oil, sugar and flower, they also called for an end of corruption and *El Hogra*. The government deployed security forces to end the protests but also introduced subsidies in order to reduce the prices. These two tactics; the deployment of the security forces to contain the demonstrators and the use of financial incentives to appease protestors, have been the hall mark of the Algerian authorities in dealing with dissent.

With Ben Ali fleeing Tunisia and the wall of silence broken in neighbouring Egypt, a number of political parties and several civil society organizations created the National Coordination for Change and Democracy (NCCD) which called for, among other things, the end of the state of emergency in place since February 1992, political reforms and social justice. The Coordination planned to hold peaceful demonstrations every Saturday until their demands are met. The first of these demonstrations was held on 12th February and attracted several hundred protestors only. The failure of the call to demonstrate against the regime can be explained by the three following reasons. The first is that Algerians claim to have had their 'spring' back in October 1988 which resulted in a relatively more liberal political system compared to that of the rest of the Arab countries.

Secondly, the 'spring' led to a quasi-civil war in the 1990s in which around 200,000 people had lost their lives. Algerians are simply tired and do not wish to go back to the 1990s. Thirdly, the important role played by the security forces in controlling the demonstrators. The streets leading to the main square, *Place du 1er Mai*, in Algiers from where the demonstrators were to begin, were blocked, access to internet was closed and public transport coming into Algiers was carefully monitored. The number of security forces deployed was estimated at 30,000, a number that far exceeded that of the demonstrators. (Layachi, 2011)

Nonetheless, despite this heavy approach to dealing with demonstrations, the Algerian authorities have also taken some steps in order to diffuse the volatile situation. On the socio-economic front, generous financial support such as subsidies for the basic food stuff and an increase in salaries for employees in the different sectors of economic activities are used. Furthermore, the conditions for government loans to the unemployed to set up their own small businesses were relaxed. Hence, several unemployed youth benefited from the generous loans, in many cases without any proper guarantees to secure the loans. It is, however, in the political front some of the most important developments took place that served to absorb some of the popular discontent. Indeed, in a speech on 24th February 2011, marking the fortieth anniversary of the nationalization of hydrocarbons,

President Bouteflika announced the lifting of the state of emergency which has been in place for the previous two decades. (Canal Algerie, 24th February, 2011) This was a popular decision that dealt a huge blow to those calling for demonstrations and provided, at least in theory, the foundations upon which further political reforms can be undertaken. Hence, on 15th April, in a televised speech, a visibly very ill president, announced the outline for a series of reforms that would open up the political space even further and pave the way for a more democratic system. (Canal Algerie, 15th April, 2011) A commission was set under the leadership of Abdelkader Bensalah, president of the upper chamber of parliament, the Council for the Nation, to conduct of series of consultations with political figures, leaders of political parties and civil society associations. The finding were further discussed in the Council of Ministers and subsequently debated in the parliament. These steps have resulted in the adoption of laws pertaining to political parties, associations.

Consequently, more political parties were legalized and no less than 21 of the newly created ones took part in the election and at least two privately owned television stations started broadcasting. The law also provided for a female quota in the different elected assemblies. According to the provisions of this new law, party lists have to include women otherwise the party is not allowed to compete in the election. Given the generally conservative nature of the Algerian society, especially in small villages and remote areas, a number of political parties resorted to offering financial incentives for women simply to have their name of the party's list. [2]

On paper, these reforms suggests that the Algerian authorities were able to open up the political space further, but in reality, these steps served only a double purpose. Firstly, it showed the *pouvoir's* ability to absorb discontent and pre-empt any dissent. Secondly, it increased its legitimacy inside and, in particular, abroad. These reforms, however, did not address some of the most important aspects of the Algerian political system and did not resolve the stalemate that Algerian politics has been experiencing since reform began in 1988. The amendment of the constitution, a crucial component for any process of reforms, which would define the nature of the political system and define the rules of the game, was left to the new parliament that would be elected in May 2012.

May 2012 Legislative Elections

Algeria has thus far been able to be at arm's length from the events that characterized the MENA countries. With the possibility of the lowest turnout in Algeria's electoral history looming, the authorities in Algiers, in an attempt to convince Algerians to vote, likened the event to two historical dates in Algeria's history. President Bouteflika compared it to November 1954, which marked the beginning of the armed struggle against French occupation (*El Khabar*, Algiers, 25th February, 2012) and his Prime Minister, Ahmed Ouyahia compared it to July 1962, which saw the holding of the referendum which brought Algeria its independence. (*El Khabar*, Algiers, 20th April, 2102) Furthermore, the authorities have also engaged in a political discourse that did not differ much from that coming from Tunis, Tripoli, Cairo, Sana'a and Damascus: there is a conspiracy against the country and the only alternative to foreign intervention is a high turnout in the upcoming election. Indeed, the Algerian authorities not only attacked those who called for the election to be boycotted, but also stated that the only alternative to voting is NATO intervention. (*Echourouk Al Yawmi*, Algiers, 30th April, 2012)

Hence, according to the authorities in Algiers, a higher turnout would not only prevent the anarchy of the 'Arab Spring', but results in a representative institution that would continue the reforms by adopting a new constitution. On May 8, 2012, two days before polling day, the president in his last public address so far, referred to himself as *tab edjnanou* (past its sell by date) in the strongest possible hint that he would oversee the handling of the county's affairs to a 'new generation' retiring from public life.

Three major observations can be made from the results of the election. The first is the confirmation that the Algerian authorities have mastered the arts of change that preserves the status quo. Despite the number of parties represented in the National Assembly has increased, as result of the reforms undertaken the year before, to almost thirty, parties that enjoyed the majority in the previous parliament kept their positions albeit with more or less seats. Hence, the former ruling party, the FLN, despite some internal in fighting gained most seats and almost won the majority. The National Democratic Rally (RND) came second, while the newly created Islamic coalition, Alliance of Green Algeria, secured third place. Secondly, unlike post-Arab Spring elections, Algeria continues to be the exceptions: the Islamists failed to make any significant gains and have seen their share of the seats fall. Finally, the elections confirmed Algeria as the leading country in the Arab world in terms of female representation; about one-third of the membership in the National Assembly is female.

Table 2.1: Seat Distribution by Party in Algerian Parliament

No.	Party	No. of Votes	No. of Seats
1.	Front de Libération Nationale	1,324,363	204
2.	Rassemblement National Démocratique	524,057	69
3.	l'Alliance Algérie Verte	475,049	50
4.	Front des Forces Socialistes	188,275	27
5.	Indépendants	671,190	19
6.	Parti des Travailleurs	283,585	24
7.	Front National Algérien	198,544	9
8.	Front pour la Justice et le Développement	232,676	8
9.	Mouvement Populaire Algerien	165,600	7
10.	Parti El-fedjr El-Jadid	132,492	5
11.	Others	3,439,148	40

While one of the main tasks of the Assembly, the ailing president promised in his last speech, was the adoption of a new constitution, almost two years later, little, if anything, has done on this front. Not only the President and his entourage have not delivered on their promises, the country seemed to have been run unconstitutionally. In April 2013, he was taken ill and spent over three months in a French hospital. Despite calls by several political figures to invoke Article 88 of the

Algerian Constitution and declare the president unfit for office, this move was resisted. The president has not carried out any of his duties and has not addressed his people for almost two years. Furthermore, given the uncertainty surrounding his health and with it the future of governance in Algeria, he reshuffles the cabinet and appointed to key positions his close allies. Hence, the Ministry of Interior, of Justice and the chairmanship of the Constitutional Council, with key roles to play in any elections went to his cronies. With these appointments that, at least guaranteed him, success in a presidential campaign, decided to run for a fourth term in office in April 2014.

The President, despite his deteriorating health and not running his own campaign, is confident of winning. His entourage has promised that one of the first acts the incumbent President will do if he is re-elected, is to change the constitution. Whether Algerians, and particularly the fraudulent administration, will give him this chance and most importantly whether he will deliver on this promise, given his previous failures, only time will tell.

Tunisia: Launching the Arab Spring

December 2010 saw the beginning of what has come to known as the Arab Spring and Tunisia was the launching place for it. A month later, January 2011, the then president Ben Ali fled the country. The removal of Ben Ali, until then, a miracle in the eyes of many students of Middle East and North African politics became a reality. Tunisia was one of the most stable countries in North Africa that made significant steps forward on the economic and social fields. Consequently, the experience of Tunisia needs to be analysed very closely.

Tunisia, the aspiring 'Asian Tiger' of the Maghreb, and with some verifiable statistical indices, looked economically healthy in the 1990s and up to the 14th of January 2011 Revolution. In practice, the government manipulated figures. As it turned out after close scrutiny following the revolution the socio-economic model for so long taken for granted by most scholars and policy-makers showed the country to be no more than a paper or 'clay' tiger. (African Development Bank, 2012) In the past ten years of Ben Ali's rule, annual growth averaged 4 to 4.5 percent. For a non-hydrocarbon economy, this was taken to be proof of solid performance. The National Solidarity Fund (NSF), like other schemes created during Bin Ali's time in power, calls for a re-assessment. Though the statistics and data came from the regime and were partly massaged, some progress was certainly made through these schemes in poverty alleviation. (Sadiki, 2002, p. 136)

Hussein Dimassi, a leading Tunisian economist, in a private conversation with Larbi Sadiki in February 2011 in Sousse, affirmed the hidden corruption related to the NSF with millions a year of donated monies misappropriated by Madame Leila Ben Ali and others administering over the fund. [3] Nonetheless, Dimassi, who also works for the country's trade union movement, also added that NSF had to allow for some poverty alleviation with intervention in less than 2,000 so-called shadow zones.

Over ten years, an estimated 100,000 micro-credits were given, helping people with all kinds of small projects and businesses. Credit for this initiative goes to the Tunisian people. One-fifth of all Tunisians—that is the adult working population—have in some way or another contributed to these voluntary funds. Yet, poverty alleviation and helping improve life for the have-nots is not the same as job-creation. This is a point not to be missed when assessing development funds anywhere. The NSF funds improved the quality of poverty but did not go towards eradicating it. In addition, the funds were instrumental in keeping the have-nots in check through fairly successful distributive mechanisms. One may venture the idea that the NSF delayed the inevitable: 'bread riots'. Note that this kind of activism is in the case of Tunisia always triggered by protests over issues of bread and butter.

However, bread riots always lead to demands for political

freedoms. Mohamed Bouazizi doused himself in petrol on the 17th of December 2010 not because he was hungry; rather, he did so because he felt his sense of self-worth, freedom to change his situation, and a dignified opportunity to self-actualise were not within his grasp as a result of state negligence to his plight and other youth in his situation, especially in the disadvantaged central and southern regions of Tunisia. This rings true of Tunisia as well as of other impoverished and populous Arab states where the Bouazizi's are in the millions.

Three observations must be made in relation to the NSF:

1. All statistics produced in the past may be over-stated by the state since it was the only source of information on the fund's performance;
2. The NSF allowed the state a measure of control to alleviate poverty whilst inhibiting the rise of society-managed charities; and
3. According to new information released after the ousting of Ben Ali, the NSF was not free of the widespread corruption and embezzlement practiced by the former first lady, Leila Ben Ali. This is a space to be watched for more precise revelations of the severity of corruption involved once the trials of the regime's henchmen and former high cadres begin after the July 2011 election.

On paper, Tunisia ranked first in Africa in terms of economic performance. (World Bank, 2009) Under Ben Ali, the economy's capacity to train exceeded the capacity to employ. About 60,000 to 70,000 graduates are produced each year, a quarter of whom will see little or no employment. Thus, the numbers of those on the margins were swelling and the government relied on the National Solidarity Fund and other mechanisms to placate the needy. There are problems with all indicators produced and all of which rank Tunisia favourably in comparison with other developing states. Generally, this led to upholding the 'myth' of a solid and dynamic economy.

From 'Moral Economy' to 'Immoral Distribution'

Ben Ali had created some wealth for Tunisia. But generally, whilst public expenditure largely maintained a distributive economy–namely investment into education, health and food subsidies–the state's rush to the 'Washington Consensus', EU hand-outs and markets, the reliance on small and medium sized businesses and an emerging spare parts industrial sector, FDI, cheap tourism, and the sluggish textile industry was bound to cause the economy to lose steam. (Hibou, 2006) Unemployment rates of up to 40 percent in the marginalized regions are considerably higher than the national average of 14 to 16 percent mostly in the North and Sahel, the country's lush coastal regions.

Marginalization of the residents of phosphates basin towns, for example, led to tensions with the national company managing the phosphates sector. Intervention by Ben Ali temporarily calmed the situation, but how proceedings from phosphates as well as other sectors will be more equitably distributed remained to be seen. With 60 percent of the population under 25 years, the need to engage in sustainable economic development is urgently needed. For youth empowered by education to be marginalized by economic mal-distribution is the fodder of protest and social upheaval.

Arab Spring's First Election

Five issues dominated the political agenda in the prelude to the October 23, 2011 election. These issues—political, economic and social—led to the postponement of the polls more than once.

1. The interim president and government want not to waste public money at a time when the country's coffers are near empty, and the cost of the election was estimated at the time at 40 million dinars (20 million Euros). So pressure was made on the Electoral Commission to get it right as the poll's success was deemed to be vital for Tunisia's transition, and the Arab Spring in general.

2. The Electoral Commission was keen to get it right and did bid for time to ensure first and foremost a full and accurate register of eligible voters, replacing the one from the days of Ben Ali, was in place for the election day. The pre-revolution register was designed whimsically and un-democratically by his Interior Ministry.
3. The Democratic Transition Commission worked at the time so hard in consortium with the Electoral Commission to ensure that an additional two-and-a-half million voters missing from the register were added in order to maximise participation and representation, given the importance of the first election aimed at inaugurating a new democratic post-Ben Ali order.
4. As the date of the historic vote neared, the country was experiencing continuous agitation and social upheaval, typical of revolutionary transition, with workers' and labour protests happening on a daily basis. Thus a great deal of hope was pinned on the election to put an end to demonstrations. The interim President (Fouad Mbazza) and government (Beji Caid Essebsi) called for the ending of all strikes ahead of the polls, stressing that social peace was necessary for democratic, orderly and fair election. (Kirkpatrick, 2011)
5. Ahead of the polls, the country's economy was thought to have shrunk by up to 9 percent; and the interim government was happy to blame this on strikes and protests' damaging effect on business confidence and overall performance.

It was therefore on the basis of wide debate and consensus that the interim government and the Electoral Commission delayed the poll, initially planned for July 24, 2011, to October 23, 2011. All agreed, when promoting the idea, that what mattered most was electoral transparency not urgency. The historic moment and mission helped ease the political elite into acquiescence, including political parties such as the Nahda Party, which initially opposed the delay. (Moshiri, 2011) For, the task at hand of electing a Constituent Assembly tasked with drawing up a new constitution, a prerequisite for burying the ousted dictatorial regime, made the postponing of the poll acceptable, especially that newly created parties and newly-found freedoms needed time to measure up to the challenge of political renewal. Here secularists such as *Afek* (Horizon), *Al-Moubadarah* (The Initiative) or the leftist *Ettakatol* to the Islamist Nahda agreed that the delay was for the best. The arduous behind-the-scenes negotiations by the Electoral Commission Chief, Kamel Jendoubi, paid off; and the relief at the delay was universal. Tunisia had firmed a date for a proper debut with democratic transition: the Arab Spring's first multi-party election.

It is early days to critically assess Tunisia's transition following the 2011 election. Nonetheless, the poll itself went smoothly and voter turnout was sufficient to lend credence to the first electoral test after the long-time dictatorship of Ben Ali. By any standards, the poll was a success—Larbi Sadiki was witness to the event in the Sousse branch of the Electoral Commission. The Carter Electoral monitoring team were impressed by not only the satisfactory levels of freedom and fairness, but also by the degree of passion and interest shown by voters many of whom waited for hours as long queues snaked out for more than 12 hours on that historic day. The figures said it all: a total of 11,686 candidates on 1,517 lists contested the Arab Spring's first election. Of these 828 belonged to partisan lists, with 655 belonging to independents, and only 34 forming party coalitions. In the first election in post-Ben Ali Tunisia, one hundred political parties contested the election. The results (Table 2.2) signalled the birth of multi-party politics proper in the country's first democratic election. Each governorate voted into the Constituent Assembly between four and ten representatives divided between 33 constituencies.

It is not the figures that matter here. Rather, it is the coalition-building spirit in which the poll was conducted and new political elite came to the fore. Specifically, following the 2011 election, the victorious party, the Islamist Nahda, led by its leader Rached Ghannouchi, stretched its hand to political partners, showing the kind of good needed for confidence-building in a nascent democracy. Soon after the poll, a process of bargaining began, leading to an impressive partnership that was to become the mainstay of Tunisia's transitional framework. Nahda, as the party with most seats, emerged as a clear favourite for leading the executive branch of government: Hamadi Jebali, Nahda's Secretary-General, succeeded Essebsi as the country's new Prime Minister (PM). This was symbolically important: a formerly long-time political prisoner becoming PM.

Another victim of the Bin Ali regime, the Republican Congress Party's leader Moncef Marzouki, who was till the 14th of January 2011 Revolution residing in exile, became President—with Nahda's blessing and after endorsement from the newly-elected Constituent Assembly. With similar political astuteness and skill, Nahda approved Mustafa Ben Ja'afar, chief of the leftist Ettakatol, House Speaker. A 'troika' was born and with it a modus operandi that, at least at the time of its inception, promised to advance partnership, compromise and confidence-building as key values in Tunisia's nascent democratic transition.

Morocco's Monarchical Arab Spring

For now, the Arab Spring has not changed Morocco; rather, Morocco seems to have changed the Arab Spring. This is one story in the advent of the Arab Spring that calls for critical attention.

Contextualising Morocco's Arab Spring: There is historical pedigree that equips the monarchy in Morocco to adapt itself to the winds of change. This it does with skill, proving the adage that the most intelligent species, in nature as in politics, are those that reinvent themselves adaptively, in response to the exigencies of time and space. Times have changed in the Arab Maghreb, or west, since the January 2011 Revolution in Tunisia followed a month later by Egypt and then Libya. Morocco, by comparison, opted for a monarchical Spring, stamping it with a touch of makhzan (the monarchical centre) politics in which the young King, Mohammed VI, deftly practices, proving himself to be a political animal, one well trained by his late father, Hassan II, who bequeathed the throne to his eldest son in 1999.

Table 2.2: Party Distribution of Seats: 23rd October, 2011

Political Party	Seats	Membership of Governing Coalition/Opposition
Nahda Party	90	Prime Minister (Hammadi Jebali)
Congress of the Republic Party	30	President (Moncef Marzouki)
Democratic Forum for Labour and Liberties (Ettakatol)	21	House Speaker (Mustafa bin Ja'far)
Popular Petition	19	Opposition
Progressive Democratic Party	17	Opposition
The Initiative	5	Opposition
Afek Tounes	5	Opposition
Democratic Modernist Pole	5	Opposition
Tunisian Workers' Communist Party	3	Opposition
Socialist Democrats' Movement	2	Opposition
Democratic Patriots' Movement	2	Opposition
Popular Movement	2	Opposition
Independents	9	Opposition
Minor Parties (8)	1 seat each	Opposition

Almost invariably across the Arab region, the Arab Spring

imposed its own dynamic and rules on many an existing polity. The qualified exception is Morocco where, to an extent, King Mohammed VI was able to impose his own rules of political engagement in order to protect his throne from being tattered by an unstoppably infectious Arab Spring (Cohen, 2012), which terminated rigidly authoritarian-bureaucratic states (e.g. Egypt and Tunisia) and claimed an under-performing oil-rich dynasty (e.g. Libya).

At least for now, he has succeeded to divert the Arab Spring's current away from the Sherifi monarchy. In so doing, the King has creatively refigured polity in a way that has made Morocco reap dividends from a carefully calibrated reform agenda, which simulated Arab Spring revolutionary transformation and transition. There is one specificity that stands out in the Moroccan version—the king executed his reforms without affecting the balance of power, or downsizing the Makhzen political clout and control over the pace and substance of change. (Catusse, 2011) This he has executed in two distinctive ways.

Firstly, he instigated a quasi 'revolution' that redistributed roles within the traditional opposition. He promoted the opposition to government, and demoted to opposition the historical parties he partnered with in steering the ship of the state. Secondly, he redefined the rules of political engagement by upgrading legitimation of the monarchy before and after the Arab Spring, thus 'padding' his rule in a fashion that it absorb the shocks of popular and global pressure for change.

An Arab Spring *á la Marocaine:* Partly, the Arab Spring is defined by cascading change. Morocco simulates change in a way in which things stay more or less the same. This is an art, the art of the possible Moroccan Sherifi rulers have done for centuries to reproduce their authority and stranglehold on the reins of power.

Morocco's November 2011 parliamentary multi-party election illustrates this point. In a stunning political turnaround, and a sign of the winds of change blowing through

North Africa, the moderate Islamist Justice and Development Party (JPD) scored a resounding victory. It was unprecedented in the country's 30-year history of largely cosmetic election. The Islamists more than doubled its share of seats. It secured an additional 61 seats, bringing its new total to 107 from 46 in the 2007 polls. Two observations are in order in relation to the 2011 election: voter turnout was low, around 45 percent. A quota system reserved 60 seats for females and 30 for males under the age of 30 to increase inclusiveness of youth.

This outcome is partly fortuitous, given the JPD's dynamism and hard campaigning in the November 2011 election. Without a doubt, however, there is an element of contrivance. It is this contrivance that may be traced to the makhzen. The JPD is given an opportunity denied to the other Islamist party (e.g. the Justice and Charity Association, the party founded by the Charismatic Sufi leader, the late Abdessalam Yassine) that the King will not legalise within the current context, much less sanction its participation in the electoral process. (Karam, 2011) It has the potential to upset the balance of power and may be usher in the kind of 'revolutionary' change neither the *makhzen* nor a measurable segment of the loyal opposition would like to see precipitated at this historical juncture.

The operative term here is 'loyalty'. The king is highly educated and is an intelligent reader of changing political landscapes around him. His political sense tells him that Islamists in power makes good political sense. They are everywhere buoyant, in Egypt and Tunisia they have shown themselves to command wide support and enjoy popular appeal. The king facilitated the ascent of his chosen Islamists as electoral victors, spearing him revolutionary upheaval. Yet the act simulates revolution, being new and breaks with political custom whereby the secular Parties such as the Istiqlal (Independence) are routinized as the makhzen's loyal partners in the running of government.

As can be seen from the party map below (Table 2.3), the

2011 election are the first after the July 2011 constitutional referendum (voter turnout was 75 percent), which was strongly endorsed by the public. Official figures say 'yes' voters formed nearly 98 percent.

Table 2.3: New Map of Morocco's Political Parties, 2007-2011 Elections

Party	2011 Results	2007 Results
Parti de la Justice et du Developpment (JPD)	107	47
Parti de l'Istiqlal (Istiqlal Party)	60	52
Rassemblement National des Indépendents (Independents' National Rally)	52	41
Parti Authenticité et Modernité (Modernity and Authenticity)	47	Founded after 2007 by Fuad Ali al-Himma, friend and current security advisor to King Mohammed VI
Union Socialistes des Forces Popularies (Socialist Union of Popular Forces)	39	38
Mouvement Populaire (Popular Movement)	32	41
Union Constitutionelle (Constitutional Rally)	23	27
Parti du Progrès et du Socialisme (Progress and Socialism Party)	18	17
Parti Travailliste (Workers' Party)	4	5

For more details of election results, see Portail National du Maroc, 2011 and *Le gouvernement du Maroc*, 2007.

More importantly, the reforms assign the Premiership to the party with the highest share of seats in the new bicameral parliament. In this instance, for the first time in Morocco's history, the Premier, in this case Abdelilah Benkirane, appoints government ministers and is empowered to dissolve parliament. (Belkeziz, 2012) Both were previously kingly prerogatives before the 2011 July 1st referendum.

Benkirane's has a majority of seats that catapulted his party to centre-stage but not the know-how of governance. This is one reason why his shift from opposition to government necessitated coalition-building with powerful parties such as the Istiqlal Party, a loyalist-centrist party, the Popular Movement and the Progress and Socialism Party. The Bloc for Democracy made up of eight parties, including two who partake in the governing coalition, have coalesced to ensure the opposition is dynamic in the new parliament where the winning party has wider powers than under previous administrations before the July 2011 referendum.

Legitimation: Securing the Makhzen: The newly shaped party scene and government-opposition map in Morocco is informed by a modus operandi through which the king, Mohammed VI like during his father's reign, defines the terms of the political game, demarcates its boundaries and red lines, and controls the pace and scope of reform.

Mohammed VI, commander of the faithful in the tradition of the Sherifi Monarchy claiming Prophetic lineage, remains regal in every sense of the term. Islamists and non-Islamists, elected or non-elected, revolve around him as the fulcrum of power. And in religious matters, like in security and even the economy, with the king being one of the richest men in Morocco, Mohammed VI, calls the shots. It is a game of concentric arenas of power: in theory the Premier runs government, and to an extent he does, but he presides over cabinet and the country's Security Council, by following agendas scripted by the king.

This is one reason why the constitutional reforms are rejected by the February 20 protest movement, which boycotted the July 2011 referendum. (Maddy-Weitzman, 2012) Mohammed not only astutely knew how to respond, in his own terms, and swiftly to the challenges posed to his reign by Arab Spring. More importantly, he almost anticipated them and worked to reform his rule years before it erupted in the Maghrebi scene. The Equity and Reconciliation Commission (IER—*Instance Equité et Réconciliation*) sought to distance his rule from that of his father, courageously opening the sensitive files of torture and oppression under Hass II's rule. Similarly, the *mudawwanah*, another piece of legislation, equivalent to a Personal Status Code was made law in 2003 after initial Islamist opposition. It gives women protection against male abuses, including unilateral divorce. The newly-created office of female judges and religious guides is specific to Morocco.

Le Plus ça Change: Morocco under Mohammed VI is ahead of the learning curve. It has engineered its own version of the Arab Spring, keeping for now vociferous and centrifugal forces in check. The moral flame of peaceful protest for political equality and participative governance instigated by the February 20 protest movement has made the system appreciate the 'light' of reform—even if makhzen-managed. They have for now spared Morocco the kind of social unrest unfurling in Jordan, a monarchy that can do with borrowing a leaf from the Book of Mohammed VI.

However, the ceiling of reform is Morocco can never measure to the high aspirations of the new protest movement and urban youth, amongst other marginal, eager for inclusiveness in polity, economy and society. Hundreds of those today either suffer actual or potential threat of coercion and detention. The judicial system is still at it, working loyally for the makhzen, with or without the king's knowledge.

Basically, in a moment of crisis, King VI felt the pressure, if not the threat, of the Arab Spring, scrambling fast to find new partners to widen his power base. Benkirane was willing to oblige a tactical king. Now that the protests have waned, and the protest movement is divided and weakened, the king seems to reclaim some of his old balance of power. In

September 2012 he even by-passed Benkirane by deciding with the Ministers of the Interior and Finance, in a meeting attended by military and security chiefs, the arrest of 130 allegedly corrupt customs officers working in Tangier's port. Basically, this renders the new laws passed in the constitutional July 2011 referendum null. Constitutionally, the King's instructions are amongst the Prime minister's powers.

Thus the persistence of the *makhzen*'s control over politics presage difficulties in Morocco's carefully calibrated own version of the 'Arab Spring', in which some things have stayed the same.

Conclusion

The Arab Spring is neither even nor monolithic. The experiences of the Arab Maghreb show that where democratization is concerned, there are three distinct routes. In the case of Algeria, politics is experiencing inertia. Despite being hailed as a turning point in Algeria's modern history, the outcome was nothing more than an episode in the never ending and frustrating process of transition and reforms. Instead of introducing far reaching reforms, the Algerian authorities have simply introduced a number of incremental changes, just enough, to diffuse tension and buy time. The election shows that the pouvoir in Algiers, faced with the changes that have been taking place in the countries of MENA, was able to overcome the prospect of a whole scale uprising a la 'Arab Spring' countries.

While the majority of these countries saw changes and the old guard eliminated, developments in Algeria suggest that for the time being, in the words of the legendary Bob Dylan, 'the times are not a changing'. The Algerian authorities cannot continue to ignore the legitimate aspirations of their own people for a more open, inclusive, democratic and most importantly accountable government. Circumstances have played in the hands of the regime and it was able to weather the storm, the situation is bound to change. The forthcoming presidential election will prove decisive as the main candidates, president Bouteflika and his former Prime Minister, Ali Benflis, promise to change the Constitution to further open up te political space. Algeria, for the time being, seems to be a work in progress.

In Morocco, King Mohammed VI used the Arab Spring to his advantage, showing skill and instinct survival. He more or less invented his own Arab Spring, choosing the pace, content and substance of the key reforms he had to introduce in the face of mounting street pressure that was inspired by protests in neighbouring countries in 2011. What distinguished his fine-tuning of the monarchical system was preference for self-serving gradualism over sudden and street-driven change. He included four key components as the centrepiece of his reformist agenda. Firstly, the King learnt from Arab Spring events that violence was not the answer to dealing with unrest and protest. He allowed society a margin for self-expression and organisation, which indirectly allowed him to assess the real weight of the youth and Islamist-based opposition. He absorbed their messages and fed them into his own reform agenda as one way of killing the momentum of Arab Spring-like protests.

To this end, the long time- shelved off project to re-write the constitution made sense at a time when political spin alone would not placated the angry youth wanting some change, that is, change short of removing the King. Removal of the King was not an item on the agenda of Moroccan protesters. They wanted radical reform and the King knew exactly how to make constitutional reform the second most important strategy of responding to the wave of protests in 2011. The King remained the locus of power despite a move to shift some power to other institutions, including government and parliament.

The November 2011elections came as the first test of the King's reforms. Their most important result in terms of state-society relations was inclusion of the Islamists in power, with an Islamist Prime Minister entrusted with the running of government. The choice was well-calculated: (a) Islamists at the time seemed to be rising to power as demonstrated by events in Egypt and Tunisia. Morocco's King wanted them in power on his own terms; and (b) he chose the Islamists for the running of government knowing too well that—like all Islamists in the Arab World—they prefer gradual reform and were not keen on revolutions. This suited the King's concept of reform: top-down, inclusive, controllable and incremental.

Tunisia has fared better than most in the Arab Spring—especially when compared to either Egypt and Libya or fellow Maghrebi states, Algeria and Morocco. The country was able to ratify a new constitution, beginning the third year of its Arab Spring revolution with a solid foundation for continuing democratic transition.

Tunisia's constitution is modern and rooted in universal democratic principles, not only championing values of equal opportunity, civil and political freedoms, equal citizenship, pluralism and the rule of law, but also setting institution-building on a legal course. The legal-institutional path followed by Tunisia's democratic transition sets apart from other Arab Spring revolution. To an extent, this has been possible thanks to civic dynamism and the proactive leadership role taken up by secular and Islamist organizations and parties, creating a 'coalition of the willing' for the greater sake of democratization. Every step of Tunisia's reform process has been helped by contractual steps, committing legally to realization of the declared objectives, and these continue to be guided by a voluntary 'National Dialogue' vehicle that has facilitated better communication between vehemently opposed ideological foes.

Tunisia's way has been the 'legal-institutional-legal' way. Thus far this has resulted in a new constitution, a transitional justice law, an electoral commission, and is now paving the way for the newest legal foundation for boosting democratic transition: a new election law. With these milestone achievements, Tunisia is emerging not as a model—as Tunisian politicians tend to describe their transition—but rather, and more correctly as a relevant and powerful symbol of the Arab Spring, with Tunisia being its very birthplace. What is certain is that this relevance will be most likely noted in Tunisia's immediate neighbourhood: fellow Maghrebi states Algeria and Morocco, in additional to Egypt and Libya where the Arab Spring has had a checkered career since the 2011 uprisings that ousted the authoritarian regimes there.

Without a doubt, however, the 'Arab Spring' has changed the political landscape of some countries in the Middle East and North Africa beyond recognition. Tunisia, the country that saw the launch of the 'Arab Spring' had seen the most changes in the Maghreb. By contrast, Algeria and Morocco saw modest and controlled changes. Change, it must be stressed, inevitably bring uncertainty.

It is how this change is managed that determines what the reaction to the uncertainties is going to be. Tunisia had begun a process of a transition to democracy, but this process is, thus far, proving very difficult to negotiate. With the opening up of the political space, many political parties tried to capitalize of the newly found freedoms. One of these is the Islamic *Nahda* that won the legislative elections in the country. This win and particularly the direction that the country is taking had put Nahda at loggerheads with secular opposition parties, especially in early 2013.

These developments should be followed very closely and Nahda should learn valuable from Algeria's experience, if the country is not to is to be sparred violence. In Algeria, the authorities have managed to wither the storm, but the country is still in a volatile situation an prone to an uprising. So far the authorities have time on their hands and the period after the 2014 presidential election will be significant for the future development and stability of the country. Morocco, given the central and unquestionable position of the King and the modest reforms undertaken since the beginning of the Arab Spring seems to have worked. These concessions, in theory, should represent a platform upon which to build.

Endnotes

1. Bouandel's interview with Abdelhamid Brahim, London, 2nd December, 1998.
2. Interviews of Youcef Bouandel in Algeria in July 2012 in Eastern Algeria.
3. Sadiki's interview with Hussein Dimassi, 14th February 2011, Sousse, Tunisia.

References

African Development Bank; Development Centre of the Organisation for Economic Cooperation and Development (OECD), United Nations Development Programme (UNDP) (2012), *Tunisia: African Economic Outlook 2012*, available at, http://www.afdb.org/fileadmin/uploads/afdb/Documents/Publications/Tunisia%20Full%20PDF%20Country%20Note.pdf, accessed: 01/01/2012.

Belkeziz, A. (2012), "Morocco and Democratic Transition: A Reading of the Constitutional Amendments: Their Context and Results", *Contemporary Arab Affairs*, Vol. 5, No. 1, pp. 27-53.

Bouandel, Y. (1993), "Algerian National Popular Assembly election of December 1991", *Representation*, Vol. XX, No. XX, pp. 10-14.

Bouandel, Y. (2003), "Political Parties and the Transition from Authoritarianism: The Case of Algeria", *Journal of Modern African Studies*, Vol. 41, No. 1, pp. 1-22.

Bouandel, Y. (2010), "Algeria's Arduous search for Peace" in David Neville-Wright and Anna Halafoff (eds.) *Terrorism and Social exclusion: Misplaced Risk-Common Security*, Cheltenham: Edward Elgar, pp. 88-101.

Boukhobza, M. (1991), *Octobre 88. Evolution ou rupture*? Algiers: Editions Bouchene.

Catusse, M. (2011), "Le "social": une affaire d'Etat dans le Maroc de Mohammed VI", *Confluences Méditerranée*, Vol. 78, September, pp. 63-76.

Cohen, S. (2012), "L'Empire des sultans: Anthropologie politique au Maroc", *The Journal of North African Studies*, Vol. 17, No. 3, pp. 567-568.

Dillman, B. (1992), "Transition to Democracy in Algeria", in *State and Society in Algeria*, J.P. Entelis and P. C. Naylor (eds.), Boulder: Westview Press, pp. 31-52.

Elections au Maroc, 2007, '*Résultats définitifs des élections législatives du 7 septembre,* available from, http://www.elections.gov.ma/index.aspx.

Hibou, B. (2006), "Domination and Control in Tunisia: Economic Levers for the Exercise of Authoritarian Power", *Review of African Political Economy*, Vol. 108, No. 108, June, pp. 185-206.

Iratni, B. and Tahi, M. S. (1991), "The Aftermath of the Algeria's First Free Local Elections", *Government and Opposition*, 26(3), pp. 273-296.

Karam, S. (November 24, 2011), "Morocco Election Tests Depth of King's Reforms,' *Reuters*.

Kirkpatrick, D. (October 4, 2011), "Interim Tunisian Leader With Ties to Old Ruler Defends a Gradual Path", An interview with Beji Caid Essebsi, *The New York Times*.

Kramer, G. (2001), Democracy without Democrats. A Comparative Study of Egypt, Jordan and Tunisia" in Salemi G. (ed.) *Democracy without Democrats*?, London: I.B. Tauris, pp. 200-226.

Layachi, A. (2011), "Algeria's Rebellion by Instalments", *Middle East Research and Information Project*, (MERIP), 12th March.

Maddy-Weitzman B. (2012), "Is Morocco Immune to Upheaval?", *Middle East Quarterly*, Winter issue, pp. 87-93.

Moshiri, N. (2011), "Interview with Rachid Ghannouchi", *Al Jazeera*, February 7, available at, http://www.aljazeera.com/news/africa/2011/02/2011233464273624.html, accessed: 17/12/2012.

Portail National du Maroc (2011), *Résultats définitifs des élections législatives du 25 novembre,* available at, http://www.maroc.ma/PortailInst/Fr/logoevenementiel/Dossier+Elections.htm, accessed: 22/12/2012.

Roberts, H. (1992), "The Algerian State and the Challenge for Democracy", *Government and Opposition*, Vol. 27, No. 4, pp. 442-464.

Roberts, H. "Algeria's national protesta", available at, http://mideast.foreignpolicy.com/posts/2011/01/09/algeria_s_national_protesta, Monday, January 10, 2011.

Quandt, W. (1998), *Between Ballots and Bullets. Algeria's Transition from Authoritarianism*, Washington, DC: Brookings Institution Press.

Sadiki, L. (2002), "Political Liberalization in Ben Ali's Tunisia: Façade Democracy", *Democratization*, Vol. 9, No. 4, pp. 122-141.

Tahi, M. (1994), "Algeria's Democratisation Process: A Frustrated Hope", *Third World Quarterly*, Vol. 16, No. 2, pp. 209-224.

World Bank (2009), *World Development Indicators 2009,* Washington: The World Bank.

3

Arab Spring in Egypt: Causes and Implications

Ahmad Mohamed Ahmad Abdel Rahman

Introduction

The Arab Spring did not spring from a vacuum; rather, it was the culmination of decades of suppression and accumulated economic, social and political problems. The inertia that the Arab society had been suffering from all these years made the Arab rulers fail to realize the magnitude of the problem. This sheer unawareness of public mood on the part of the rulers made it easy for the youth activists who had hitherto refrained from active politics to rise against these injustices. Moreover, the Islamists had all along taken advantage of the suppressive policies of the regimes to get close to the people through a variety of social welfare programs thus solidifying their base and gaining public sympathy and support.

It is noteworthy that the Arab countries where the revolutions took place did not all have the same socio-political and economic structure. Although all these movements sought to overthrow the yoke of dictatorship, the political colour and roots of these dictatorships were not the same. For example, in Tunisia the revolution was sparked by a youth setting himself ablaze due to poverty and the resultant confrontation with security forces. In Egypt, the movement was a call for better economic conditions and opposition to inheritance of power. In Libya, it was against suppression and the rule of one man without any political institutions. In Yemen, it was against the dictatorship of one man and his tribe. In Syria, it is against family and sectarian dictatorship.

However, we find that all these revolutions, though

triggered by different factors and their own unique socio-economic and political structures, have one unifying factor: *they have been all youth-led movements*. Despite their presence in countries like Egypt and Tunisia, the opposition parties had hitherto failed to bring about any change. It is for this reason that the uprisings with one common slogan—"the people want" surprised the ruling elite out of their complacency. Another point to note is that the beginning of all these movements was peaceful though all of them have since been marred by violence.

This paper focuses on the Egyptian Revolution as an example of the Arab Spring and deals with two major aspects, viz.:

1. The causes of the January 25, 2011 Revolution, and
2. Its implications within the country, in the Middle East region and beyond.

In particular, this paper will attempt to give the future vision of the post-revolution Egypt.

Causes of the January 25 Revolution

In general, the purpose of a revolution is to change an obsolete social, economic or political order that has outlived its utility and to establish in its place a new system that meets the needs and aspirations of modern society. Usually a revolution is accompanied by violence because opposing forces—those of change and of continuity—come into conflict with each other.

The roots of the Egyptian Revolution lay in the following factors:

1. An entrenched dictatorship vs. the people's desire for freedom and democracy.
2. Widespread corruption on the part of the ruling elite and a coterie of businessmen that were either part of the government or close to the powers that be.
3. Frequent violation of human rights and brutal repression by the national security force.
4. The entry of big businessmen into politics especially over

the last ten years of Mubarak's regime that saw the rich-poor divide getting wider.

5. High cost of living that was constantly on the rise and low income.
6. Lack of adequate job opportunities and the high rate of unemployment among the educated youth.
7. Rejection of the idea of the "inheritance" of presidency.
8. Social network media—namely, Facebook and Twitter—which served to rally the youth who compared Egypt with other countries and found the comparison unfavourable to their country.
9. The parliamentary election of November 2010 in which Mubarak's National Democratic Party swept the polls amidst blatant unfair practices. This was the last straw on the camel's back.

These internal factors gained momentum due to two external factors, viz.

1. The fall of Zine El Abidine Ben Ali in Tunisia that encouraged the Egyptian protestors, and
2. The fact that Egyptians saw that their country had lost its clout in the Arab region and in Africa.

Chief Features of the Egyptian Revolution

The Egyptian Revolution had certain distinctive features. It was basically an internal revolution that soon found international sympathy. Starting as a white revolution, "*silmiya*" (peaceful) was its slogan. However, it soon took a violent turn when security forces sought to silence the voice of protest with brutal force.

The Revolution started as a youth movement which was soon joined by all sections of people. The youth played a major role in mobilizing their peers through social network media. During the last five years of Mubarak's rule a number of protest groups had come into the limelight. These groups used various means to mobilize the people making sure that these means were such as to keep them out of sight of the security network which sought to distance ordinary Egyptians from any political and civil activities. Prominent among these movements were:

1. Youth Movement for Change.
2. April 6 Youth Movement.
3. National Association for Change.
4. Khaled Said Group.
5. Kefaya (enough) Movement.

During the revolution, all these groups came together under the name "Coalition of the Youth of January 25 Revolution".

The youth form one third of the total Egyptian population and throughout the country's history they have played a major role in all fields of life. During the British occupation in the first half of the 20th century and especially in 1935, students rose against foreign occupation. In 1967, the students were the first to ask President Gamal Abdel Nasser to try those who were responsible for Egypt's defeat in the war against Israel. During President Anwar El Sadat's rule, in 1972 students organized a huge agitation in universities to pressurize President Sadat to liberate Sinai. (Helal, 2010)

At the beginning of the 21st century the youth began to surface on the political scene once again because of a number of regional and international developments. Some of these events were Al-Aqsa uprising of 2000 and the invasion of Iraq in 2003 at the regional level and the events of September 11, 2001 at the international level. The events of 9/11 in particular led the international community to give more importance to the Arab region as western powers were convinced that terrorism is linked to the absence of political freedom, widespread corruption and the poor life of the people. Thus, Arab rulers came under pressure from the west to adopt political reform and to give political freedom to their people. This culminated in the concept of the Greater Middle East put forth during the G-8 meeting in June 2004. (Shehata, 2011)

Some national forces in Egypt benefited from this

environment and started to form political movements and parties, e.g. the Kefaya Movement, the National Association for Change, the Democratic Coalition and the Democratic Front for Change, Al Ghad Party and Ikhwanul Muslimeen (Muslim Brotherhood). From 2004 on, these organizations started asking for democracy and constitutional reform. There is no doubt that the Kefaya Movement played a major role in spreading the culture of agitation in Egypt by focusing on domestic issues that needed reform. In 2005, Ikhwanul Muslimeen organized a number of agitations to compete with the Kefaya Movement for public attention.

The negative political and social environment forced people to come on the political scene. For example, the rise in the price of bread and other essential commodities in 2007 and the international economic crisis of 2008 that had its repercussions on Egypt made the limited income employees of different public sector enterprises take to the streets to agitate for pay raise. All these political activities helped break the culture of fear among the people who had for a long time kept away from any kind of political activity. Among these people were university teachers, judges, members of different syndicates such as medical, engineering etc., the Mahalla labour union that agitated in 2008 and the real estate employees who followed suit in 2009. So far the demands were all economic not political. (Shehata, 2011)

The last straw on the camel's back was, however, the parliamentary elections of November 2010. These totally fraudulent elections removed all opposition parties from parliament. The National Democratic Party (NDP) won 98 percent of the seats. The real opposition was thus removed and only some orchestrated opposition was allowed to remain to give the parliament a semblance of having an opposition. This turned the whole country against NDP.

The blatant rigging escalated the demand for political change especially since there were indicators that Egypt was heading towards a transition of power with the presidential elections scheduled for 2011. That is why opposition parties and movements escalated their agitation against the inheritance of power (there was widespread speculation that Gamal Mubarak was being groomed to succeed his father as president).

In order to offset this move, opposition parties proposed different names to contest the presidential elections such as those of Amr Moussa, Mohamed El Baradei, Ahmed Zuweil, Ahmed Shafiq etc. to replace Mubarak. A youth group emerged to support Baradei and succeeded in mobilizing a large number of young people to support him.

Meanwhile, the atrocities committed by the national security forces against the agitators made the youth in all governorates of Egypt use facebook and twitter to ask their peers to rise and demand constitutional changes. They established a Facebook page called, “We are all Khaled Said”. (Khaled Saeed was a young man from Alexandria who was brutally tortured and killed by the police for exposing their atrocities.) This page made even those who had hitherto been indifferent to politics take an interest in politics. The “We are all Khaled Said” group called for a massive agitation on January 25—the police day in Egypt—to demand the resignation of the interior minister and lifting of emergency law.

The success of the Tunisian revolution that led Zine El Abidine Ben Ali to flee to Saudi Arabia on January 14 inspired the Egyptian youth to call for protests in all major squares in every city. These people decided to keep away from the slogans of religious and political parties as they were not following the agenda of any political party. Their slogan was “bread, freedom and human dignity”.

On January 25, even Egyptians were surprised at the response to this call when large numbers of people came out to gather in the major squares of Cairo, Alexandria, Suez, Assiut and other cities.

Reasons for the Success of the Revolution

1. **The Social Media Network:** The internet played a major role in mobilizing people especially since it was beyond the control of security forces.
2. **The Tunisian Revolution:** This revolution sent a profound message: the people can change the system.
3. **The Weakness of the Political System:** Mubarak's regime was top-heavy. It had no firm foundation in the form of public support. Mubarak ruled with an iron hand stifling all political dissent.
4. **The Atrocities of the National Security Forces:** These atrocities made people support the protestors because they wanted to take revenge from the police.
5. **Military Support for the Protestors:** The army remained restrained throughout and refused to fire on civilians. It stood by the people's right to peaceful protest.
6. **Media Coverage:** The coverage of the events by the international media and citizen journalists played a significant role in disclosing the fact that the protestors could not be silenced and that the regime, despite it brutality, was powerless in the face of this mass movement.
7. **The Determination of the Protestors:** The protestors remained firm even in the face of violence and stood by their decision not to leave Tahrir Square unless the regime went no matter what they faced.
8. **Popular Support:** It was a people's movement and there was no one leader who started the protests or led the masses. All sections of the people regardless of their different ideologies and socio-economic backgrounds joined the protests.
9. **International Sympathy:** Although the world reacted with caution in the initial stage of the revolution, the high-handedness of the regime and the legitimate democratic aspirations of the people soon turned the tide in favour of the protestors. The international community demanded that

Mubarak listen to the voice of the people and the one-time strong ally of his government, the US, openly asked him to step down.

Phases of the Revolution

The Egyptian Revolution did not end with the ouster of Mubarak. It continues and may be broadly divided into the following four phases.

Phase One: The protestors' main demand was for the removal of the old regime as it symbolized corruption in all aspects. They also demanded social justice and a better standard of life.

Phase Two: Some objective people like Ahmed Shafiq took power and started introducing some reforms. However, the protestors rejected these people because of their link with the old regime especially since Ahmed Shafiq, though otherwise a respected figure on the Egyptian political scene, had been appointed prime minister by Mubarak.

Phase Three: The protestors succeeded in removing people with connections to the old regime and asked for Essam Sharaf to be appointed prime minister. Sharaf's government formally dissolved the NDP and called for a referendum on what should come first: the framing of a new constitution or the elections to parliament. People voted overwhelmingly in favour of parliamentary elections taking place first. However, Sharaf's government soon lost the confidence of the people because of its failure to control sectarian violence and the domination by the Supreme Council of Armed Forces (SCAF). SCAF was seen to be tying the hands of the prime minister who consequently was unable to take much action. Persistent demands for Sharaf's removal finally led to his resignation in November 2011.

Phase Four: Sharaf's resignation was followed by the formation of a National Salvation Government under Dr. Kamal El Ganzouri despite opposition by certain sections of the people who would not accept anything short of SCAF handing over power to a civilian authority. Although until an elected civilian president forms a new government, no interim transitional government can take any major decisions, El Ganzouri came with more powers than any other prime minister in the past. The chief mandate of his government was to maintain security and stability.

Ganzouri's appointment was followed by the announcement of a definite date for the transfer of executive power to civilians by the end of June 2012 and a reduction in the period of election. It was also announced that a Constituent Assembly would be formed after the parliamentary elections to frame the new constitution before the presidential election. The process of nominations for this election is scheduled to start in April.

Elections to the People's Assembly (the lower house of parliament) that started towards the end of Sharaf's government and ended under El Ganzouri have brought the Islamists to power with an overwhelming majority. Elections to the Shura Council (upper house of parliament) are currently taking place and it is expected that Islamists will sweep the polls there too.

Ganzouri's government seemed to have started well. The police were back on the streets and there was some security. The stock market rebounded and the general situation of the country seemed to be taking a turn for the better. However, the violence that followed an Egyptian Premier League match in Port Said resulting in 74 deaths and thousands injured shook the country once again. There were large scale protests in several cities. In Tahrir Square, protestors tried to storm the interior ministry which they want "purged of the remnants of the old regime" and clashed with the police which was blamed for the tragedy. Demands for SCAF to give up power gained momentum and the government has been called to account by the people and by the newly elected People's Assembly.

As mentioned earlier, the world reacted with caution towards the Egyptian Revolution in its initial stage. However, later on most countries supported the protestors' right to make their demands. America and other western countries asked Mubarak to heed the voice of the people. Some Arab countries supported the protestors from the beginning while others were hesitant to support them for fear of repercussions at home. A number of countries promised financial help that, however, never materialized.

Implications of the Revolution

The Revolution is bound to have far-reaching effects not only within Egypt but also on its position in and relations with the international comity of nations.

Implications at Home: The Revolution will undoubtedly have far reaching implications at home in the political, economic as well as socio-cultural spheres. There is no denying the fact that the interim period—the period immediately following the Revolution—has been marred by a lack of security, an economic downturn, loss of confidence by the investors and sectarian and other kinds of violence. There is an all-round eruption of emotion after 30 years of suppression. A mute nation has suddenly found a voice which it is using in full measure sometimes, as its detractors may say, to its detriment. None should deny people their right to self-expression and peaceful protest. However, taking the law in one's own hands will only add to lawlessness and instability in the country and will tarnish its image and that of its Revolution both at home and abroad.

Analysts feel that once an elected government takes office under an elected civilian president, the country will stabilize.

Political Sphere: One year on, it has to be admitted that much has changed despite some claims that nothing has changed or that nothing has changed for the better. The Revolution has shown what the people of Egypt really want and which was denied to them for decades.

On the first anniversary of the Revolution, SCAF announced the lifting of the emergency law except in acts of thuggery. Emergency had remained in force all through Mubarak's rule and even earlier.

Egypt's universities have seen a transformation of leadership, with deans and heads of faculty now directly elected by their colleagues and peers.

Al-Azhar is regaining its rightful position in the world as the pre-eminent voice of moderate Sunni Islam. This will have lasting effects both in Egypt and the world.

Television, radio and the press are now enjoying unprecedented freedom. In fact, now everyone has a voice. All Egyptians are now entitled to an opinion and they are equally free to express it.

The Egyptian Revolution, as mentioned earlier, was essentially a people's movement without a unified leadership. The positive aspect of this feature is that it was essentially a spontaneous outpouring of the will of the masses that were not led or dictated to by any single leader. However, the negative aspects of the lack of leadership have emerged since the Revolution because during the various protest movements in the past year, SCAF and other governmental authorities have found it almost impossible to negotiate with different protest groups and come to any sort of unanimous or even consensual understanding.

Most protest groups have the "take away fast food culture" where they want what they demand to be delivered to them on the spot. They are not prepared to wait for their demands to be met. In the entire history of mankind no revolution has produced instantaneous results. It takes time for demands to be met and for gains to appear. Today, different groups have different demands and Tahrir Square of today is not the same as Tahrir Square of one year ago in the sense that it neither projects a unified stand nor the will of all Egyptians. It might even seem that some of these groups are behaving in the same autocratic manner as that of the regime they opposed and overthrew.

The Islamists have come to power but with a reformed

rhetoric. In fact, they can be said to be more democratic than certain other groups as they take all their decisions through *Shura* (consultations). The leaders of their organizations change frequently through elections. The proof of their grassroots popularity is that they have come to power even in those countries such as Morocco and Kuwait where there was no revolution. Here, one question arises: *why did the liberals fail despite being the leaders of the revolution.* The answer for this lies in the better organization of the Islamists. They faced the atrocities of the old regime. In addition, they have the funds as they get financial support from some Arab countries. However, the last factor can be refuted on the basis of the fact that some of the liberals are richer and could spend on their electoral campaigns.

The main cause for the success of the Islamists is flexibility in their approach. They said they did not want to dominate. Rather they wanted to be partners in changing the country and the life of the people for the better. Ikhwanul Muslimeen is thus part of a coalition under the name Democratic Front. This Front consists of the Freedom and Justice Party (the party of Ikhwanul Muslimeen) along with Ghad, Karama and Hadara parties (these three parties are all moderate).

In parliament, they will definitely seek the support of liberal parties like Wafd. Wafd was a part of this coalition at the beginning, but later decided to go it alone. However, Wafd declared its support for Ikhwan in Parliament. Thus, the Speaker of the newly elected People's Assembly is from the Freedom and Justice Party of the Ikhwanul Muslimeen, and of the two deputy speakers one is from the Wafd Party and the other from the Nour Party of the Salafis. The *murshid* (spiritual leader) of Ikhwanul Muslimeen has declared that the group will support a secular civilian presidential candidate. Ikhwan has declared that it will not field a candidate of its own in the presidential elections. Moreover, they have declared they do not want to implement either the Iranian or the Saudi model of Islam in Egypt.

There is no denying the fact that Ikhwan hold the balance in the country. If they strike a deal with SCAF, the scenario of Pakistan will emerge with a civilian government in power but the military calling the shots. If they embrace the aims of the revolution and democracy, Egypt will go the way of Turkey. If they follow the path of the extremists, the Iranian model will emerge.

It must not be forgotten that unlike the armies in Syria, Libya and Iraq, which were deployed to quell the uprisings, the Egyptian army protected the revolution and the demonstrators. The army will most likely stick to the agenda of transferring power to a civilian authority. However, it will want to retain the special privileges and benefits it has always enjoyed and will be reluctant to come under civilian scrutiny. This might bring it into confrontation with future civilian governments.

Economic Sphere: Egypt is facing and will continue to face economic problems at least for some time in the coming period. The Revolution has led to lack of investments, closure of factories, strikes demanding pay raise and lack of tourism. All these factors have led to a rise in unemployment. The foreign exchange reserves dropped from US$ 34 billion to US$ 18 billion at the end of December 2011. This figure is expected to further drop to USD 12 billion by the end of 2012. Egypt has negotiated a one billion dollar loan from the International Monetary Fund to bail it out of the present crisis.

However, these are short-term setbacks that can be overcome once security and stability are restored to the country. These two factors will restore the confidence of both investors and tourists. This will happen once a stable civilian government is formed and a smooth transition of power takes place by the end of June.

Greater attention to establishing small-scale industries will absorb unemployment and speed up development in a short time. It will also restore stability and security to the country because with a secure job and a regular source of income, the poverty of unemployed youth will not be exploited by destabilizing elements who hire them as thugs to vandalize and cause anarchy in the country.

Corruption in all fields will definitely decrease. This will lead to the national income not being confined in the hands of a few people. There will thus be a more equitable distribution of the national income leading to a better pay structure. As a result, the standard of living will improve and one of the major aims of the Revolution will thus be fulfilled.

Socio-cultural Sphere: The culture of tolerance will increase among Egyptians notwithstanding certain instances of sectarian violence that have taken place since the Revolution. The primary aim of the Islamists who are dominating parliament will be to restore stability in the country. The Egyptian people too are not in favour of violence. The average Egyptian by nature is moderate not extremist. It is notable that during both the Revolution and the anniversary celebrations of the revolution there was no incidence of sectarian violence.

Any post-Revolution government that comes to power knows full well the role of the masses as an element of change. The proof of that are the March 2011 referendum and the parliamentary elections.

The barrier of fear has broken for good. People are no longer afraid to come out to demand their rights. They also believe that any change has to come from within the country and not imposed by any external forces.

Implications Abroad: Events since the Revolution have clearly indicated that Egypt's foreign policy will henceforth reflect the will of the people and not serve the selfish interests of a regime or a coterie. The purpose of foreign policy is to serve domestic interests. However, if foreign policy and foreign trade agreements are detrimental to national interests, they need to be looked at afresh. Despite the fact that the major demands of the protestors were related to problems at home, there were also demands for changes in foreign policy as the people felt that under Mubarak, Egypt had lost its pre-eminent position in the region.

Egypt's foreign policy will be examined here in the following aspects:

1. Towards the Arab countries and the Middle East region.
2. Towards the African continent.
3. Towards other countries.

Egypt's Foreign Policy towards the Middle East: Following are the major aspects of Egypt's foreign policy towards the Middle East region:

Palestine: The Mubarak regime did not take any firm stand against Israeli atrocities on Palestinians. Mubarak was asking for peace knowing fully well that hard-line Israeli governments will never bring peace. After the Revolution, Egypt's policy towards the Palestinians has changed. Egypt has reopened the Rafah border to allow Palestinians to travel easily (Rafah is the only opening to the outside world for the residents of Gaza).

Egypt has succeeded in bringing Fatah and Hamas closer towards reconciliation. It must be mentioned here that the Egyptian Revolution influenced the Palestinian youth in demanding that Fatah and Hamas reconcile their differences, leave their own interests aside and seek national interests.

Ismail Haniya came to Egypt shortly after the second phase of Egypt's parliamentary elections and declared that Hamas is the "jihadi" branch of Ikhwanul Muslimeen. He also visited Jordan for the first time in 12 years (previously Hamas leaders were not allowed into Jordan).

Israel: In 2009 Haaretz newspaper conducted a survey that showed that 89 percent of Israelis were in favour of reoccupying Sinai! Even the current foreign minister of Israel —who Egypt has refused to welcome—threatened to attack the High Dam in Aswan which supplies electricity to the whole of Egypt and prevents the annual flooding of the Nile from inundating parts of the country.

Israel is fully aware that democracy in Egypt means that the decisions of any future government will be influenced by popular will. Relations with Egypt and other Arab countries depend on Israel's policies towards Arabs in general and the Palestinians in particular. Israel's claim to be the only democracy in the Middle East is no longer valid as Egypt and some other Arab countries are firmly on the road to democracy.

Israel is fully aware that things have changed since the days when Egypt, under Mubarak, was a strategic ally that helped it against rivals like Hamas and Hizbollah. Now, Israel and the world powers will have to deal with Arab public opinion and not with regimes.

In an attempt to test the waters perhaps, in August 2011, Israel raided the Egyptian border and killed five Egyptian guards, which provoked public anger. Although Egypt's interim government demanded an apology from Israel and threatened to withdraw its ambassador from Tel Aviv, thousands of protesters took to the streets to express their anger. They called for the end of diplomatic ties, an end to subsidized gas exports to Tel Aviv and even an end to the 1979 Peace Treaty. The protests escalated when dozens stormed the Israeli Embassy building and forced the emergency evacuation of the ambassador and his staff. Though Israel expressed its regret for the Egyptian deaths and said it was investigating the incident, pressure was growing in Egypt for sterner sanctions. Any future democratically elected governments in Egypt are likely to have a more balanced stance towards Israel, based on the will of the people. These governments will have to reconsider their relationship with Israel.

Egypt's Camp David Accords with Israel will remain. All Islamists have declared their commitment to this treaty. However, certain voices are asking for the modification of certain clauses in the treaty, e.g., an increase in the number of Egyptian armed forces stationed in Sinai and a revision of the price of gas supplied to Israel. The gas pipeline has already been blown up more than ten times. Dr. El Ganzouri's government is seriously considering raising the price of gas supplied to Israel.

Arab Countries: Egypt supports the stability of the Gulf region and for this reason it was against the uprising in Bahrain. Among other things this stand emanates from national interests as Egypt earns valuable foreign exchange from these countries in the form of remittances from Egyptian expatriates working there.

Egypt supported the Libyan Revolution since its inception. The first visit of Field Marshal Hussein Tantawi, the head of SCAF was to Libya. Egypt will continue to support the interests of the Arab people.

Iran: One of the first statements of Dr. Nabil El Araby as foreign minister was in favour of restoring full diplomatic relations with Iran based on mutual interests. Egypt's relations with Iran are expected to improve. Iran is a neighbour for Arab countries and as such our relations should be based on cooperation and mutual understanding for the best interests of all.

Africa: Egypt's relations with Africa were affected with Mubarak's government ignoring the significance of Africa, especially the Nile Basin countries, to Egypt. The policy of Egypt towards Africa has to change especially after the division of Sudan and the increasing relations between Israel and the African countries. These relations can threaten Egypt's national security.

After the Revolution, Egyptian diplomacy has focused on Africa. Dr. Essam Sharaf visited Sudan and some other Nile Basin countries immediately after taking office. He convinced these countries that Egypt recognizes the importance of Africa to Egypt. Dr. Sharaf's visit was followed by a public delegation consisting of different political parties and leading public figures including some revolutionaries to convince Ethiopia not to build a dam on the Nile as it would restrict the flow of water into Egypt. In January 2012, the Egyptian Foreign Minister visited a number of Nile Basin countries. This shows the important place of Africa in Egypt's foreign policy.

The West: In fact, it is mutual national interests that will henceforth form the basis of all foreign relations. This will restore Egypt's position in the Arab and African region as a major player in the political arena. Egypt's foreign policy will no longer be predominantly pro-West.

As far as Egypt and other Arab countries are concerned, the recipients of economic and financial aid from the US and European countries should depend entirely on their own resources. It is also time for Arab countries to shift their attention to Asia and Africa. Colonialism of the 20th century, which witnessed wars of independence against occupying forces in different parts of the world, are being repeated in the 21st century though in a different form. The powers that divided and ruled much of Africa and Asia in the last two centuries continued their policy just changing their tack. Thus, they propped up dictators with financial aid to maintain their dictatorial regimes while at the same time financing and training local adversaries who were campaigning to remove these dictators from power. The role of NGOs is notable in this regard. Even after the toppling of dictators, west-backed and financed NGOs and human rights organizations continued their activities to prevent reconciliation and promote divisionism among the people.

For the first time, the Egyptian government questioned the role of non-governmental organizations (NGOs) and prevented heads of certain American organizations from leaving the country because of a judicial order that has called for investigation into their suspicious activities during the January 25 Revolution. These NGOs receive financial and logistical aid from the US Congress. Two of them also belong to the Republican and Democratic parties. As a result, Egypt has come under intense pressure from Washington to take its hands off these NGOs accused of running suspicious activities. Washington threatened more than once to cut off its economic and military aid, unless the SCAF ordered the reopening of NGOs in Cairo.

Some suspects who have been arrested following incidents of violence have admitted that they received training in camps organized for young Egyptians abroad. Legal investigations would reveal the facts behind these training camps which are instigating instability and anarchy in the country.

Conclusion

Democracy is a practice but ruling is a responsibility. Thus, enlightened political Islam will be more suitable for Arab and Islamic countries for the coming decades provided it does not transform into a rigid theocracy.

There is no doubt that a number of far-reaching changes have taken place in Egypt over the past year viz.:

1. For the first time since the Revolution of July 1952, Egypt has had free and fair elections.
2. The emergency has been lifted after more than 30 years.
3. Parliament is to act as a watchdog over the government's policies and activities rather than being a subservient tool for vested interests.
4. A new constitution is to be drafted soon.
5. Presidential elections will take place soon with the president's term of office reduced to four years and any president allowed to seek re-election only once. Thus, no president can remain in office for more than two terms, i.e. eight years.
6. The trials of members of the old regime for corruption and killing of protestors during the Revolution currently taking place will take their due course. The slow pace of justice has prompted many bereaved families to vow to take the law into their own hands to avenge the brutal death of their family members. However, such behaviour will only add to national chaos.
7. The Speaker of the newly elected People's Assembly has declared that the Revolution is not yet over. According to him, the Revolution will continue until all its aims are fulfilled.

8. The interim period is marred by instability and economic downslide. However, most analysts feel that once an elected government takes office and forms a government, the country will become more stable and go on the right track towards economic development and fulfilment of the aims of the Revolution.
9. The Egyptian public will not accept anything short of a civilian president. An evidence of this is that demands for the SCAF to give up power are made almost daily from different quarters. There is now talk of the presidential elections being expedited. The SCAF too seems to be ready to transfer power to a civilian president because governing the country has become a burden for it now.
10. However, the army will want to retain its privileges. A majority of the people are not against this because the Egyptian army has, throughout its history, defended national interests including the rights and interests of civilians. No one can forget that the success of the January Revolution is to a large measure due to the sympathy of the army for the demands of the protestors and its refusal to harm the civilians in any way.
11. It may be said that all elected members of parliament belong to the opposition now because the National Salvation Government is a transitional government that was appointed and not elected. Thus, members of parliament are loyal to the people and not to any regime. For the first time since the 1952 Revolution the head of government, i.e., the Prime Minister, was summoned by Parliament for questioning after the Port Said events. Some members even asked for the head of SCAF to be summoned. This was unthinkable a year ago.
12. Analysts are projecting two future scenarios for Egypt:

Optimistic View: The Egyptian Revolution will change the social, economic and political life of the country by cutting off relations with the misdeeds of the last regime. *There will be real democracy, a constitution and a constitutionally elected* *government. This will lead to increased stability.* Unemployment will decrease and production will increase thus giving an impetus to the economy. The military will give up some of its privileges and the country will be ruled by a civilian president elected for no more than two four-year terms. Thus, the Revolution's demands for bread, freedom and social dignity will be realized.

Pessimistic View: Egypt will metamorphose into a theocratic state now that Islamists have swept the polls. The protagonists of such a scenario are of the view that despite some moderate statements made by the Islamists, tourism will suffer. Egypt's relations with the international community, particularly with the West will turn sour leading to an economic decline that could come with the West cutting off much needed aid to Egypt.

In my opinion, Egypt will not go in this direction because an average Egyptian is moderate by nature and not an extremist. For the first time in Egypt's political history, one-third of the newly elected members of parliament are highly educated holding Ph.D. degrees. They will bring enlightenment and an intellectual edge to parliamentary discussions and legislation. A quarter of the members of parliament do not own a car—an indication that they are ordinary middle class citizens who will empathize with the ordinary Egyptian. This is also an indication of the fact that it was not money power that brought them to power nor was it their Islamist background. It was their proximity to the people at the grassroots level that resulted in their victory. The new parliament is also quite diverse with all sections of public opinion represented there ranging from liberals and socialists to Islamists.

1. Relations with Israel will be based on national interests because while it may be easy to pressurize a dictatorial regime, it is not easy to do so with an elected government that is accountable to the electorate for its actions. Even the interim National Salvation Government is talking

about renegotiating the gas deal with Israel in favour of more favourable terms for Egypt. Moreover, some provisions of the Camp David Accords could come up for a review, like the presence of the number of Egyptian troops in Sinai.

2. Relations with the West and other countries of the world will go along the same lines as relations with Israel. National interests and public opinion will be the lynchpin on which these relations will be based.

There is thus no denying the fact that changes in Egypt and the rest of the Arab world are coming and are irreversible whether one accepts them or not.

References

Abdullah, Ahmed (2008), "The Student Movement and National Politics in Egypt 1923-1973", Cairo: The American University in Cairo Press, 2008.

Al Ahram Al Siyasa Al Dawliya, Issue No. 184, Cairo, April 2011.

Al Ahram Al Siyasa Al Dawliya, Issue No. 187, Cairo, January 2012.

Helal, Ali El din (2010), "Al Nizam Al Siyasi Al Masry, 1981-2010", Cairo: Al Dar Al Masriya Al Lubnaniya, 2010.

Shehata, Dina (2011), Al Harakat Al Shababiya wa Thawrat 25 Yanayar, Kurrasat Istrategia, Issue No. 128, 2011.

4

Turmoil in Libya: Internal Dynamics and External Linkages

A.K. Pasha

US/Western Attempts to Overthrow Gaddafi

The overthrow of the Libyan Monarchy by Gaddafi in September 1969 and the expulsion of the US from the huge Wheelus Air Base was a blow to the Americans. He soon after sought and got higher oil prices and increased Libyan participation in the oil companies. He also stridently opposed all US attempts to bring about partial agreements on the Arab-Israeli conflict (AIC). US-Libyan views on major world issues diverged widely and relations between them remained considerably strained under the administrations of Presidents Richard Nixon, Gerald Ford and Jimmy Carter.

The Reagan administration very early identified Libya as a main perpetrator of state-sponsored international terrorism and made determined efforts to bring down Gaddafi's regime. He was accused of involvement in terrorist activities as early as 1972 and the US put Libya in the state Department's list of states, which sponsor international terrorism. Gaddafi was painted in the darkest colours of being an international terrorist. The CIA spared no efforts to kill Gaddafi. Soon the US attacked Libya on 14 April 1986 mainly with the intention of killing Gaddafi, but the Libyan leader survived. Following the footsteps of the Reagan and Bush administrations, President Bill Clinton intensified his efforts to overthrow Gaddafi, this time using the UN as a tool to portray scattered Libyan political violence as state-sponsored terrorism.

The first incident was the Lockerbie issue. On 21st

December, 1988, a Pan American World Airways jumbo jet flight 103 travelling from London to New York exploded over Lockerbie, Scotland, killing 243 passengers and crew. The US mobilized the UN and on 20th January, 1992, the UN Security Council unanimously adopted Resolution 731, which was a blow to Libya. The West again had its way in the UNSC when Resolution 748 was passed on 31st March, 1992. The adoption of UNSCR 748 clearly indicated the extent to which the West would go for regime change in Libya. It signalled new heights of Western hostility towards Libya and an indication of harsher steps to follow. The manner and speed with which the US mobilized the UNSC clearly indicated US impatience with the Gaddafi regime. Actually US move helped Gaddafi to consolidate his base and tighten his grip on power. But most Libyans were convinced that the West after subjugating Iraq wanted to gain control of Libyan Oil.

The US led UN sanctions imposed on Libya on 15th April, 1992 remained in place for more than a decade. Gaddafi through his extensive contacts in Africa mobilized at many African summits urged them to lift or suspend or ease the UN sanctions on Libya. Soon Libya reconciled to the trial in Europe of the alleged Lockerbie bombers and handed over in August 2003 the two suspects with imprisonment for one of the suspects when he was found guilty. Subsequently, Libya agreed to pay several billion US dollars to the victims with Gaddafi accepting responsibility for the Lockerbie bombing. For Gaddafi the coming to power of the neo-con team in US in 2001 and the policy of George W. Bush after 9/11, together with the solidarity of PM Tony Blair of Britain and PM Ariel Sharon of Israel, represented danger. More significantly, US invasion of Iraq in March 2003 and lack of countervailing support to Libya from Russia or China and his own isolation in the Arab world propelled him to work for rapprochement with the West.

In August 2003, Libya formally accepted responsibility for the 1988 Lockerbie bombing and in September 2003 the

UNSC voted to lift economic sanctions against Libya. No wonder Gaddafi in a stunning decision in December 2003 decided to publicly renounce terrorism and agreed to destroy long-range missiles and WMDs. He also abandoned Libya's quest for nuclear weapons and gave up Libya's nuclear programme. In January 2004, Libya was approved as the 109th country to ratify the NPT and in February 2004 Libya formally became the 159th country to join the Organization for the Prohibition of Chemical Weapons. Soon after this unprecedented Libyan initiative, the West especially UK and US worked to lift UN sanctions on Libya.

On 11th February, 2004, Italian PM Silvio Berlusconi met Gaddafi in Tripoli. In February 2004, Libyan Foreign Minister and UK Foreign Secretary Jack Straw met and UK restored diplomatic ties. Soon the British PM Tony Blair visited Libya along with other Western leaders who followed him thereby ending Tripoli isolation and boycott. In the tense standoff over Lockerbie, Libya had to ultimately make several concessions and at the same time the West also realized the futility of its policy towards Gaddafi's Libya. Finally, on 15th May, 2006, the US decided to restore full diplomatic ties with Libya after a break of more than 25 years. The US also removed Libya from a state department list of states sponsoring terrorism. It must be recalled that the US had closed its embassy in Tripoli, in 1980 and had declared Gaddafi as a supporter of international terrorism. But what led to Libya's normalization of its international relationships was Gaddafi's decision in December 2003 to renounce terrorism and destroy long range missiles and WMD'S, Pan Am flight over Lockerbie controversy in 1988 for which Libya was blamed and Libyan decision to accept responsibility for it and pay compensation and hand over the two Libyan suspects who were put on trial that led to gradual rapprochement with the US and West.

Genesis of Domestic Opposition

After a failed coup in mid-1970s led by two of his

colleagues, Gaddafi purged the military of dissent and many were executed. Since then sensitive posts were allotted to close personal acquaintances of Gaddafi or to members of his immediate family or tribe. So by 1975, Libya had come to assume all the characteristics of a militant, radical, repressive and ruthless authoritarian regime in power. Soon Libyan society and polity were gradually radicalized with popular committee system being extended in 1975. And in 1977 March, the Libyan Jamahiriya was established. Soon people discovered that the main purpose of the popular committees was to eliminate those who did not conform to Gaddafi's thinking. Hence, people who did not conform to the new thinking simply did not participate in Libyan affairs. This Libyans call the period from 1978-1988 as the "dark decade" because of the political repression and the extreme economic hardships. Only the revolutionary committees and their leadership experienced no shortages during this period. Gaddafi's economic reforms laid the foundation for the final split between

Libya's religious elites and Gaddafi: The nationalization of the economy, by implication also rendered waqf nationalized as well. The Ulema attacked the move on religious grounds, as an attack on the sanctioned right to private property. Sheikh Al-Bashti in Tripoli continued to attack Gaddafi's actions. The 1990's saw the proliferation of the ranks of the opposition to Gaddafi's revolutionary ideas. The middle class, educated professionals with degrees but severely limited opportunities, and the growing numbers of students who perceived an equally disturbed future had begun to voice their contempt for rampant corruption and the absence of an independent civil society. Apart from the Sanusi religious elites who slowly remerged, the Muslim Brotherhood also surfaced as a network of resistance in Libya, opposing Gaddafi's attempt to dismantle the religious bloc.

The National Salvation Front—also emerged as a grave threat to Gaddafi since 1981 led by Muhammad Yousef al

Maqarayah. Many who defected from the regime found place in the Front. The main aim of the NSF became the overthrow of the Gaddafi regime. Two other groups also emerged to challenge Gaddafi: Islamic Martyrdom founded in 1993 by Amir al Haim and the Libyan Islamic Group led by Omar Rashid. Both had Libyan veterans who had returned from the Afghan conflict or Jihad. All of these groups and the numerous supporters they had, reflected nothing less than utter resentment towards Gaddafi's tyrannical rule of Libya. Among the several groups that opposed Gaddafi the Islamist militants were particularly daring and aggressive.

The first anti-regime protest began in 1995 June in Benghazi when the religious forces clashed with Libyan security forces leading to a protracted struggle in various parts of Benghazi areas. A number of attempts were made on Gaddafi's life by the Libyan Islamic Group, Islamic Martyrdom Movement and other Islamic guerillas in June 1996 and June 1998. Not sure of his support in the military, Gaddafi started building alternative popular militias and staffing key security posts with expatriate East Germans, Cubans and other mercerenies. According to Hussein Soloman, "It is this increasingly isolated situation that compels the regime to re-assess its foreign policy as it seeks to make common cause with the USA and its allies in the fight against militant Islam".

But the major issue was whether Gaddafi could offer political stability in future as he had provided since September 1, 1969. Most of Libya's population is young and has great expectations especially after the severe UN-USA economic sanctions for well over a decade. Women particularly had been hard hit and had endured the worst phase in their recent memory. This along with a largely authoritarian political system despite the Green Book propaganda and People's Committees and Congresses, the people had a legitimate question i.e., after decades of struggle against the West, why did Gaddafi virtually surrender in December 2003 to the West?

Ever after this 180-degree turn around, the plight of the ordinary Libyans did not improve fast enough and there was bound to be turmoil in the future.

An indication of what was to come became visible during the 2005 protest over the publication of Prophet's cartoons controversy when Islamist Libyans suddenly attacked the Italian consulate in Benghazi and the police resorted to indiscriminate firing resulting in heavy causalities. Most Libyans wondered what Gaddafi was going to do with the more than US$ 100 billion foreign exchange reserve he had. Was it for emergencies to him and his family in case things get out of hand to his iron-fist rule or for what else?

Arab Spring and Libya

The overthrow of Zine El Abidine Ben Ali and Hosni Mubarak in Tunisia and Egypt in early 2011 and the protests for political reforms sweeping across the Arab World did not spare Libya as well. Small protests erupted in Benghazi since February 2011 which was put down by Gaddafi's security forces. From the very start, Gaddafi faced many rebellions in the Benghazi area and his responses were to the crush or destroy the prestige of the existing religious elites particularly those connected with the Sanusi in the Cyrenaica. Soon matters were getting out of hand attracting global attention focused at the highhanded measures adopted by the Gaddafi regime's security forces. Gaddafi himself called the protesters names and vowed to crush them. There were reports of heavy civilian casualties and soon the West called for effective steps to protect the civilian population. In this connection the GCC states and Arab League called for a no fly zone over Libya to prevent Gaddafi from using his air force to suppress the civilian protests in the Benghazi area.

Towards the end of February 2011 the US imposed sanctions and soon the UN also imposed sanctions. The UN approved curbs on travel, freezing of financial assets, weapons sales and a reference to ICC in The Hague. India supported the first UN Security Council Resolution. India also had to evacuate over 15,000 of its citizens from Libya by special flights and ships. India also "deplored" the use of force "which is totally un-acceptable and must not be resorted to". It "earnestly hoped that calm is restored at the earliest without any further violence". The UNSC adopted another resolution no. 1973 to impose UN NO Fly zone in which India, China, Russia, Brazil abstained. Soon UK, France, USA and others in the NATO plus Qatar, UAE started bombing Libya apparently to protect the civilians but actually to kill Gaddafi and bring down his regime.

There was no doubt about Western hostility to Gaddafi and his regime but what actually triggered was Libya's decision to allow China, Russia and others unhindered access to Libya's oil assets and role in infrastructure development and Gaddafi's refusal to join US led Africa Centcom and his influence over many African states not to join. The Libyan opposition under the banner of National Transitional Council [NTC] with NATO support especially heavy bombing of entire Libya and huge destruction of both civilian and military assets claimed victory and control over Tripoli, Benghazi and other coastal cities. Bin Walid and Sirte appear to have been retaken by pro-Gaddafi forces. But in effect Libya is in a civil war and Libya *de facto* divided into two or more parts. Libyans are killing Libyans and the West and Arab states of GCC [especially Qatar and UAE] are adding fuel to the fire. Libya with the highest score on the UN's human development index (HDI) of all African countries has been deliberately destroyed in a barbaric fashion.

The NTC is a divided house and still unable to form a government as sharp differences have arisen between Secularists and Islamists, tribal vs. outsiders among other differences. Ali Sallabi emerged as a leading Islamist in new Libya who claims that relations between Islamists and secularists are "strong". He also said, "We support pluralism and justice. Libyans have the right to build a democratic state and political parties". But many critics fear that Mr. Sallabi may show his true colours only after he has scaled current obstacles and assumed a position of power. More significantly, the Chairman of NTC in his first press conference said that Islam will be the main source of new Libya's laws.

There is feeble talk of elections and virtually no talk of political reforms as the West and Libyan opposition's main goal was Gaddafi's removal from power. Although some members of Gaddafi's family have fled to neighbouring states but Gaddafi's supporters continue to fight and challenge the foreign backed NTC. These threats cannot be ignored as they have large quantities of light and heavy weapons. Some Berbers and other tribes in the south of the country in the vast Sahara desert also have huge weapons and may join the fight. There is fear of a low intensity warfare being waged by the tribes based in Sahara who not only control vast areas but might blow up oil and water pipelines, and other oil facilities thereby crippling Libya's oil exports. Since the NTC is not in full control of all Libya the militias have inflicted revenge killings, torture and rape especially on the population of Tawergha for allegedly supporting Gaddafi and his supporters. Other black Africans have also suffered for being suspected Gaddafi mercenaries and nearly a million have reached neighbouring Niger.

Libya under Gaddafi had already decided to break with the past in most sectors and initiate bold economic reforms as part of a broader campaign to reintegrate the country into the international economy from which it was isolated due to its conflictual relationship primarily with the US. Libya had already started aggressively vowing foreign investors to take a larger role in the reconstruction of its battered infrastructure/economy. The new political set-up is likely to privatize its largely state run industries. High on the list of prioritize are the telecommunication industry and infrastructure. Already the new regime has given priority to companies of the West.

In an extremely rare departure from its usual anti-Arabs

and pro-U.S. propaganda, the *Guardian* of London commented, "If stopping the killing had been the real aim, NATO states would have backed a ceasefire and a negotiated settlement, rather than repeatedly vetoing both. Instead, after having lost serious strategic ground in the Arab revolutions, the Libyan war offered the US, Britain and France a chance to put themselves at the heart of the process while bringing to heel an unreliable state with the largest oil reserves in Africa". (Seamus Milne, the *Guardian,* 24th August, 2011) Colonel Muammar al-Gaddafi was willing to negotiate a peaceful solution, but after more than four decades of dealing with al-Gaddafi, U.S.-NATO leaders rejected any peaceful negotiation.

The control of Libya was the goal and peace did not meet that goal. The overwhelming majority of the Libyan population is against the violence unleashed by the militias and NATO bombings which is the only thing that sustains their violence. U.S.-NATO bombings of Libya "are in derogation of international law, actions that are criminal in terms of their consequences: the killing of children, the killing of people in their own homes, and this has been well documented", said Michel Chossudovsky of Global Research in Montréal. Although Colonel al-Gaddafi had some popular support across Libya but unlike in Tunisia, Egypt and Bahrain, there were no popular peaceful uprisings except in Benghazi and rebellion in other areas was a Western-backed armed insurrection.

The Transitional National Council (TNC) was a Western-backed "Libyan rebels"—a collection of expatriate criminals, C.I.A. operatives ("Al-Qaeda"), xenophobic and racist hoodlums, and religious extremists" as one writer put it. They are not peaceful ordinary Libyans struggling for democracy and human rights. They were backed by U.S.-NATO ground forces as also from Morocco, Jordan, UAE Qatar and other pro-US Arab states. Again to quote the *Guardian* (25th August, 2011), "British and French special forces along with special forces from Qatar and some eastern European states are on the ground in eastern Libya, calling in air strikes and helping co-ordinate units as they prepare to assault Sirte, the last coastal town still in the hands of pro-Muammar Gaddafi forces". The militias were financed, trained and armed by the U.S. and U.S. allies.

The West/U.S. has been using the volunteer and largely untrained militias as a façade of "democratic" government to control the country. There is hard evidence of mass killings of non-combatants, detainees and the wounded by the U.S.-NATO backed armed militias. For six months Libya was subjected to a barbaric U.S.-NATO military siege. U.S.-NATO aggression has been responsible for war crimes and crimes against humanity. According to NATO's own record, over 25,000 air missions have been flown over Libya, including 9,000 combat sorties by U.S.-NATO warplanes destroying hospital, schools, homes, water supply and communication. Thousands of innocent civilians have been killed. The country's civilian's infrastructure, including hospitals, schools, water supply plants and roads have been destroyed and ruined. Some of these militias now control key areas including Tripoli airport and have become self-appointed guardians. Sadly many have clashed with others and there is no national army to absorb these armed militias and establish a disciplined force.

Eric Schmitt and Steven Lee Myers of the *New York Times* observed, "Through Saturday [20th August, 2011], NATO and its allies had flown 7,459 strike missions, or sorties, attacking thousands of targets, from individual rocket launchers to major military headquarters. The cumulative effect not only destroyed Libya's military infrastructure but also greatly diminished the ability of Colonel Gaddafi's commanders to control forces, leaving even committed fighting units unable to move, resupply or coordinate operations". (NYT, 21st August, 2011) Indeed, it was the heaviest bombardment. Once the way was cleared, the militias stormed the capital, inflicting mass atrocities against the civilian population. A Libyan eyewitness told Kim Sengupta of the *Independent* (24th June, 2011), "The militias are saying they are fighting government troops here, but all those getting hurt are ordinary people, the only buildings being damaged are those of local people. There has also been looting by the rebels, they have gone into houses to search for people and taken away things. Why are they doing this?"

In another piece in the *Independent* (27th June, 2011), Sengupta exposes the Western-backed militias. She writes, "the mounting number of deaths of men from sub-Saharan Africa at the hands of the rebels, lynching's in many cases, raises disturbing questions about the opposition administration, the Transitional National Council (TNC) taking over as Libya's government, and about Western backing for it". The U.S. and its allies will back any group as long as they serve their imperialist interests. It is important to remember that the so-called "Independent" is one of the most anti-Arab papers of all the British newspapers. As the *Independent on Sunday* editorial reveals, "This newspaper supported NATO military intervention, and Britain's part in it, when it began in March, but it was a choice between hard and complex options—and so it remains". (Independent *on Sunday,* 28th August, 2011) The aggression against Libya was in flagrant violation of international law and UN Security Council Resolutions, including Resolutions 1973 adopted in March 2011 to "use all means necessary to protect Libyan civilians". There was no legal mandate to attack Libya and start a war.

The sovereign Government of Libya committed no crimes. It is clear that the aim of U.S.-NATO powers is to divide Libyans in order to seize control of Libya's financial assets and oil reserves and strengthening imperialism's grip on Libya and set the stage of the re-colonization of Africa. Undoubtedly it is a broad daylight robbery. "In 1950, Libyans saw their country deliberately divided by Britain and France, and [the] seeds of division planted among them", writes the renowned Canadian Middle East scholar, Henri Pierre Habib. After more than four decades of "independence", the old seeds of division have germinated. Meanwhile, U.S. politicians are euphoric by what they are doing in Libya and see it as a template to implement around the world. "It is a good indication of the kind of partnership and alliances that we need to have for the future if we are going to deal with the threats that we confront in today's world", said U.S. Defence Secretary, Leon E. Panetta. In other words, the aggression against Libya will be used as a template to commit future aggression against other nations, such as Syria and Iran.

The NTC is beset with numerous internal problems as also aggravated by spiralling violence, assertion by tribal groups and renewed old hatreds. Among many others, the Amazigh tribal leaders and people are also angry about their exclusion from NTC and also being targeted for their black colour. Its decisions lack transparency and have been attacked for its secretive nature and people have demanded resignation of all but a few members of NTC. Already Vice-President Abdul Ghoga has resigned.

Growing public opposition which is frustrated by lack of progress towards democratization turned violent in Benghazi recently which delayed the finalization of the new electoral law. The NTC has not been able to increase oil output to pre-Gaddafi levels because various militias are guarding many oil plants and are refusing to give up weapons. It is this incompetence of the NTC which is pushing the country to chaotic violence and fragmentation as also bringing Islamic groups including Muslim Brotherhood to prominence. The promised elections in 2013 may or may not be held given the polarization in the country along tribal and religious lines, not to speak about the huge weapons available with all groups. NATO brought about regime change in Libya and ordinary Libyans who expected democracy, improvement in their economic conditions and above all peace are sadly witnessing their country slowly sliding into civil war.

References

A.K. Pasha, *Libya and the US: Gaddafi's Response to Reagan's*

Challenge, New Delhi; Détente Publications, 1984.

—*Libya in the Arab World: Gaddafi's Quest for Arab Unity*, Aligarh: CWAS, AMU, 1988.

—Libya and the UN Sanctions, in Lalima Varma (ed.), *UN in the Changing World*, New Delhi: Radiant Publications, 1997, pp. 120-139.

—"Recent Developments in Libyan Foreign Policy", *Détente,* Vol. 3, No. 2, December 1983-January 1984, pp. 9-19.

—"US Challenge to Libya: The Reagan Era", *Détente,* Vol. 3, No. 2-3, July-October 1989, pp. 9-18.

—"Libya and the US: A Study in Disquiparant Relationship", *Détente,* Vol. 3, No. 6, August-September, 1984, pp. 3-11.

—"US Policy towards Libya", Paper presented in a Seminar on "International Terrorism and State policy", March 29-30, 1994, National Security Programme, SIS, JNU, New Delhi.

—"The US Goal to destroy Libya", *The Pioneer*, 3rd April, 1992.

—"India's West Asia Policy: Continuity and Change", *Strategic Analysis,* Vol. 16, No. 6, September 1993, pp. 792-795.

—*India and OIC: Strategy and Diplomacy*, New Delhi: Centre for Peace Studies, 1995, pp. 102-104.

—"Libya and India's Foreign Policy", *The Middle East*, New Delhi, No.1, March 1993, p. 32.

—"USA and Radical Muslim States in WANA", in Riyaz Punjabi (ed.), *USA and the Muslim World: Cooperation and Confrontation,* London: Brunel, 2005.

—*India and West Asia: Continuity and Change,* Delhi: Gyan Sagar, 1999.

—"A New Bounce in India and Libya Ties", *Africa Quarterly*, New Delhi, Vol. 46, No. 2, May-July 2006, pp. 32-41.

—"India and the Maghreb States: Challenges and Opportunities", *Africa Quarterly*, Vol. 48, No.1, February-April, 2008, pp.38-45.

—"Emerging Challenges to India in the Gulf/ West Asian Region", *World Focus*, Vol. 29, Annual Number [347-348], November-December 2008, pp. 419-429.

—"India's Changing Threat Perception from West Asia", *Strategic Studies*, Bahrain, Vol. 5, No.16, Autumn 2009, pp. 9-52.

—"India and Turmoil in West Asia: Challenges and Emerging Responses", *World Focus*, Vol. 30, Annual Number [359-360], November-December 2009, pp. 484-490.

——"Turmoil in Libya and India", *World Focus*, Annual Number, Vol. XXXII, No.11-12, November-December 2011, pp. 922-930.

——Turmoil in the Arab World: Arab Spring or Hot Summer", *Journal of Peace Studies*, Vol. 18, Issue 3 and 4, July-December, 2011, pp. 3-21.

C.S.R. Murthy, "UN Sanctions against Libya: A Perspective", *Journal of West Studies,* Aligarh, No. 8, 1992, p. 17.

C.S.R. Murthy, "India at the UN", *World Focus*, Vol. 13, No. 5, May 1992, p. 19.

Marc Weller, "The Lockerbie Care: A Premature End to the New World Order", *African Journal of International and Comparative Law*, No. 4, 1992, pp. 1-15.

Part II: Arab Spring in Mashreq and Gulf

5

Arab Spring: Saudi Exceptionalism?

Gulshan Dietl

The term exceptionalism in the Arab context harks back to Samuel Huntington's thesis that envisages democracy progression in waves. The third wave was frozen after its initial advances in the seventies. It never washed the shores of the Arab/Muslim world, according to this thesis. Hence, the Arab exceptionalism. Today, the term has been reinvented in the context of the Arab Spring. The Spring is a year old, and not a single crowned head has rolled so far. Hence, the monarchical exceptionalism.

The institution of monarchy does provide a buffer between the monarch and his subjects in the form of a government structure. The king has the privilege of sacking a besieged government and still remaining in power. In the case of Saudi Arabia, the oil-wealth, a small population, huge government patronage, welfare economy, etc., provide additional immunity. On the other hand, an aging leadership, an internet-savvy and educated youth, assertive women, sectarian divisions, and a contagious "Arab Spring" all around in the neighbourhood indicate a partial and potential vulnerability of the Saudi King.

The paper proposes to examine the Saudi domestic situation, the King's response and the country's diplomacy towards the neighbourhood Springs.

Youth, Women and Minorities

The condition of the youth, the women and the minorities is the barometer of a country's socio-political health. A closer scrutiny of these three segments of Saudi society is necessary to understand the general ethos in the country. A critical assessment of the government responses is equally necessary to gauge the deeper undercurrents and possible outcomes.

Al-Mamlak al-Arabiyya al-Saudiyya or the Kingdom of Saudi Arabia has the dubious distinction of being named after its ruling dynasty. Its ruler derives his legitimacy from a blend of tribal, Islamic and temporal props. As a tribal chief, the ruler is the patriarch of his people. Khadim al-Harmain (Servant of the Two Holy Shrines)—the official title of the ruler—confers religious aura to the authority. Till now, the two exercises in temporal legitimacy have been the elections for the municipal councils in 2005, and after a long hibernation, in September 2011.

There is no uniform mobilisation and no widespread protests in the country so far. The Saudi youth, women and the Shias in the east of the country have voiced their grievances separately, nonetheless. In the aftermath of the oil boom, there was a virtual baby boom in the country as elsewhere in the Gulf, with the result that the demographic structure resembled a pyramid. Within a couple of decades thereafter, it acquired the shape of a diamond as the baby boomers moved up the population ladder forming a "youth bulge". It is at this stage that the societies tend to become the most violent. Expected to look after the dependent previous generation and raising the next, the youth tend to get increasingly frustrated in the absence of adequate opportunities. If the better-endowed societies of Europe and the US found it difficult to contain the rage of their baby boomers in 1968, the Saudis are even less prepared. The youth unemployment in the country is estimated to be twenty percent or even higher.

Last year, the groups advocating greater political freedom in Saudi Arabia planned to hold a "day of rage" in the Kingdom. Friday 11 March was the designated day. On 6th March, the Council of Senior Scholars issued a statement calling for unity, declaring that this concept is fundamental to Islam and strongly supported by Prophet Muhammad. The

Ulama also noted that Saudi Arabia is blessed with wise leadership, that the government is legitimate, and that the Kingdom should never allow foreign notions to distort its Islamic identity or wreak havoc. They drove the latter point home by warning against anything that might cause sedition.

The next day, the government's unelected advisory body—the Consultative Council, or Majlis al-Shura—endorsed the Ulama's position and noted that Islamic law prohibits demonstrations in the Kingdom. It instructed the public not to pay attention to "misleading calls for demonstrations, sit-ins, and marches" and warned against "deviant intellectual and partisan links". "Deviant" is Saudi code for Al-Qaeda, while "partisan" usually refers to Saudi Shias, who are suspected of treacherous links to their coreligionists in Iran. [1] In addition, Majlis Speaker Sheikh Abdullah bin Muhammad Al al-Sheikh reminded citizens of the Kingdom's "unique, open-door" approach to satisfying demands and settling grievances by "writing directly to the leadership or any official". The same day, the Council of Ministers—meeting under the chairmanship of King Abdullah, who is also the prime minister—added its own endorsement.

Two distinct threads of protest were likely to emerge on Friday's "day of rage". Sunnis were expected to demonstrate in Riyadh and other cities. At the same time, Shias were planning demonstrations complaining about their disadvantaged status in Saudi society. Sunni dissenters themselves fell into two categories: those who wanted greater freedoms, and those who regarded the royal family as illegitimate and unwilling to administer a sufficiently religious state. The latter are often perceived as being sympathetic to Al-Qaeda. At present, however, the former are the most vocal. Inspired by political change in Egypt and Tunisia, they are calling on the House of Saud to be more accountable. On the day, massive numbers of forces were deployed on the streets. The "day of rage" did not materialise except in the east of the country.

Within a few days of the failed day of rage, the Ministry of

Interior announced that there were five thousand and eighty people charged with terrorism-related crimes and one thousand six hundred and twelve out of them were sentenced to several years in prison by a Saudi court. [2] A few months later, the Amnesty International leaked a proposed draft law against terrorism that the country was poised to approve and implement. The Amnesty criticised the law for "vague and broad" definition of terrorism ranging from "destabilising society" to "harming the reputation of the state". [3] The political activities were severely threatened as a result.

The cyberspace provided an alternative space to mark the popular protests. The internet activists resorted to it in a big way. The Saudi flag that carries two crossed swords over a palm tree was reinvented to carry two mops over a stack of buckets. The reference was to the floods in Jeddah that the authorities failed to tackle. The garbage cans holding the dictators were depicted. There were many other signs of derision. Blogs appeared to express the anger; documentaries were made to expose poverty that has never been acknowledged. One hundred and nineteen Saudi citizens signed a petition asking for a constitutional monarchy. More petitions followed. There was an attempt at forming a political party named Hizbe Umma al-Islam or the Islamic National Party. The founders were arrested almost immediately.

The Saudi women live under the guardianship of their male relatives. Their decisions to get education, to work, to travel or to receive health care must be endorsed by their guardians. The Saudi women are not permitted to drive or ride in a vehicle driven by someone who is not a close male relative or an employee. They may enter the public buses from the designated entrances at the back. King Abdullah evoked a flurry of expectant speculation, when he stated that the Saudi women would "one day be able to drive". That was soon after he inherited the Saudi monarchy. After waiting for several years for that "one day", the women have become restive. Late last year, some drove and pasted the videos of themselves behind the wheels on the YouTube and other social networks. Their cases are pending before the courts and they will not go unpunished. Shaima Jastaina, convicted on the crime of driving and sentenced to lashings has been pardoned by the King. The future women drivers may not necessarily be shown royal generosity.

On 25th September, King Abdullah announced in a five-minute speech televised live that he was granting women the right to vote in future municipal elections, the right to run as candidates, and that they would be appointed to the Shura Council, the 150-member body that advises the King on legislation and policy. [4] This time around, fewer Saudi women are reported to be excited about it. Some are sceptical, and many more cynical.

All Saudis follow Islam. The official theology of the state is Wahhabism that can be traced to the Hanbali School of jurisprudence. The Sunni Islam is understood in four classical schools of jurisprudence: the Hanbali, the Shafii, the Maliki and the Hanafi. The latter three have continued to simmer under the weight of Wahhabism. There have been fatwas issued questioning the Wahhabi theology and challenging the Saudi rule. Separatism or open defiance has not manifested itself widely, so far.

The major sectarian cleavage is between the Wahhabis and the Shias. The Shias are the largest minority in the country, constituting anywhere between four and fifteen percent of the population and numbering anywhere between one and four million. What makes the Shia situation crucial is the fact that the oil wealth is located under their soil and in the water around their land. Left to themselves, theirs could be the richest state in the entire region. Inspired by the Islamic Revolution in Iran and emboldened by the seizure of Makkah at home, the Saudi Shias defiantly observed the Ashura in late1979-early 1980. King Abdullah met the Shia leaders early in his rule, sending a signal of greater inclusiveness to the community in the religious domain of the country. The meeting did not lead to action.

Protests erupted in Eastern Province on the "Day of Rage". It coincided with the popular uprising in neighbouring Bahrain, [5] which has a Shia majority and a Sunni royal family. About four hundred people have been arrested since March, of whom seventy remain in custody, including the author Nazir al-Majid and the human rights activist Fadil al-Munasif. The protests in Bahrain, as also in the Eastern province of Saudi Arabia continued to simmer. In November, four Shia men were shot dead by security forces over four days in the city of Qatif. The interior ministry said they had been armed and operating on "foreign orders"—code for Iran. Earlier in January this year, the authorities named twenty-three suspects in connection with the disturbances in Eastern province, accusing them of possessing illegal weapons and opening fire on the public and police. At least one person was killed and three others injured in clashes between security forces and Shia protesters, the activists said. Issam Mohammed, 22, reportedly died when troops fired live ammunition after demonstrators threw stones at them in al-Awamiya, a town in the Qatif region. Officials said a security vehicle was shot at and attacked with petrol bombs. The violence came as the British Prime Minister David Cameron arrived in Saudi Arabia for his first official visit. [6]

King Abdullah has issued a series of decrees to protect the internal security of the Kingdom. Involving the disbursement of hundreds of billions of dollars, these orders can be grouped into three types:

1. Satisfying the citizenry through salary increases and other incentives. [7]
2. Satisfying the armed forces through creating more than 60,000 new officer level positions, offering promotions for military officers whose promotions had been on hold due to the lack of vacancies and the creation of a new committee to solve the problems of members of the army and police.

3. Most importantly, a series of decrees providing more funding and powers to strengthen the authority of the Wahhabi religious establishment; including an order directed to the media to refrain from criticizing or challenging the religious establishment and to support the Commission for the Enforcement of Religious Law. [8]

In May last year, the Saudis signed a mega deal amounting to US$ 60 billion for purchase of arms from the US. It would include F-15 combat aircraft to ensure Saudi air superiority over Iran for years. A "Facilities Security Force" expected to grow to at least 35,000 members would be trained and equipped by the US personnel to be overseen by the US Central Command. A formerly secret State Department cable released by the Wikileaks described the Force's mission as protecting "Saudi energy production facilities, desalination plants and future civil nuclear reactors". [9] The equipment and the personnel indicate not just the external attack, but also the domestic sabotage as their mission. The Saudi oil assets have repeatedly come under terrorist attacks for the past few years, and the security cordon around them have progressively thickened to foil them.

There has been at least one powerful voice from the younger generation of the Saudi royalty in support of the popular uprising. Prince Waleed bin Talal wrote an op-ed in the New York Times exhorting the Kingdom to open up and to move ahead with times. "But we can succeed only if we open our systems to greater political participation, accountability, increased transparency and the empowerment of women as well as youth. The pressing issues of poverty, illiteracy, education and unemployment have to be fully addressed", according to him. "It would be a folly" to suppose that the winds of change blowing across the region would dissipate. The Arab governments could no longer afford to take their populations for granted, or to assume that they will remain static and subdued. Nor can the soothing instruments of yesteryear, which were meant to appease, serve any longer as substitutes for meaningful reform, he wrote. [10] He followed up the op-ed with an interview with the Reuters on 9th March 2011, in which he made a concrete suggestion: the women could be allowed to drive, which would send over 750,000 foreign drivers home. [11] Implementing his prescriptions would not have diminished the royal authority; only lent it more acceptability. That has not happened so far.

Survival, Sectarianism and Iran

The Saudi responses to the Arab Spring in its neighbourhood can neatly be summarized in three words: survival, sectarianism and Iran. Zainul Abedin ben Ali, Hosni Mubarak and Muammar al-Gaddafi did not survive the onslaught of the Arab Spring. The signs of its nascent arrival in the Kingdom are already evident. Taken to a successful conclusion, the Saudi Spring could spell an end to the monarchy—at least in its present unbridled form. An active foreign policy to claim leadership of the Sunni Arabs, therefore, is an imperative for the royal survival. Iran, a Shia non-Arab power across the Gulf waters, to that extent, is the prime target of Saudi activism.

The Saudi involvement with the Arab Spring has seen a progression with each case. They were reportedly disappointed by the US abandoning the besieged Hosni Mubarak and offered to step in with monetary assistance that the US withdrew from him. King Abdullah came out in support of Mubarak from his sickbed in Morocco. The Saudi response to the Libyan developments was one of reticence, even as they went along with the Qatari lead in inviting foreign intervention.

Yemen is a complicated and multi-layered conflict situation. There is struggle between the families of President Ali Abdullah Saleh and the al-Ahmars. There is an Arab Spring between the ruling elite and the youth. And then, there are two rebellious groups; a separatist one in the south and the Houthi rebels in the north. The Saudis have three major concerns in the situation. One, the Saudi-born-and-bred al-Qaeda have found a safe haven in Yemen. Some of the "most wanted" Saudi suspects are believed to be operating from there. Two, the long and uncontrolled border has been a regular route for illegal immigration, arms smuggling and narcotics trade. Three, the Saudis see twenty-four million Yemenis—hungry, heavily armed, and envious of Saudi wealth—looking across the border. If civil war erupts, the Saudis will not be able to stop the waves of refugees. [12] The Saudis sought to rescue Saleh by granting him a political asylum. His sudden return to Yemen and the consequent chaos has not mitigated the Saudi concerns. Yemen may yet prove to be a complex bee hive full of aggressive hornets. [13]

It was the Spring in Bahrain that jolted the Saudis into action. The Bahraini "Day of Rage" on 25th February was to mark the ninth anniversary of King Hamad's announcement of reforms. As the reforms never saw the light of the day, and as the Spring in the North African states produced dramatic results, the Bahraini youth took to the streets. A small island Kingdom with a Sunni ruler and roughly seventy percent Shia population, Bahrain has always been divided along the sectarian cleavage. The Spring, predictably, turned into the Shia struggle for equality. Political stability and a compliant regime in Bahrain is of utmost importance to the US, as the American base on the island is considered the most important strategic territory outside the US proper. Any disturbance in the country would be unacceptable to the US and its Saudi ally.

As the violence erupted beyond the Bahraini authority's capability to tackle it, the Saudis stepped in. A convoy of 150 armoured troop carriers and about 50 lightly armed vehicles carried about a 1,000 Saudi soldiers across the King Fahd Causeway into Bahrain in mid-March. A Saudi security official told the Associated Press that the troops were deployed to protect critical buildings and installations like the oil facilities. [14] The Shia protesters, however, saw the Saudi troops as a military occupation. It was an uncharacteristically ferocious response, in comparison to the traditional low-key style of Saudi diplomacy, and was a sign that they felt genuinely in danger and would take the initiative to protect themselves. [15] In the middle of the mayhem in Bahrain, the Gulf Cooperation Council appointed Abdul Latif Al-Zayani, an adviser to the Bahraini Ministry of Foreign Affairs, as its Secretary-General.

As the Bahraini and the Yemeni cauldrons continue to simmer, the Saudis have reverted back to their time-tested dollar diplomacy. They have granted the post-revolutionary Egypt US$ 4 billion in aid to appease its generals and as much as US$ 20 billion are lavished on Bahrain and Oman. [16] In addition to throwing money at the problems, it has invited Jordan and Morocco to join the Gulf Cooperation Council. Egypt is a candidate for inclusion at a later date. At the last GCC Summit in Riyadh, the leaders have agreed to King Abdullah's proposal to transform the group into a single entity. [17] The attempt is to expand the GCC and tighten its structure.

Beyond the GCC states, the Saudis have projected Sunni Islam as the force of stability and unity. Sunni states in the region, including Turkey, Egypt, Morocco and Tunisia are vital to the new foreign policy initiative and are being courted through the traditional method of consensus-building. The King sent the foreign minister Saud al-Faisal to Turkey, Egypt and elsewhere to share thoughts and gain perspective. The Turkish President Abdullah Gul visited Saudi Arabia in August 2011. [18] Emissaries were sent to China, Russia, and Japan to sign technical partnership agreements. Capping the diplomatic traffic was the visit of the US National Security Advisor Tom Donilon in April.

The Saudi stand on Syria, unlike on Egypt, Yemen and Bahrain, is to support the uprising. In early August, in the first week of Ramadan, the King recalled the Saudi ambassador from Damascus. In a written statement read out on the al-

Arabiya satellite television, he warned, "Syria should think wisely before it's too late and issue and enact reforms that are not merely promises but actual reforms". [19] Shortly following the King's speech, Morocco issued a statement expressing deep concern, adding that it "traditionally refrained from interfering in the internal affairs of other countries", while Jordan, a neighbouring state to Syria whose relations weren't always ideal, expressed "rejection and regret over the continued killing" in Syria. [20] Saudi Arabia's influence in the region was evident when a few hours after it withdrew its ambassador to Damascus, Kuwait and Bahrain followed suit.

Lest there be a doubt about its motive in castigating President Bashar al-Assad's repressive policy, the Saudi Prince Turki al-Faisal explained it thus, "Saudi Arabia recently played a leading role in isolating Syrian President Bashar al-Assad's brutal government by demanding an end to the killing of protesters and recalling the Saudi ambassador from Damascus. The impending fall of Mr. Assad's barbarous regime provides a rare strategic opportunity to weaken Iran. Without this vital ally, Tehran will find it more difficult to foment discord in the Arab world. Today, there is a chance for the United States and Saudi Arabia to contain Iran and prevent it from destabilizing the region". [21] The quote is an open admission; even an assertion. The Saudi path to Iran runs through Syria.

In general, the Saudi response to the Arab Spring is driven by Iran. Iran's enhanced status in Iraq, Bahrain, Lebanon, and indeed among the Saudi Shias is a challenge. The Iranian nuclear programme is perceived as a threat. The Iranian motives in developing its missile capabilities are seen to be directed against its Arab neighbours (the ones providing basing facilities to the US), Israel and against the US naval assets in the region. The Iranian confrontation with the US has created tremendous uncertainties and instability in the regional politics. The Iranian threats to close the Strait of Hormuz have introduced further strains in an already charged situation. For

Saudi Arabia, Iran is an immediate and existential threat.

The Saudis have chosen to take the challenge from Iran beyond the politico-strategic sphere into a sectarian one. Since the Islamic revolution in Iran, the two have constantly questioned each other's Islamic credentials. Today, Saudi Arabia projects itself as the guardian of the Sunni Arabs. It seeks to channel the energy and fervour of the Sunni Arab Islamist groups and the Arab tribes and focus them on the "threat" of Iran. Specifically, it seeks to diminish Iranian influence and Iranian-supported Shia institutions and leaders in the Arab heartland. [22]

What Next?

The Saudis have sought to manage the youth and the women discontent by appeasement and punishment in equal measure. The two track policy involves a delicate tight-rope walking and may be directed at wrong recipients. The ones to be appeased probably are politically correct anyway, and ones to be punished may not opt for course correction. The strategy of appeasement requires a further tactful balancing between a conservative society and a restive youth. It also accords the King a comfortable position of a reform-minded ruler and a social mediator.

The Shia discontent has been met by harsh punishment, and no appeasement to-date. There are two serious problems with the sectarian politics. One, more the Saudis proclaim their salafi puritanism, more vulnerable they become to an even harsher version of salafism. The jihadi version of salafi movement is as violently anti-Saudi as it is anti-Shia. The Saudi leadership believes that it has the Al-Qaeda in the Arabian Peninsula (AQAP) threat under control, but their current actions could be providing them a safety net and a fertile ground to recruit new members. [23] Two, the Saudis have sought to exclude the Arab Shias from an all-Arab phenomenon. The approach alienates the Arab Shia and opens the door to the Iranian influence.

The House of Saud itself seems to be divided over the concessions to make and compromises to reach. Crown Prince Naif and Prince Turki Al-Faisal are seen to be against any change or compromise. King Abdullah projected a reformist agenda in his initial years, but did not follow it through. Prince Waleed bin-Talal has been outspoken in advocating reforms.

The Saudis have reacted in differing and diametrically opposite fashions to the Spring in different states. Their responses cover a wide spectrum all the way from passive resentment to a military intervention. Money power, tribal affiliations, sectarian cleavages have been deployed to the fullest measure. The GCC proposals to invite the rest of the two Arab monarchies and to transform itself into a single entity are powerful signals that the Saudis will not allow the Spring in the royal courtyards. Iran would be contained and its influence in the Arab world would be rolled back.

Tunisia, Libya and Egypt in North Africa have been the harbingers of the Arab Spring. All three of them have witnessed regime changes and are in the process of taking stock and moving forward at their own individual pace. Whether the Spring will spread eastward in a typical domino fashion to the rest of the Arab world remains to be seen. Whether it eventually brings about a comprehensive reshaping of the region is uncertain at best. What is certain is that the decades-old winter of frozen and fossilized structures and systems in the Arab world is thawing. And Saudi Arabia is no exception.

Endnotes

1. Simon Henderson, "Saudi Arabia's Planned Day of Rage", Washington Institute, Policy Watch number 1774, 9th March, 2011.
2. Ghazanfar Ali Khan, "5,080 People Charged with Terrorism", Arab News, 3rd April, 2011.
3. Al Jazeera, "Draft Saudi Security Law Faces Criticism", 1st December, 2011. http://www.aljazeera.com/news/middleeast/2011/12/20111214525395336l.ht.
4. All members of the Shura Council are appointed by the King.

Their mandate is to advise, neither to vote a legislation nor to veto one.

5. The Bahraini youth, Sunni and Shia both at that stage, had observed their own "day of rage" on 25th February, which marked the ninth anniversary of King Hamad's reforms; the reforms that had not materialized.
6. "Shia Protester Shot Dead in Saudi Arabia", http://www.bbc.co.uk/news/world-middle-east-16543013, accessed on 15th January, 2012.
7. In February, King Abdullah introduced a domestic aid program worth US$ 37 billion. The King rolled out an even more comprehensive $97 billion aid package on March 18. He provided US$ 70 billion alone for five hundred thousand units of low-income housing and sent $200 million as a reward to the religious establishment. Additionally, the King upped unemployment benefits, paid a bonus worth two months' salary to public servants, and increased the education allowance for all students (Robert M. Danin, "Is Saudi Arabia Next?", Council on Foreign Relations, 5th December, 2011).
8. Carol A. O'Leary, Nicholas A. Heras, "Saudi Arabia's Iran Initiative and Arab Tribalism: Emerging Forces Converge in the Arab World", *Terrorism Monitor*, Vol. 9, Issue 38, 21st October, 2011. http://www.jamestown.org/single/?no_cache=1&tx_ttnews%5Btt_news%5D=38555&tx_ttnews%5BbackPid%5D=7&cHash=80812bf625d6ca0316fc61874cab6961
9. Associated Press, "US Quietly Expanding Ties with Saudis", 19th May, 2011.
10. Alwaleed bin Talal bin Abdulaziz Al-Saud, "A Saudi Prince's Plea for Reform", New York Times, 24th February, 2011, http://www.nytimes.com/2011/02/25/opinion/25alsaud.html?_r=1&ref=middleeast.
11. Quoted in Joshua Teitelbaum, "Saudi Arabia Faces a Changing Middle East", *Meria Journal*, Vol. 15, No. 3, September 2011, http://www.gloria-center.org/2011/10/saudi-arabia-faces-a-changing-middle-east.
12. Bernard Haykel, http://www.project-syndicate.org/commentary/haykel4/English 16th August, 2011.
13. Madawi Al-Rashid, "Iran, Turkey and Saudi: The Regional Race

for the Arab Spring", Al-Akhbar English, 28th August, 2011.

14. Ethan Bronner, "Saudi Troops Enter Bahrain to Help Put Down Unrest", New York Times, 14th March, 2011.
15. Rami G. Khouri, "The Saudi Iranian Cold War", Agence Global, 18th October, 2011.
16. Soumaya Ghannoushi, "By Propping up the Arab Monarchy, Saudi Arabia is Reverting to its Old Anti-Revolutionary Role", The Guardian, 8th June, 2011.
17. Ghazanfar Ali Khan, "GCC Leaders Back Call for Union of Gulf states", Arab News, 21st December, 2011.
18. The Saudi-Turkish alliance is indispensible for Turkey as well. Its quest for leadership, especially within the context of the emerging conflict in Syria, would require an Arab partner. Despite a great amount of goodwill that it enjoys in the Arab world, it cannot justify any unilateral actions without Arab support. Saudi Arabia could prove a partner in the eventuality.
19. "Saudi King Recalls Ambassador and Demands End to Bloodshed", http://www.todayszaman.com/news-254174-turkey-and-saudi-arabia-the-buildup-to-syria-by-sultan-sooud-al-qassemi*.html, 8th August, 2011.
20. Sultan Saood Al-Qassemi, "Turkey and Syria: The Buildup to Syria", http://www.todayszaman.com/news-254174-turkey-and-saudi-arabia-the-buildup-to-syria-by-sultan-sooud-al-qassemi*.html, 18th August, 2011.
21. Turki al-Faisal, "Veto a State, Lose an Ally", New York Times, 11th September, 2011, http://www.nytimes.com/2011/09/12/opinion/veto-a-state-lose-an-ally.html.
22. O'Leary and Heras, n. 8.
23. Gregory Gause lll, "Is Saudi Arabia Really Counter-revolutionary?", http://mideast.foreignpolicy.com/posts/2011/08/09/is_saudi_arabia_really_counter_revolutionary, 9th August, 2011.

6

Syrian Uprising: March Towards Further Instability

Prasanta Kumar Pradhan

Introduction

The protests in Syria against the regime of Bashar al-Assad began in March 2011 in the city of Darra and then spread quickly to the other parts of the country. Initially the government used force to suppress the protests and believed that the protests could be suppressed by using the military and other security forces. But soon it came to realise that it can achieve only limited success by the use of force and there is need for a national dialogue with the various sections of the society to understand their demands and fulfil them. But by the time the regime called for a national dialogue, it was clearly too late and people rejected the offer for a dialogue and instead asked the regime to go. Slowly, the protests continued to spread and the Assad regime responded by launching large scale military operations which, among others, included use of tanks and artillery. This further multiplied the popular anger against the regime and the determination of the protesters to call for removal of Assad became stronger and more pronounced.

The crisis in Syria is aggravating with the number of casualties and refugees growing day by day. The regime has remained adamant and has clung to power despite the huge opposition from the people. He has also defied the appeals by several members of the international community to quit and let a democratic system of government begin in the country. The opposition has started its own political and military campaign to remove Assad for power. It is in this intricate situation that Syria is passing through. In the process, the protest for change has now reduced to a conflict between Assad's stubborn determination to continue in power and a fragmented opposition's struggle to overthrow him.

Humanitarian Crisis

The continuing fight between the regime's forces and the rebels has created a humanitarian crisis in Syria. Though no exact statistics available, more than 100,000 people have been killed in the fighting in Syria. They include civilians, opposition forces and the military as well. The UN Office for the Coordination of Humanitarian Affairs (UNOCHA) estimated that 9.3 million people inside Syria are in need of humanitarian assistance which includes 6.5 million internally displaced people of which 46 percent are children. [1] In addition, there are another 2.5 million Syrian refugees living in the neighbouring countries. Destruction of their houses has been one of the reasons for the displacement of the people. Around 1.2 million houses have been damaged with 400,000 totally houses destroyed since the beginning of the conflict in 2011. [2] A report by the UN Secretary General [3] states that with the aggravation of conflict, children have been severely affected in the country.

According to the report, in the initial stages of the conflict, violations were committed primarily by the Government forces. But increasing number of violations were reported as the conflict intensified and the opposition became more organised and armed. While the government forces have been accused of committing grave sexual violence's against children, the opposition forces have been accused of recruitment and use of children in the conflict. According to the report, known perpetrators of grave violations against children include the Syrian Armed Forces; Syrian intelligence forces, Government-associated militias such as the Shabiha; the popular committees (later formalized under the National

Defence Forces); Syrian Kurdish armed groups; FSA-affiliated groups; Jabhat al-Nusra; Ahrar al-Sham; ISIS; and other independent or unidentified armed groups. [4]

Similarly, there has been widespread violence against women committed in the country during the ongoing civil war. Due to the current instability it is difficult to find out the exact number of women who has been suffering from such violence and atrocities. But the UN and different human rights groups have raised concerns over the sufferings of the women in the country. The UN's independent international commission of inquiry found that 'rape, sexual torture and sexual violence were perpetrated by government forces and militia against men, women and children. These acts constitute crimes against humanity, war crimes and violations of international human rights law'. [5]

The Euro-Mediterranean Human Rights Network, in one of its reports, finds that women have been raped, kidnapped, sexually harassed during raids and in detention, used as human shields and used as hostages in Syria. [6] The International Federation for Human Rights (FIDH) in its reports says that women are subjected to rape and other forms of sexual harassment by the government forces as well as the anti-government armed forces. [7]

The reports states that rape and other forms of sexual violence took place during house searches and at checkpoints and while in detention. Fear of rape has been main reason for many women fleeing the country. Women are also abducted and used as an 'instrument of terror'. Clearly, the humanitarian situation is worsening day by day in Syria and as the UNSC resolution on humanitarian situation in Syria says that 'humanitarian situation will continue to deteriorate in the absence of a political solution'. [8]

Use of Chemical Weapons

The reports of the use of chemical weapons by the Assad regime against the opposition raised serious questions regarding the future of the ongoing civil war in Syria. Evidences of use of chemical weapons came out in August 2013 when it was found to have been used in Ghouta. Initially, both the regime and the opposition alleged each other for using such weapons but later it became clear that it was the regime that used chemical weapons against the opposition. The use of chemical weapons elicited strong international reactions against Assad regime with US President Barack Obama stating it as the 'red line' for the US.

Thus, owing to the increasing international pressure, Syria signed the Chemical Weapons Convention in October 2013 and, subsequently, agreed for destruction of all its chemical weapons. The Organisation for the Prohibition of Chemical Weapons (OPCW) is playing a very important role in supervising the process of destroying the weapons. In October 2013, OPCW found 1,000 metric tons of Category-1 chemical weapons stocks which includes most important varieties such as Sarin, 290 tons of Category-2 chemical agents and 1,230 unfilled chemical weapons delivery systems. [9] In the very same month OPCW and the UN established a joint mission to oversee the elimination of all the chemical weapons from Syria. The Joint Mission has been mandated to 'achieve the timely elimination of the Syrian chemical weapons programme in the safest and most secure manner possible' [10] and Sigrid Kaag has been appointed as the Special Coordinator for the OPCW-UN Joint Mission.

The OPCW has laid out a plan to destroy all the Syria's chemical weapons stock by June 2014. In January 2014, the OPCW reported that the first consignment of priority chemicals were removed from Syria. It is also facing difficulty to remove the chemical weapons from the war zones which is causing delays for the OPCW. For its sincere efforts towards eliminating chemical weapons in Syria, the OPCW has received the 2013 Nobel Prize for peace. The OPCW has also received enormous international support in its efforts to remove all the chemical weapons from Syria. In February

2014, Japan donated €13.25 million (US$ 18.37 million) to a special OPCW Trust Fund, and in January 2014 Canada announced to contribute of CAD10 million (around US$ 9 million) to the Trust Fund for the operations to destroy the Syrian chemical weapons. [11]

Assad and Military

Assad's stronghold over his military is one of the most important reasons for his survival against the opposition. Military has been a very powerful institution in Syria and the regime has used the military for regime stability and survival. The trends in the Arab Spring has shown that leaders who have lost controls over the military, where the top commanders have defected to the opposition, have lost power. Muammar al-Gaddafi in Libya, Hosni Mubarak in Egypt, Ali Abdullah Saleh in Yemen are the most recent examples who have fallen after a number of their senior commanders have defected. But in Syria, though some senior military leaders have defected to join the opposition, the impact of that has not been too dear for Assad.

The secret of a highly loyal military in Syria lies in the fact that a large number of the higher ranks of the military are held by the Alawites and the Baathists. The Republican Guard is mostly manned by the Alawis. The irregular armed groups known as the *Shabiha* are also fighting alongside the military further strengthening the regime's position. Most of the *Shabiha* members belong to the Alawite sect thus further adding to the military advantage of Assad. [12] The opposition alleges that the *Shabiha* is 'manipulated by the secret intelligence apparatus' and it does the dirty job 'with no written orders so the state can deny responsibility'. [13] There are also a number of elite security services who are extremely loyal to the regime and constitute both offensive and defensive forces. Importantly, there are political and ideological factors that keep these forces bind with the regime. They would fight with the regime till the end also feel that their fate is closely linked to the survival of the regime. [14]

Military and paramilitary forces play a very defining role in the present situation in Syria. It has turned out to be a military conflict between the regime's forces and the anti-government forces. While the government forces are trying to retain its stronghold all over the country, the anti-government forces are trying to gain new territories every day.

Hezbollah Joins the War

Participation of Hezbollah in the civil war has further strengthened the regime's position. Though, initially, Hezbollah leaders refuted the claims of the Syrian opposition about the involvement of Hezbollah in the conflict, it has slowly become clear since late 2012 and early 2013 that Hezbollah fighters are actively involved in the fight. They have now become a vital force for the Assad regime. In April 2013, Hezbollah chief Hassan Nasrallah confirmed that his forces are fighting in Syria, [15] and later in November 2013 stated that his forces will fight alongside Assad's forces as long as necessary. [16] He has recently stated that Hezbollah fighters will withdraw if the Arab countries stop interfering in the affairs in Syria.

There are a large number of opposition groups and parties in Syria active against the Assad regime. Several armed opposition groups are involved in fighting against the regime's forces. Both political and military opposition to the regime has been fragmented and has lacked cohesion and unity among themselves. Though there a large number of political parties of different sizes operating from various parts of the country, none of these political entities has become successful to claim leadership all over the country and represent such diverse sections of the society.

Syrian National Council (SNC)

The SNC is one of the first major political bodies to be formed against Assad regime in the aftermath of the beginning of the protests. The SNC is a coalition of groups and individuals, including signatories of the Damascus Declaration (2005), the Syrian Muslim Brotherhood, various Kurdish factions, representatives of the Local Coordination Committees, other political parties or platforms including Damascus Spring and the National Bloc, representatives of the Alawi and Assyrian communities, and some independent figures. [17] Immediately after its formation it emerged as the only political opposition to the Assad regime and thus many countries around the world started to recognise the SNC as the legitimate representative of the Syrian people.

The SNC sought to secure political support for the Syrian revolution, to promote national unity, to ensure that there is no political vacuum, to develop a roadmap for democratic change in Syria and to deliver the voice of the Syrian revolution and its demands to the international community. [18] Though it has clear objectives, the organisation soon came to face the hurdles for lack of unity among the groups and individuals within the organisation. The trouble with the internal cohesion of the party looked imminent as there were several groups and they represent diverse interests and the leadership do not have any past experience of working together for their national interest. A common agenda of overthrowing the Assad regime united them together but working to achieve long term goal of establishing a democratic country needs unity, commitment and dedication that was found lacking in the organisation.

For this reason, there has been frequent changes in the leadership in the SNC which is not a healthy sign for the organisation. Burhan Ghalioun was named as the first chairman of the council. But he was replaced by Abdelbaset Seyda in June 2012. But Seyda also could not stay for long as the leader of the party and resigned in November 2012. Since then George Sabra has taken over as the chairman of the SNC. The SNC has been recognised some countries around the world as the legitimate representative or dialogue partner, prominent among them are the USA, UK, EU, regional countries such as Turkey, Egypt and Arab League.

The Muslim Brotherhood has been playing a major role in the SNC. Muslim Brotherhood's superior organisational strength is one of its strengths in playing an active part in the SNC. Also, the Muslim Brotherhood took the advantage of absence of any other prominent Islamist political organisation working in the country and thus it became popular among the masses as the protests became stronger. Their external linkages with the countries like Qatar and Turkey also make them a powerful entity in the country as they receive both ideological and financial support from them. Though it has often been accused of radicalising the protests, it has, nevertheless, been an important part of the movement against the regime.

Syrian National Coalition

But because of the lack of unity and cohesion it seemed that the SNC is not living up to the expectation of the Syrian people and of the international community. In October 2012, the then US Secretary of State Hillary Clinton stated that "the SNC can no longer be viewed as the visible leader of the opposition", adding that, "It can participate but that opposition must include people from inside Syria and others who have a legitimate voice that needs to be heard". [19] There was apprehension in the US that the SNC is dominated by the Muslim Brotherhood and that the council failed to attract the minorities such as the Kurds, Alawites, Christians, Druze, and so on. [20]

Thus, in November 2012 the National Coalition for Syrian Revolutionary and Opposition Forces was formed in Doha which included the SNC and several other political factions and groups. The Coalition became a larger umbrella body and looks more inclusive in its formation with the SNC being the largest component. At present, there are 114 members with Ahmed Jarba heading the coalition. The stated goal of the coalition is to establish a 'democratic, pluralistic Syria based on the rule of law and civil State, where all the Syrians will be equal regardless of their ethnic, religious and sectarian background'. [21] It also declares to uphold the sovereignty, unity and territorial integrity of the country.

The national coalition, since its formation, has received widespread international recognition. The coalition has been recognised by the US, EU, Arab League, GCC, Turkey along with some other countries as the legitimate representative of the Syrian people. The Arab League has granted the Syrian National Coalition the Syria's seat in the organisation and has been designated as the main interlocutor with the Arab League. International recognition certainly gives more legitimacy to the coalition to function but it should be able to function unitedly as there is always a risk of internal differences keeping in view the various segments of the society are involved in the coalition. There are some media reports of internal differences in the coalition with different factions being backed by different external players.

The national coalition has established an interim government in November 2013 with Ahmad Tomah as the prime minister and nine other cabinet ministers. In a statement, Tomah has said that, "the interim government is the authority that oversees the implementation of the Syrian Coalition's policies". [22] As it is only a few months in to the formation of the interim government it remains to be seen how well it is accepted by the people of Syria and the international community.

Free Syrian Army (FSA)

The FSA is the military structure under the control of the Syrian national coalition. The FSA was formed in 2011 by the defected officers from the army after the protests against Assad began. These are the officers and soldiers who refused to shoot at the protesters and chose to fight with the people against the regime. Earlier, the FSA was associated with the SNC but with the SNC weakening because of the internal rift and the national coalition formed taking in to its fold more number of groups, parties and individuals; the FSA came under the national coalition.

In December 2012, in a meeting of the military commanders in Turkey, the FSA founded the Supreme Military Council (SMC) [23]—a 30-member body to coordinate operations and strategic planning. The SMC coordinates the military operations undertaken by the FSA. It is also trying to bring all other rebel armed groups under the umbrella of a unified military command so that a robust military front can be formed against the regime. The SMC is also creating a platform for the development of a countrywide military strategy [24] to fight against the regime's forces. At present, the FSA looks to be the only armed for which is united with a command and control structure. It has been financially supported and provided with arms and weapons by countries like the US, Saudi Arabia and Qatar.

Different sources of funding is one of the challenges the FSA is facing today. Though all the rebel armed groups have come under a unified FSA, their funding and weapons come from different sources. The FSA or the SMC has little control over the funding of their affiliates. These small groups get funding or weapons by dint of their personal connections or social networks. [25]

It has also been reported that Saudi Arabia and Qatar are funding different groups of rebels in the FSA and are trying to exert more power and influence and impose their ideology on the groups they are funding. All the funds received by the FSA and its affiliates must be united for a better coordination and to avoid any rift in the organisation. There are also reports of rivalries within the ranks of the FSA which has been a cause of embarrassment for the rebels. In February 2014, the chief of the FSA Salim Idriss was removed for being 'ineffective' and lacking in experience to lead military operations on the ground. [26] He has been replaced by Abdul-Ilah al-Bashir who earlier header the rebels' operations in the Golan Heights is also considered to be a moderate.

Islamist Resistance

Islamists are playing a very crucial role in the opposition to the Assad regime. They have emerged strongly taking the opportunity of the chaos and confusion in the aftermath of the beginning of the protests. There are a number of such organisations who give strong ideological and military resistance to the regime. They are inspired and driven by their own ideology and objective. They do not seem to be united against the Assad regime because of their differences and prefer to fight independently though they are fighting against the common enemy that is Bashar al-Assad. Rather they are found to be involved in intermittent clashes among themselves. The Jabhat al-Nusra Front is the Al-Qaeda affiliated front [27] which wants the removal of Assad and the establishment of an Islamic state.

There have been heavy clashes between the Al-Nusra and the Islamic State in Iraq and Levant (ISIL) which is another radical armed group active in Syria. Recently, Al-Nusra has given an ultimatum to the ISIL to accept mediation to end their infighting or else it will launch an assault and remove the ISIL from Syria. ISIL is an Al-Qaeda splinter group based in Iraq but it has started its activities in Syria. Al-Qaeda, recently, cut off all ties with the ISIL [28] which, certainly, would be a boost for the Al-Nusra Front. Involvement of the rebels in fighting among themselves has, to some extent, undermined the fight against the Assad regime.

The Salafists have also strengthened their outfits to fight against the Assad regime. There are a number of Salafist groups who are active in the country. [29] In order to give a united combat to the regime the several Salafi rebel armed groups came together in November 2013 to form the Islamic Front. [30] The Salafi rebel group is reportedly supported and funded by Saudi Arabia and some other Gulf countries. This group has also rivalry with the FSA and in one of the incidents the Islamic Front raided ten warehouses of the FSA and seized a large number of weapons. [31] The ideology of the Islamic

Front runs contrary to the FSA. While the FSA believes in a democratic and pluralistic Syria, the Islamic Front wants to establish an Islamic state. There have been efforts by Turkey to mediate between the two groups but there have not been any positive results so far.

The Sectarian Dynamics

Sectarian dimensions play an important role in the Syrian conflict. The nature of Syria's demography and population has been a propellant of the conflict as it has taken serious sectarian colour. About 74 percent of the Syrian population is Sunni Arabs, while 16 percent are other Muslims which includes the dominant Alawites, and about 10 percent of the population is Christians. The Assad family belongs to the Alawite Shias and are ruling over the country since decades. The Sunnis allege that the Alawites man the top political, bureaucratic and military leadership in the country and the Sunnis are neglected and side-lined. Thus there exists a deep seated feeling of anguish among the Sunnis of the country.

Though the conflict started as an opposition to the Assad regime, subsequent internal and regional political and diplomatic developments have turned the conflict into predominantly sectarian in nature. The Assad regime is supported and backed by Iran—a Shia dominated country. Iran and Syria enjoy a warm and cordial relationship and both are important for one another. The Lebanese Hezbollah has also joined the war in favour of Assad against the opposition. As it is well known, Hezbollah is a predominantly Shia organisation and has close links with the Assad regime and Iran. Hezbollah gets direct help from Iran and the Assad regime, most of the time facilitates the supply of weapons from Iran to reach Hezbollah. Thus, the joining of the Hezbollah in the conflict to fight alongside the government's forces substantiates the existence of sectarian nature of the conflict in Syria.

On the other hand, the opposition forces are supported by the prominent Sunni countries such as Saudi Arabia, Qatar and others who have thrown their political and diplomatic behind the opposition apart from providing them with funds. Also, Saudi Arabia and Qatar have openly advocated arming the opposition to protect themselves and fight against the regime's forces as they see no hope of a political or diplomatic solution to the problem. The involvement of the Al-Qaeda and Muslim Brotherhood—who are Sunni dominated organisations- in the conflict against the regime leaves no ambiguity about the sectarian dimension of the conflict. Thus, at all levels—political, ideological and military—the sectarian dimension plays an important role. Though the sectarian dimension of the conflict is not the sole determinant of the developments in the country, it is certainly playing a crucial role in the developments taking place in Syria.

Syria and the Evolving Regional Politics

The developments in Syria have impacted the regional balance of power in the region. As violence and instability has prevailed for a long time and the internal situation has unstable, the regional players come in to have their influence in the country. An exciting blend of power politics, ideology and sectarianism is at play in Syria. All the major internal players in Syria are supported by some or other external players. For instance, the regime has been supported by Iran, Russia and Hezbollah from whom the regime gets arms, funding and the military support on the ground. Similarly, the various rebel groups have also different mentors outside the country. Muslim Brotherhood is alleged to have strong links with Qatar and Turkey. Similarly, Saudi Arabia has been accused of funding and supporting the Salafi groups in Syria. The national coalition has got wider international recognition and it has been getting support from a large number of countries including the US, Turkey, Saudi Arabia, Qatar among others.

Syria has also further aggravated the relationship between Saudi Arabia and Iran—two major players in the region—with many observers stating that there is a 'proxy war' going on between the two countries. In the past these two countries have been found supporting opposite factions in countries like Iraq and Yemen. Taking opportunity of the existing situation in Syria, both the countries have been trying increasing their own spheres of influence in the country and using the Syrian conflict to maximise their political gains. While Iran supports the Assad regime and Hezbollah, Saudi Arabia supports the Salafists who are fighting to remove Assad. For Tehran, Syria is a major geo-strategic ally in dealing with the United States, Saudi Arabia, Israel and Sunni dominated groups. For Iran, the Lebanese Hezbollah is the most precious asset. [32]

On the contrary, for Riyadh, the Assad regime is a hindrance in its interests in Syria and the region as well. There has been no indication from both these countries to mutually discuss the Syrian issue and make attempts to normalise the situation. Rather the involvement of these powers only led to strengthening of the different groups and thus leading to further worsening of the conflict.

Syria is also one of the important reasons for the recent conflict within the Gulf Cooperation Council (GCC). Saudi Arabia, UAE and Bahrain recalled their envoys from Qatar alleging the latter's failure to implement an agreement among GCC countries not to interfere in each other's internal affairs. [33] They alleged that Qatar did not respect the agreement it signed which reads, "Anyone threatening the security and stability of the GCC whether as groups or individuals - via direct security work or through political influence, and not to support hostile media". [34]

Though members of the GCC, there are ideological differences between Saudi Arabia and Qatar. As mentioned earlier, Saudi Arabia supports the Salafists but the Qatar backs the Muslim Brotherhood. There has been an internal tussle between these two countries to increase their power and influence in Syria as both Salafists and the Muslim Brotherhood are actively engaged in opposition to the regime.

As the Muslim Brotherhood has played a very important role in the formation of the SNC and has been a dominant force in the national coalition, it has emerged as a major political force in opposition to the Assad regime.

For, Saudi Arabia, growing profile of the Muslim Brotherhood in Syria would mean increasing influence of Qatar in Syria and a marginal role for Saudi Arabia in any future political dispensation in the country. Keeping this in mind, Saudi Arabia has strengthened the Salafi rebels by uniting them to form the Islamic Front and, now, it has banned the Muslim Brotherhood as well. Such decisions points to the existence of differences between the two over crucial issues which has been brought to the fore because of the developments in Syria.

Conclusion

It is clear from the above discussions that Syria is going through a very difficult phase of its history. The politics and the society has become highly disintegrated and violence and brutality has become an integral part of the approach of both the regime as well as the opposition. The international community has expressed its concerns over the death and destruction happening in Syria. The UN and countries around the world have come forward to support the people of the country but it is up to the Syrians themselves to chart out a future path for themselves. As it has been reiterated by the UN and many other countries, the future should be led by the Syrians and the international community can only help them achieve their goals.

Both the regime and the opposition are adamant in their respective positions. The regime has not hesitated to use force against its people and it has even gone to the extent of using chemical weapons on them. The reaction from the armed rebels has also been equally, though not more, brutal. The present irony is that a political and diplomatic solution looks too remote and the armed violence cannot bring any long term solution to the Syrian conflict. Moreover, the fragmented opposition lacks unity and cohesion among themselves to put up a united challenge to the Assad regime. None of the parties involved look militarily too powerful to completely defeat and destroy the other nor are they in a mood to talk and negotiate. International efforts have also not given any tangible results. The situation at present looks very discouraging for peace and stability in the country and the conflict seems to continue and aggravate in the near future.

Endnotes

1. The UN Office for the Coordination of Humanitarian Affairs (UNOCHA), available at, http://syria.unocha.org/, accessed on March 7, 2014.
2. OCHA Humanitarian Bulletin, "Syrian Arab Republic", Issue 43, February 13-26, 2014, available at, http://syria.unocha.org/sites/default/files/Syria_Humanitarian_Bulletin_43_140226_EN.pdf, accessed on March 7, 2014.
3. United Nations Security Council, "Report of the Secretary-General on children and armed conflict in the Syrian Arab Republic", January 27, 2014, available at, http://daccess-dds-ny.un.org/doc/UNDOC/GEN/N13/627/07/PDF/N1362707.pdf?OpenElement, accessed on March 4, 2014.
4. Ibid.
5. United Nations General Assembly, Human Rights Council, 7th "Report of the independent international commission of inquiry on the Syrian Arab Republic", February 12, 2014, available at, http://www.ohchr.org/EN/HRBodies/HRC/IICISyria/Pages/IndependentInternationalCommission.aspx, accessed on March 8, 2014.
6. Euro-Mediterranean Human Rights Network, "Violence against Women, Bleeding Wound in the Syrian Conflict", November 2013, available at, http://www.euromedrights.org/eng/wp-content/uploads/2013/11/Doc-report-VAW-Syria.pdf, accessed on February 21, 2014.
7. International Federation for Human Rights (FIDH), "Violence Against Women in Syria: Breaking the Silence", available at, http://fidh.org/IMG/pdf/syria_sexual_violence-web.pdf,

accessed on March 1, 2014.

8. See the UNSC Resolution 2139 (2014) available at, http://www.securitycouncilreport.org/atf/cf/%7B65BFCF9B-6D27-4E9C-8CD3-CF6E4FF96FF9%7D/s_res_2139.pdf.
9. "Syria: Inspectors find 1,300 tons of chemical weapons", *The Telegraph*, October 29, 2013, available at, http://www.telegraph.co.uk/news/worldnews/middleeast/syria/10411375/Syria-inspectors-find-1300-tons-of-chemical-weapons.html, accessed on February 1, 2014.
10. See, "Joint Statement from the Organisation for the Prohibition of Chemical Weapons (OPCW) and the United Nations (UN)", October 16, 2013, available at, http://www.opcw.org/news/article/joint-statement-from-the-organisation-for-the-prohibition-of-chemical-weapons-opcw-and-the-united/, accessed on January 23, 2014.
11. Organisation for the Prohibition of Chemical Weapons (OPCW), available at, http://www.opcw.org/news/article/joint-statement-from-the-organisation-for-the-prohibition-of-chemical-weapons-opcw-and-the-united/, accessed on March 2, 2014.
12. "Syria unrest: Who are the Shabiha?", *BBC News*, May 29, 2012, available at, http://www.bbc.com/news/world-middle-east-14482968, accessed on February 15, 2014.
13. "Syria's paramilitary gangs a law unto themselves", *Reuters*, July 2, 2012, available at, http://www.reuters.com/article/2012/07/02/us-syria-crisis-shabbiha-idUSBRE8610N620120702, accessed on January 29, 2014.
14. Bassam Haddad, "Syria's Stalemate: The Limits of Regime Resilience", *Middle East Policy*, Vol. XIX, No. 1, Spring 2012, p. 88.
15. "Hezbollah is helping Assad fight Syria uprising, says Hassan Nasrallah", *The Guardian*, April 30, 2014, available at, http://www.theguardian.com/world/2013/apr/30/hezbollah-syria-uprising-nasrallah, accessed on January 20, 2014.
16. "Nasrallah: Hezbollah in Syria for long haul", *Al Jazeera*, November 15, 2013, available at, http://www.aljazeera.com/news/middleeast/2013/11/nasrallah-hezbollah-syria-long-haul-20131114146174301 32.html,

accessed on February 2, 2014.

17. "The Syrian National Council", Carnegie Middle East Centre, September 25, 2013, available at, http://carnegie-mec.org/publications/?fa=48334, accessed on January 10, 2014.
18. See, http://www.syriancouncil.org/en/objectives.html, accessed on March 2, 2014.
19. "As Fighting Rages, Clinton Seeks New Syrian Opposition", *The New York Times*, October 31, 2012, available at http://www.nytimes.com/2012/11/01/world/middleeast/syrian-air-raids-increase-as-battle-for-strategic-areas-intensifies-rebels-say.html?_r=0, accessed on February 22, 2014.
20. Ibid.
21. "Declaration by the national coalition for Syrian revolutionary and opposition forces", available at, http://www.etilaf.org/en/coalition-documents/declaration-by-the-national-coalition-for-syrian-revolutionary-and-opposition-forces.html, accessed on March 10, 2014.
22. "Tomah: Interim Government Will Not Hamper Geneva II", November 16, 2013, available at, http://www.etilaf.org/en/news/tomah-interim-government-will-not-hamper-geneva-ii.html, accessed on March 11, 2014.
23. "Rebel Groups in Syria Make Framework for Military", *New York Times*, December 7, 2012, available at, http://www.nytimes.com/2012/12/08/world/middleeast/rebel-groups-in-syria-make-framework-for-military.html?_r=0, accessed on February 2, 2014.
24. Elizabeth O'Bagy, "The Free Syrian Army", Middle East Security Report 9, Institute for the Study of War, March 2013, available at, http://www.understandingwar.org/sites/default/files/The-Free-Syrian-Army-24MAR.pdf, accessed on January 12, 2014.
25. "Who is the Free Syrian Army?", *France 24*, August 10, 2012, available at, http://observers.france24.com/content/20120810-syria-free-syrian-army-structure-funding-ideology-methods-fight-against-assad-regime, accessed on December 22, 2013.
26. "Free Syrian Army fires military chief", *Al Jazeera*, February 18, 2014, available at,

http://www.aljazeera.com/news/middleeast/2014/02/free-syrian-army-fires-military-chief-201421742719901171.html, accessed on March 10, 2014.

27. For a detailed discussion see Seth G. Jones, "Syria's Growing Jihad", *Survival: Global Politics and Strategy*, Vol. 55, No. 4, 2013, pp. 53-72.
28. "Al-Qaeda Breaks Link with Syrian Militant Group ISIL", *Reuters*, February 3, 2014, available at, http://www.reuters.com/article/2014/02/03/us-syria-crisis-qaeda-idUSBREA120NS20140203, accessed on March 2, 2014.
29. For an analysis of the Salafists in Syria see Aron Lund, "Syria's Salafi Insurgents: The Rise of the Syrian Islamic Front", UI Occasional Papers-17, The Swedish Institute of International Affairs, March 2013, available at, http://www.ui.se/eng/upl/files/86861.pdf, accessed on February 10, 2014.
30. The Islamic Front includes seven groups namely, Liwa Al-Tawhid, Ahrar Al-Sham, Soqour Al-Sham, the Al-Haq Brigades, Ansar Al-Sham, the Army of Islam, and the Kurdish Islamic Front.
31. "Syria: FSA, Islamic Front Face-off", *Asharq Al Awsat*, December 11, 2013, available at, http://www.aawsat.net/2013/12/article55324955, accessed on March 2, 2014.
32. Mohsen Milani, "Why Tehran Won't Abandon Assad(ism)", *The Washington Quarterly*, Vol. 36, No. 4, 2013, p. 88.
33. "KSA, Bahrain, UAE recall ambassadors from Qatar", *Arab News*, March 5, 2014, available at, http://www.arabnews.com/news/535101, accessed on March 7, 2014.
34. Ibid.

7

Bahrain Crisis and Iran-Saudi Arabia Contestation

M. Mahtab Alam Rizvi

Introduction

The "Arab Spring" that began early in the West Asia and North Africa (WANA) region in 2011 has shaken the entire region. Rulers who had ruled for decades have been ousted such as Tunisia, Egypt and Libya; and the few countries that are defying changes are still undergoing severe unrest. Scores of demonstrators have taken place on the streets in Syria, Jordan, Yemen, Algeria, Bahrain, Saudi Arabia and Oman against their ruling governments and insisting for more economic and political reforms. The major demands made by the protesters are: political and constitutional reforms, employment, economic and social equality, improving human rights conditions, political participation of the people.

Within the Gulf region it was Bahrain that was most affected. There were/are two main reasons for this: first, Bahrain's sectarian division; and second, the involvement of two major regional players—Iran and Saudi Arabia—in a form of proxy conflict on Bahraini soil. Although the majority of the protesters belong to the Shia community, this was not initially a sectarian demonstration. Rather, it was motivated by calls for political and democratic reform and the decentralisation of power from the Al Khalifa family to the elected parliament. [1] Initially demonstrations were peaceful and eluded directly condemning King Hamad. However, after a long period of clashes with security forces, and several deaths, the demonstrators were succeeded to capture Pearl Square in

Manama. Though on March 14, one month after the protests started, Bahrain requested GCC countries for their support that led to the arrival of Saudi and Gulf Cooperation Council (GCC) forces under the aegis of the Peninsula Shield Force.

Given the awkward nature of identity incongruence within Bahrain, it is argued that the kingdom witnesses grave internal-security challenges. Internal clashes in Bahrain also reached and influenced to the other regional countries especially in Saudi Arabia and Iran, for Riyadh the stability of the country is strategically significant. Bahrain is a sectarian fault line between Sunnis and Shiites, placed within a few kilometres of both Iran and Saudi Arabia. [2] It is a station where a confrontation between the two regional rivals Iran and Saudi Arabia could happen, with overwhelming international consequences. Both Iran and Saudi Arabia realize the significance of Bahrain, contribution in the strategic calculations and performance of each country. Clash between Iran and Saudi Arabia for Bahrain has a long history. [3]

In the light of this development this paper analyzes the factors behind the event of 2011 in Bahrain that culminated in Saudi-led GCC forces to extend help and support to the Al Khalifa ruling family. This paper also argues that Bahrain has offered a proxy arena of rivalry between Tehran and Riyadh that possesses key strategic importance for both countries.

Brief Background

Bahrain has been ruled since 1783 by the Khalifa family, members of the Bani Utbah tribe, who banished the Persian Empire. The king is the sovereign authority and members of the ruling family enjoyed the key positions including the political and military positions. In 2001 Bahrainis strongly backed proposals placed by the Emir—now the king—to turn the country into a constitutional monarchy with an elected parliament and an independent judiciary. The first parliamentary election held in 2002 and elected 40 members which included a dozen of Shia MPs. [4] There are long-running conflicts between Bahrain's

Sunnis and the Shiite Muslim majority. On occasion, these have spilled over into domestic turbulence and spread in the Gulf region.

The majority of the population of Bahrain belongs to the Shiite community. But the Sunni minority, which includes the Al Khalifa's family, runs the government and relishes higher living standards. One of the major demands from the demonstrators in Bahrain is to stop widespread discrimination against Shiites. The other demands of the protesters are: rewrite the constitution and to establish a body with a "full popular mandate to investigate and hold to account economic, political and social violations. Bahrain's population increased to 1.2 million in 2010, of which 568,399 were Bahraini citizen and 666,172 were non-nationals. [5] While a majority of the population is ethnically Arab, a considerable number of people from South Asia also live in Bahrain including around 290,000 Indian nationals in 2008. [6] There are no official data of Shia and Sunni Muslims of Bahrain, though around 65-70 percent of Bahraini Muslims are Shias. [7] Despite majority of population belong to Shia community, nearly half of the government was comprised of Al Khalifa family in 2010.

Bahrain's parliament also known as National Assembly is consist of two houses: first one is the Shura Council (*Majlis Al-Shura*) with 40 seats and second one is the Council of Representatives (*Majlis Al-Nuwab*) with 40 seats. The 40 members of the Shura Council are directly appointed by the king. However, the members of the Council of Representatives are elected by popular vote for a period of 4-year term. [8] Before Arab uprising half of the elected members were came from shia community represented by Al-Wefaq opposition group. However, 18 members of Al-Wefaq have resigned from the post due their disagreement with government on power sharing. The opposition Al-Wefaq bloc strongly condemned the government and added that the power sharing envisioned in Bahrain's constitution of 2002 had not yet been appropriately implemented. The country's cabinet is presently appointed by Bahrain's king.

The roots of the Arab uprising in Bahrain can be traced back to the appointment of Hamad Al Khalifa as Emir, when his father died in 1999. Upon his accession, King Hamad proposed a programme of reforms in a bid to move Bahrain away from its authoritarian tradition. [9] The other main features of reforms were: announced elections for Parliament, gave women the right to vote and introduced the National Action Charter. However, due to the lack of implementation of many of these reforms augmented to the mounting unhappiness among the Bahrainis especially among the Bahrainis Shia.

The protests began on February 14, 2011, when protesters, imitating events in Egypt's Tahrir Square, took over the Pearl Square roundabout in Manama. Despite killing of scores of people demonstrations still continue. Recently in October 2013 Bahrain's security forces again clashed with anti-regime protesters in Manama's western suburb of Sanabis. A petrol bomb hurled at a Bahrain police patrol on November 13, 2013, left one policeman wounded. Attacks on security forces have become frequent in Bahrain, while protesters frequently clash with security forces in Shiite villages. Though the majority of the protesters were Shia, this was not initially a sectarian demonstration. Rather, it was motivated by demands for political and democratic reform and the change of centre of power from the king's palace to the elected parliament. The other demands of the protesters were/are: rewrite the constitution and to establish a body with a "full popular mandate to investigate and hold to account economic, political and social violations. However, one of the key demands from the protesters is an end to widespread discrimination against Shiites.

King Hamad bin Isa Al Khalifa of Bahrain tried to compromise with the protesters, and made a number of important concessions. [10] The government of Bahrain also started to announce financial incentives including cash distribution, and assured political reforms. The ruling government promised cash payments of about 1,000 dinars to each family on the occasion of the 10th anniversary of the National Action Charter and as a mark of gratitude by King Hamad bin Isa Al Khalifa. [11] The King also offered to increase social spending and to release minors jailed after the August 2010 protests.

On February 15, 2011, on television King Hamad called condolences for the deaths of protesters, said that a parliamentary committee to investigate the deaths would be created, and affirmed that peaceful protests are legal. [12] He called for "dialogue" with protesters, promising dialogs would focus major demands such as strengthening the power of parliament and that any deal could be put to a referendum. He said dialogs would also include electoral and governmental reforms, as well as examining into appeals of corruption and sectarianism. [13] King also formed the Bahrain national dialogue forum on July 1, 2011, for the discussion and promotion of reform. He also established the Bahrain Independent Commission of Inquiry (BICI), chaired by noted human rights lawyer M. Cherif Bassiouni, on June 29, 2011 to investigate the events of February and March 2011 and their consequences.

Saudi Arabia and Iranian Involvement

The political turmoil within Bahrain has presented Iran and Saudi Arabia with the scope to involve in a proxy conflict. Indeed, the involvement of Saudi-led GCC troops in Bahrain enhanced an additional level of rivalry for regional supremacy. [14] In light of the beliefs of Shiism and *veleyat-e-faqih* (guardian of Islamic jurists)—the readiness of encouragement for the subjugated of the Muslim world—it has been accused that Iran was increasingly involved in the demonstrations in Bahrain. This conviction, coupled with the red line for Saudi Arabia of protecting the government rule by Al Khalifa's family, offers justification for the Saudi involvement in

Bahrain. When contemplating the basis for the involvement of Saudi Arabia and Iran within Bahrain, one must consider the internal dynamics of both the countries and how the motion of internal security dilemmas has nurtured increased tensions between Riyadh and Tehran. [15] The case of Bahrain hence also necessitates examination of the importance of internal factors within Iran and Saudi Arabia that have shown state behaviour towards Bahrain.

Saudi Arabia Intervention

The arrival of Saudi-led GCC troops in Bahrain revealed the apparent severity of the security situation within Bahrain. The presence of these troops was to safeguard the survival of the royal regime, regarded as a red line by Saudi Arabia. By March 16, 2011, the Bahraini security forces, supported by GCC countries, had succeeded in crushing the protesters. [16] Saudi Arabia deployed about 1,000 troops with armoured support, and the United Arab Emirates (UAE) deployed about 500 police officers. The GCC countries in general and Saudi Arabia in particular has taken initiative to extend full-fledged support to Bahrain. The GCC has not only supported and sent troops to Bahrain but has also created a fund of US$ 20 billion for Manama and Oman. [17] Rulers of the Gulf countries also planned to form a GCC Developmental Programme (GCCDP) to finance development projects in member countries and establish an ad hoc committee comprised of representatives of member countries to build the essential mechanism to launch and implement this programme. [18]

The mission of the GCC troops was "to support the government against its domestic opponents and prevent Iran from becoming embroiled in the clash". [19] In seeking to end the protests at least for time being, security forces also targeted opposition headquarters, demolished unlicensed Shia religious structures and, according to Shia clerics, allegedly demolished at least 38 mosques. [20]

Saudi Arabia enjoys strong ties with Bahrain, stemming in

part from the Al Khalifa's tribal roots in Saudi Arabia, and also from economic links, helped by the sale of oil. Additionally, Bahrain also plays a significant role for Saudi Arabia, acting as a valve for social pressures stemming from the implementation of its religious doctrine. The importance of Bahrain for Saudi Arabia is also due to some other reasons. First, there are geopolitical anxieties about increasing Iranian influence within the Gulf and across west Asia. Certainly, Saudi Arabia is willing to block growing Iranian involvement within Bahrain, granted such close proximity to the kingdom, and they realise the stability of the Al Khalifa's regime as essential for attaining this goal. [21] In adding to financial and ideological support, links between Saudi Arabia and Bahrain have been gelled by the marriage of a daughter of King Abdullah of Saudi Arabia to a son of King Hamad of Bahrain.

Secondly, Bahrain's significance stems from worries within Saudi Arabia about common ethnic bonds between the Shia of Bahrain and the Shia of the Eastern Province of Saudi Arabia. Hence, for Saudi Arabia, increasing Shia power in Bahrain may lead to an encouraged Shia community in the Eastern Province. Saudi Arabia's worry over growing Iranian involvement in Bahrain is not merely a new development. Undoubtedly, this can be found during the time of the Shah of Iran and the expansion of the King Fahd Causeway. This project was originally designed in the 1960s, during which time the shah asserted Iranian prerogatives to Bahrain. Yet suspicion of Iranian interference across the region, particularly within Bahrain, increased with the revolution of 1979 and Ayatollah Khomeini's desire to export the revolution in other regional countries. The Islamic revolution led by Khomeini had an additional emphasis on "the export of the revolution". For him, the establishment of an Islamic government in Iran was not enough and he talked about the export of the revolution to other countries in the region.

In this milieu, the crisis in Bahrain brought some key challenges for the regional countries including Saudi Arabia.

First, the turmoil had the power to arouse the gripes of the country's own Shia population, many of whom live in Saudi Arabia's most significant strategic provinces in the east—where most of the Saudis oil is pumped. Second, with the urgent and most serious threat out of the way, Saudi Arabia has focused on its larger geopolitical goal of isolating Iran, a goal that has backed by United States of America. From day one, the Iranian boogeymen have been a major factor of the way that Saudi Arabia, Bahrain, and other GCC states speak about the unrest in the kingdom. Fear of a pan-Shia movement has also demonstrated itself in the efforts towards political accommodation which various Gulf States particularly GCC countries have at times adopted towards their domestic Shiites minorities such as allowing of certain religious rights, as in Qatar; giving of political and economic rights, as in Bahrain; or the involvement of Shiites leaders in the institutional reform process, as in Saudi Arabia. [22]

Saudi foreign policy has always given high importance to the Gulf region with the purpose of growing Riyadh's weight over the smaller neighbours. Saudi Arabia is also worried about the current development in Bahrain, contributed that around 70 percent of Bahrain's population is Shia and, in addition, Iran is said to have significant influence over them. GCC countries in general and Saudi Arabia in particular is also concerned that Iran may take the advantage of the situation, hence challenging the Saudi role and put hold on Bahrainis Shia and influenced over Bahrain. Saudi Arabia has also warned Iran for any intervention in Bahrain. Moreover, it is also possible that the Saudi-led GCC involvement in Bahrain has done more to enflame Shia populations in both Saudi Arabia and Bahrain. It is also believe that Saudi-led GCC intervention in Bahrain will provoke these populations closer to Iran.

Indeed, Saudi Arabia has taken up the challenges seriously and, so far, has been able to deal with them suitably. [23] Saudi Arabia has also successfully controlled the domestic turbulence by promising social and economic measures and increasing security in the country. Riyadh has also succeeded to maintain intact influence on its neighbours while at the same time confining the place for Iran to increase its influence within Bahrain.

Iranian Response

While Saudi Arabia's intervention within Bahrain was unquestionable, Iranian involvement within the kingdom is also undeniable. Bahraini government, including GCC countries have alleged Iran of meddling within Bahrain. Though there is uncertainty as to the extent of Iranian involvement in the demonstrations across Bahrain, the reality of links between Bahraini Shia clerics and Tehran is noticeable. Thus, Sheikh Isa Ahmad Qassem, the spiritual leader of the key opposition party, Wafaq, and the leader of Friday prayers at a mosque in the predominantly Shia-populated Diraz City, is an ardent follower of Khamenei, collecting taxes for the Supreme Leader, publicising his religious ideology, and motivating people to follow him rather than other 'sources of imitation. [24] Iranian Supreme Leader, Ayatollah Ali Khamenei has been also praised him and said that Qassem as a "star in the sky" of Shiism. Most of the Shia clerics of Bahrain were trained in Qom and thus speak Persian language. Even several Shia clerics wrote to Khamenei requesting him to support the Shia population of Bahrain when clashes erupted in the country. The letter was extensively published in the Iranian media. [25]

Considering the relationship between Iran and opposition groups working within Bahrain is necessary to study the historical relationship between Tehran and opposition groups, particularly al-Jabha al-Islamiyya li Tahrir al-Bahrayn (the Islamic Front for the Liberation of Bahrain, the IFLB). The IFLB was accused by the ruling government of attempting a coup d'état in 1981, blaming that the group got support from Tehran in order to achieve this goal. The Bahrain's ruling family also accused that the IFLB received support and training from the Islamic Revolutionary Guards Corps (IRGC), [26] which helped to promote Tehran's ideology across the region after the 1979 revolution. Iranian immersion inside Bahrain can be analysed in this ways too: in terms of spreading the ideological views of Khomeini, while also challenging the influence of Saudi Arabia. [27]

A second interpretation of the crisis argues that Iranian involvement within Bahrain was a result of military calculations during the Iran-Iraq War (1980-88), signifying again how ideological beliefs can sustain into geopolitical calculations. Hasan Alhasan's work on the IFLB offers an important insight into links between the opposition groups and Iran. Alhasan also suggested that there are five areas in which Iran has been tied with the IFLB: ideology, leadership, media support, logistics and military training. [28] Alhansan's work also draws the IFLB aims:

The immediate goals of the group were: (i) the toppling of the Al Khalifa regime, (ii) establishing a "free Islamic order", (ii) obtaining true independence for Bahrain, (iv) achieving cultural and economic independence, (v) eradicating illiteracy and implementing mandatory education, and (vi) the scientific and technological advancement of the country. Its long-term objectives revolved around three axes, namely: the development of the individual as one educated in Islam, embodying its morals, carrying its message, and being prepared to sacrifice himself in its defence; building the believing community through a vanguard capable of leading it to glory; and finally the erection of Islamic civilization, which would be the end result of the Islamic Revolution. [29]

Perceptions in Iran of the nature of the "Arab Uprising" vary. While describing it as an "Islamic awakening" inspired by Iran's 1979 Islamic revolution. Official Iranian comments to the Bahrain crisis came quickly but were usually more carefully than reactions to the Egyptian and Libyan crises. Iranian media described that the influx of GCC troops in general and Saudi Arabia in particular is an invasion. The statements from the Bahraini opposition, broadly cited in the official Iranian media, signalled very much like a prelude to Iranian involvement. Iran cited opposition groups calling Saudi actions an "occupation". [30]

Supreme Leader of Iran Ayatollah Ali Khamenei described that "your brother in region," portrayed President Hosni Mubarak as a "traitor dictator," and said that the events in Tunisia and Egypt were "natural extensions of Iran's Islamic revolution of 1979". [31] Bahrain, with its majority Shiite population, had long been claimed by Tehran as its own (as discussed above). Some Iranian officials including high ranking have maintained the small Gulf emirate, with its majority Shiite population, as Iranian territory. In 2007, *Kayhan*, an Iranian newspaper controls by conservative and close to Supreme Leader, published an editorial asserting that it had seen "undeniable documents" specifying that "Bahrain was a part of Iran's territory until 46 years ago". [32] Additionally, the editorial rejected the idea that Bahraini independence from Iran was attained in a legitimate way. A second example of these remarks came in 2009, when Ali Akbar Nateq Nuri, former speaker of the *Majlis* and head of the accountability bureau in the supreme leader's office, asserted that Iran enjoyed sovereignty over Bahrain, [33] also mentioning that Bahrain had been "the fourteenth province of Iran until 1970". [34] Yet these comments may have been employed merely as a rhetorical tool.

Not only has this *Kayhan* editor Hossein Shariatmadari has on various times expressed that president Mahmoud Ahmadinejad's visit to Bahrain as "a provincial tour." [35] On March 15, 2011, the then Iranian Foreign Minister Salehi urged the United Nations (UN) chief to support the legitimate demands of anti-government Bahraini protesters in line with the international commitments of the United Nations. Later on April 15, 2011 Salehi once again called on the UN to take firm and immediate measures to halt Bahrain's crackdown on the protesters. He also requested UN Security Council to take "serious and immediate action" to prevent the killing of innocent Bahrainis. [36] The Speaker of the *Majli*, Ali Larijani also strongly condemned and warned that GCC countries including Saudi Arabia will pay the price for military intervention in Bahrain. The sectarian division in the region has grown especially due to the Arab uprising in the WANA region.

Undoubtedly, the case of Bahrain is one of the occurrences where Iran and Saudi Arabia were in disagreement even before 1979 Islamic Revolution. However, the problem was sorted out, with Iran saving face, when the shah of Iran advised that the Bahrainis should be able to determine their own fate. The Shah proposal was open a new chapter for a UN mission to realize that the people of Bahrain sought independence and freedom. However, the crisis spilled over periodically.

Conclusion

Despite the crackdown, opposition anger has continued to bubble, sporadically erupting in anti-government protests. Recently in September 2013, tens of thousands of people have marched through the Bahraini capital in solidarity with an arrested leading Shi'a politician and former member of the Council of Representative Khalil al-Marzooq. Khalil is being held on suspicion of inciting violence on September 18, 2013. The another opposition leader and secretary general of the Al-Wefaq, Sheikh Ali Salman was also interrogated for an opposition exhibition which authorities shut down due to being illegal and inciting hatred. However, he released after five hours of questioning, and charged with insulting Bahrain's interior ministry.

The contentious decision to permit Bahrain to host the Formula 1 Grand Prix in April 2012 further stimulated protests. Bahrain is a milestone for the Gulf region. If the problems cannot be addressed by the ruling government, then Bahrain will spread trouble to the region—sharpening Shia-Sunni division—and the dangerous competition between the

Saudis and Iran. In fact the ruling Al Khalifa's family— which controls the government—is divided on how best to respond to opposition demands for a more meaningful dialogue. It is believed that Prime Minister Sheikh Khalifa bin Salman al-Khalifa belongs to the hardliner camp who is unwilling to give any concessions to the protesters on the bases that they will only inspire opposition leaders to make more demands. However, Crown Prince Salman al-Khalifa, on the other hand, is observed as a moderate, and the opposition is hopeful that he should be involved in any dialogue. Recently he stated that "We all aspire to a better tomorrow, in which nothing but development, progress, respect for the rule of law, and coexistence represent the utmost goal we all seek to achieve". [37]

On the other hand, the Shia opposition groups in Baharian also suffer from internal factionalism. Recently, the Al-Wefaq (main Shiite opposition group) and other main Shiite factions began discussion with government officials and Sunni envoys last week to resolve the Bahrain crisis. However, some radical Shiite factions oppose dialogue. Many Shiites groups believe that any negotiations with the ruling family will not weak the Al Khalifa regime and power will continue to enjoy with them even in future. Thus the national dialogue started in February 2013 remains block in stand-off due to disagreement from both sides.

In the light of current tensions roiling Bahrain, it is expected that the kingdom is opening the door to external intervention, to offer support either for the ruling family or for the opposition. The time has arrived for the leaders of the WANA region including Bahrain to understand that the incidents in Tunisia, Egypt and Libya have revealed that economic incentives alone cannot help authoritarian regimes for longer period. The adequacy of leaders among the people, acknowledgment of the aspirations of the youth, social and economic equality, political and constitutional reforms, etc. are essential in today's world.

The involvement, either perceived or actual, of Iran and Saudi Arabia in Bahrain has severe implications for the security of the Gulf region and wider west Asia. Given the internal dynamics inside both Iran and Saudi Arabia, the legitimacy of regimes in both the countries is opposed on the basis of religious differences and factional divisions. Both Iran and Saudi Arabia have sought to manage to the situation through the use of religious and nationalist sentiment. Undoubtedly, it is feasible to track both Iran's and Saudi Arabia's behaviour externally as an outcome of internal dynamics. As such, the instinct that defending the ruling regime in Manama has been a red line for Saudi Arabia has compelled direct military intervention inside Bahrain. Both Bahrain and Saudi Arabia accused that Iran has encouraged protesters and offered backing to opposition groups. This has also proved historically that the clerics in Bahrain have had close ties with Iranian Supreme Leader Ayatollah Khamenei as observed during the discussion above. Given this assumption, the GCC troops was intended to support the ruling family and tried to prevent increasing Shia power and Iranian influence in Bahrain.

Bahrain can be observed through the geo-strategic importance for both Iran and Saudi Arabia, competing for legitimacy in the region. However, this is true that the face-off between the two rivals Iran and Saudi Arabia has never seemed so risky. Both Iran and Saudi Arabia understand that all-out armed conflict between them could prove catastrophic, and that knowledge will act as a powerful deterrent. But there are other forces at play, and those could prove even more powerful.

After all, the Arab uprisings seek to permanently reshape the landscape of the West Asian region. For both countries, the stakes are huge. Saudi Arabia may not be all-powerful in Bahrain for ever, though alarm about what it might do has given the precise justification to avoid solving the crisis. The Saudis, who are thought to be funding a huge shortfall in Manama's budget, wouldn't allow Bahrain for any compromises with the opposition groups. Although, obviously, at present Saudi Arabia is in win-

win situation in Bahrain.

Endnotes

1. Michelle Dunne, "The Deep Roots of Bahrain's Unrest", *Carnegie Endowment for International Peace*, 2011.
2. Frida Ghitis, "World Citizen: Saudi Arabia and Iran Face Off in Bahrain," *World Politics Review*, March 17, 2011, available at, http://www.worldpoliticsreview.com/articles/8215/world-citizen-saudi-arabia-and-iran-face-off-in-bahrain.
3. Simon Mabon, "The Battle for Bahrain: Iranian-Saudi Rivalry," Middle East Policy Council, 2013, available at, http://www.mepc.org/journal/middle-east-policy-archives/battle-bahrain-iranian-saudi-rivalry.
4. "Bahrain profile", *BBC News*, September 19, 2013, available at, http://www.bbc.co.uk/news/world-middle-east-14540571.
5. Bahrain's Census 2010, available at, http://www.census2010.gov.bh/results_en.php.
6. "290,000 Indians in Bahrain", *Gulf Daily News*, July 5, 2008, available at, http://www.gulf-daily-news.com/NewsDetails.aspx?storyid=222148.
7. "Why Bahrain blew up: An ill omen for the Saudis", *New York Post,* February 17, 2011, available at, http://www.webcitation.org/6BA6ukktF.
8. "Bahrain", International Foundation for Electoral Systems. 26th July, 2010, retrieved on March 22, 2011.
9. Ibid.
10. Frida Ghitis, "World Citizen: Saudi Arabia and Iran Face Off in Bahrain", *World Politics Review*, March 17, 2011.
11. "Bahrain Doles out Money to Families," *Al Jazeera*, February 12, 2011, available at, http://english.aljazeera.net/news/middleeast/2011/02/201121251854857192.html. See also IDSA issue Brief, March 31, 2011, available at, http://www.idsa.in/system/files/IB_ProtestsinArabWorld.pdf.
12. Peter Pearson, "Bahrain and the Arab Spring: time for some realism," *Telegraph*, August 4, 2011.
13. "Thousands Stage Anti-Government Protest in Bahrain", Reuters, February 25, 2011, available at, http://www.reuters.com/article/2011/02/25/us-bahrain-protests-

idUSTRE71O4VS20110225.
14. Michael Slackman, "The Proxy Battle in Bahrain," *New York Times*, March 20, 2011, available at, http://www.nytimes.com/2011/03/20/weekinreview/20proxy.html?pagewanted=all.
15. Simon Mabon, "Saudi Arabia and Iran: Soft Power Rivalry in the Middle East", IB Taurus, 2012.
16. "Timeline: Anti-government Protests in Bahrain", *Reuters,* March 16, 2011, available at, http://www.reuters.com/article/2011/03/16/us-bahrain-protests-events-idUSTRE72F4RR20110316?pageNumber=2.
17. IDSA Issue Brief, March 31, 2011, available at, http://www.idsa.in/system/files/IB_ProtestsinArabWorld.pdf.
18. "GCC Foreign Ministers Reject Foreign Interference and Appropriate $20 Billion for Development in Bahrain and Oman", *Saudi Press Agency*, March 10, 2011, available at, http://www.spa.gov.sa/English/index.php.
19. Simon Henderson, "State of Emergency", *Foreign Policy*, June 7, 2011, available at, http://www.foreignpolicy.com/articles/2011/06/07/state_of_emergency.
20. Joost Hilterman, and Kelly McEvers, "Barricaded in Bahrain", *The New York Review of Books* (blog), December 27, 2011, available at, http://www.nybooks.com/blogs/nyrblog/2011/dec/27/barricaded-bahrain.
21. Simon Mabon, "The Battle for Bahrain: Iranian-Saudi Rivalry", Middle East Policy Council, 2013, available at, http://www.mepc.org/journal/middle-east-policy-archives/battle-bahrain-iranian-saudi-rivalry.
22. Muhammad Hosni Mubarak quoted in Frontline, "An Unanticipated Shia Awakening", PBS, available at, http://www.pbs.org/wgbh/pages/frontline/showdown/view. See also Pierre Pahlavi (CFC), Shia Crescent, ISA, 2008.
23. "Saudi Arabia and the Crisis in Bahrain", February 26, 2011, available at, http://www.raceforiran.com/saudi-arabia-and-the-crisis-in-bahrain.
24. Mehdi Khalaji, "Iran's Policy Confusion about Bahrain", *Washington Institute for Peace*, 2011, available at,

http://www.washingtoninstitute.org/templateC05.php?CID=337

25. Ibid.
26. IRGC also known as *Pasdaran* is Iran's most powerful security and military organisation, responsible for the protection and survival of the regime.
27. Simon Henderson, "Iran's Shadow over Reform in Bahrain", *Washington Institute for Near East Policy,* 2010, available at, http://www.washingtoninstitute.org/templateC05.php?CID=334 7.
28. Hasan T. Alhasan, "The Role of Iran in the Failed Coup of 1981: The IFLB in Bahrain", *Middle East Journal,* Vol. 65, No. 4, 2011, p. 604. See also Simon Mabon, "The Battle for Bahrain: Iranian-Saudi Rivalry", Middle East Policy Council, 2013, available at, http://www.mepc.org/journal/middle-east-policy-archives/battle-bahrain-iranian-saudi-rivalry.
29. Ibid., p. 605.
30. Frida Ghitis.
31. Ali Alfoneh, "Mixed Response in Iran Middle Eastern Upheavals", *Middle East Quarterly*, Summer 2011, available at, http://www.meforum.org/3006/mixed-response-in-iran#_ftn14#_ftn14.
32. Mehdi Khalaji, "Iran's Policy Confusion about Bahrain", *Washington Institute for Near East Policy,* 2011, available at, http://www.washingtoninstitute.org/templateC05.php?CID=337 6.
33. Lamine Ghanmi, "Morocco Cuts Ties with Iran over Bahrain", *Reuters*, March 7, 2009, available at, http://af.reuters.com/article/topNews/idAFJOE52601D2009037.
34. Mehdi Khalaji.
35. Ali Alfoneh, "Mixed Response in Iran Middle Eastern Upheavals", *Middle East Quarterly*, Summer 2011, available at, http://www.meforum.org/3006/mixed-response-in-iran#_ftn14#_ftn14.
36. "EU Urges Dialog to End Bahrain crisis", *Press TV,* April 19, 2011, available at, http://www.presstv.ir/detail/175658.html
37. Simon Henderson, "Iran's Shadow over Reform in Bahrain", Washington Institute for Near East Policy, 2010, available at, http://www.washingtoninstitute.org/template.php?CID=3347.

Part III: Social Media and Arab Spring

8

Social Media and Arab Spring

Sashi Kumar

"The revolution will not be televised,
Will not be televised, will not be televised, the revolution will be no re-run brothers,
The revolution will be live".

The Gil Scott-Heron song of the seventies has, over the succeeding decades, become a mixed metaphor of sorts, invoking at once the mutuality and the disjuncture between the media and historic moments of political upsurge. We have seen military coups and putsches in Africa, Asia or Latin America acquire a media coefficient, with the broadcasting station becoming as much a seat of power to be targeted as, and even before, the parliament or the presidential building. We have seen airwaves unleashed in the mid eighties by the new Direct Broadcast Satellite (DBS) technology—wireless TV signals which do not respect national boundaries—sweep away the hitherto insulated communist regimes of East Europe.

Moving into the 'globalising' and 'unipolar' era, we have seen a brazen counterrevolution (even if it collapsed in two days) by the US-backed Venezuelan oligarchs and fuelled by their private owned TV channels against Hugo Chavez's democratically elected government in 2002. We have seen too a spate of colour coded revolutions ranging from the Tulip Revolution of 2005, which typifies those of various hues in the CIS states culled out of the former Soviet Union, to the anti-Ahmedinejad Green revolution in Iran of 2009, and the pro-Shinwatara Red shirt movement in Thailand in 2010—which are seen as engendered by the new found connectivity and virtual community capabilities of the user driven digital cyber media, cumulatively dubbed the 'social media' of our times.

The Arab Spring, the latest in the series, takes the social media determinism hypothesis to a new high and into contending camps arguing respectively that the revolution will, and will not, be tweeted. The buzz generated online at such momentous junctures is certainly more than mere static and transforms, by novel means like hashtagging, into a concerted agenda with a burgeoning agitated engagement around it. Twitter, Facebook, YouTube, wikis, blogs, vlogs and podcasts not only mirror, but feed into, the dynamics on the ground in terms of mass mobilization, unblinking blow by blow chronicling of direct action, signaling flash strikes and demonstrations and tactically staggering them to outwit the police, coordinating succour to those involved in street battles and piercing the smokescreens that the authorities raise around such situations.

In Tunisia, Egypt, Yemen, Syria, Jordan, Libya, Bahrain and other Arab countries, the digital social media became so imbricated in the peoples' movements kindled by the fire that consumed the Tunisian street vendor Mohamed Bouazizi in his iconic act of self immolation in December 2010, that the sense was not so much of an online chatterati with a ringside view of the action driving the traffic as of cyber agit propagandists driving the action themselves. In the jargon of the medium, the *twitterati* it seemed, had become, or been overwhelmed by, the *tweeple*.

The *twitterati-tweeple differentiation*, in a manner of speaking, digitally parallels the *liberalisation-democratisation dichotomy* in the Arab world—where liberalisation was a top-down initiative launched in the late 1980s by the regimes in tandem with the traditional oligarchs co-opting an emerging economic elite, and thereby keeping grass root popular democratic churning at bay. This calibrated liberalisation saw fairly free parliamentary elections in Jordan (1989) and Yemen

(1990), the Syrian parliament accommodate seats for 60 new independent candidates (1990), robust and competitive local elections in Algeria (1990), and even rigid Saudi Arabia experiment with a 60-member consultative body, the '*majlis ash-shura*' and a code of basic civil rights, the '*al-hukum al-asasi*'.

By the mid-1990s, however, the regimes on this path had reached their respective thus-far-no-further thresholds, and took a U-turn into a counter phase of active de-liberalisation marked by draconian laws against the press, suspension of elections and clampdown on, particularly the Islamist, opposition. The process was uneven across the region, but broadly, if paradoxically, the regimes which were legatees of Arab nationalist, Baathist or Nasserite takeovers seemed quicker than the rest to cut short the liberalization exercise, because it was seen as opening up the space for the Islamist groups to flex their muscle. The Gulf kingdoms, on the other hand, continued with a gradualist liberalization of a beneficent patriarchal variety—in July 2002, Qatar drafted a new Constitution with provision for secret ballot by the population including women; Bahrain released political prisoners and held out assurances of elections.

In sum, as Holger Albrecht and Oliver Schlumberger point out in their essay, 'Waiting for Godot: Regime change without democratisation in the Middle East' (published in the October 2004 issue of *International Political Science Review*), this qualified liberalization helped a permutation and cooptation in the structure of the governing elite, and thereby in "avoiding regime change by change in regime". It did not, was never meant to, lead to democratization. On the contrary, as the cited authors observe, "the common denominator of all these changes in the functional logic of these regimes is that they served to foreclose the emergence of autonomous rival forces".

The regimes managed to keep things from spilling over into the street by soft-pedalling the structural adjustment programmes in the eighties, and by rampant NGO-isation of society since then, so that class based protests by trade unions or the peasantry were marginalized and Islamisation seemed the only oppositional act in town. Thus, the 'Arab Street', as it came to be called, was stereotyped in the western consciousness as a rallying point or barometer of pan-Arab sentiment rather than a site of local specific struggles. Asef Bayat in his article, 'The Street and the Politics of Dissent in the Arab World' (published in the Spring 2003 volume of *Middle East Report*) discusses how this sweeping orientalist Arab Street fixation misled western policy makers and media into strange assumptions and stranger deductions.

In the aftermath of 9/11 and the looming threat of the US war on terror, the expectation was that the Arab street would rise in support of Osama bin Laden. When the street did not stir, the conclusion was that the street did not matter any more, rather than that the street may not be in empathy with bin Laden. *The Economist* declared the 'death' of the Arab street and Condolezza Rice went on to postulate that since the Arabs, sans street power, could not liberate themselves, the US must deliver them from their despots. "In the narratives of the western media", Asef Bayat cryptically concludes, "the Arab street is damned if it does and damned if it doesn't".

Bayat goes on to recount how the Arab street responded very differently and defiantly to the Israeli invasion of the West Bank in the end of March 2002 and to the US led invasions of Iraq and Afghanistan. Millions of Arab citizens poured out on to the streets of West Asian capitals in a massive show of solidarity and strength, often defying local laws and authorities. There was a coordinated boycott of American and Israeli goods including McDonald's, KFC, Starbucks, Nike and Coca Cola. Coca Cola, which lost between 20 and 40 percent of its market share in many Arab countries, was replaced by the Iranian Zamzam Cola which sold 10 million cans in the Gulf kingdoms in just four months. A counter cola market thrived briefly with Zam Zam exported to European states including Belgium and Denmark. Another brand, Mecca

Cola, surfaced in Paris and sold 2 million bottles in 2 months to European Arabs. All this pointed to the political and economic potency of the Arab street.

Cyberactivism was in its early days yet, although it had proved crucial and decisive in organizing the Seattle protests against the WTO towards the end of 1999. The incipient internet did not yet have the digital social media complement; Wikipedia had just been launched (2001) and Facebook and YouTube were yet to hit cyberdom. Indeed, a recent article in *The Economist* ('How Luther went Viral', December 17, 2011) reminds us that social media as a genre or phenomenon is not unique to the digital era and was marked by the same irrepressible energy and frisson five hundred years before Facebook.

When Martin Luther's nailed his 95 Theses against Papal indulgences to the church door in Wittenberg in October 1517—heralding the Reformation—they were swiftly disseminated by a set of retail media including printed pamphlets, woodcuts, ballads, to become common currency across Germany and Europe in a matter of weeks.

There was already, at the dawn of this century, an established practice of agitation and indignation on the Arab street being spawned by a variety of what Asef Bayat calls 'small media'. Audio and video cassettes of popular, if controversial, Islamic folk heroes like the Egyptian theologian Yusuf al-Qaradawi (in exile in Qatar since the sixties and well until the recent upsurge when he returned to Cairo), Sheikh Abd al-Hamid Kishk (whose hilarious Friday sermons were a huge draw until they were proscribed by President Mubarak in the eighties), the Lebanese Ayatollah Fadlallah considered the spiritual mentor of the Hezbollah, and the Egyptian television evangelist, Amr Mohammed Khalid, were widely circulated.

They jostled and vied for attention with a repertoire of hot selling recordings and albums by a constellation of Arab icons—ranging from the adulated evergreen divas, Umm Kulthum of Egypt and Fayroz of Lebanon, to the Moroccon satirist Ahmed

Sanoussi and the more contemporary stars of Egyptian pop and fusion, Amr Diab and Mohammed Munir. The undercurrent of aspirational Arab-hood and political identity in this eclectic spread of rhetorical, satirical and musical work heaved again to the surface with the Israeli action on the West Bank in 2002 when these cultural products were in popular demand afresh.

When it came to internal domestic criticism in the authoritarian regimes of the region, the creative media seemed to pack more punch than the formal news media which, when not run by the state, was under its systematic scrutiny. The Egyptian film, 'The Yacoubian Building' made in 2006, based on Alaa-el-Aswany's novel of 2002, was a powerful allegory on a society corroding from within. Set in and around an old Armenian building in the centre of Cairo, the film deals boldly with the quotidian and larger moral challenges faced by its disparate residents, who include, in the description of the director Marwan Hamed, "a corrupt politician, an autocratic womanizer, a destitute young woman who lives on the roof of the building and is sexually abused at work, a talented student who mutates into an Islamic terrorist after he is denied the opportunity to study at the police academy because his father works as a janitor and has a low social status, a journalist who suffers because of his homosexuality, and a shoe shine boy who rises to become a member of parliament and misuses religion to pursue his own interests".

That recipe was bad enough, sampling as it did real life characters and situations in Egyptian society. The conservative sections and ruling class of Egypt came heavily down on the film with 112 members of the parliament demanding cuts. But the box office gave it a rousing welcome and a follow up television serial of the same story the next year made 'The Yacoubian Building' almost a household name and an oblique precursor of Tahrir square. For, to quote its director Hamid again, "the film is a document of the time we live in because it shows very openly what many are thinking in secret. Corruption has eaten its way into all areas of Egyptian life". A dialogue between the skirt chasing, ageing grandee, Zaki, and the exploited young Busayna towards the end of the film sums up its allusive potency.

"If you can't find good in your own country", Zaki tells Busayna, "you won't find it anywhere else".

"Then you will know why we hate Egypt", is Busayna's tormented reply.

Not all creative gambits paid off like 'The Yacoubian Building'. The first graphic novel in Egypt, 'Metro', produced by Magdy el Shafee in 2008, about a computer engineer's futile fight against a system dankly and hopelessly corrupt, was banned by the authorities. Magdy was taken to task for testing public morals, subject to a long trial, convicted and fined. This censorious atmosphere notwithstanding, a corpus of new and pioneering writing emerged, its authors strongly informed, even shaped, by the internet, and hazarding a different language: among them Ahmed Alaidy whose novel 'Being Abbas El-Abb' (2006) deployed a new hybrid vocabulary; Mohammed Aladdin who wrote up all of his 60-page novel, The Gospel according to Adam' (2006), in one paragraph; Mansoura Ez Eldin with her oneiric brinkmanship in 'Maryam's Maze' and 'Beyond Paradise' (2009); and the graphic artist, Ahmed Negy, whose face and T-shirt designs became familiar in the Tahrir square tumult.

The digital social media which burst on the scene with the YouTube tagged 'Sidi Bouzid' campaign after Mohammed Bouazizi's self immolation in that coastal town of Tunisia and merged into the chant "Ben Ali, out" on Facebook and diverse other online fora, and then spread virally to feel and feed the pulse of revolt as it expanded into the streets and public squares of Egypt, Libya, Syria, Jordan, Morocco, Yemen, and Bahrain and other Arab states, are generally approached as exogenous to the social and cultural logic of each situation. The same fallacies applied in taking stock of the Green Revolution in Iran were in evidence here. There is a body of analysis now questioning the assumption that social media played a decisive role in the pro Moussavi and anti Ahmedinejad rallies after the Iranian elections of 2009 on the ground that the preponderant volume of tweets and online messaging were in English and not Farsi, aimed at western rather than local netizens, and unlikely to have intervened in, or crucially impacted, the course of events on the ground. The online excitement around the event then was ostensibly greater among the observers than the participants.

The Arab spring, on the other hand, does seem to have integrated the social media in far greater measure. But it still appears to hover above the ground reality like a universalizing tech-veneer and unable to acquire a *raison d'etre* in terms of each specific context. This is perhaps partly a function of the nature, scale and pitch of internet technology, which lends itself to a non-hierarchised and loosely networked cyber flatland. But without the underpinnings that relate them to local practice, custom and lore do they tend to freewheel into a global rather than local realm and consciousness?

Brian T. Edwards in his article, 'Tahrir: Ends of Circulation' (published in the Fall 2011 issue, Vol. 23, No. 3, of 'Public Culture') reflects on this tension informing the digital social media. "What are the ends of circulation", he wonders. "Does the digitally enabled circulation of revolutionary images, ideas, even advice—and in literary production of forms, genres, motifs—*end* in places like Cairo, where it is incorporated into a local idiom and national context? Or, is it precisely the abstraction and compression of representations of local meanings—a necessary precondition for forms to make their way across publics, from one mode in the circularity matrix to another—that allows them to flow globally, where they might achieve various *ends*?

The application of the social media across the Arab states was also uneven for reasons of connectivity, censorship and local politics. Digital media as a player in the protests was more vibrant and visible in Tunisia and Egypt. They were relatively subdued in Libya, where the state controlled the internet and in Yemen with its low internet penetration. Syria with only 15 percent of its population online seemed to produce more noise because the pro and anti Assad forces were logged on at logger heads with one another. The opposition has also accused Twitter and Facebook of lending a helping hand to the Assad regime by blocking tweets and posts in the country. There were similar hurdles to free circulation of social media in the region with other regimes too resorting to time, location and content specific blocks.

In Egypt, the social media initially bypassed the Muslim Brotherhood, which subsequently emerged as the group with the best electoral prospects. Cadres of the Brotherhood stayed away from the Day of Rage protest of January 25, 2011 which was mobilized in good part by Twitpic, Facebook and YouTube and for which more than 90,000 people signed up on Facebook alone. By January 28, the government was cracking down on the this mobilization through internet and mobile phones by pressuring the operators to suspend services in selected locations. The opposition groups, particularly the Baradei Action for Change, countered this attempted blackout by hitting the streets and exhorting people to join them to the slogan "Down with Mubarak".

The authorities responded by imposing curfews and driving the protestors back indoors and, ironically, to their computer keyboards with a vengeance. The regime could not, apparently, keep them away from both the streets and their computers at the same time. Thus it went until February 10 when the Vice President, Omar Suleiman, announced Mubarak's resignation. In the weeks leading up to his ceding power there was an estimated ten fold increase in the tweets on the situation. Videos on the protest consumed gigabytes of Youtube space, the top two dozen fetching nearly five and a half million views.

There were through all this the flash narratives of net heroism. Tunisian activist blogger, Salim Amamon, was pitch forked from Ben Ali's jail to Minister of Youth and

Government, a position he gave up soon. The Egypt based Facebook group, "We are all Khalid Said" commemorating the young man who had been killed by the police in 2010 had over 80,000 followers on the Thursday, January 27, 2011, before the massive Friday turnout—which was a sudden spike from the 20,000 registered the previous day. The *New York Times* ran front page stories in February 2011 about an Egyptian who named his new born daughter 'Facebook' and another eulogizing Google's Egyptian chief,. Wael Ghonim, for waging the revolution via Facebook groups.

But sobering thoughts temper the enthusiasm. The key social platforms mediating the Arab spring—Facebook, Twitter and YouTube—belong to US-based private corporations. Indeed, e-diplomacy is the latest plank in US foreign policy, of which information, hegemony and control have been an integral part since the end of the Second World War. Some of these media organizations were also complicit with the regimes in removing videos from, or cutting access to, their sites at critical junctures. In some of the Gulf States, skype was completely blanked out.

There are reports of Egyptian youth planning to sue internet companies which colluded with Mubarak. The issue of censorship becomes intriguing with news of Twitter agreeing to be accommodative to requests from governments and organizations to remove tweets that run foul of the law of their land. Coming, as this does, a month after Saudi prince Walid bin Talal took a US$ 300 million stake in Twitter, and in the light of Facebook's market foray with a US$ 5 billion initial public offering, it may not be just cussed conspiracy theory to see a pattern in these developments.

The social media was both combative against, and buttressed by and dovetailed into, the dominant mainstream pan regional media, Al Jazeera. The channel's programme 'The Stream' aggregated citizen journalism and a lot of the activist social media. Soon after Mubarak ceded power, the managing director of the channel, Wadah Khanfar, acknowledged the mediatory role of the citizens of Tunisa ad Egypt: "the youth of the Middle East, choosing universal values from within while embracing tolerance and diversity—they are our reporters." Al Jazeera also re-broadcast its social media generated content to the United States through Free Speech TV, a non profit satellite network accessed by an estimated 35 million homes there.

The nature and scope of the agency of the social media in the Arab spring are, given the continuing flux in the region, a developing story. But the reading in western capitals that this leavening of aspirations across the region, leveraged by cutting edge digital media, is *ipso facto* a popular demand for the western liberal democratic model, is proving premature and misplaced, with the Islamist parties best placed to win the polls marking the regime change in each country. The medium is clearly not the message in this case. Are the assorted social media manufacturing a public sphere or people-hood which cuts across the traditional categories of the *ummah* (or Islamic nationhood) or the *millet* (for the minorities), or which challenges the *assabiyah* (tribal or clan affiliation) factor, even while upholding the *sharia* as the ultimate arbiter?

The distinction between *liberalism,* with its emphasis on individual liberty, human rights and rule of law, and *democracy* understood as combining the principles of equality, majoritarian rule and sovereignty of the people, may make a difference to that question. The rhetoric of the social media has, typically, been stridently western-liberal and impatient with the deliberative representative process organic to the political ethos of the Arab states.

The street scuffles breaking out in Egypt and Tunisia between the Islamists, who probably see themselves as the democratic heirs of the Arab spring, and the freer-wheeling protesters—many of them poster boys and girls of the social media—who are wary of a 'counter revolution' by the remnants of the old regime in league with the Islamists, keep the margins of the movement, even where it has been successful so far, restless. The social media, as is their wont, flock to the dizzy fringes of the movement and root for dramatic and drastic changes. In the process they may well be getting ahead of themselves and not helping the transition they have helped usher in crystallise.

9

New Media and Arab Spring

Pallav Kumar

Historically, the importance of mass media was restricted to certain domains of communication but in the present context its role has been defined as a multi-tasking tool that fits in every sphere of the society. Further the revolution in the field of mass media and new media technologies added its role to a great extent. The influence of new media technologies is very prominent in the present societies of the world. The last two decades have seen the rapid transformation into media which are predicated upon the use of digital computers, such as the satellite TV, internet and mobile. Actually, emergence of new information and communication technologies signals a potentially radical shift of who is in control of information, experience and resources. Today, we are witnessing the evolution of a universal interconnected network of audio, video, and electronic text communications that is going to blur the distinction between interpersonal and mass communication and between public and private communication. Internet, provide the potential for a democratic post-modern public sphere, in which citizens can participate in well informed, non-hierarchical debate pertaining to their social structures.

For social and political scientist, significance of the media is not limited to the content of media messages but it becomes an important source for the flow of information. The ways in which we receive information, and the information to which we have access, are beginning to change the dynamics of social institutions. New media offers exciting possibilities for social change, not just through support of explicitly political structures, but through the restructuring of personal relationships, social interactions and organizational dynamics. Social change leaders were some of the earliest adopters of new media because its ability to engage supporters mapped onto their focus on mobilizing and deepening supporter relationships.

But the social change potential of new media goes far beyond its use by political organizers, campaigners and civil society activist. Individuals and organizations who use new media are subtly but profoundly transformed in an atomized world, new media reconnects us to our communities, to one another, and to our own creative potential; from the most explicitly political and social online communities to the frivolous social networks that bring us back to our deeply social and political nature; new media is rewriting the rules for social change.

The new technologies, especially the Internet, are inherently democratic, provide the public and individuals with access to information and sources and enable all to participate actively in the communication process, thus helping to strengthen the organizations of civil society. These civil society's organisations have embraced the new media as a means of exchanging, collecting, and disseminating information quickly and cheaply. It gives a real exposure to the mass audience about right and wrong. Even we can say that without media, people in societies would be isolated, not only from the rest of the world, but from governments, law-makers, and surroundings.

News and entertainment media institutions do not exist independently of their environment but rather take on the form and coloration of the social and political structures within which they operate. There is an intimate and organic relationship between media institutions and society in the way that those institutions are organized and controlled. Neither the institution nor the society in which it functions can be understood properly without reference to the other. In an era of globalization, the new media technologies have become a strategic weapon for most countries. So it has become an essential pillar of the information age and the knowledge economy.

Society, groups and organizations in the Arab world are no exception. However, Arab world lagged behind most of the world in adopting the new media technologies such as internet and satellite television. Arab world's political structure is very different from the West because most of the countries are governed mainly by the authoritarian rule; however at some places it is so called elected government.

And it was not surprising that government censors or punishes speech critical of the authorities or the regime. Even, most of the media organisations are directly or indirectly owned by the government or regime.

The satellite television and internet reached the Arab world in the early 1990's, but its proliferation rate has really been booming since the turn of the millennia. In its second decade in the Arab world, the internet has been increasingly challenging many of the region's governments because they impose strict limitations on civil freedoms while on the other these tools of new media technologies requires freedom from all limitations.

It has brought about the formation of pressure groups for social and political change on social networks such as Facebook, Twitter, YouTube etc. because it allows real time coverage of events through the websites.

Under such climate, world wide web is playing the role of "the other". On one hand, the new media technologies provide unlimited communication and allow diversity in opinions and approaches without the permission of "those in charge". In Arab world, the approaches of journalists, political and human rights activists, and a large number of youths are completely contradicting those of "officials in charge" (i.e., governments). On the other hand, the responsible authorities used to offer their own opinions and to protect them by allowing only the exchange of the information which support their approaches. They imposed harsh restrictions on traditional media, freedom of press, and freedom of expression. [1]

Today, widespread presence of new media technologies in Arab world, people became more interested in the internet because of the ease of accessing it from many places. With the increase of this interest in internet, the number of bloggers in Arab world increased. It turned into one of the characteristics of the technological revolution. Bloggers are playing an increasingly important role in broadening the scope of acceptable political and social discourse, and self-expression. For example, only in Egypt there is an estimated 160,000 bloggers who write in Arabic, and sometimes in English, about a wide variety of topics, from social life to politics to literature. [2] Some blogs achieved great fame among internet users, and became an essential information source as it reveals the news that semi-formal media is not interested in. That led authorities to attempt to suppress bloggers.

Political activism and awareness has increased many fold due to these tools of new media technologies. Earlier camera used to be dedicated to the leader's great achievements, unforgettable speeches, and blessed projects; now it has turned against the leader to show his mistakes and record his errors, changing the world and awakening people. The decision about who will stays and who will exits, now in the hands of globalised satellite channels and the internet. The leader's slogan no longer rules because now the picture opposes it and nullifies it. [3] This is a new form of socialization that is occurring in a unique way because information is democratized and youth have much more influence in what they are exposed to. This new way of socialization can link different cultures and generations from all over the world.

It is not long ago when Arab youth were called the 'lost generation' by the Arab experts because they were frustrated and politically helpless to press for change. They were thoroughly intimidated by the Mubaraks, Ben Ali and Salehs, together with their ubiquitous, Orwellian spies and secret police; they were disillusioned by the failed attempts at rebellion by their parent's generation. It was believed that the only outlet for youthful dissent lay in Islamic extremism and violence. A much cited 2003 Brookings Institution report on Arab youths warned that they were being raised in an environment of religious radicalism and anti-Americanism. "These values", the report argued, "thus become the formative elements of a new and dispossessed generation, auguring badly for the future".

But the new Arab youth's survey 2010 released in March 2011 by the ASDA'A Burson-Marsteller showed that they ranked democracy as a greater priority than good civic infrastructure, access to the best education or even fair wages. It is important to note that Arab youth are talking about a pure version of Arab democracy, unlike the unpopular neo-conservatives' democracy that was brought to Iraq through military invasion, which was followed by sectarian violence and division. Arab youth's this trend has validated its earlier report's finding which were published in 2009, in which the highest priority for young people in the region was participation and representation in the political life of their country of residence. Recent events in Tunisia, Egypt, Libya and elsewhere are the manifestation of this fundamental truth: Arab youth have a deep and enduring desire for democracy.

The role of new media as a tool of social, economic and political change had seen first time in Egypt in 2008 when some of the bloggers used this new media as a tool to organize a movement for the fulfilment of their righteous demand.

Youth Movement was an Egyptian Facebook group started by Ahmed Maher, a 30-year-old civil engineer, and Israa Abdel Fatah in Spring 2008 to support the workers in El-Mahalla El-Kubra, an industrial town, who were planning to strike on April 6. Activists called on participants to wear black and stay home the day of the strike. Bloggers and citizen journalists used Facebook, Twitter, Flickr blogs and other new media tools to report on the strike, alert their networks about police activity, organize legal protection and draw attention to their efforts.

The New York Times has identified the movement as the political Facebook group in Egypt with the most dynamic debates. In January 2009, it had 70,000 predominantly young and educated members, most of whom had not been politically active before; their core concerns include free speech, nepotism in government and the country's stagnant economy. Their discussion forum on Facebook features intense and heated discussions, and is constantly updated with new postings.

The uprising of Egypt lasted for 18 days against the Hosni Mubarak, the President of Egypt, who ruled the country for long 30 years was obviously extension of new media's social and political role. After the Egyptian uprising of 2011 it became clear that it was not lead by the traditional political leader or big personalities but by the young professional who do not have any political background or political agenda but only had a great cause. This revolution was led by urban professionals like Google executive Wael Ghonim and dentist Mustafa Nagar. In an interview on Dream TV, Ghonim said that, "*Everyone was contributing small pieces, bits and pieces. We drew this whole picture of a revolution. No one is the hero in that picture.*" Ghonim was the creator of the Facebook page *"We Are All Khaled Said,"* on which he called for the January 25, 2011 protest that launched the uprising in Tahrir Square. Said was a 28-year-old techie and businessman who was believed to have been brutally killed by police in Alexandria in 2010.

Ghonim and the tens of thousands, who took part in the historic uprising, hope that new system of government will be a democratic one and work is already being done to figure out how to get the ball rolling. For the making of new future of Egypt, Ghonim created a page using Google moderator asking people what are you dreaming about. It was astonishing that within a week there were more than four thousands suggestions and over ten thousand votes for that page.

Everyone is now dreaming. Everyone wants to do something. And it was new media and their interactive nature through which everyone can now express their ideas and concerns.

Perhaps one of the greatest achievements of the Arab uprising is that it was indeed exclusively indigenous. The Jasmine Revolution of Tunisia and Egyptian revolution has shown the world that democracy and freedom in the Arab world needs no military funding, no political doctrines, no Great Arab World Democracy Projects, and no foreign invasions or foreign-backed military coups. It only needs ordinary people to unearth their own, innate and extraordinary strength. The uprising has finally restored the power back to the people, orchestrated their return as the rightful owners of their own country and shapers of their own destiny as a collective experience that many of them will always remember, with pride, and some will always fear, for good reason. And it all happened due to the far reaching impact of new media. Satellite television based on their home region such as Al Jazeera and others, who can understand the feelings and sentiments of their own people which were ignored by their own government and also from West and the social networking which is highly interactive in nature assimilated the whole country in one single point.

These new social groups were composed of modern educated population. Some of those, who were educated in American and European Institutions, were connected to their native homes through the modern means of communication, turned out to be new western-oriented elites. These new western oriented elites were mainly composed of IT professionals, lawyers, medical practitioners, teachers and business entrepreneurs. Similarly, due to the development in this new media technology and its product Internet helped the emergence of absolutely new groups that is bloggers. These bloggers finally took the position of torch bearer for the society and we can easily see its importance in the current uprising of Arab world, which started from Tunisia and spread all over the Arab world. And it is quite interesting that current uprising do not have any traditional political leader but a group of young professionals who have will to change the society for the betterment of masses. [4]

Today's Arab world is considered very young because its more than fifty percent population is young. And one anonymous scholar said that "*youth is a type of madness and old age is a type of wisdom*". So that young population of Arab's is in confusion today. They are stuck between the traditional belief and modern thinking. [5]

Emergence of Satellite Television and the Arab World

The Gulf war brought about by the Iraqi invasion of Kuwait opened a new chapter in the history of the media in the region. The Arab states seeing the impact of CNN on international scale, grasped the strategic importance of satellite television on times of conflict. Several governments, in particular Saudi Arabia, encouraged their rich compatriots to invest in the installation of satellite television channels in Europe. MBC, ORBIT and ART were able to build their hegemonies and set up thrones under the Arab sky. Other countries followed suit by launching their own national channels.

Satellite channels set in motion the emergence of modern TV journalism. Programming has expanded to include news broadcasts, talk shows, live debate, and reality TV game shows. Actually with the emergence of satellite channels the Arab soil was ripe for a new crop. The strongest catalyst for radical change in the Arab media landscape was CNN's live coverage of the Gulf War in 1991. Until then, Arab audiences had virtually no access to international news coverage. Watching live reports from the fields, often broadcast in real time, jolted the viewers across the Arab world, exposing them to the modern face of TV journalism and leaving them longing for more.

The last decade of the twentieth century saw considerable

innovation in the media sector of the Arab region. This innovation can be recounted in different ways. The developments in new media technology, especially in satellite television created an environment of more media outlets, and most of these outlets managed outside the direct control of governments, and was more responsiveness to the competition for viewers created by the proliferation of satellite channels. The qualitative breakthrough came in the sphere of new cross-border Arab media. Specializing in news and current affairs, Al Jazeera broke the mould of the satellite channels set up by governments and by private Saudi and Lebanese entrepreneurs. It was a real revolution in the Arab world. [6]

Al Jazeera, financed by Qatar government could dare to establish a free ranging and independent news channel in the region. The channels provide free ranging public affairs; interviews and talk shows with viewer's participation which did never existed in the region before. A year after drawing international scrutiny for its coverage in Afghanistan the channel continued to attract both fans and critics with its bold, uncensored news and debate programs. [7]

Since its launch in 1996, "It created a consciousness in the Arab world" said Adel Iskandar, an instructor at Georgetown University and author of the book '*Al-Jazeera*'. Further he says, "It capitalized on a public that was so disenchanted with the blandness of the regional broadcasting which was broadcasting the kind of myopic presentation that completely insults the intelligence of the viewer who were literate and educated consumers of news. That is a key turning point". [8]

Al Jazeera, which is headquartered in Doha, Qatar, reaches Arabic-speaking audiences with a very specific model: aggressively opinionated talk shows, a manic style of up-to-the-minute reporting from the streets, and a mandate to give a voice to ordinary citizens, including those who clash with government interests. In many ways, it is considered as Al Jazeera's movement, not only because of the role it has played in the Arab uprising spreading across the Arab world, but also because the channel has helped to shape a narrative of popular rage against oppressive Arab governments (and against Israel) ever since its founding. That narrative has long been implicit in the channel's heavy emphasis on Arab suffering and political crisis, its screaming-match talk shows, even its sensational news banners and swelling orchestral accompaniments. The Channel's motto "The opinion and the other opinion" has literally reflected by the Al Jazeera from its inception.

According to Marc Lynch, a professor of Middle East Studies at George Washington University who has written extensively on the Arab news media, "They did not cause these events, but it is almost impossible to imagine all this happening without Al Jazeera". [9]

One interesting incident will be useful to site here about the description of Al Jazeera. On a visit to Doha, former Egyptian President Hosni Mubarak wanted to satisfy his curiosity about the most famous satellite TV station in the Arab world, one that has annoyed him and many other Arab rulers. It was past midnight when he arrived unannounced at Al Jazeera's studio, located in the compound that houses Qatari Radio and Television. After touring the station's compound, he turned to Safwat Sharif, leader of Egypt's vast media empire, and exclaimed: "*All this trouble from a match box like this?*" [10]

During the political crisis of winter 2010-2011 in Arab world, the Arabic satellite TV channel Al Jazeera has set the benchmark of media's ideal role, which has been giving rock solid support to people's causes, inspiring Tunisia's brave people who ended Zine El Abidine Ben Ali's 23-year rule, and also supported the Egyptians too. Actually Al Jazeera played a role of the standout voice of aggressive, independent journalism in the Arab world, in channeling popular discontent throughout the region. Where one side, state owned media only advocating the political and internal interest of their own regime, while on the other side, Al Jazeera representing transnational Arab voice and people's rights, against authoritarian governments. So that channel faced serious obstacle.

Tunisian government had barred its reporters from the country, but Al Jazeera managed to gather report from the ground through his local contacts. Similarly, Egyptian authorities also shut down Al Jazeera's office, complaining that its continuous coverage was biased toward protesters and may encourage more unrest as the uprising in Tunisia drove its long-ruling leader from power. But the channel has become a voice for people who have been voiceless for decades because of the authoritarian nature of the regime.

The protestors in both countries, Tunisia and Egypt, made active use of social networking tools for mobilizing large crowds, encouraging the popular revolt, and publicizing their cause to foreign audiences. Many commentators have dubbed this being the "social revolution". There is even a joke on the internet of how "Sadat was assassinated and Mubarak was 'facebooked'", which has cemented the role of the internet as a tool in the hands of the revolutionaries. However, behind all the mass support for the protestors, and the remarkable organizational capacity developed through these social networking sites, an overlooked aspect of the protests is the critical coverage provided by the Al Jazeera.

In his blog 'Al Jazeera and the Promise of the Arab Revolution', Nabil Echchaibi, [11] says that, this Arab revolution is without a doubt the poster child of Al Jazeera. He says, "if we frame the question around purist expectations of journalistic objectivity, then Al Jazeera will simply appear as a propaganda tool. But if we situate its controversial coverage in a general climate of political profiteering and impunity of leaders, then Al Jazeera appears more a network on a mission, not only to report but to restore Arab dignity and replace muzzled politics with a new culture of civil dialogue". [12]

Faisal Al-Qasim (anchor at Al Jazeera), once told a student at the American University in Sharjah who was worried about the loud tone of guests on his show, "We have been sorting out our problems in the Arab world with bullets and iron. Why don't we sort them out for a change with shouting? So let us shout. To awaken them, tell them, wake up wake up. There is a world around you. Something is happening in the world. You're still sleeping. Wake up. This is the message of Al Jazeera". [13] And through this shouting and waking Al Jazeera has done more than its share and has been instrumental in funnelling every sentiment of pent-up frustration and humiliation found in Arab world.

Uprising in Arab World

This instant technology is wonderful. It shows the whole world in real time. Governments and large businesses no longer have total control over the media and public opinion. This is a great counterbalance to the power struggle in the world. Dictatorships can only thrive when they can control information. As long as those who are being repressed can find a way to get the information out, the dictators will have a hard time and will likely crumble all the more quickly. Social media is only one way to spread information. As long as the internet exists, there will be ways to use it. After 22 years of repression, the Tunisian dictator fled away from the country. Similarly, after 30 years of repression, Mubarak is doomed. It seems democracy would be the logical choice since Facebook and Twitter are the very essence of free speech. Social media are redefining the dynamics of popular revolt. The need for a central figure to drive a revolution is replaced by the collective consciousness of the masses.

Social media allows people to communicate with other people who have freedoms, and this comparison brings on an uprising. Gradual freedom brings on an evolution of democracy, what the people of Tunisia and Egypt has been struggling for 30 years. It has allowed the people to speak louder than the dictators. These social websites will eventually be the means of helping people across the globe identify with each other. This uprising in Tunisia, and Egypt being discussed through these websites, shows that all have similar needs despite culture differences. Freedom and equality are key principles that are valued and spread through social networks like Facebook and YouTube. If we analyse the strength of these tools then one can easily recognize that it took only 5 days for Egypt to have a vice- president after a wait of 30 years and it all happened due to the vibrant nature of social media such as Facebook, Twitter and YouTube.

From the winter uprising of 2010-2011 in Tunisia and Egypt to the protests in the streets of Yemen, Algeria Jordan and Lebanon, social media had played a role in helping protesters being organized and draw international attention. It got importance when Secretary of State Hillary Clinton urged to authorities in Egypt to allow for peaceful expression and to not block social media sites. Egypt blocked Twitter and Facebook in the wake of the protests. [14] Plans for the protests in Egypt, saw record numbers pouring out into the streets, calling on President Hosni Mubarak to step down, and were widely broadcasted on the social networking site Facebook.

Given the magnitude of grievances in each country, revolt would almost certainly have come eventually. But social media simply made it come faster to organizing protest, before Egypt shut off the Internet and mobile phones, before it even started blocking Twitter and Facebook, those tools were used to coordinate and spread the word about the demonstrations that were scheduled for January 25, 2011. Without these mass organizing tools, it's likely that fewer people would have known about the protests, or summoned the kind of courage that's made possible during the protest. It also started shaping the narratives, soon after the protest started in Egypt, hooligans were turning the city upside down. Order needed to be restored and the narratives could easily have shifted in favour of the government.

And it was easy for any regime to make it look like

protesters have turned ugly, giving them an excuse to clamp down. But the tweets belied that narrative. And indeed, a New York-based female Egyptian blogger interviewed by CNN, suggested as much, She "appealed to the media to not fall for what she described as a Mubarak regime plot to make the protests in Egypt seem like dangerous anarchy," according to the New York Times' blog "*The Lede*". "Urge you to use the words 'revolt' and 'uprising' and 'revolution' and not 'chaos' or 'unrest". "We are talking about a historic moment". [15] The narrative was reset. Soon thereafter, CNN changed it's on-screen headlines from "*Chaos in Egypt*" to "*Uprising in Egypt*". [16]

Social media put the pressure on Washington to act more quickly. During the first week of protest the tone of US was very controlled and supportive for the government in the interest of maintaining stability because Egypt has been always a close ally of US in Arab world. So it was tough for them and there certainly must be concern about a domino effect leading to even more instability in the region. But when protest increased and so much information leaking out, it became impossible for the U.S. to downplay what was going on and stay out of it. US started shifting his stand. Officials began speaking of a "transition". They declined to articulate explicit support for Mubarak. And later US officials started telling its embattled president, Hosni Mubarak, to step down but clearly laying the groundwork for his departure."

A wave of civil unrest is continuing to spread across the Arab world following the uprisings in Tunisia and Egypt and history shows that where Egypt goes, other Arab countries soon follow. There have already been started insurrection's ripples in Bahrain, Libya, Algeria, Jordan, and Yemen. No one had thought that citizens of the Arab world, suppressed for so long and denied both political and economic opportunities, would be in a position to rise in revolt against the dictators. But Tunisia showed the way and a firestorm is sweeping across the Arab world. Now Arab peoples are no longer afraid to confront their own regimes. They have been facilitated by a newfound fearlessness and feeling of empowerment.

The protesters on the streets of Cairo who, in just 18 days, ended the three-decade rule of Hosni Mubarak were not merely demanding the end of an unjust, corrupt and oppressive regime. They did not merely decry poverty, unemployment or the disdain with which their leaders treated them. They had long suffered such indignities. What they fought for was something more elusive and more visceral. It has breathed life into an exhausted idea: Arab self-determination.

An article published in The Guardian of Britain, *"Egypt protester: Tunisia showed us something different was possible"* in which a Cairo graduate Shady Alaa El Din said his story that he wanted to leave Egypt because of the lack of freedom and opportunity, but protests in Tahrir Square have made him feel he can help bring change. "I was never involved in politics before, not because I didn't think things were in need of change, but just because there was nobody who convinced me that they could make a difference. None of the so-called opposition leaders really cared about the country; they were all just showing off and acting like the president but in a smaller way; lots of mini-dictatorships headed by guys who are out for themselves. The regime allows these people to exist deliberately, it prevents any genuine opposition from emerging". [17]

But when revolution occurred in Tunisia in which long and oppressive regime had fallen it gave a new and totally different messages to the youths like Shady that something different is possible. Now they got new courage to oppose the government for the betterment of society. Before the Jasmine Revolution of Tunisia and their own struggle against the government, the Arabian youth were in dilemma but after the success of uprising they do not have any confusion and they himself wants to change the society for better future. And they got this strength from the like minded people who are online and connected with each other and share their feelings. [18]

Arab states suffer from a curse more debilitating than poverty or autocracy. They have become counterfeit, perceived by their own people as alien, pursuing policies hatched from afar. One cannot fully comprehend the actions of Egyptians, Tunisians, Libyans, Jordanians and others without considering this deep-seated feeling that they have not been allowed to be themselves, that they have been robbed of their identities. Where the United States and Europe have seen moderation and co-operation, the Arab public has sensed a loss of dignity and of the ability to make free decisions. Popular uprisings are the latest step in this process. Taking to the streets is not a mere act of protest. It is an act of self-determination. And it is interesting in this regard that while the focal point was the huge crowd in Tahrir Square in Cairo; small revolutions were taking place in virtually every section of society. The business and financial district was rebelling, as were the medics and health careers, factory workers, media professionals, teachers and lecturers and students. Even police officers have been marching to request the forming of a union that defends their rights.

The entire Arab world is witnessing a tectonic shift. There is a fragile, if for many sublime, expectations that democracy may now spread in this region. A new generation has come of age. Creativity, new communication technologies and the use of rational peaceful protest have restored Arab self-esteem. Cairo concluded what Tunisia had hinted at. It seems to have united east and west in the understanding that true security begins with the dignity of the human being, and is based upon what we often refer to as *hurriya*, or "freedom". Recent events have shown that men and women make their own history, and are capable of controlling their own destinies. Anti-government protests inspired by popular revolts that toppled rulers in Tunisia and Egypt are gaining pace around the Arab world despite political and economic concessions by nervous governments. Clashes were reported in tightly controlled oil producer Libya, Bahrain, Yemen, Algeria, Jordan, Albania,

Iraq, Iran and Turkey.

With young people able to watch pro-democracy uprisings in other countries on satellite television or the internet, and to communicate with like-minded activists on social networks hard for the secret police to control, authoritarian governments across the region have grounds to fear contagion. Actually, what new media did for the Arabs is that they narrated the basic problems of Arabs in a very different manner from the extremist.

Religious extremist's diagnosis essentially says that the poverty, oppression, and humiliation that Arabs experiences are due to the fact that they are not obeying God's rules, especially about dress and behaviour, and so God has turned His face from them. The cure for all these ills, therefore, is precise and universal observance of all God's rules and injunctions, as interpreted in their peculiarly narrow and intolerant version of Islam. The Islamists never talked about the Arabs, of course. They spoke only of "the Muslims", for their ideology rejected all distinctions of history, language and nationality.

While from Turkey to Indonesia, most non-Arab Muslim countries enjoy reasonable economic growth, and some are full-blooded democracies. Their governments work on behalf of their own countries. But new media, on the other side, which don't know the geographical boundary, establishes the new solution for these ills found in their society. New media gave the insight to the educated young Arabs who can easily spread their concern to other fellow young of Arab world, because they speak their language, they can understand their feelings and finally they can lead them for the betterment of their nation. And it is not surprising that current uprising of Arab world has no definite leaders but everyone is participated in a equal manner and Google executive Wael Ghonim excerpted it in an interview with Dream TV on February 7, 2011 that, "Everyone was contributing small pieces, bits and pieces. We drew this whole picture of a revolution. And no one is the hero in that picture". [19]

Contradictory Approach to Big Man Theory

What happened in the Arab world in recent past is worth noting that it has basically changed the trends of change. For most of the last century, the world operated on the big-man theory of politics: Towering personalities were required to drive big changes. Now it seems to have moved into the small-person era of history, in which seemingly insignificant people are setting off sweeping movements. This may be the most significant example of how the new media tools especially the satellite TV and Internet is changing the Arab world. The most important figures in Arab world undergoing historic ferment may well be the following people, all unknown and seemingly insignificant before now become icons of revolution:

Mohamed Bouazizi, a 26-year-old fruit vendor in Tunisia. He set himself on fire to protest humiliating treatment at the hands of the police in his hometown, Sidi Bouzid—the kind of treatment he and others accepted quietly before. Word of his act spread on the internet, inspiring a street uprising that toppled President Zine el-Abidine Ben Ali, helping fuel a similar one in Egypt.

Khaled Said, a 28-year-old businessman from Alexandria who had the temerity to post on the internet a video of Egyptian policemen stealing marijuana after a drug bust. After doing so, he was grabbed by police officers at a cafe, dragged outside and beaten to death. When photos of his beaten body began spreading on the internet, he, like Mohamed Bouazizi, became an inspiration for revolution.

Wael Ghonim, Google's head of marketing in the Middle East. He picked up the story of the beating of Khaled Said and began turning it into fodder for a people's uprising in Egypt by establishing a Facebook page devoted to the death, as well as working on other sites advocating political reform. Egyptian security forces tried to isolate him in silence by the arrest but failed to reckon that acted as a catalyst and intensified the uprising, his Internet following only increased with his disappearance.

Ahmed Maher is a 30-year-old civil engineer and a leading organizer of the April 6 Youth Movement. After a strike that march in the city of Mahalla, Egypt, Mr. Maher and his friends called for a nationwide general strike for April 6. To promote it, they set up a Facebook group that became the nexus of their movement, which they were determined to keep independent from any of the established political groups. Mr. Maher and others organized their own brigade, *Youth for Change*.

The new media technology provided these stories instant political power and that couldn't possibly have acquired this much intensity in the age when information moved slowly and bureaucracies had the ability to craft the narratives they desired for the masses to consume. The changed dynamic also made possible a remarkable event: a broad-based revolution in Tunisia and Egypt in which there was no obvious individual leader.

One may interprets the revolutions and uprising in the Arab world in their own way. But the fact remains that the youthful populations, high unemployment, grotesque inequality, abusive police, reviled leaders, and authoritarian systems that stifle free expression are realities of today's Arab world. The Arab world has for far too long suffered from religious extremism and dictatorship as well. But in today's connected world, where every one has similar access to what's happening across the world, it is tough to have any repressive religious viewpoint or regime attempting to tie people down for too long and the new media technology has provided a tool to masses to unite and fight against the long established repressive regimes that have been obvious in Egypt, Tunisia, Yemen, Libya, Bahrain, Jordan, and other Arab countries. It is time for the Arab world to accept this reality. This current wave of revolution may hopefully replace religious extremism and authoritarian dictatorships in the region by much more moderate values of the kind that will help the Arab world to integrate in a far more democratic manner with the rest of the world, something similar to what Indonesia is attempting.

Endnotes

1. Open Arab Net, available at, http://www.openarab.net/en/node/347.
2. "US Embassy Cables: Egypt's Bloggers Take on Key Role as Political Activists", Posted by guardian.co.uk on 28th January, 2011, available at, http://www.guardian.co.uk/world/us-embassy-cables-documents/199582.
3. "Reality Television and Arab Politics: Contention in Public Life" by M.M. Kraidy, Cambridge University Press, New York, 2010.
4. 'New Media and Public Relations', by Sandra C. Duhe, Peter Lang Publishing Inc. New York, 2007; and 'Transnational Media and Social Change in the Arab World' by Jon B. Alterman, *TBS Journal*, Issue No. 2, Spring 1999.
5. "Population Levels, Trends and Policies in the Arab Region: Challenges and Opportunities", by Barry Mirkin, United Nations Development Programme, Regional Bureau for Arab States, Arab Human Development Report, Research Paper Series 2010; available at, http://www.arab-hdr.org/publications/other/ahdrps/paper01-en.pdf.
6. Al-Jazeera: The Inside Story of the Arab News Channel That is Challenging the West, by Miles Hugh Grove Press, NY, 2006.
7. 'Al-Jazeera: How the Free Arab News Network Scooped the World and Changed the Middle East' by Mohammad El-Nawawy and Adel Iskandar, Cambridge Westview Press, 2002; and 'Al-Jazeera, the Inside Story of the Arab News Channel that is Challenging the West' by Hugh Miles, Grove Press, New York, 2005.
8. 'Al-Jazeera: The Story of the Network that is Rattling Governments and Redefining Modern Journalism' by Mohammad El-Nawawy and Adel Iskandar, Cambridge Westview Press, 2003.
9. 'Seizing a Moment, Al-Jazeera Galvanizes Arab Frustration' by Robert F. Worth and David D. Kirkpatrick, an article published in New York Times on January 28, 2011, accessed on February

4, 2011, available at, http://www.nytimes.com/2011/01/28/world/middleeast/28jazeera.html?_r=1.

10. "The new Arab Media Phenomenon: Qatar's Al-Jazeera", available at, http://www.thefreelibrary.com/The+new+Arab+Media+phenomenon:+Qatar's+Al-Jazeera.-a080013132.
11. Assistant professor of journalism and media studies and associate director of the Centre for Media, Religion and Culture at the University of Colorado-Boulder.
12. 'Al-Jazeera and the Promise of the Arab Revolution', by Nabil Echchaibi, accessed on February 2, 2011, available at, http://www.huffingtonpost.com/nabil-echchaibi/al-jazeera-and-the-promis_b_821105.html?ir=Media, Posted on February 9, 2011.
13. Ibid.
14. "Social Media Playing a Role in Arab World Protests", Article published in Voice of America, 26th January, 2011, available at, http://www.voanews.com/english/news/middle-east/Social-Media-Playing-a-Role-in-Arab-World-Protests-114672924.html.
15. 'How Social Media Accelerated the Uprising in Egypt', by E.B. Boyd, January 31, 2011, accessed on February 4, 2011, available at, http://www.fastcompany.com/1722492/how-social-media-accelerated-the-uprising-in-egypt.
16. Ibid.
17. "Egypt Protester: Tunisia Showed us Something Different Was Possible"' by Jack Shenker, February 14, 2011, available at, http://www.guardian.co.uk/world/2011/feb/14/egypt-youth-protest.
18. Ibid.
19. BBC News Service, http://www.bbc.co.uk/news/world-middle-east-12400529.

Part IV: Islam and Arab Spring

10

Turkish Faith-Based Civil Society's Transformative Influence on Islamism as an Inspiration to the Middle East

Ihsan Yilmaz

Introduction

Turkey could be an inspiration with its successes and failures for the Muslim World but not a model. When we talk about a model, are we talking about Turkey's record of authoritarianism that the Middle Eastern countries of the world have enough of it? Or are we talking about being a model with our Turkish nationalism that the Middle East has had enough of it too? The Turkish state has preferred the Sunni Turks over Alevi Turks and Kurds and has preferred non-practising Muslims over the practicing Muslims. Alevis, Kurds, practicing Muslims, together with the leftist, socialist, and so on, are perceived by the establishment as the major arch enemies of Turkish nationalism. And I believe Middle Eastern nations have enough of that as well.

So in that sense, the Turkish model could not work, or it is not a required model for the Middle East. Even in the era of multiparty politics, since 1950, we have had a military coup every ten years, every decade. The last one being on 27th of April, 2007, only five years ago when the military chief of staff was directly involved in politics, declaring the military's attitude against a presidential candidate whose wife wears a head scarf. And funnily enough, in the declaration which we call E-memorandum or e-coup, because it was on the internet website of the military chief of staff, they also could criticize Islam's prophet's birthday celebrations which were taking place all over Turkey. Can you imagine a military general criticizing Christmas celebrations in a country with predominantly Christian population? Ninety-nine per cent of Turkey's population is Muslim.

Nevertheless, is this a success? Of course from a nationalist perspective, it was, unfortunately, a success, in the lands of the Ottoman empire, which was a multi-national, multiethnic, multi-religious empire. The Young Turks who ruled Turkey single-handedly without allowing political opposition for about four decades until 1950 have succeeded in establishing a so-called homogeneous society but the Kurds have been resisting that. They have resisted being Turkified and they keep sticking to their lingual and ethic identities to the dismay of the Turkish generals. So I believe that Turkey with its tradition of military tutelage and direct interventions in politics could not be a role for the Middle Eastern nations for they have also enough of that as well.

What about the elite approach to democracy and the belittlement of the masses by the bureaucracy or the oligarchy (as we call it in Turkey) or the establishment, bureaucratic establishment together with the, of course, Istanbul business-tycoons that are, unfortunately, represented by some of the members of TUSIAD? And as the 2007 elections showed, when the AKP party won it with a landslide victory, receiving forty-six percent of the votes while the main opposition party received only about twenty-five percent of the votes, several secular elites called Turkish nation a stupid nation. And just after the 12th of June, 2011 referendum when the majority of the Turkish nation, fifty-eight percent of them voted in favour of pro-EU, pro democratization referendum, many of them also said the Turkish nation was stupid. I believe, with its Jacobinist elitism, disrespect for the nation and top-down social engineering, Turkey is not a required model for the Middle East.

So, if the traditional political setting in Turkey is not a model, is there anything in the Turkish experiment that is worthy of being emulated? I suggest that we should look at the transformation of the Turkish society vis-à-vis politics, secularism, democracy, and Islam. I believe this experience of Turkey could be inspirational for the Middle East. If in the post-9/11 world, if we keep talking about winning the hearts and minds of Muslims, then we need to look at the hearts and minds of Muslims in Turkey especially the practicing Muslims who have had their normative framework transformed as a result of several factors—not only one or two, but several—and also, we should look at the AK Party experience and how they have transformed themselves, their normative framework, their mental maps and so on from Islamism to post-Islamism, and to even, as I call it, non-Islamism.

I believe that the Turkish civil society has been influential in this transformation and especially faith-based movements established and operated by practicing Muslims in Turkey such as the Gulen movement—and of course, there are several others as well—have been instrumental in the Islamists' transformation to non-Islamism. This civil society model can be either a model or inspiration for the Middle Eastern nations especially when we take into account the fact that there are revolutions taking place in Middle Eastern societies nowadays. While Turkish Islamists' recent transformation that has brought about their rise to the power has been applauded at home and abroad, there are relatively very few studies that analyze their transformation by taking into account the unique experience of Turkish Islamism starting from the 18th and 19th centuries' Ottoman secularization, young Ottomans of the 1860s and the Ottoman constitutionalism and democracy.

Moreover, structural materialist analyses of Islamism and post-Islamism take globalization and Westernization as independent variables and try to analyze how they have influenced Islamists' behaviour. Although academics have drawn our attention to the globalization, international opportunity structures and failure of Islamist government experiences both in Turkey and abroad as the factors that have influenced the Islamists' transformation, the socio-cultural variable needs to be taken into account as well. [1] Dynamics that affected the change in the Turkish Islamists' Islamic normative framework have not been analyzed in detail.

Thus, this study endeavours to analyze the main factors behind the newly emerged tolerant normative framework of the JDP (Justice and Development Party) leaders who were formerly Islamist.

After showing that there are good historical reasons arising from the Ottoman experience of secularism and democracy and arguing based on a brief theoretical discussion of the plurality of Islamisms, I will discuss that the Turkish Islamism has always differed from the other Islamist experiences. Then, I will move on to the contemporary times and will attempt to show that Islamic groups' physical and discursive interaction has been a crucial factor in the Turkish Islamism's transformation.

I argue that the Gülen movement has been the most influential factor that has helped the JDP leaders to develop a more tolerant normative framework and to eventually jettison their Islamism. It is of course difficult to establish casual relationship between two social phenomena but we can underscore correlations. By focusing on the Gülen movement, I in no way disregard the other domestic influences such as the transformation of the formerly Islamist scholars and the newly emerged nascent Anatolian bourgeoisie. But still, I argue that the Gülen movement has been the most dominant factor, because, compared to the other factors, it is the most influential and widespread one with its schools, dormitories, businessmen associations, charities and the media organizations.

Secondly, when we look at the discourses of all main Islamic actors mentioned in this study from an historical perspective, we find that while Gülen has been advocating almost the same views for the last four decades, the other actors have had to adapt their views during the course of the same time span and what is more, their views converged to

Gülen's views. Needless to say, as I mainly focus on the socio-cultural factors that have influenced the transformation of the JDP leaders' normative frameworks, I will not be looking at the external factors such as global opportunity structures and domestic institutional constraints imposed by the aggressively laicist establishment that have already been discussed elsewhere.

As my main hypothesis is that the Gülen movement has been the most influential factor in the normative transformation of the former Islamists' mental frameworks and their religio-political worldviews, I will try to provide a comparative discourse analysis between Fethullah Gülen's and Islamists' ideas on several issues that have been relevant for both Islamism and newly-emerged post-Islamism.

Emergence of Republican Turkish Islamism

The Khalidi branch of the Nakhsbandi has been the most politically engaged of the brotherhoods, whose debut in national politics was led by Sheikh Mehmed Zahid Kotku (1897-1980) who preached that it was the duty of observant Muslims to take an active interest in national affairs. (Smith, 2005: 316) He did not perceive the secular state as an absolute enemy and, in that sense, did not hold much esteem for radical Islamists in the Muslim world. (Mardin, 2005: 158) He created a new version of the "operational code" of the brotherhood, synchronized with the political code promoted by the secular state, that of constitutional legitimacy. (Mardin, 2005: 158) By the 1970s, Kotku started promoting a second layer of legitimacy, working in tandem with Islamic legitimacy, was that of political institution building. (Mardin, 2005: 158) It was an aspect of a positive view of the state as an institution, also part of the Nakhsbandi tradition from Mevlanâ Halid to Bediüzzaman Said Nursi. (Mardin, 2005: 158)

Kotku's circle would include many prominent right-wing politicians. The first prominent Islamist party in Republican Turkey, the National Order Party (*Milli Nizam Partisi*, MNP)

(1970-71), and the National Salvation Party (*Millî Selamet Partisi*, MSP) (1972-81) were established through his promotion and support and he had supervised their activities. (Cakir, 1994: 22 cited in Mardin, 2005: 157) [2] The leader of these parties, Prof. Necmettin Erbakan, was a disciple of Kotku. Most of the leaders of Erbakan's the National Order Party, were also disciples of Kotku and political parties founded by the leadership of Erbakan always carried a deep communitarian identity. (Yildirim et al., 2007: 6) His parties were composed of strong grassroots organizations reflecting communitarian, family, and religious order mentality and "communitarian imaginations and aspirations dominated his parties". (Yildirim et al., 2007: 6)

Erbakan's Islamist movement is known as *Milli Görüş* (National View or Outlook) that embraced a set of aspiring yet ambiguous references to the Ottoman past, and directed criticism against "cosmopolitanism" as opposed to the "national" (Dagi, 2005: 24) Here, nationalism, a primary motto of the secular Turkish Republic, promoted as religio-nationalism by Erbakan's parties, was not an obstacle but a shared feeling of pride—first "Ottoman" then "Turkish"—that had been building since Abdülhamid II. (Mardin, 2005: 157-158) Erbakan's intellectual sources and industrial connections to the Anatolian middle-sized conservative capitalists brought about "an interesting amalgam of traditional Sunni-based Islamic culture and Sufi worldview embedded within a developmentalist discourse". (Yildiz, 2003)

The first of several Islamic parties led by Necmettin Erbakan, National Order Party (MNP), was established in January 1970. It espoused a discourse of new economic and social order based on "national" as opposed to Western principles. In MNP's view, Turkey's identity and future was with the Muslim world, rather than with the West. The party was shut down after a military intervention in 1971 on the ground that it was against the secularism.

The National Salvation Party [*Milli Selamet Partisi*

(MSP)] was founded in October 1972 after the generals called Erbakan back from voluntary exile in Switzerland with a hope of dividing Suleyman Demirel's centre-right Justice Party's [*Adalet Partisi* (AP)] share of the votes. MSP's ideology was almost the same as the closed MNP. The MNP argued that the Westernization had fragmented Turkish society. Erbakan envisaged that based on Anatolian heavy industry, a stronger Turkey would loosen the ties with the West and would become the leader of the Muslim world under the umbrella of a Muslim Common Market, with the Islamic *dinar* as its common currency. Also, a Muslim Defence Alliance would be developed.

After the military coup in 1980, the MSP was also closed down together with all other political parties. When the army returned back to its barracks in 1983, Erbakan founded a new party under a new name—the Welfare Party [*Refah Partisi* (RP)]. The Welfare's ideology was not different from that of the MSP. Welfare had steadily increased its share of the votes and after the 1994 general local elections; mayors of several major cities such as Ankara and Istanbul (current Prime Minister Recep Tayyip Erdogan became the mayor of Istanbul at that date) were Welfare members. The trends in the political and economic aspects of the Turkish society from the 1980 military intervention through the 1990s were advantageous for the Islamists and '(b)oth the military and the government were supportive of a nationalist view of Islam. Islam gradually became politicized. For the new middle and bourgeoisie classes, Islamic movements and networks provided social capital with which to establish business links and NGOs". (Yildirim et al., 2007: 7)

In 1996, as the bigger partner of a coalition government with the True Path Party [*Dogru Yol Partisi* (DYP)], Necmettin Erbakan became Turkey's first Islamist prime minister. One of his first acts was to invite—officially non-existent—Islamic brotherhoods' leaders to an *iftar* dinner to the Prime Ministry. Not surprisingly, secularists were all up in arms. He then went on to establish an economic cooperation pact with 8 biggest Muslim nations under the name D-8. He had not had any friends in the West and this attempt increased the number of his foes both at home and abroad. A psychological warfare accompanied by a media campaign was launched trying to prove that the country was under the occupation of radical and strange-looking Islamists. On February 28, 1997, the military dominated National Security Council presented Erbakan with a list of "recommendations" (read orders) to curb the alleged anti-secular activities.

Meanwhile, the generals invited the top echelons of bureaucracy (governors, judges and all others) to a series of secularism-in-danger briefings and mobilized the establishment against the Welfare Party, eventually forcing Erbakan to resign in June 1997 in what has been called a "post-modern" coup. In January 1998, the Constitutional Court closed down Welfare Party and banned Erbakan from politics for five years. Acutely being aware of history's repetition, this time Erbakan's new party was already ready before the closure decision. The Virtue Party [*Fazilet Partisi* (FP)] continued operating under Erbakan's close friend Recai Kutan's leadership until it was also shut down by the Constitutional Court in June 2001.

The Virtue Party was a post-Islamist party and thus we will analyze it in a separate section. For all the other parties that Erbakan formed and led, serving the religion was a crucial factor. These parties heavily used religion as the dominating parameter of their "political discourse, among the characteristics of which were: confining religious concepts and values to a certain group, nationalizing, modernizing, secularizing and politicizing them, making use of political opinions held by Muslims in the generic sense as the criterion for the religious brotherhood, the sectarian possession of its contributions to religious life and hence causing people of different political convictions and preferences to feel cold against the religion and making them hold anti-religion attitudes, functioning as a non-systemic party while operating within systemic boundaries, if necessary, by instrumentalizing the religion". (Yildiz, 2003) Erbakan had intolerant and exclusivist rhetoric. His discourse justified itself by the alleged existence of a monolithic "other".

He constantly blamed all others as blind imitators of the West. He was upset with many religious brotherhoods and communities that never voted for his parties and he did not think they were good Muslims as he believed politics was based on "the truth versus wrong", him representing the truth. His followers were quick to label people as the voice of America or even worse as CIA agents. Erbakan himself "was accusing those who did not vote for RP as belonging to "religion of potato," instead of Islam". (Kuru, 2007: 145) He was of the opinion that "the political party means the religion" and, accordingly, those Muslims who have not belonged to the party or lent support to it have been warned that they may be subject to spiritual sanctions/hazards". (Yildiz, 2003) In Erbakan's view "elections are the counting of Muslims in Turkey". (Yildiz, 2003); (Yildiz, 2003: f. n. 19) On October 4, 1973, *Milli Gazete's* headline was "Not Parties but Beliefs are in Collision in the Election". (Yildiz, 2003: f. n. 19) Erbakan was not always exclusivist: "The Prophet Adam was Welfarist. Likewise, all the past prophets were partisans of WP, so was the Sultan Mehmet II (The Conqueror)". (quoted in Yildiz, 2003)

In the beginning of the multiparty politics in 1950s, both nationalism and Islamism were represented in the centre-right parties. The coexistence of nationalism and Islamism is one of the reasons "why Islamism emerged in the form of Islamic nationalism even when it gained an independent existence. Thus, the conception of an anti-Western Islamism structured by a national Islamism/Islamic nationalism, with a heavy emphasis both in NSP and WP, became one of the main leitmotifs characterizing their politico-religious discourse". (Yildiz, 2003) Similar to the world wide Islamist discourse, the Turkish Islamists have also envisaged capturing the state and using it to socially engineer top down Islamist transformation in society by adopting the centralism of the state.

Fethullah Gülen's Civil Islam Discourse and Hizmet Movement

Now, we turn our attention to the most resonant voice of non-Islamist (apolitical) tradition in Turkey, the roots of which are older than the Islamist tradition. Fethullah Gülen's apolitical Islamic understanding is not of course unique neither in Turkey nor in the Muslim World but his both intellectual power and *alim* credentials and wide influence over the Turkish society as a whole makes him and his influential movement relevant for our discussion. To see if and to what extent, Gülen and his movement have influenced the transformation of Turkish Islamism to non-Islamism, from Milli Görüş to JDP, we will now analyze the discourse of Gülen on secularism, pluralism, democracy, rule of law, nationalism, state, Islamism, religiosity, the other, borders and dialogue.

In Gülen's view, the faithful can comfortably live in secular environments "(i)f secularity is understood as the state not being founded on religion, hence it does not interfere with religion or religious life; and as the faithful living his religion does not disturb others; and furthermore if the state will accomplish this task in a serious neutrality, then there is no problem". (Armagan and Unal: 108, quoted in Altunoglu, 1999: 103) He makes a reference to an Anglo-Saxon understanding of passive secularism and argues that within the boundaries of this type of secularism, Islam and secularity of the state could be compatible. (Yilmaz, 2000: 5) As for secular law-making, in his view, Islam does not have a problem with it.

In Islam, the legislative and executive institutions have always been allowed to make laws. These are based on the needs and betterment of society and within the frame of general norms of law. On domestic issues in the Islamic community and its relationship with other nations, including economic, political and cultural relations, Muslims have always developed laws. The community members are required to obey the laws that one can identify as "higher principles" as well as laws made by humans. Islam has no objection to undertaking *ijtihad* (independent reasoning), *istinbat* (deductive reasoning), and *istikhraj* (derivation) in the interpretation of *Shari'ah* principles. (Gülen, 2005: 450)

Gülen's views on democracy are well-known. He has been underlining for a long time that "Islam does not propose a certain unchangeable form of government or attempt to shape it. Instead, Islam establishes fundamental principles that orient a government's general character, leaving it to the people to choose the type and form of government according to time and circumstances". (Gülen, 2006: 14) Fundamental principles Islam prescribes, accruing to Gülen, are social contact and election of a group of people to debate common issues. (Gülen, 2006: 17) Gülen summarizes the theological reasons why Islam considers that people are responsible for their own fate and thus governance:

Islam considers a society to be composed of conscious individuals equipped with free will and having responsibility toward both themselves and others. Islam goes a step further by adding a cosmic dimension. It sees humanity as the "motor" of history, contrary to fatalistic approaches of some of the nineteenth century Western philosophies of history such as dialectical materialism and historicism. Just as every individual's will and behaviour determine the outcome of his or her life in this world and in the hereafter, a society's progress or decline is determined by the will, worldview, and lifestyle of its inhabitants. The Koran (13:11) says, "God will not change the state of a people unless they change themselves [with respect to their beliefs, worldview, and lifestyle]". In other words, each society holds the reins of its fate in its own hands. The prophetic tradition emphasizes this idea, "You will be ruled according to how you are". This is the basic character and spirit of democracy, which does not conflict with any

Islamic principle. As Islam holds individuals and societies responsible for their own fate, people must be responsible for governing themselves. (Gülen, 2006: 16)

Gülen's understanding of majority rule does not permit a tyranny of majority, "members of minority communities should be allowed to live according to their beliefs. If these sorts of legislations are made within the norms of international law and international agreements, Islam will have no objection to any of these. No one can ignore the universal values that the Qur'an and the *Sunnah* have presented with regard to the rights mentioned above". (Gülen, 2005: 451)

Whenever speaking on the issue of democracy, Gülen constantly reminds us that Islam is a religion and thus is more than a political method, system or ideology.

On the issue of Islam and democracy, one should remember that the former is a divine and heavenly religion, while the latter is a form of government developed by humans. The main purposes of religion are faith (*iman*), servanthood to God ("*ubudiyyah*), knowledge of God (*ma*"*rifah*), and beautiful actions (*ihsan*). The Qur'an, in its hundreds of verses, invites people to the faith and worship of the True (*al-Haqq*). It also asks people to deepen their servanthood to God in a way that they may gain the consciousness of *ihsan*. "To believe and do good deeds", is among the subjects that Qur'an emphatically stresses. It also frequently reminds people that they must develop a conscious relationship with God and act as if they see God, or as if they are seen by God. (Gülen, 2005: 451-452)

Gülen has been defined as nationalist but when analyzed in detail it will be seen that he cannot be a nationalist for various reasons. First of all, as an observant Muslim, he can only be a patriot and love his people but this cannot be to the exclusion of others. Secondly, he has followers and sympathizers all over the world, including many Kurds in Turkey. A nationalist stance would deter all these people. Third, one of his intellectual predecessors, Said Nursi, was a

Kurd and Gülen has Kurdish friends in his close circle. Overwhelming majority of Gülen's close friends is from Western Anatolia, a region that is not known for its strong nationalist sentiments unlike several inner Anatolian cities. Last but not the least, whenever Gülen talks positively about Turks, he makes clear that the main reason of his respect is Turks' heroic service to the cause of Islam. Any nation that fares better will be appreciated by Gülen as he appreciates and admires past successful eras of several non-Turkish Muslim individuals and nations such as Abbasids and so on.

Fethullah Gülen has stayed away from ideologisation and instrumentalisation of religion in politics. While Islamists had conceived Islam as identity, ideology and politics and focused on religion instead of religiosity, Gülen had been harshly critical of Islamists. "The distinction between political ambition and religious activism is crucial for a correct understanding of Gülen's mission". (Ozdalga, 2000)

The phrase, "Sovereignty belongs to the nation unconditionally", does not mean that sovereignty has been taken from God and given to humans. On the contrary, it means that sovereignty is entrusted to humans by God, that is to say it has been taken from individual oppressors and dictators and given to the community members. To a certain extent, the era of the Rightly-Guided Caliphs of Islam illustrates the application of this norm of democracy. Cosmologically speaking, there is no doubt that God is the sovereign of everything in the universe. Our thoughts and plans are always under the control of the power of such an Omnipotent. However, this does not mean that we have no will, inclination or choice. Humans are free to make choices in their personal lives. They are also free to make choices with regard to their social and political actions. (Gülen, 2005: 453)

Gülen also flatly rejects the totalizing ideology of Islamism. This vision of Islam as a totalising ideology is totally against the spirit of Islam, which promotes the rule of law and openly rejects oppression against any segment of society. This spirit also promotes actions for the betterment of society in accordance with the view of the majority. Those who follow a more moderate pattern also believe that it would be much better to introduce Islam as a complement to democracy instead of presenting it as an ideology. Such an introduction of Islam may play an important role in the Muslim world through enriching local forms of democracy and extending it in such a way that helps humans develop and understanding of the relationship between the spiritual and material worlds. I believe that Islam also would enrich democracy in answering the deep needs of humans, such as spiritual satisfaction, which cannot be fulfilled except through the remembrance of the Eternal One. (Gülen, 2005: 452)

He is also well aware that generally speaking Islamism is a reactive and reactionary ideology that is formed by contemporary human and social needs rather than what actually religion dictates. Put differently, he strongly refutes the claim of the Islamists that what they advocate is indeed the true, authentic, original and pure Islam. (Gülen, 2005: 455)

He repeatedly declared that there is no particular model for either the method of election or the system of administration. He explains that,...in Islam it is not possible to limit the concept of governance and politics into a single paradigm, unlike the principles of faith and the pillars of Islam. History shows us that in the Islamic world, since the time of the Prophet, there have been many types of states. This is so even if we exclude the elections in the early period of Islam and the qualities that were exhibited in those elections. Even if one cannot see some major methodological differences among these types of governance, there are many differences in the details. Those who are not aware of the principles of these different methods of governing have understood each of them as a separate system. I have to note that these differences were the result of the aspects of religion that are open to interpretation and related to the field of independent reasoning (*Ijtihad*). (Gülen, 2005: 454)

Recently, Gülen has been arguing that in this age Islam does not need a state support, which is a new ijtihad. He does not oppose to the idea of mutual autonomy of state and Islam. He puts that "(i)f a state...gives the opportunity to its citizens to practice their religion and supports them in their thinking, learning, and practice, this system is not considered to be against the teaching of the Qur'an. In the presence of such a state there is no need to seek an alternative state". (Gülen, 2005: 451) He also told Ali Bulac that establishing and Islamic state is not a religious duty for Muslim individuals and that in this age civil society can independently maintain Islam even where Muslims are not in majority.

Gülen is a modern version of *alim* (singular of *ulama*) and *ulama* never engage in a selective reading of the sources as Islamists do. While Islamists did not respect the authority of the *ulama*, Gülen, backed up by his intellectual power too, helped *ulama* profile regain its prestige back among cosmopolitan urban middle class white collars, a base Islamists were trying to address. [3] Gellner argues that development and education have been conducive, rather than detrimental, to teaching the orthodox practices of Islam because, in the past, the knowledge-based orthodox (*ulama*-formulated) observance was generally limited to more educated and urbanite Muslims; while the practices of the rural periphery were intermingled with superstition and, in some cases, remnants of pre-Islamic practices. (Gellner, 1992: 2-22) Today it is possible for many more Muslims to adhere to the orthodox practices. This observance is not seen as a sign of backwardness. (Gellner, 1992: 2-22) This is definitely the case with white-collars and cosmopolitan middle classes that compose majority of Gülen's followers and sympathizers.

Ulama, unlike the Islamists, look at the issues from a holistic point of view. For instance that is why Gülen could see many verses in Qur'an that strongly encourage dialogue while many Islamists were busy portraying all non-Muslims in the same manner. While Islamists focused on political acts, Gülen keeps reiterating that hereafter is much more important and his life in the 5th floor revolves around worship. Gülen transcends the strictly scripturalist and literalist Salafi epistemology by attempting to rehabilitate Sufi concepts and by focusing on the renewal of inner faith. This is reminiscent of the approach adopted by previous Islamic activists and intellectuals who, like al-Banna (d. 1949) in Egypt, Muhammad Iqbal (d. 1938) in colonial India, and Said Nursi (d. 1960) in Turkey who were conscious of the spiritual dimension of Islam.

Paul Tillich coined the term "the *ultimate concern*" that is, what a community or individual considers to be of most importance, "Whatever concerns a man ultimately becomes god for him...and conversely, it means that a man can be concerned ultimately only about that which is good for him". (Tillich, 1951: 211) Gülen's ultimate concern in this life differs from many Islamists at least in the sense that what they do in practice. While Islamists focus on political acts, a socially active Gülen reiterates that hereafter is much more important and worship is vitally important. He does not see the Qur'an as a political book or project.

The Qur'an is a translation of the book of the universe, which comes from the divine commands of creation, an interpretation of the world of the unseen, of the visible and invisible. It is an explanation of the reflections of the divine names on earth and in the heavens. It is a prescription for the various problems of the Islamic world. It is a guide for bliss in this life and in the life to come. It is a great guide for the travellers in this world moving towards the hereafter. It is an inexhaustible source of wisdom. Such a book should not be reduced to the level of political discourse, nor should it be considered a book about political theories or forms of state. To consider the Qur'an as an instrument of political discourse is a great disrespect for the Holy Book and is an obstacle that prevents people from benefiting from this deep source of divine grace. (Gülen, 2005: 456)

Gülen's discourse has been influential primarily in the

movement named after him. Atay (2007: 459, 467) gives details about how his discourse and praxis in relation to piety, spirituality and worship influence also his movement.

It is obvious that Gülen is not a socially inactive thinker and practitioner who formulates a discourse and practices it and then only passively observes if people discover and emulate them. Gülen seeks to actively engage with this world by teaching and presenting his weltanschauung and its praxis. Atay's observations are also confirmed by Vicini (2007: 439) who did a field research among the movement's adherents and sympathizers, "I am not arguing disciplinary aspects disappear from Gülen's view on Islam. Firstly, because Gülen is a strenuous defender of Islamic pillars and the need to accomplish them. Adherents to the movement—overall people who aim at becoming educators—perform *namaz* five times per day and often even perform the meritorious one during the night. Secondly, volunteers of the movement, by endlessly engaging in activism, really follow a very disciplined life".

Unlike Islamists, Gülen does not pursue an identity politics and does not define himself by the Other. In other words, he does not have a constitutive other. In his discourse, "(o)therization and adversary component is weak" (Komecoglu, 1997: 86), which is not reactive but proactive, not having "us" versus "them" coarse schism. To put it differently, "unlike the confrontational New Social Movements, the Gülen movement has engaged in 'moral opposition', in which the movement's actors seek to empathize with the adversary by creating (what Bakhtin calls) 'dialogic' relationships". (Gurbuz, 2007: 104)

Gülen does not see the world in political terms and does not draw imaginary boundaries. As skilfully expressed by Klas Grinell (2010), Gülen is a "border transgressor". Gülen's frequently used term *dar al-hizmet* (country of service) reflects his border transgressing vision. (Yilmaz, 2003: 234) By employing *ijtihad*, he bases this border transgressing understanding on and also extends to the Islamic jurisprudence (*fiqh*). He does not divide the world by employing mutually exclusive concepts of *dar al-harb* (abode of war) and *dar-al Islam* (abode of Islam, peace) but sees it as an almost coherent place, as it were, that needs to be served continually by utilizing the concept *dar al-hizmet* (abode of service to humans, thereby God). (Yilmaz, 2007: 35) Gülen stresses that wherever a Muslim is, even outside a Muslim polity; he or she has to obey the law of the land, to respect others' rights and to be just, and has to disregard discussions of *dar al-harb* and *dar al-Islam*. In Gülen's understanding, *umma* is a transnational socio-cultural entity, not a utopian politico-legal one. (Yilmaz, 2003: 235)

He does not see the world not in terms of Muslims versus others. He also does not think that trying to revive the Caliphate is feasible, "I would say that the revival of the Caliphate would be very difficult and making Muslims accept such a revived *Khilafah* would be impossible. The perception of the modern world regarding the revival of *Khilafah* must be considered". (Gülen, 2005: 457) Gülen "subscribes to a remarkably different interpretation of the Muslim world and realistically draws the boundaries where Turkey can play a leadership role. He did not regard D-8 optimistically and considered it Erbakan's cheap message to his constituency. Such initiatives are, for Gülen, quite adventurous and risky, and therefore a waste of time". (Kosebalaban, 1999: 175)

He rejects that a clash between the "East" and "West" is necessary, desirable or unavoidable. In Gülen's worldview, an abstract West is not the enemy of Muslims but ignorance, poverty and disunity are: "unlike many Islamic revivalist movements, the Gülen movement shaped its identity against the perceived threat of a trio of enemies, as Nursi named them a century ago—ignorance, disunity, and poverty. This perception of the opposition is crucial to understanding the apolitical mind-set of the Gülen movement's followers". (Gurbuz, 2007: 104)

He has been supportive of Turkey's accession to the

European Union. (Ünal and Williams, 2000: 189) "Gülen's pro-Western attitude has played a key role in the domestication and softening of other Islamist groups' anti-Europe and anti-U.S. positions. Although many Islamists eventually came closer to embracing this idea, a majority of them initially criticized Gülen for his pro-Europe views. He was one of the first Islamic leaders to embrace the idea of EU membership and at a time when Islamists in general regarded it as a threat to Turkish security and Islamic culture". (Kosebalaban. 1999: 176)

Gülen's self-confidence and positive view of the world are "in contrast to Wahhabism, Tablighism, and Jihadism". Sufism as advanced by the Gülen movement has a positive view of the world entire. The internal workings of the universe—science, history, politics, art and culture, philosophy—are not something Muslims should fear or stuff into an Islamized box but rather engage positively in view of the spiritual insight of Islam". (Heck, 2007: 645)

Gülen's "acceptance of the two Turkish identities—European and Islamic—as complementary rather than contradictory was innovative at a time when both secular and Islamist identities totally rejected this duality. Gülen's national-security identity encourages Turkish foreign-policy decision makers to remain fully on track with EU membership. As a leader of a significant Islamic movement, he gave his approval to this policy goal. Many Turkish Islamists joined him later, unloading the Islamic element in the anti-EU camp. Yet Gülen also defends the argument that the success of Turkish diplomacy in the West lies with its success in the East". (Kosebalaban, 1999: 182)

In comparison to Islamism's simple but abstract assertion to surrendering to the ancestors, i. e. returning to the golden age of pristine Islam will solve all problems of Muslims; Gülen endeavours a concrete socio-economic and cultural analysis of the current spatio-temporal context and based on this analysis offers concrete solutions to tackle Muslims' enemies rather than insisting on abstract rhetoric. If ignorance is one of three major enemies, then the Gülen project's offer would be education at different levels, not only at schools or not only religious education. Gülen's educational project covers life. It is not only confined to mosque nor is it only confined to secular schools. It also includes family education, child upbringing (see his book *Cekirdekten Cinara*), educating religious scholars (Atay, 2007), educating by example (*tamsil*) not only in classrooms etc. If poverty is Muslims' second enemy, then Gülen's offer would be establishing charity organizations (Kimse Yok Mu?) in addition to education's indirect help to lift people's socio-economic status. If dissention or internal conflict is the third major enemy, then, dialogue, tolerance and mutual understanding are the remedies to tackle this conflict. As can be seen, Gülen movement's major projects all focus on either of these three areas and the movement's media organizations play also supporting roles in this global civil activism.

Non-Islamism: Justice and Development Party (JDP)

The renewalists of the Virtue party continued to adhere to their renewalist discourse and as JDP leaders have frequently asserted universal values and value-based discourses such as human rights, democracy, and free market principles. (Yildirim et al., 2007: 17) As they departed their ways with the Islamist wing of the Virtue Party, their new discourse is no longer a hybrid (post-Islamism of the Virtue Party) form of Islamism and universal liberal democratic conservative values. While acknowledging the importance of religion as personal belief, they accommodated themselves within the secular constitutional framework. (Mecham, 2004: 350) They completely jettisoned the Islamist elements in their previous post-Islamist rhetoric and underscored a non-Islamist, as it were, universal liberal democratic conservative discourse. Yet, they are in no way non-Muslims despite Erbakan's implications even though, ironically, from an Islamist point of view, there is no difference between non-Islamist and non-Muslim. As a matter of fact, "the most radical and harsh criticisms of the AKP came from the Happiness Party, which is now the single representative of the National Outlook Movement". (Yildirim et al., 2007: 17)

Erdoğan frequently states that his party is a conservative democrat party, implying a Muslim democrat party similar to Christian Democrats in Western Europe in which an Anglo-Saxon type passive secularism is espoused where public visibility of religion is tolerated but religion is only a cultural backdrop rather than an active part of the Islamist discourse. In direct contrast to Islamists' formulation of political identity based on opposition to the West, the JDP has steadily emphasized Western political values. At the same time, the party has viewed the West, especially the EU, as an important ally in democratization of Turkey. The party "successfully linked traditional identity and issues of social and distributive justice to a global 'Third Way' between a statist economy and unfettered capitalism". (Smith, 2005: 322)

The JDP has attracted the votes of a broad constituency, cutting across class, gender, and ethnic (and religious) lines, and who previously had voted for mainstream right and Islamist parties. In the 3 November 2002 election, it won 34 per cent of the votes and increased its share of the votes to 47 per cent in 22 July 2007 elections, the main opposition party receiving only 21 percent. In the 2007 elections, many Turkish-Armenians reportedly voted for the JDP as well.

Factors that Influenced the Transformation from Milli Görüş to JDP

Globalization, international opportunity structures [4] and failure of Islamist government experiences in countries such as Sudan, Pakistan and Iran coupled with the awareness of the fact that some Islamists who severed their ties with the tradition and bypassed several centuries' experiences have gone out of their way and become extremely radicalized are some of the external or non-domestic factors that influenced Turkish Islamists to change their discourse. In the domestic context, there are two major factors that contributed to the change. First is the desire to avoid from confrontation with the aggressively laicist establishment as this would prevent Islamists to stay in power even if they rise to it as the Welfare Government experience showed. Constraints imposed by the laicist establishment and state "structure have limited Islamist actions and provided distinct opportunities for the emergence of a brand of reformist new thinking". (Cavdar, 2006: 480) Second major factor is a tolerant normative framework that has brought about Turkish Islamists' transformation.

As I have tried to analyze in the preceding sections, there are several factors that influenced the emergence of this tolerant framework. Turkish exceptionalism, to use Serif Mardin's terminology, has always been a factor in the Turkish Islamism's moderation. For instance, its close ties with the Nakhsbandi tradition differentiate Turkish Islamism from the majority of Islamist ideologies and movements worldwide. Turkish constitutional and democratic history starting from the Ottoman times and the fact that the country has never been colonized by the European imperialist powers have also contributed to the moderate and less than reactionary nature of the Turkish Islamism. Moreover, "(t)he state policies of creating the parameters for Islamist parties further moderated the already mild nature of political Islam in Turkey". (Cavdar, 2006: 486)

Islamic groups' both physical and discursive interaction is also a major factor in the Turkish Islamism's transformation. Whilst it is difficult to establish casual relationship between different social phenomena, it is still possible to underscore correlations. A number of academics including myself (Yilmaz, 2000, 2003, 2005; Kuru, 2007; Maigre, 2007) have argued that the Islamists' "transformation was not an isolated event, but part of a larger experience that several other Islamic groups took part in" (Kuru, 2007: 141) In the words of

Elisabeth Maigre (2007: 42) "(w)hile it is quite difficult to tell which group has had the foremost influence, researchers and academics have outlined the inter-connection between the Islamic bourgeoisie, the moderate Islamists, and the Gülen movement. It is noteworthy that many of these business people as well as some Virtue and later JDP politicians sent their children to Gülen's schools. Furthermore, Zaman is the second largest daily newspaper, the largest in Anatolian towns, and the majority of Virtue and JDP's supporters, including the businessmen, are regular readers". (Maigre, 2007: 42)

Kuru (2007: 141) also argues "that the AKP leaders' interaction with the Gülen movement, in this regard, played an important role in the formation of the party's new perspective toward secularism". With regards to politicization of Islam, it is—at least—fair to suggest that "(t)he emergence of the Justice and Development Party has shown that Muslim politics in Turkey is evolving from an instrumentalist usage of Islam to a new understanding of practicing Muslims who have to deal with daily politics. This evolution is obviously what Gülen has been advocating over the past three decades". (Yilmaz, 2003: 227) Maigre (2007: 45) concurs, "By anticipating the need to adapt Islam to the present times, confident that the Turkish republic would have to adapt too and open itself to more diversity, Gülen has been a visionary. He has unlocked the way to a new global culture that places Muslim Democrats ahead of any radical thinking and he has sent a strong message to the Muslim world showing a successful way towards democratic transition and gradual adaptation to Globalization without losing landmarks and religious background". (Maigre, 2007: 45)

Maigre (2007: 34) further argues "that Gülen's cultural and religious influence on both the business and political classes within the Islamic movement has driven the moderation of political Islam and open the way toward the integration into the new reality of globalization where the frontier between religion and business are blurred and those notions are brought together within a new conception of Culture". (Maigre, 2007:34) Gülen's competitive Islamic discourse which is not anti-western, tolerant, pluralistic, politically and economically more liberal etc. has weakened the influence of Erbakan's Islamism on the wider socially conservative masses of Anatolia including the nascent Anatolian elite. This social base was much larger than the base of Milli Görüş and has become more open to Gülen's discourse.

Export-oriented and liberalizing reforms of Turgut Ozal that integrated the country to the global structures and trends also made it possible for Anatolia's culturally conservative, religiously observant but economically liberal bourgeoning bourgeoisie to be major players in the Turkish domestic scene. These new classes are more liberal than the Istanbul bourgeoisie as they were export-oriented unlike Istanbul businesses. As observed by Barkey and Congar (2008: 66):

Following Ozal's reforms in the 1980s, this new business elite took advantage of the economic liberalization to internationalize itself. In the process, Anatolian-based businesses gained self-confidence, lessening fear of the outside world. As more flexible and adaptive newcomers, this new class tacitly endorsed the EU process and demonstrated very little, if any, opposition to privatization efforts. It is this socially conservative but economically liberal business elite that forms the backbone of the AKP's support. While they may not evidence the sophistication of Istanbul-based capital, the Anatolian tigers, as they are also known, have extensive networks and can help finance political parties and related activities. While piety is an important element of their identity, this does not interfere with their ability to participate in that most secular of institutions, the market. (Barkey and Congar, 2008: 66)

These people have sent their children to secular educational establishments where they could learn a European language, instead of sending them to *madrassah* or state's

Imam Hatip Schools. In most cases, as there were only Gülen movement's schools that could provide this opportunity, most of the new elite's children and thus indirectly themselves have become acquainted with the movement and its worldview. As a matter of fact, in most cases the boundaries between these new elites and the Gülen movement supporters are blurred and it is the members of this Anatolian bourgeoisie who actually fund and establish the Gülen schools, after seeing their success in other Anatolian towns and cities.

These new middle classes have always been in close contact with both centre-right and Islamist parties, influencing centre rights parties to be more Islamic and Islamist parties to be more centre-right. Many provincial Islamist politicians have also sent their own children to Gülen schools. We must also note that the Gülen media is the largest in almost all Anatolian cities. The Zaman daily is currently the country's most circulated newspaper with an oscillating circulation between 800,000 and 1,000,000. Samanyolu TV is one of the major TV channels in the country and it is widely watched in Anatolia especially by right-wing and conservative and religious people.

As Kuru (2007: 145) underlines, Abant Platform and the Gülen Media are the two major public mediums that the younger generation Milli Görüş politicians and the Gülen movement were able to discursively interact:

For example, in February 2000, Erdoğan and Arınç first publicized their new discourse in Zaman. In two separate interviews, these two leaders emphasized democracy as their priority and embraced (passive) secularism while criticizing the idea of an Islamic state. These two interviews received the attention of other newspapers. Assertive secularist Hürriyet positively announced them in its headline "Political Islam at the Crossroads," while Islamist Vakit criticized them arguing that Zaman corrupted Erdoğan and Arınç's mind. (Kuru, 2007: 145)

Among the attendants of the Abant platform meetings were several leaders, founding members and ministers of the

JDP such as Abdullah Gül, Bulent Arınç, Cemil Çiçek, Ali Coşkun, and Nevzat Yalçıntaş. Moreover the chairperson of the meetings, theology professor Mehmet Aydın, and some frequent participants, such as associate professor of political science Hüseyin Çelik and constitutional law professor Burhan Kuzu, joined them the new generation former—Islamists when they founded the JDP. (Kuru, 2007: 145-146)

Islamic and Islamist intellectuals' transformation is another important factor that influenced the paradigmatic shift in the minds of Turkish Islamists. After the 28th February, 1997 post-modern coup that directly aimed at terminating all Islamic activities, groups, social projects and bourgeoisie, these intellectuals also have come to the views of Gülen that he has been advocating since 1960s. They stated that under the new post-28 February domestic and post-9/11 global "conditions, the old discourse and actions of the previous parties had become "useless", and they called for an accommodationist rather than a confrontational approach". (Cavdar, 2006: 482) In fact, these Muslim intellectuals were never "unwilling urban residents yearning to return to the security of the rural town or village where there was no need to think through who one was and what one was to do.

They are very much creatures of the contemporary Turkish city, like their secular counterparts". (Meeker, 1991: 217) Dagi (2004: 135-136) observes that these Muslim intellectuals "appear to have abandoned their ideas for the construction of an alternative social and political order that in effect enabled them to seek a rapprochement with the West, Western ideas and institutions. The alternative to the established political regime is no longer searched for in Islam but rather in modernity and its political architecture". As the most prominent of these Muslim intellectuals, Ali Bulac, affirmed long ago, these intellectuals now accept that "if the meaning of political Islam is to establish a theocratic state, it is finished", pointing out that being, once, a cause for conflict and polarization, Islam is now a base for conciliation (Bulac, 2000).

These "intellectual leaders of post-Islamism have been searching for a rapprochement with the West, but not out of necessity to form a temporary alliance to confront the Kemalist state apparatus. Rather, this rapprochement is part of an effort to rethink modern political notions like democracy, human rights, and integration into the globalization process, including Turkey's membership in the European Union". (Dagi, 2004: 136) Other than being directly and normatively influenced by the new Anatolian elite, the Gülen movement, its schools and media, and the post-Islamist intellectuals, the younger generation Islamists were also aware of the fact that the new middle classes would no longer vote for an Islamist party after the failure of the Welfare in power. As Ihsan Dagi (2004: 140) observes:

Since 1997, the Islamists have seen Islam's social bases with its educational, commercial, and solidarity networks disrupted by the politicization of Islam, which exposed Islamic networks to the assault of the Kemalists. Because the visibility and power of Islam in the political realm justified only the counter-attack of the Kemalists, the threatened Islamists have become more interested in keeping Islam's social and economic structures intact as the bases for social 'conservatism'. Therefore, ideas for a 'social' rather than a 'political' Islam have gained ground, perfectly displayed by the acknowledgement of the ruling Justice and Development Party (JDP), despite its Islamic roots, that all ideologies including Islamism have died in the age of globalization.

Younger generation Islamists politicians have always been in contact with the man in the street, grassroots and periphery. Moreover, the current Interior Minister professor Besir Atalay, who is known to be close to the current president Abdullah Gul, established and directed a social research institution, ANAR, several years before the establishment of the JDP and this research institution regularly surveyed socio-political trends in society. Abdullah Gul is also known to be frequenting the offices of this institution before establishing the JDP. They must have been well aware of the fact that the society would never vote an Islamist party to the power.

The acknowledgment that the current democratic system could indeed be sufficient for Muslim individuals to live and observe their religion reminds us the views of Gülen on Islam, state and politics. We must note that Islamists came to this understanding after their experience and failure in power.

Conclusion

Islamic groups' both physical and discursive interaction is a major factor in the Turkish Islamism's normative transformation. The former Islamists have directly and normatively been influenced by the new Anatolian elite, the Gülen movement, its schools and media, and the post-Islamist intellectuals. As we noted above, the Islamic and Islamist intellectuals' transformation is an influential factor in the paradigmatic shift in the normative frameworks of the Turkish Islamists. After the 28th February, 1997 post-modern coup that directly aimed at terminating all Islamic activities, groups, social projects and bourgeoisie, these intellectuals also have come to the views of Gülen that he has been advocating since 1960s. [5] We should note that Gülen's stateless cosmopolitan Islam is still different than post-Islamism—as he puts that Islam does not need a state to survive; in this age civil society can independently maintain Islam even where Muslims are not majority. As far as the Anatolian elite's influence is concerned, it should be underlined that the Gülen movement has been an influential factor in shaping the normative frameworks of this new class as well as Ozal's reforms, export-oriented economy and global opportunities.

As Bayat (2007a: 12) argued, "efforts to make a religion democratic undoubtedly start at an intellectual level. The challenge, however, is to fuse democratic interpretations into popular consciousness". Power does not simply lie in discourse and rhetoric but, but primarily in those who formulate and advocate them. Discourse is not power, unless it is given material force. For instance, the idea that "Islam being compatible with democracy", has a different weight depending on who expresses it. There is a need to give ideas and discourses material force and to mobilize consensus around them. (Bayat, 2007a: 13) As I argued elsewhere, this is indeed what makes the Gulen movement unique. (Yilmaz, 2000; 2003; 2005) He successfully mobilized many people around his discourse "to establish institutions and to put into practice his discourse and realize his ideals". (Yilmaz, 2003: 237)

While I am unable to confirm the validity of this hypothesis, I argue that as a highly respected and knowledgeable *alim* and religious leader, Gülen and his discourse must have helped younger generation Islamists to be comfortable as far as Islam and their minds and hearts are concerned. To understand Gülen's influence we also need to be aware that Erbakan was not only a political leader but a religious one who presided over a religious community (*cemaat*) called Milli Görüş. [6]

In addition to having been influential in Turkey, Gülen's understanding of Islam, one can expect, will also be influential in the wider Muslim world in parallel to the increasing influence of both Turkey and the movement on a global scale. As Voll (2003: 247) noted a while ago, "(i)n the clashing visions of globalizations, Fethullah Gülen is a force in the development of the Islamic discourse of globalized multicultural pluralism. As the impact of the educational activities of those influenced by him attests, his vision bridges modern and postmodern, global and local, and has a significant influence in the contemporary debates that shape the visions of the future of Muslims and non-Muslims alike". (Voll, 1999: 247) Major developments in Turkey have already been followed with considerable interest by the Muslim media, thinkers and activists. The movement also increased its activities in the non-Turkish Muslim world. In addition to operating several schools in major Muslims countries such as Pakistan, Bangladesh, Malaysia and Indonesia, it has recently been opening schools, hospitals and also universities in Africa and wherever permitted in the Middle East.

Moreover, the movement, being aware of the need to situate itself and publish its ideas within the wider *ummah*, has started publishing the *Hira* magazine in 2005. (Heck, 2007: 643) The magazine "is chiefly intra-Muslim in its aims and aspirations. The magazine is published in Arabic and features articles written by both Turkish and Arabic writers; a lead article by Fethullah Gülen opens and sets the tone of each issue. The magazine acts to bring the intellectual outlook of the Gülen movement to the Arab world, serving as a cultural bridge between Turks and Arabs, as a forum in which pressing issues in contemporary Islam can be aired and treated by leading Muslim thinkers, and as a tool for the global Muslim community to consolidate a renewed vision of its relation to the intellectual and socio-political realities of the modern world". (Heck, 2007: 643) Furthermore, in 2006, the "movement, which has been criticized not paying enough attention to the Muslim World as much as they emphasize dialogue with non-Muslims, invited intellectuals from the Middle East including Arab, Jewish and Turkish to discuss the future of the Middle East in February 2007, the [Abant] platform co-organized a meeting in Egypt with the prominent Al-Ahram Institute to discuss Turkish and Egyptian experience with democracy, modernization and secularism". (Ugur, 2007: 158)

In concluding, I do not claim that the Turkish experience is totally unique; neither do I suggest that this experience could be directly copied and pasted to the other contexts. Moreover, Islamisms in other countries are also in transition. Yet, what I do envisage is that the Turkish experience and the Gülen movement's influence will interact with these experiences, paving the way for new hybrid Islamisms, post-Islamisms and even non-Islamisms.

Endnotes

1. See for a recent exception, Rabasa and Larrabee 2008.
2. In the first Islamist party, other than Kotku's disciples, some of

Nursi's followers also took part. Although, they departed their ways shortly afterwards, it will be interesting to study how they legitimised to enter into daily politics in the name of Islam, despite Nursi's unequivocal denunciation of Islamism and declaration that "I take refuge in God from Satan and politics". We must note that after this experience with politics, schisms emerged in their Nur community. We shortly discuss Nursi viz. Islamism in section 4b below.

3. *Ulama* were not always conservative in Islamic tradition and history. For instance, unlike the image portrayed by several modern scholars on Turkey, the bureaucratic ulama were progressive and were not staunchly opposing the Ottomans modernization project. Their class struggle with the other sections of the state are mistakenly interpreted as their opposition to modernization. The only opposed the change in the sense that they did not want to see their power diminishing in the state structure.
4. For a useful analysis on how global opportunity structures influenced AK Party leaders' transformation, see Kuru, 2005.
5. It must be underlined that whilst these Muslim intellectuals still base their arguments on Islamic sources and make frequent references to Islam, AK Party leaders severed their discursive ties with these sources as far as politics is concerned. That is why we can call these Muslim intellectuals post-Islamist but not the AK Party leaders.
6. At least for some segments of its partisans in the countryside, the National Outlook movement has functioned as the political messiah and, accordingly, its leader, Erbakan, has been considered to be the undisputed leader of the political jihad: "the political party means the religion" and, accordingly, those Muslims who have not belonged to the party or lent support to it have been warned that they may be subject to spiritual sanctions/hazards" , Yildiz, 2003.

References

Ahmed, Akbar (2003) "Islam under Siege: Living Dangerously in a Post-Honor World", Oxford: Polity Press.

Aktay, Yasin (2003), "Diaspora and Stability: Constitutive Elements in a Body of Knowledge", in M. Hakan Yavuz and John Esposito (eds.) *Turkish Islam and the Secular State: The Gülen*

Movement, Syracuse, New York: Syracuse University Press, pp. 131-155.

Altunoğlu, Ebru (1999), "Fethullah Gülen's Perception of State and Society", unpublished M.A. Thesis. Istanbul: Bogazici University.

Atay, Rifat (2007), "Reviving the Suffa Tradition", in Ihsan Yilmaz et al. (eds.) *Muslim World in Transition: Contributions of the Gülen Movement*, London: Leeds Metropolitan University Press, pp. 459-472.

Ayoob, Mohammed (2004), "Political Islam: Image and Reality", *World Policy Journal*, 21: 3, Fall, pp. 1-14.

Ayoob, Mohammed (2005), "The Future of Political Islam: The Importance of External Variables", *International Affairs*, 81, 5, pp. 951-961.

Barkey, Henri J. and Yasemin Çongar (2007), "Deciphering Turkey's Elections: The Making of a Revolution", *World Policy Journal*, Fall, pp. 63-73.

Barton, Greg (2005), "Progressive Islamic Thought, Civil Society and the Gülen Movement in the National Context: Parallels with Indonesia", Contributions of the Gülen Conference, November 2005, Houston, Texas.

Bayat, Asef (1996), "The Coming of a Post-Islamist Society", *Critique*, Fall, pp. 43-52.

Bayat, Asef (2007a), "Islam and Democracy: What is the Real Question?, ISIM Papers, No. 8, Amsterdam: Amsterdam University Press.

Bayat, Asef (2007b), "Making Islam Democratic: Social Movements and the Post-Islamist Turn", Stanford: Stanford University Press.

Bulac, Ali (2000), *Zaman,* 4th June, 2000.

Bulac, Ali (2007), "Islam and Politics", *Today's Zaman*, 13th July, 2007.

Çakır, Rusen (1994), s*Ne Seriat Ne Demokrasi: Refah Partisini Anlamak* [Neither the Shari'a nor Democracy: To Understand the Welfare Party], Istanbul: Metis Yayınları.

Can, Eyüp (1995), *Fethullah Gülen Hocaefendi ile Ufuk Turu,* Istanbul: AD Yayıncılık.

Cavdar, Gamze (2006), "Islamist *New Thinking* in Turkey: A Model for Political Learning?", *Political Science Quarterly*, Vol. 121, No. 3, pp. 477-497.

Dagi, Ihsan D. (2004), "Rethinking Human Rights, Democracy, and the West: Post-Islamist Intellectuals in Turkey", *Critique: Critical Middle Eastern Studies* (Summer 2004), 13(2), pp. 135-151.

Dagi, Ihsan D. (2005), "Transformation of Islamic Political Identity in Turkey: Rethinking the West and Westernization", *Turkish Studies*,Vol. 6, No. 1, March, pp. 21-37.

Denoeux, Guilain (2002), "The Forgotten Swamp: Navigating Political Islam", *Middle East Policy*, 9: 2, June, p. 61.

Esposito, John L. and John O. Voll (1996), *Islam and Democracy,* New York: Oxford University Press.

Esposito, John L. and Ihsan Yilmaz (eds.) (2010), "Islam and Peacebuildng: Gülen Movement Initiatives", New York, NY: Blue Dome Press.

Geertz, Clifford (1968), "Islam Observed", New Haven, CT: Yale UP.

Gellner, Ernest (1992), "Post-modernism, Reason and Religion", London and New York: Routledge.

Grinell, Klas (2010), "Border Thinking: Fethullah Gülen and the East-West Divide", in John L. Esposito and Ihsan Yilmaz (eds.) "Islam and Peacebuilding: Gülen Movement Initiatives", New York, NY: Blue Dome Press, pp. 43-62.

Gulalp, Haldun (1995), "The Crisis of Westernization in Turkey: Islamism versus Nationalism", *Innovation: The European Journal of Social Sciences*, Vol. 8, Issue 2, pp. 175-182.

Gülen, Fethullah (1997a), Interview with Hulusi Turgut, *Sabah*, January.

Gülen, Fethullah (1997b), *Fasıldan Fasıla III*, Istanbul.

Gülen, Fethullah (2001), "A Comparative Approach to Islam and Democracy", *SAIS Review*, Vol. 21, No. 2, pp. 133-138.

Gülen, Fethullah (2004), Nuriye Akman, Interview with Gülen, *Zaman*, 23rd March.

Gülen, Fethullah (2005), "An Interview with Fethullah Gülen", translated by Zeki Saritoprak and Ali Unal, *The Muslim World, Special Issue, Islam in Contemporary Turkey: The Contribution of Fethullah Gülen,*Vol. 95, No. 3, pp. 447-467.

Gülen, Fethullah (2006), "Essays, Perspectives, Opinions", second revised edition, Somerset, NJ: The Light.

Gurbuz, Mustafa (2007), "Performing Moral Opposition: Musings on the Strategy and Identity in the Gülen Movement", in Ihsan Yilmaz et al. (eds.) *Muslim World in Transition: Contributions of the Gülen Movement*, London: Leeds Metropolitan University Press, pp. 104-117.

Halliday, Fred (1995), "The Politics of Islam: A Second Look", *British Journal of Political Science*, Vol. 25, No. 3, pp. 399-417.

Heck, Paul L. (2007), "Turkish in the Language of the Qur'an: *Hira*"', in Ihsan Yilmaz et al. (eds.), *Muslim World in Transition: Contributions of the Gülen Movement*, London: Leeds Metropolitan University Press, pp. 643-649.

Ismail, Salwa (2001), "The Paradox of Islamist Politics", in *Middle East Report*, 221, Winter, pp. 34-39.

Kepel, Gilles (2002), "Jihad: The Trial of Political Islam", 2nd edition, London: I. B. Tauris.

Kepel, Gilles (2004), "The War for Muslim Minds: Islam and the West", Cambridge, MA: The Belknap Press of Harvard University Press.

Kosebalaban, Hasan (2003), "The Making of Enemy and Friend: Fethullah Gülen's National-Security Identity", M. Hakan Yavuz and John Esposito (eds.) *Turkish Islam and the Secular State: The Gülen Movement*, Syracuse, New York: Syracuse University Press, pp. 170-183.

Kuru, Ahmet T. (2005), "Globalization and Diversification of Islamic Movements: Three Turkish Cases", *Political Science Quarterly,* Vol. 120 No. 2, pp. 253-274.

Kuru, Ahmet T. (2007), "Changing Perspectives on Islamism and Secularism in Turkey: The Gülen Movement and The JDP", in Ihsan Yilmaz et al. (eds.), *Muslim World in Transition: Contributions of the Gülen Movement.* London: Leeds Metropolitan University Press, pp. 140-151.

Lauziere, Henri (2005), "Post-Islamism and the Religious Discourse of Abd Al-Salam Yasin", *International Journal of Middle East Studies,* 3, pp. 241-261.

Maigre, Marie-Elisabeth (2007), "The Influence of the Gülen Movement in the Emergence of a Turkish Cultural Third Way", in Ihsan Yilmaz et al. (eds.) *Muslim World in Transition: Contributions of the Gülen Movement,* London: Leeds Metropolitan University Press, pp. 33-45.

Mardin, Serif (1962), *The Genesis of Young Ottoman Thought: A Study in the Modernization of Turkish Political Ideas,* Princeton, NJ: Princeton University Press.

Mardin, Serif (2005), "Turkish Islamic Exceptionalism Yesterday and Today: Continuity, Rupture and Reconstruction in Operational Codes", *Turkish Studies,* Vol. 6, No. 2, pp. 145-165.

Mecham, R. Quinn (2004), "From the Ashes of Virtue, A Promise of Light: The Transformation of Political Islam in Turkey", *Third World Quarterly,* Vol. 25, No. 2, pp. 339-358.

Meeker, Michael (1991), "The New Muslim Intellectuals in the Republic of Turkey," in *Islam in Modern Turkey,* (ed.) Richard Tapper, London: I. B. Tauris, pp. 189-219.

Ozdalga, Elisabeth (2000), "Worldly Asceticism in Islamic Casting: Fethullah Gülen's Inspired Piety and Activism", *Critique,* 17, pp. 84-104.

Rabasa, Angel and F. Stephen Larrabee (2008), *The Rise of Political Islam in Turkey,* Santa Monica, CA: Rand Corporation.

Roy, Olivier (1995), *The Failure of Political Islam,* translated by Carol Volk. Cambridge, Ma: Harvard University Press.

Roy, Olivier (1998), "Le post-islamisme", *Revue des Mondes Musulmans et de la M'editerran'ee,* pp. 11-30.

Roy, Olivier (2004), "Globalised Islam: The Search for a New Ummah", London: Hurst and Company.

Schulze, Reinhard (1998), "The Ethnization of Islamic Cultures in the Late 20th Century or from Political Islam to Post-Islamism", in George Stauth (ed.), *Islam: Motor or Challenge of Modernity,* Yearbook of the Sociology of Islam, No. 1, 1998, pp. 187-198.

Smith, Thomas W. (2005), "Between Allah and Ataturk: Liberal Islam in Turkey", *The International Journal of Human Rights,* Vol. 9, No. 3, pp. 307-325.

Tillich, Paul (1951), "Systematic Theology", Vol. 1, Chicago, University of Chicago.

Turam, Berna (2003), "National Loyalties and International Undertakings: The Case of the Gülen Community in Kazakhstan", M. Hakan Yavuz and John Esposito (eds.), *Turkish Islam and the Secular State: The Gülen Movement,* Syracuse, New York: Syracuse University Press, pp. 184-207.

Ugur, Etga (2007), "Religion as a Source of Social Capital? The Gülen Movement in the Public Sphere", in Ihsan Yilmaz et al. (eds.), *Muslim World in Transition: Contributions of the Gülen Movement,* London: Leeds Metropolitan University Press, pp. 152-162.

Vicini, Fabio (2007), "Gülen's Rethinking of Islamic Pattern and its Socio-Political Effects", in Ihsan Yilmaz et al. (eds.), *Muslim*

World in Transition: Contributions of the Gülen Movement. London: Leeds Metropolitan University Press, pp. 430-444.

Voll, John O. (2003), "Fethullah Gülen: Transcending Modernity in the New Islamic Discourse", M. Hakan Yavuz and John Esposito (eds.), *Turkish Islam and the Secular State: The Gülen Movement*, Syracuse, New York: Syracuse University Press, pp. 238-247.

Yavuz, Hakan and John L. Esposito (eds.) (2003), *Turkish Islam and the Secular State: The Gülen Movement*, Syracuse: Syracuse University Press.

Yildirim, Ergun et al. (2007), "A Sociological Representation of the Justice and Development Party: Is It a Political Design or a Political Becoming?", *Turkish Studies*, Vol. 8, No. 1, pp. 5-24.

Yildiz, Ahmet (2003), "Politico-Religious Discourse of Political Islam in Turkey: The Parties of National Outlook", *Muslim World*, Vol. 93, Issue 2, pp. 187-210.

Yilmaz, Ihsan (2000), "Changing Institutional Turkish-Muslim Discourses on Modernity, West and Dialogue", paper presented at the Congress of The International Association of Middle East Studies (IAMES), Freie Universitat Berlin, Germany, 5-7 October, 2000.

Yilmaz, Ihsan (2003), "Ijtihad and Tadjid by Conduct: The Gülen Movement", Gülen' in M. Hakan Yavuz and John Esposito (eds.), *Turkish Islam and the Secular State: The Gülen Movement*, Syracuse, New York: Syracuse University Press, pp. 208-237.

Yilmaz, Ihsan (2005a), "State, Law, Civil Society and Islam in Contemporary Turkey", *The Muslim World*, Vol. 95, No. 3, pp. 386-390.

Yilmaz, Ihsan (2005b), "Inter-Madhhab Surfing, Neo-Ijtihad, and Faith-Based Movement Leaders", in Peri Bearman, Rudolph Peters and Frank E. Vogel, *Islamic School of Law: Evolution, Devolition and Progress*, Cambridge, MA: Harvard University Press, pp. 191-206.

Yilmaz, Ihsan (2005c), *Muslim Laws, Politics and Society in Modern Nation States: Dynamic Legal Pluralisms in England, Turkey and Pakistan*, Aldershot: Ashgate.

Yilmaz, Ihsan (2007), "Social Innovation For Peaceful Coexistence: Intercultural Activism From Rumi To Gülen", in Ihsan Yilmaz et al. (eds.), *Peaceful Coexistence: Fethullah Gülen's Initiatives in the Modern World*, London: Leeds Metropolitan University Press, pp. 25-41.

Yilmaz, Ihsan (2011a), "Il modello turco" alla prova", *La politica estera della Turchia: continuità e discontinuità*, Pavia/Italy, May.

Yilmaz, Ihsan (2011b), "Beyond Post-Islamism: A Critical Analysis of the Turkish Islamism's Transformation toward 'Civil Islam' and Its Potential Influence in the Muslim World", *European Journal of Economic and Political Studies*, Vol. 4, No. 1, June 2011, pp. 235-280.

Yilmaz, Ihsan et al. (eds) (2007a), *Peaceful Coexistence: Fethullah Gülen's Initiatives in the Modern World*, London: Leeds Metropolitan University Press.

Yilmaz, Ihsan et al. (eds) (2007b), *Muslim World in Transition: Contributions of the Gülen Movement*, London: Leeds Metropolitan University Press.

11

Islamism and Democracy: Between Tactical and Pragmatic Imperatives and Doctrinal Inflexibility

Shajahan Madampat

Does the emergence of Islamism, or political Islam, as a potentially transformative force in the Arab world augur well for democratic prospects in the region? Will Islamism graduate, under the compulsions of real politic, to become the Arab Muslim equivalent of Europe's Christian Democrats, or, use the electoral route to eventually try and establish a scripturally vindicated form of theocratic or theo-democratic tyranny?

The question assumes especial significance now, more than ever before, as political developments over the past one year have confirmed that the fall of dictatorships or monarchies in Arab countries is most likely to be followed by the rise of Islamists to power, alone or in alliance with other parties. Though the victory of Islamists in Egypt, Tunisia and Morocco cannot be described as a definitive landslide, they have undoubtedly emerged as the single largest political force with a considerable presence among all strata of the society.

Islamists seem as much surprised and baffled as others by the sudden turn of events in their favour, as the political developments that started in Tunisia at the end of 2010 took everyone by surprise. It is obvious the Islamists themselves did not expect the political battlefield to turn in their favour so soon and so decisively. However, it must be said to their credit that their tactical posturing has not only been politically correct—in most cases—but also magnanimous, going to the extent of openly promising to 'play by the book'. Though this in no way can be construed as an assurance on their part to keep their core ideology in abeyance in pursuit of the immediate greater common good, there is no doubt that they are acutely aware of the attention focused on them from around the world.

Be that as it may, but the question that refuses to die down is whether the core beliefs and ideological fundamentals that distinguish the Islamists from the rest of the Muslim society are compatible with even the elementary concepts of democracy? Will a series of tactical compromises, pragmatic somersaults and the heady experience of political power ultimately lead the Islamists to relinquish their commitment to the establishment of an Islamic State? Can they reinterpret their core ideology to such resilience that it can accommodate the fundamental postulates of a pluralist democracy based on the idea of equal citizenship and free and fair elections?

Four factors make answering these questions a rather complicated task. One is the general tendency to conflate between Islam as a faith and Islamism as a political ideology on the one hand, and between Islamism and other streams of Islamic or Muslim perspectives that view the establishment of a Sharia-based Islamic state as a favourable goal, on the other. It is noteworthy here that no mainstream Islamic sect doubts the favourability of setting up an Islamic state, should the circumstances prove conducive to it.

While the Islamists confer primacy and priority to the task of setting up the Islamic state, the others view it as an automatic development once the society in its entirety or majority turns Muslim/Islamic. Another widespread fallacy is that of looking at radical Islam and political Islam through the same lens. While it is true that radical Islam drew much of its ideological sustenance from the textual corpus of political Islam, the more popular and politically ambitious branches of political Islam, such as the Muslim Brotherhood in Egypt and Al Nahda in Tunisia, have over the decades shed much of the inflexibility and apocalyptic rhetoric that marked early Islamist writings. This process of toning down has been as much due to the imperatives of real politic as to the rigorous intellectual debates within Islamism as well as between them and their critics in several Arab countries, especially in Egypt.

The second factor is the bewildering gulf between the clearly articulated ideological positions in the core texts of all branches of Islamism and the ambiguous public posturing and tactical positions that come out of the more dominant Islamist groups in the various contexts of real politic. The third is the diversity within the Islamist bloc, which is in many ways comparable to the diversity within the communist movement, marked by intense acrimony, rigorous intellectual debates and constant rethinking and re-evaluation of positions and propositions. There are perhaps more internal debates within Islamism than between Islamism and its critics; a fact that makes any monolithic conception of the phenomenon patently flawed.

The fourth and perhaps the most important factor that complicates the study of Islamism and democracy is the fact that no Islamist group or intellectual so far put forth a blueprint for their political program or a model for the kind of political system that they envisage. Much of the discussion on the actual contours of a political system as envisaged by the Islamists comprises either mere statements of intent laced with self righteous rhetoric or selective and ambiguous references to the supposedly glorious past in relation to an 'utterly decadent present' that is at variance with everything that Islam stands for. In the absence of such an 'Islamist manifesto' acceptable to all Islamists, it is almost impossible to arrive at conclusions that can apply equally to all branches of Islamism.

Islam and Islamism

It is crucially important to state that we are not discussing the compatibility between Islam and democracy. Islam as a faith and democracy as a political concept and a cultural framework are eminently compatible with each other. Many of the core values and concepts that either permeate Islamic scriptures or manifest themselves in the life of the Prophet and his companions can be fairly interpreted as being quite in line with the fundamental concepts of democracy. Shura (internal consultation), justice, strictures against imposing faith, ijma' (consensus) and Ijtihad (independent interpretive judgment), assertions of equality are some of those values and concepts generally marshaled to clinch the democratic argument about Islam.

In any case, Islam in its long history as a lived global faith has proved itself flexible or elastic enough to accommodate changing modes of social, political and cultural patterns. It has actually coexisted with or was subsumed within many different types of political order, ranging from dictatorships and totalitarian regimes to full-fledged democracies. The question of compatibility with democracy is therefore relevant only in relation to Islamism because it is an ideology that interprets Islam as an essentially political project.

For clarity's sake, it may be appropriate to briefly refer here to the three dominant manifestations of Islam in the contemporary world in order to avoid conceptual confusions. The large majority of Muslims in the world belong to the fold of what can be called 'popular Islam'. Popular Islam is marked by traditional modes of devotion and worship, a certain degree of cultural adaptation and a sense of comfort in the socio-cultural milieu within which it functions. The second is official Islam which is usually associated with the clerical elite and the dominant fiqhi (jurisprudential) establishments. It often functions as the ideological apparatus of the state and renders its services in religiously justifying state actions. Its actual ideology is often the state and it instrumentalizes religion in the service of the state and the ruling establishment. Islamism is the third and politically most consequential manifestation of Islam, and is marked by the primacy it accords the establishment of the Islamic State.

An attempt at defining Islamism is fraught with problems, but lack of clarity on this count can lead us in contradictory directions. Though the word Islamism is a neologism that was coined in the 1970s, the Arabic equivalent for Islamists has been in vogue since at least the 10th century AD, although the word was used in a general sense referring to Muslim intelligentsia. Perhaps, the first use of the word 'Islamists' was in the book 'Maqalaat al Islamiyyin' (Opinions of the Muslims) by Abu al-Hasan al-Ash'ari (873-935). Islamism, defined broadly, is an ideological construct based on a political reading of Islam in both its history and textuality. It was an impassioned response to the two thriving ideologies of the early twentieth century, capitalism and communism—and this response rose in the context of colonialism and against the backdrop of a widespread sense of defeatism and self-pity that gripped Muslim societies. In other words, Islamist thinkers of the period sought to project their version of Islam as an alternative to the two 'isms' then competing with each other for global dominance. According to them, the primary duty of a Muslim was to strive for the establishment of an Islamic state, without which Islam will remain a 'house half-built'. In this sense, Islamism could be described as a "form of instrumentalization of Islam by individuals, groups and organizations that pursue political objectives". [1]

Needless to say, the Islamist zest for the capture of power reflected an unquestioning internalization of the idea that the state represented the entire emancipatory, therapeutic and transformative potential of a society. Once you establish the kind of state that conforms to your lofty ideals, every other virtue automatically follows, as had supposedly happened in the early days of Islamic glory. In short, the most crucial invention of Islamist thinking was the notion that Islam has unfortunately and wrongly been internalized by its followers as a mere instrument of persuasion, to the utter exclusion of its potential as a powerful instrument of coercion. The proper and just utilization of this coercive potential, many Islamist writings argued, will liberate the Muslims from all kinds of bondage. The pacifist sociality rooted in a ritualistic and anesthetic conception of Islam must give way to a militant politicality based on the 'hakimiyyah' (Authority, Sovereignty) of Allah. That alone is the solution to liberate the society from both 'internal decadence and external domination'. Success in this pursuit will guarantee justice on earth, and salvation in the hereafter.

Maududi articulated it eloquently as follows: "Human relations and associations are so integrated that no state can have complete freedom of action within its own principles, unless those same principles are in force in a neighbouring country. Therefore, Muslim groups will not be content with the establishment of an Islamic state in one area alone. Depending on their resources, they should try to expand in all directions. On one hand, they will spread their ideology and on the other they will invite people of all nations to accept their creed, for salvation lies only in it. If their Islamic state has power and resources it will fight and destroy non Islamic governments and establish Islamic states in their place". [2]

The Islamists argued the primary task of the Muslim Umma was to establish an Islamic order that will serve as a divinely sanctioned alternative to all existing models of social, economic and political organization. They tried hard, through rhetoric, exegetical overdrive and selective appropriation of aspects of Islam and modernity (it involved the twin processes of Islamisation of modernity and modernization of Islam), to present their view as both modern and authentic. The claim to modernity was meant to convince followers and critics that they were anchored in the concrete realities of the present, while claims to Islamic authenticity were intended to monopolize and privilege their interpretation above all else.

It is interesting to see how the process of selective appropriation of certain aspects of Islam and modernity takes place within the Islamist discourse. As Gudrun Kramer pointed out, "Interesting, if contradictory, signals come to light which seem to support the thesis of the "Islamisation of modernity" (or is it rather the "modernisation of Islam?"). Present day authors, including committed Islamists, identify justice and the jihad, i.e., any effort on the path of Islam, as basic values of an Islamic order. But they also list freedom, equality and responsibility, which were not part of classical doctrines of Islamic governance, at least not in the politicized sense meant here. This reveals the influence of modern political thought not only in the domain of "techniques", but also in the area of "values". It is true that many Muslims will argue that freedom, equality and responsibility are nothing but the expression of true and unadulterated Islam, which was falsified during the course of history through a combination of error, tyranny and usurpation. Nevertheless, from an outsider perspective it is the integration of the concepts of freedom and equality into the project of an Islamic state that matters". [3]

Islamism: Moderate and Extremist

Although scholars tend to divide the Islamist movements into neat categories such as 'moderate' and 'extremist' or 'Ikhwani' and 'Jihadi', such binaries fail to encompass the rich diversity within Islamist thinking and the many contradictions within each categories. A minority of scholars, like Dr. Nasr Hamid Abu Zeid, reject the distinction between moderates and extremists on the ground that "the difference between the two in the discourse is merely that of degree, not of character because there are no disagreements between them in their intellectual orientation or mechanisms...The disagreement between moderation and extremism is minor, not fundamental. It is a disagreement over the scope of the implementation of the principle, not about the principle itself...The goal is clear and openly articulated in the extremist discourse while it remains hidden and veiled in the moderate discourse". [4]

Both the moderate/extremist argument and the rejection of any internal differentiation within Islamism do not reflect the actual reality of political Islam. Indeed there are moderates and extremists within the broad category of Islamism, but it goes much beyond this binary. Moreover, Islamists in different countries pursue policies and push ideas that are specific to the contexts within which they operate. Al Nahda in Tunisia and the Muslim Brotherhood in Egypt are both products of political developments in their respective countries and the common ground between them has been decreasing substantially over the years. Al Nahda, thanks to its proximity to Western, especially French, intellectual traditions, shows much more preparedness to move away from many of the basic postulates of Islamism than, say, the Muslim Brotherhood. Brotherhood is still unable to jettison some of the rigidity that it inherited from the founding fathers, claims to flexibility and adjustments in the realm of real politic notwithstanding. An approach that ties both these disparate groups under the same yoke for analysis will be utterly misleading.

The Jamaathe Islami in India is another interesting example. In practice, the Jamaathe has discarded almost all the ideas of Abul A'la Maududi and is openly advocating secular democracy, but at the same time continues to promote Maududi's writings and ideas. The result is the organization has over the years turned so schizophrenic that it is forced to wear a secular mask to the outside and a Maududian mask inside, showing all signs of a serious identity crisis. The jamaathe Islami is actively involved in promoting secular democracy in India, while exulting at the possibility that secular democracy may never find acceptance in the Arab world!

It may be noted that there are two clear concepts of Islamist state within the Islamist discourse. One is the idea of an Islamic State which is articulated in a populist conciliatory idiom. Representatives of this idea do not accuse the entire civil society of Kufr (Unbelief) or Jahiliyya (a state of pagan ignorance and moral decadence); nor do they dub the lands of non- Muslim Darul Harb (Land of War). According to them, the Islamic Ruler, the Caliph or Imam, is a civilian ruler whose legitimacy and authority are derived from the people's endorsement, which is expressed by Ahl al Hall wal Aqd (people who loose and bind). Hasanul Banna, Hassan al

Hudaibi, Mustafa Al Sibai', Rached al-Ghannouchi and several others promote this concept of an Islamic state. The other idea, represented by the likes of Abul A'la Maududu, Syed Qutub, Mohamed Abdussalam Faraj, Saeed Hawa, Fathi Yakun and others, represents the Islamic ruler in the garb of a theocratic figure, who is elevated to the status of no less than God's representative on earth. He derives his authority not from the people, but from God Himself and 'shura' for him is a mere consultation that is not binding on him.

All the mainstream Islamist groups, it must be stated clearly, argue for a civilian ruler who derives his authority from the community.

The only difference worth noting between the so called radicals or extremists and the moderates is that while the former's project aims at the seizure of power through revolutionary means and violence, the moderates try to change the system from below and rely heavily on social and charitable activities, in addition to political mobilization. Guilain Dinoeux notes that the strategy of the radicals follows a Leninist approach. "It envisions the creation of a small, well-organized "vanguard" party led by committed, professional Islamist revolutionaries who will overthrow existing governments and then use state power to restructure society from above, along "Islamist" lines". [5]

Even within the so called moderate camp, we often see extremely radical vestiges of the foundational doctrines of political Islam coexisting rather uncomfortably with highly refined and conciliatory ideas that are compatible with the requirements of democratic pluralism. For example, Rachid Ghannouchi, the Tunisian Islamist thinker behind the success of Al Nahda, categorically stated that open expressions of atheism will be not only tolerated, but also protected in the Islamic state that he envisages. Another moderate, the famed journalist and fellow-traveller of Islamism from Egypt, Fahmy Huweidi, is ambivalent on the punishment meted out to apostasy in Islam.

Writing in the context of the assassination of seven

intellectuals in Algeria by the Islamists on charges of apostasy, he tries to express criticism against the brutality in a rather patronizing tone. His main argument was not that the killing was unacceptable in principle or because expressing one's opinion on something should not be ground for murder. Rather, his criticism was that only the judiciary has the right to pass a judgment on whether or not a person had committed apostasy, and if yes, what punishment should be given. Not fully satisfied with his own ambivalent position, especially since he was flooded with critical letters from Islamist sympathizers from around the world, including from Pakistan, he seeks counsel with the celebrated 'moderate' Islamist cleric Sheikh Yousuf Al Khardawi.

The learned scholar, while emphasizing the legal option of death against apostasy, tries to appear benevolent in the end and says there are precedents for apostasy being either punished rather lightly or not being punished at all in the hope of eventual repentance on the part of the alleged apostate. Moderate this may be, but there can be no doubt that this position is at odds with the essential requirement of free speech in any democratic polity. The issue of apostasy is of utmost relevance in our present discussion, because all art and literature, let alone academic and intellectual pursuits, can be brought under the scanner and judged blasphemous if the law of apostasy is given teeth.

Apostasy as Sword of Damocles Hanging over Free Speech

The case of Dr. Nasr Hamed Abu Zeid is a frightful example of what could happen to intellectual life if the state of Islamist dream comes into being. Dr. Abu Zaid was not only declared an apostate by an Egyptian court, but his divorce from his wife was also decreed on the basis of the argument that a Muslim woman should not be married to an apostate or blasphemer. Dr. Abu Zeid, a prominent scholar of Islamic studies and author of a number of profound books, was judged an apostate in Hosni Mubarak's supposedly secular Egypt. Dr.

Abu Zeid's crime was that he had expressed some opinions that ran counter to popular positions on the Quran and its interpretations. More shockingly, the verdict was manipulated through convoluted legal procedures and on the basis of a Hasba (third party) petition because Egypt did not have a law on apostasy. He had to flee the country with his wife and seek shelter in the Netherlands because the Islamic Jihad declared its intention to murder him on the basis of the judgment.

Two points need to be noted here. First, Dr. Abu Zeid's books, especially the one that brought him under attack, were all academic books. He did not indulge in polemical offensive against the religion nor declared himself blasphemous. Second; he repeatedly declared himself to be a Muslim who had the right to express his views on the religion even if they differed from the popular views on the subject. This is what he said in his defence: "I'm sure that I'm a Muslim. My worst fear is that people in Europe may consider and treat me as a critic of Islam. I'm not. I'm not a new Salman Rushdie, and don't want to be welcomed and treated as such. I'm a researcher. I'm critical of old and modern Islamic thought. I treat the Qur'an as a naṣṣ? (text) given by God to the Prophet Muhammad. That text is put into a human language, which is the Arabic language. When I said so, I was accused of saying that the Prophet Muhammad wrote the Qur'an. This is not a crisis of thought, but a crisis of conscience".

The judges would not concede any of that. They rejected his defence, declared him an apostate and ordered him to divorce his wife. It is important to note here that one of the issues that clinched the verdict of apostasy on Dr. Abu Zeid was his criticism against the secondary status accorded to religious minorities in the Islamist discourse. What is shocking in this whole episode is that this verdict came out in a political order that is opposed to the Islamists.

"The defendant's proposition that the requirement of Christians and Jews to pay jizyah (poll tax) constitutes a reversal of humanity's efforts to establish a better world is contrary to the divine verses on the question of jizyah, in a manner considered by some, inappropriate, even for temporal matters and judgments notwithstanding its inappropriateness when dealing with the Qur'an and Sunnah, whose texts represent the pinnacle of humane and generous treatment of non-Muslim minorities. If non-Muslim countries were to grant their Muslim minorities even one-tenth of the rights accorded to non-Muslim minorities by Islam, instead of undertaking the mass murder of men, women, and children, this would be a step forward for humanity. The verse on jizyah, verse 29 of Surat al-Tawbah, which the defendant opposes, is not subject to discussion". (p. 16 of the judicial opinion)

If a highly reputed thinker of Dr. Abu Zeid's stature could meet with such a cruel fate under the influence of Islamists in a political system notoriously opposed to them, imagine the situation when they actually govern the country! Fahmy Huweidi, whom we mentioned earlier, wrote articles empathizing with Dr. Abu Zeid's detractors. It is instructive to elucidate Huweidi's take on the issue, which is marked by cleverly veiled fanaticism and outward expressions of moderation.

The ominous title of Huweidi's first response on the Abu Zeid controversy is "Beware of Playing with Fire". This article, published before the court verdict came out and dealt with the controversy that raged about the denial of promotion to Dr. Abu Zeid, articulates clearly what a moderate Islamist considers to be tolerable limits of free expression, beyond which one is 'playing with fire'. Stating that the whole issue was merely one of administrative procedures in a university, Huweidi makes his position on freedom of expression clear. In our context in India, this statement bears frightening resemblance to many of the declarations from Sangh parivar ideologues on many occasions, most recently, during the debate on A.K. Ramanujan's essay on the Ramayanas.

"We need to frankly make a comment about the issue of the freedom of scientific research and the uproar raging around it. Those who are calling for unlimited freedom without any regard for the society's values and its public order are wrong in their understanding of freedom. They are playing with fire at the same time, especially if they, on the basis of this mistaken understanding, open the doors to mess around with the faith and sanctities of people".

"We want to clarify the issue this time, citing the opinion of one of the legal luminaries of Egypt, Dr. Asmat Saif Al Daulath, who wrote in a study about the topic: The safety of the society, in terms of its existence, limits, territory and humanity, is an objective condition for the right to free expression, in the sense that whoever expresses a thought that occurs in his head which subverts the society, the society has to, by all means, incriminate him, outlaw him, prevent him and to restrict him. All constitutions and laws in the world comprise rules that incriminate, outlaw and prevent transgression committed on the pretext of freedom of expression against those elements essential for the shaping of a society".

"In light of the above, we would unambiguously determine that messing around with religious texts, the Quran and the Sunnah precisely, should be out of bounds for those who invoke freedom of expression or research and promote claims that aim at the invalidation and termination of the texts in the name of the historicity of the text and relativity of religious rules, or other pretexts for aggression against the faith of the society and its conscience".

"With the same amount of clarity, we will say that acceptable and legitimate Ijtihad (independent reasoning) on religious text is only that which springs from conformity to it, meant to put it in its right frame in order to extract from it utmost possible energy for the revival and advancement of the society and for the good of people in this world and in the hereafter. Any adverse Ijtihad aimed at assaulting the religious texts and pulling down their fabric and texture will not include most definitely in freedom of expression. It will be banned and the society has to prevent and outlaw it, particularly if the constitution stipulates Islam to be the state religion and Shariah to be the principal source of legislation. This is because messing around with texts is an act of aggression against not only the faith of the community, but also the constitution and the public order of the country. [6]

Interestingly, in another article that appeared as a sequel to the one from which I quoted above, Huweidi continues his tirade against secularists, but this time he takes the example of Israel and the criminalization of holocaust denial in many western countries to support his argument. Here is a paragraph:

"There is the widespread Israeli opinion that there are Jews in Israel who do not believe in God, but they believe that God granted the land of Israel to them! This position articulates the sense of responsibility that people feel within the framework of the Zionist project. They do not care if someone believes in God or not, but the point is for his voice to join that of others in holding fast on to the idea of promised land in Palestine, considering that it is a prerequisite for the setting up of the project and the continued sustenance of the state". (Ibid, p. 108)

Though Huweidi does not want to go to extreme positions such as holocaust denial, he concludes with a passionate call for the establishment of what he fondly calls "a safe zone" in the world of thought where the religious faith and beliefs of people are preserved away from critical approach. This precisely is the core issue that comes to the fore when we look at the extent to which Islamists can incorporate democratic values when they come to power. The presumption of a mandatory inviolable safe zone in the sphere of thought (please do not mistake that we are talking here about defamation or libel, we are talking about thought) is a deeply anti-democratic idea. That the whole argument was made at a time when an academic was condemned to a life of exile and declared an apostate merely for the crime of expressing his opinion is an ample proof that the Islamists hardly care about free speech and democratic freedoms. Rachid Al Ghannouchi, who is often described as the most moderate of mainstream Islamists, considers apostasy a political crime committed against the nation (although he does not use the word treason).

Democracy and Islamism

Islamist views on democracy can be classified essentially into two approaches. The main current of Islamism views democracy as being closer to Islam than other political systems while the Jehadi approach rejects democracy on the ground that it derives sovereignty/authority from the people instead of from Allah.

Graham E. Fuller succinctly summed up the dilemma staring the Islamists in the face even as they inch closer than ever to the achievement of their foundational goals. "The irony for political Islam in the twenty first century is that *only the integration of broad aspects of Western political thought and political experience will enable Islamism to survive as a meaningful political force*—particularly in the area of democratic institutions. But conversely, the evolution of broader political thought in the Muslim world cannot decisively advance or flourish unless it specifically comes to incorporate and digest Islamic political thought and traditions as well. Western political models for governance in the Muslim world will shrivel like transplanted trees unless they include the nourishment of Islamic culture from which political Islam emerges. This process is both inevitable and essential for the advancement of genuine and "authentic" political thought in the Muslim world". [7]

Fuller also points to the other major dilemma that the Islamists face: "Islamists often seem caught between two poles: guardians of tradition, or vanguard of change. Most of them recognize that change is essential across Muslim society. But pursuit of a reformist role requires them to cooperate, or even compete with liberal secularists. In philosophical terms, reaching a compromise is manageable, but in the rougher world of practical politics, each party is competing for a slice of the electorate. Islamists cannot neglect courting the conservative constituency of society, but that may automatically condemn them to adopt highly conservative positions and even to support the social status quo". [8]

In this context, it is interesting to note that arguments of Arab Islamic exceptionalism, authenticity and cultural specificity as a counter to votaries of democracy are now coming forth not from Islamists, but from the defenders of the present autocratic status quo! Islamists of the main currents are now of the near consensual opinion that the best method of bringing about an Islamic state is to establish a democratic system with Islamic legislative, legal and moral content. But they make it amply clear that it does not spring from any conviction about the virtues of democracy as a whole, but because it is the best bet in the given circumstances to somehow get to power. They are clear that they adopt democracy only to the extent of procedures and institutions and not beyond its formal structures. In his foreword to the famed book by Rachid Al Ghannouchi 'Common Freedoms in Islamic State,' Mohamed Salim Al Awa, the Egyptian Islamist scholar, makes these points clear:

1. Democracy is nothing more than a means to organize rotation of power.
2. Democracy is part of larger integrated system that comprises economy, society, public policy and individual life.
3. In all these aspects, Islam has its own rules of permission, prevention, and prohibition and only when all these Islamic rules and regulations are implemented will the Islamic project be accomplished.
4. The difference between means and procedures on the one hand and principles, values and ideas on the other are clear. The former can be adopted from any source regardless of its faith and communal affiliation.

Ghannouchi, ever more generous and liberal than his fellow Islamists, goes a step further and asserts that democracy means granting recognition to all, equality, rotation of power, the right of people to choose. Islam has the capacity to internalize the democratic form and direct it. [9] His approach is more accommodative, since he goes beyond the form and describes democracy as a culture and value system that calls for dealing with extremism though dialogue.

Ghannouchi's approach is, however, more nuanced than it appears on the surface. He accepts democracy as the best bet among the given alternatives in the absence of the Islamic system. According to him, a society ruled by a defective law is better than a society whose law is the will and whims of the tyrant. A reading of his various writings together provide a clearer idea of his approach to democracy. There is a need to distinguish the legal legitimacy of democracy from the religious legitimacy that only an Islamic system can claim. He sees the transition from dictatorship towards democracy as a natural and necessary stage leading up to the eventual establishment of the Islamic order.

Mohamed Imarah, the prominent Egyptian Islamist, gives a hand of support to pro-democratic voices within Islamism by saying that the Islamic concept of Shurah does not differ from democracy in their experiences, institutions and mechanisms, but there is a fundamental difference between them, in the sense that democratic notion of freedom is absolute while Shurah curtails these freedoms on the basis of the primacy of Allah's rights over those of human beings. [10]

Imarah's candid admission about curtailing freedoms in the name of the primacy of divine rights over lesser mortals is significant. It is the hermeneutical hair splitting on this aspect that determines the dividing lines between the so called radicals and moderates within the Islamist bloc. The radicals are honest and straight forward on this point: they do not prevaricate or equivocate about the inevitable curtailment of freedoms and the discrimination inherent in a confessional system against 'outsiders'. The moderates prevaricate and indulge in semantic gymnastics in order not to appear undemocratic and discriminatory in their approach to 'outsiders.' When they claim the political order they envisage is democratic, they overlook two cardinal facts: First, unlike other confessional systems, the Islamic state as envisaged by the Islamists derives its legitimacy primarily from its adherence to the Sharia, a legal framework of divine origin. The problem with such a system is that soteriological and eschatological postulates and concerns, which are absolutist in their essence and abstract and unempirical by their very nature, underpin the entire business of governance and political activity.

Therefore it is incapable of running the affairs of a polity that consist of not only a plurality of faiths and belief systems, but also a large number of people who prefer to either remain outside the fold of faith or live according to their own subjective understanding of their faith away from institutional mechanisms of religion. Second a confessional political party that makes soteriogical and eschatological convictions the basis of its political program is sure to turn the logic of democracy upside down because it is premised on the notion of permanent majorities. Democracy is secure only when the majority keeps shifting on the basis of 'competitive interests' of the citizens rather than on the basis of confessional consolidation. The moment a permanent majority around confessional calculations gets solidified in a democracy, it ceases to be a democracy and turns into tyranny. The following statements by two major intellectuals, one an academic sympathetic to the Islamist cause and another a prominent Islamist scholar, are sufficient to represent the ethical dilemmas and undemocratic potential implicit in the Islamist idea of state in regard to religious minorities and dissenting groups:

"It might be objected that what Islam grants with one hand by positing the basic equality of all human beings, it takes away with another by ruling that non-Muslims living in an Islamic state should be inferior to Muslims by incurring heavier financial liabilities and civic deprivations. The answer to this objection is that no egalitarian school of political thought provides for absolute equality—unless it is hopelessly utopian, or has no intention of achieving political power". (Hamid Enayat, Modern Islamic Political Thought, Kuala Lumpur, Islamic Book Trust, pp. 188-189)

"And the decisive fact is that the limitations placed by the Shariah on the rights of non-Muslims are not permanent and irremovable, because non-Muslims always have the option to convert to Islam, and thereby overcome their political incapacity". (Ibid, p. 189)

Muhammad Asad, the Polish convert to Islam and one of the most celebrated figures of Islam in the 20th century, wrote his famous book on Islamic government with a view to provide a theoretical framework for state and government in his adopted country Pakistan. He is candid in admitting that an Islamic state is impossible without allowing for certain amount of differentiation between the majority and minority. He is also clear that members of the minority communities—however great their integrity and loyalty to the state—cannot be expected to work wholeheartedly for the 'ideological objective' of Islam. The resemblance between this rhetoric and Sangh Parivar discourse on Muslims is striking!

"To be sure, this fear of discrimination relates only to the theory and not to the practice of government; for in countries where Muslims form an overwhelming majority (and only these can justifiably be termed "Muslim countries"), the leadership of the state automatically accrues to them. Nevertheless, in the context of modern political thought, which is strongly influenced by Western concepts and prejudices, even a theoretical discrimination on the ground of religion might be unpalatable to many Muslims, not to mention the non-Muslims living in their midst.

One must, therefore, frankly admit from the outset that

without a certain amount of differentiation between Muslim and non-Muslim there can be no question of our ever having an Islamic state or states in the sense envisaged in Quran and Sunnah. One cannot escape the fact that no non-Muslim citizen—however great his personal integrity and his loyalty to the state—could, on psychological grounds, ever be supposed to work wholeheartedly for the ideological objectives of Islam; nor, in fairness, could such a demand be made of him...those who are to wield supreme authority in the Islamic state and are to be responsible for the shaping of its policies should always be Muslims; and this not merely *de facto*, by virtue of their majority in the country, but also de jure by virtue of a constitutional enactment. If we are resolved to make Islām the dominant factor in our lives, we must have the moral courage to declare openly that we are not prepared to endanger our future by falling into line with the demands of that spurious "liberalism" which refuses to attribute any importance to men's religious convictions; and that, on the contrary, the beliefs a man holds are far more important to us than the mere accident of his having been born or naturalized in our country". [11]

"It would seem like a "presidential" system of government, somewhat akin to that practiced in the United States, would correspond more closely to the requirements of an Islamic polity than a "parliamentary" government in which the executive powers are shared by a cabinet jointly and severally responsible to the legislature. In other words, it is the *amir* alone to whom all administrative powers and functions should be entrusted, and it is he alone who should be responsible to the *majlis*—and through it, to the people—for the policies of the government. The ministers ought to be no more than his administrative assistants or "secretaries," appointed by him at his own discretion and responsible only to him". [12]

"We know that the ulu 'l-amr (holders of authority) in an Islamic state must be Muslims. If the executive powers of government were to be vested in a cabinet of ministers chosen from the legislature on the basis of party representation—as is customary in the Western European parliamentary democracies—it is these ministers who, together with the amir, would constitute the executive ulu l'-amr by virtue of the mandate they have received from the majlis: in which instance the holding of ministerial power by a non-Muslim would contravene the clear-cut shar'i stipulation which reserves the executive leadership of the state to Muslims. Hence, the community would be faced with the alternative of either statutorily debarring non-Muslim citizens from all ministerial posts (which might make it difficult for the non-Muslims minorities to cooperate loyally with the state), or of blandly disregarding a fundamental injunction of the shariah (which would strike at the root of the Islamic concept of state).

However, if all executive powers and prerogatives are vested in the amir alone, he would obviously be the sole dhu l-amr responsible for the activities of his government, where as the ministers would be no more than his secretaries or administrative assistants whom he would appoint at his will and to whom he would delegate certain tasks inherent in his office. Because they would not be responsible for policy making, these secretaries could not be regarded as ulu 'l-amr in their own right—and so there could be no shar'i objection to appointing a non-Muslim to a cabinet post. This would not only prevent an unfair discrimination against non-Muslim citizens, but, in addition, would make it possible for the government to utilize, on merit alone, all the best talent available in the country...The mere fact that there are considerable non-Muslim minorities in most of the Muslim countries should, therefore, tip the balance in favour of the so called presidential system of government". [13]

I did not try to paraphrase these extensive quotes lest I should be accused of misrepresenting the text under discussion. From all these, it will not be unfair to conclude that Islamism in all its diversity is fundamentally incompatible with democracy—in the sense of a liberal, competitive political system that does not discriminate against certain groups and constituencies. A democratic state is impossible to sustain unless it is able to maintain some sense of neutrality with regard to people's faiths and other markers of identity.

Conclusion

Although claims of moderation and adherence to democratic values by Islamists must be taken at face value, the fact remains that Islamism and democracy are inherently incompatible with each other at their core.

While Islam as a faith and lived reality and democracy as a culture and political system are compatible, Islamism as a political ideology is premised upon the total negation of all the fundamentals of pluralist democracy, most importantly the idea of equal citizenship. However, if the Islamists wholeheartedly embrace the fundamental premises of democracy as many Islamists and their supporters claim, then they cease to be Islamists and enter a post-Islamist phase, which is welcome.

If such a metamorphosis actually takes place and the Islamists accept the ideas of equal citizenship and pluralism and reject their insistence on the primacy of an Islamic state, they are then comparable to the Christian Democrats in Europe and Latin America or the parliamentary communists in India. And as such, there is nothing that warrants scepticism about their legitimate role in the democratic process, even if their embrace of democratic principles is a mere tactical ploy.

But if the tactical espousal of democracy is to be dropped when they feel the context is ripe to return to the original dogma based on the notion of 'establishing God's Sovereignty (Hakimiya) on Earth', all hell will break loose and the resulting scripturally vindicated tyranny will be far more lethal than the ones that the revolutions toppled. So far, we have not heard any Islamist ideologue rejecting the defining concepts of Political Islam.

Therefore, treating tactical remarks by ideologues like

Ghannouchi as evidence for a sea change of ideology and mindset will be rather naïve. Equally naïve and counterproductive will be attempts at denying the Islamists their legitimate right to participate in the democratic process. The utterly noisy and public nature of democracy has over time diluted many a dogma and adapted it to suit the functioning of democratic politics. But what if the compulsions of pragmatism give way to the temptations of mistaken idealism?

If increasing popular support or internal pressures lead the Islamists over time to revert to the ideological purity of their original worldview, it can undermine democracy in three significant ways.

Firstly, the practice of equal citizenship—the idea that all citizens are entitled to equal rights regardless of class and creed, an idea central to democratic politics—will be undermined because in Islamist ideology official hierarchization of all religions practiced within the state is an essential pillar of statecraft. Dissenters, liberals and free thinkers from within the Muslim community stand to suffer the most in an Islamic state as envisaged by the Islamists.

Secondly, political formations based on religious ideology or identity tends to gain and hold on to power by creating permanent majorities. The notion of permanent majority throws democracy out and brings tyranny in because a polity can remain democratic only if the majorities are constantly in a state of flux. If permanent majorities based on primordial identities are politically consolidated, totalitarianism will prevail in the name of democracy.

Thirdly, the wanton use of religion as an instrument of coercion, power and political mobilization and its consequent de-sacralization will adversely impact on the polity in ways that goes far beyond the immediacy of electoral politics. It will not only undermine and distort the democratic processes and unleash physical and emotional violence at all levels, but also kill the soul of a culture. While religion as faith as well as an instrument of persuasion has historically played a humanizing role, religion as ideology and an instrument of coercion has only resulted in structures of violence, hidden and manifest.

History is full of wasted revolutions. Will democracy be ill-fated to usher in theocracy in the Middle East?

Endnotes

1. Guilain Denoex, The Forgotten Swamp: Navigating Political Islam, in *Political Islam: A Critical Reader*, Frederic Volpi (ed.), London and New York, Routledge, 2011, p. 60.
2. Abul A'la Maududi, *Haqiqat-i-Jihad*, p. 64, Taj Company Ltd., Lahore, Pakistan 1964.
3. Visions of an Islamic Republic: Good Governance According to The Islamist, in *Political Islam: A Critical Reader*, Frederic Volpi (ed.), London and New York, Routledge, 2011, pp. 89-90.
4. Nasr Hamid Abu Zeid, Al Khitab al Dini al Mu'a'sir, Aaliyaatuhu, Wa Muntalaqatuhu al Nadhriya (Contemporary Religious Discourse: Its Theoretical Mechanisms and Orientations, Page 45, quoted in Mohamed Jamal Barut, yathrib al jadeeda: Al Harakaat al Islamiya al Rahina (New Yathrib: Current Islamic Movements), London,
5. Guilain Denoex, The Forgotten Swamp: Navigating Political Islam, in *Political Islam: A Critical Reader*, Frederic Volpi (ed.), London and New York, Routledge, 2011, p. 70.
6. Fahmy Huweidi, al muftaroon (Slanderers), Cairo, Dar al Shuruq, 1996, pp. 100-101.
7. The Future of Political Islam: Its Dilemmas and Options, in *Political Islam: A Critical Reader*, Frederic Volpi (ed.), London and New York, Routledge, 2011, p. 419.
8. Ibid., p. 414.
9. Muntalaq magazine, No. 110, 1995, quoted in IbrahimA'rab, Al Islam al Siyasi Wal Hadatha (Political Islam and Modernity), Casablanca, Afriqiya Al Sharq, 2000, p. 10.
10. Ibid., p. 105.
11. Muhammad Asad, The Principles of State and Government in Islam, Kuala Lumpur, Islamic Book Trust, 1980, pp. 40-41.
12. Ibid., p. 61.
13. Ibid., pp. 62-3.

12

Contesting Visions of the Nation-State: Past and Present in the Making of Egypt

Mohammed Moussa

Introduction

Civic expressions of the nation-state are inspired by political affiliations derived from central and marginal identities. The Arab world is the location of contested visions on the legitimacy and content of nationalism. Ethnicity is enmeshed with religion, politics and violence. For states in the region, the political regalia of the nation-state are to be found in the army and other social-wide institutions. Since the introduction of a standing military force, gradual and manifest changes to the social fabric in this part of the world have been noticeable. The maintenance of this institution has been perceived to be urgent in safeguarding Egypt's borders and territorial integrity. Further evidence attesting to the prominent role played by the Egyptian army can be discerned in the period between 1952 until 2011 when every head of state hailed from its officer ranks.

The Arab Spring interrupted, albeit temporarily, the high profile position of the military occupying this office. Democratic elections brought a civilian, a first in the political record of contemporary Egypt, to the presidency in a remarkably free and fair poll. Muhammad Mursi, a senior Islamist from the Muslim Brotherhood, had narrowly beat Ahmed Shafiq, a former officer in the Egyptian air force and Hosni Mubarak's last Prime Minister, in the second round of presidential elections. Nonetheless, the victory of an Islamist did not entail a rejection of the idea of Egypt as a nation-state. To the contrary, the Egyptian nation was to be shored up by other affiliations: namely Islamic. However, the restoration of the army's role in politics arrived in a very public coup d'etat witnessing the Defence Minister, Abdel Fattah al-Sisi, announcing on 3rd July, 2013 the removal of Mursi. In one fell swoop, the Egyptian army re-emerged as the primary institution in its self-image as the custodian of the nation-state. Popular protests against Mursi preceded the bold yet not atypical move on the part of the heads of the military to shuffle out a civilian from the presidential palace.

This chapter seeks to explore the contests surrounding the idea of the nation-state in Egypt since the beginning of the twentieth century with particular focus on events prior and after the ousting of Hosni Mubarak. A century of continually unfolding debates about the political identity of Egypt is characterised by agreements and disagreements on a whole plethora of issues. Various facets of nationalism enjoyed broad consensus in one period only to be replaced with other positions affirming the contingent nature of public discourses not only in Egypt but elsewhere in the world. Movement, rather than fixity, defined the complex mosaic of the nation-state with a constant stream of political actors dissatisfied with the status quo. Certainly, the inherent instability of the meaning of what is the nation-state always accompanied the emergence of a consensus on its content. Further, the presence of Islamists, commensurate with the formation of the Egyptian nation-state, posed particular problems to this consensus. From outright rejection of the very foundations of the nation-state to acceptance of the notion of nationalism, Islamists have disagreed profoundly among themselves on this very recent introduction to the Arab world.

Thus, this chapter will examine the contest over the nation-state by Egyptians from different political backgrounds varying from Sa'd Zagloul to Khalid Muhammad Khalid to Abul Alaa Mady. Particular attention will be paid to the revival of the contentious debate on the public role of Islam in a post-Mubarak nation- state. The following is a breakdown of the discussion of this subject in four sections: a theoretical exposition on the interpretability of the past in the formulation of the nation-state; Islam and the idea of the nation under the monarchy of the descendants of Muhammad Ali Pasha in the former part of the twentieth century; the period from 1952 until the first decade of the twenty-first century which witnessed the creation of a regime based on nationalism; and finally the resurgence of the nationalist-Islamist dynamic in public forums during and after the ousting of Hosni Mubarak in February 2013.

Islam, the Past and Nationalism

The past is not an objective reality that simply reveals itself to historians or other curious observers. Inevitably, inquiries into what took place then are also constructions of what is taking place now. Those in the present duly bring into being a process of constructing the past. A single event can be interpreted in a multiplicity of ways by an equally multiple number of actors pointing to the bottom- less well of stepping into the past. Thus, ambiguity characterises the presence of the past in the present. Unequivocal ventures to endow a particular and exclusive meaning to the past flounder on the rocks of the capricious nature of human subjectivity: whether individual or collective.

Many voices speak the language of the past in a fashion that frustrates the hegemonic constructions that attempt to negate their existence. Ashis Nandy, an Indian political psychologist, has produced an incisive critique of the current dominant discipline on the past, history, unravelling its presumed superiority. Indeed, alternative ventures vie with history to offer, particularly in the non-West, a repertoire of 'myths' bringing what Ashis Nandy describes to be "the here-and-the-now" with its immediate sense of the past into the present. [1] Elsewhere, contrary to the efforts of historians to monopolise the past shorn of an explicit ethical content, Nandy argues that the past is comprehended in light of the "morality of everyday life". [2] Consequently, the challenge to interpret the past is not merely an exercise in academic competence but a venture situated in the present seeking authoritative import in one's current moral and political positions.

Nowhere is this impetus towards time so acutely felt than in the Arab world. The role of Islam has been instrumental in cultivating a sense of the past that constantly seeks inspiration from its founder, the Prophet Muhammad, and other prominent figures including scholars and warriors. War and peace are interwoven into the tapestry of a tradition that continues to offer a compelling and dynamic set of ethical themes to Muslims. Simultaneously, backward looking and progressive, according to Serif Mardin, the "lifeworld" of Islam has indubitably endured in the activism of contemporary Islamists. [3] The idea of a golden age appears with a forward motion galvanising a devout citizenry to participate in shaping the present for the purpose of reform. For Olivier Roy, the converse is true. Islamists are largely indebted to modernity in the essence of their project in the rejection of "the real tradition" for "an imaginary Tradition". [4]

Although the account put forward by Roy eschews the sweeping generalisation of attributing all things Islamic to a single and fixed Islam, he neglects the insight that all traditions are contrived imaginatively in some fashion. Traditions exist in a state of ambivalence with one generation either accepting or rejecting its previous forebears conventional wisdom on a variety of matters. The past thus emerges from the interpretations of individuals who select, within certain boundaries, the assortment of symbols, themes and values in their immediate context. Purposeful ventures of change within a tradition often can and do acquire a robust appearance that attack, adapt or accept its numerous elements. Revivalism is no stranger in the constructions of Islam with Ibn Taymiya, a medieval Syrian jurist, and Muhammad bin Abd al-Wahhab, the eighteenth century zealous revivalist from central Arabia, demonstrating the sporadic yet ever-present impulse to 'renew' Islam. [5]

The emergence of nationalism in the Arab world posed a challenge to both the then current meanings of the past and the processes of perceiving it. Whereas change was previously understood to possess cyclical connotations, primarily the renewal of the collective understanding of Islam, it soon acquired the urgent notion of progress. All spheres of human life were to be subjected to the onward march of the nation-state: at once breaking with the past and pursing an inevitable path of evolution. Nationalist historiography has offered various arguments on the issues of women, class, religion and anti-colonialism in support of the objective reality of the nation. [6] Such a reinvention either marginalised or excluded other understandings of the past. While Islam was not removed from the overt symbols of the state in the Arab world, it could no longer claim to be the primary component of a regime's identity. Further, the pride of place of Islam in public life was previously manifested in a diversity of expressions that belied a single interpretation of the past to provide religious legitimacy to a ruler. Responses from the 'traditional' *ulema* (religious scholars) have also varied.

Whether occupying the positions of state functionaries or dissident scholars, this diverse group of individuals has sought to provide religious justification for or against the nation-state. And moreover, interpretations of the sacred texts of Islam are pregnant with political ramifications. The past produced by nationalists in the Arab world offered a convincing language, although shaded by religious imagery, to states for the purpose of constructing a nation. Nonetheless, the very idea of the nation-state continues to be a contested experience that betrays an exceedingly constructed and fluid character whereby debates on the religion of the state, languages to be afforded official status, recognition of hitherto ignored ethnic identities and disputes over territories recur with increasing force. In each one of these areas, the conflicting postures towards the past undermine the seemingly closed discussion on the definition of the nation-state.

Populism and the Nation under Monarchy

Absolutism on the scale of the modern state had to wait until after Napoleon's short-lived occupation of Egypt in the late eighteenth century. At a groundbreaking juncture, Egypt became a competing power to the Ottoman Empire. Further, the arrival of Muhammad Ali Pasha, an Ottoman officer, led to the development of political institutions that equally depended on the traditional Muslim notion of legitimacy, the application of Islamic law, and foreign methods—a standing army. Religion, bureaucracy and the force of arms coalesced together to create the modern state during the nineteenth century in a process that is still unfolding. What Elie Kedourie describes to be Muhammad Ali Pasha's "military modernization" brought his Egyptian subjects into a tighter embrace with political authority with new impositions. [7] And moreover, the conscription, particularly of *fallahin* (peasants) from the countryside, introduced to this end required the establishment of a state bureaucracy to maintain records. [8] The prestige of the emerging state was developed into a dynastic rationale to ensure the succession of the descendants of Muhammad Ali Pasha in agreements with Ottoman Istanbul first in the position of *wali* (governor) in 1805 followed by the bestowal of *khedive* (viceroy) in 1867. From a province administered by ephemeral governors in a large empire at the turn of the nineteenth century to an autonomous state with its own imperial aspirations, the Egypt of the Khedivial dynasty of the Muhammad Ali Pasha yearned for greater recognition of their power.

During this period, nationalist sentiments such as those expounded by Rifa'a Rafi al-Tahtawi in a nascent form after his return from Paris in 1831 would have to wait half a century to acquire popular appeal. Paradoxically, the search for legitimacy by the rulers of Egypt was also accompanied by the increasing consciousness of nationalism. These parallel developments would meet and depart in a contentious mixture of constitutionalism, Muslim reformism, autocracy and colonialism. Towards the end of the 1870s, the pen of Yaqub Sanu, from a mixed Egyptian-Italian Jewish background, was devoted to cause of 'Egypt for the Egyptians'. His time in exile in Paris, after falling foul of the incumbent Khedive Ismail due to his writings, included severe denunciations of colonialism. A perennial Egyptian nation under the yoke of successive occupations of Persians, Greeks, Romans, Arabs, Turks and latterly the English is a central theme of Sanu's prolific writings. [9] At the same time, Sa'd Zaghloul, a youthful disciple of Muhammad Abduh and Jamal al-din al-Afghani, perceived Islam, particularly the Shari'ah, to encourage the spirit of constitutionalism sanctioned by the verses of the Qur'an to restrain the tyranny of rulers. [10]

For Abduh and his diverse group of followers, the inspiration for Muslim revival alternated between the golden ages of Islam, both Salafi and Abbasid, and the modern West. [11] The turban and the fez symbolised an emerging divide between a past understood to be tradition and a past that needed to be unshackled for the purpose of a new identity. Importantly, the latter was becoming an increasingly salient facet in the public life of Egypt emphasising Sanu's constant celebrations of *al-ummah al-misriyya* (the Egyptian nation). Another no less rousing figure was Mustafa Kamil, a lawyer by training, and his struggle to define Egypt as a nation within a broader pan-Islamic context. Colonial occupation was contrary to the sense of *wataniyya* (patriotism) present in the shared homeland of Egypt and Sudan. [12] Liberation of these lands was driven by an anti-colonial fervour. Pan-Islamic sentiments and Ottomanism were part of the stock-in-trade ideas of Kamil's fight against colonialism motivated by his nationalism.

Although the specific demands for independence were initially restrained in the beginning of the twentieth century, the cause of the nation-state was adopted by an older Zaghloul with no less vehemence. Acceptance of the very premise of British colonialism by the Zaghloul and the delegation he led known as the Wafd was transformed into a rejection of their protectorate over Egypt. [13] Dissatisfaction with the prevailing set of direction of the political arrangements between the British colonial administration and the Khedive was palpable in the political climate of Egypt. Continuous rejection of the efforts of Zaghloul and many others before him to propose statehood for an Egyptian people desiring independence provoked this reaction. Woodrow Wilson's principle of self-determination at the end of the First World War, pitting the imperial powers of Europe against one another, resonated with many in the colonial territories including Egyptians who were paying attention to the destructive events in the imperial metropole.

For Zaghloul, the nation was embodied in his person, at a time when he held no official political position, competing against both the Khedive and the government to negotiate with the British on the matter of independence. [14] Nationhood could be manifested in the single voice of a charismatic individual, garnering support from citizens, without the institutional trappings of formal political authority. Thus, the Khedive Fouad, enjoying a somewhat circumscribed exercise of stately power under British auspices, was involved in a fragmented political environment where nationalists questioned the bounds of his authority. Joseph Kechichian argues that the motivation behind the adoption of the title of *malik* (king) by Fouad was to showcase both the independence of Egypt to the British and "worldly legitimacy" of his power to Egyptians. [15] The institution of the monarchy was intended to assert the regal and national nature of the Khedivial dynasty within Egypt amid the growing populist nature of nationalism. Palace-led constructions of the nation were challenged by those of Zagloul and the Wafd aiming to align more closely the idea of popular sovereignty of the nation with the state.

The newly enacted constitution of 1923 contained provisions on the hereditary nature of the Egyptian monarchy, parliamentary sovereignty and the position of Islam as the religion of the state. These three elements, scattered in articles throughout the founding document a new political order, incorporated the contending debate over the nation-state. Dynasticism and constitutionalism were juxtaposed next to each other in an uneasy tension. Significantly, however, the king was to swear an oath spelled out clearly in Article 50 that recognised the authority of the constitution and the nation. The Wafd's initial rejection of the entire process of constitutional drafting was soon replaced with enthusiasm once it turned out that the constitution tilted towards its populist elements. Successive electoral victories seemingly challenged the legitimacy of the monarchy thereby precipitating the largely uninterrupted suspension of the constitution for nearly a decade until 1935. Throughout this period, the Wafd under a new leadership of Mustafa Nahhas, Zaghloul had passed away in 1927, perceived the task to the restoration of a sacred document protecting the nation. [16]

A voice was raised, not necessarily from a typically traditional quarter, in support of an alternative conception of political affiliation. Abd al-Razzak al-Sanhuri, the architect of the revised 1948 Egyptian legal code, proposed the reformulation of the caliphate, after its abolition in 1924, to preserve the unity of the East. [17] Notwithstanding the apparently irresistible drive towards a specifically Egyptian state, under both monarchy and constitutionalism, the contradiction between the nation-state and the *ummah* was not resolved. An astute observation made by Tamim Barghouti focuses on the ideal of the *ummah* that evades any sense of territoriality with legitimacy proffered to a *dawla* based on its ability to safeguard the interests of Muslims. [18] While the *dawla* was in essence a temporary institution, the nation-state was timeless brooking no doubts concerning its provenance and continued existence.

Republicanism and Religion in the Nation-State

A new period began after the last ruler from the descendants of Muhammad Ali Pasha was unceremoniously overthrown in the popularly known '23 July Revolution'. Monarchical legitimacy was rejected for a republican system. However, a vociferous debate on the position of religion in the state had ensued prior to this moment. Khalid Muhammad Khalid, a graduate from al-Azhar seminary, had revived the arguments of Ali Abd al-Raziq, an earlier contemporary, concerning the essentially non-political nature of Islam. In a sharply worded response, Muhammad al-Ghazali, also formerly a student at al-Azhar, defended the need for a public role of Islam. The nation-state was accepted by both to varying degrees. The primacy of Islam for "orthodox Muslims" is interpreted by Ansari implying that *wataniyya* does not hold any import despite al-Ghazali arguing that it is an undeniable fact in the quote cited. [19] For Khalid, the existence of *al-hukuma al-qawmiyya* (the nationalist state), in contradistinction to *al-hukuma al-diniyya* (the religious state), would better serve the protection of religion. [20] Further, the priority of the affiliation to *al-watan* (the homeland) is firmly located in the struggle for the betterment of the nation. [21]

A clear separation between religion and the state accompanies Khalid's definition of the nation-state that is republican. Opposition to this position was expressed in a robust fashion by al-Ghazali in his advocacy of an Islamic state. Nonetheless, this state is not religious in the narrowest sense of the word where those running the state must possess religious knowledge. [22] Other forms of government, including nationalist, are not necessarily rejected if they ensure the public prominence of Islam and combat despotism. [23] Hamid Enayat posits that nationalism was vehemently rejected by al-Ghazali in the celebration of *al-watan al-Islami* (the Islamic homeland). [24]

Although the constitutional identity of the state in the early 1950s was commensurate with Islam for al-Ghazali, the need to curtail the influence of religion in public life was urgent for Khalid. After the events of 1952, Egypt pursued a rapid movement towards the latter's vision with the *ulema* increasingly under the control of the state. Religious authority entered the all-encompassing ambit of the new regime that emerged from the cadre of young officers who overthrew King Farouk. This novel political arrangement witnessed the rise of Jamal Abdel Nasser to the office of president.

Contending ideologies were accommodated within the state. Arabism and Islamic socialism were cornerstones for republican Egypt. The nation-state was neither confined to the territory of Egypt, belonging to the wider nation of Arabs, nor exclusively dominated by Islam. And moreover, Abdel Nasser was transformed into the personification of pan-Arabism. A new relationship between the state and religious institutions was inaugurated during the rule of Abdel Nasser that would continue uninterrupted into the present. The 1961 reform of al-Azhar, transforming it from a seminary to a university, accompanied the critique of *rijal al-din* (men of religion) which paradoxically created a salaried class of religious scholars beholden to the state. [25]

Thus, the independence of Islam, more precisely the body of scholars enjoying the authority to interpret it, was severely constrained. Religion was merely a dimension of a broader and eclectic political identity that was at once Arab, Third Worldist and African. The definition of the nation-state was influenced by territorial, linguistic and political considerations. Egypt was part of the Arab nation, despite its short-lived union with Syria in United Arab Republic, in a politically fragmented region. Arabism's rise followed the receding shadow of the universalism of the Ottoman Empire according to Fouad Ajami whereupon the Arab nation mirrored the Turkish nation. [26]

Such a broad appeal for the Egyptian nation-state disappeared to make way for two contending political affiliations: Islam or nationalism. An interplay between these two identities has been present since the turn of the twentieth century. Following the defeat of the Arab armies in 1967, expressions of nationalism in Egypt have made use of the *turath* to foster a return to religion. [27] Ibrahim Abu Rabi observed an intellectual shift on the part of Muhammad al-Ghazali that increasingly stressed the Islamic dimensions of Arabism rejecting its subordination to nationalism. [28] The Muslim past has also been appropriated by Egyptian secularists to argue against their religiously-minded opponents. Tensions gradually arose when a constitutional position was awarded first to Islam and subsequently to the Shari'ah. Additional references in the constitution to religion aimed to shore up the legitimacy of the existing regime of Anwar al-Sadat. Succeeding Abdel Nasser, who died in 1970, Sadat departed as president from his predecessor's policies. Renewed prominence was given to religion.

In Article 2 of the Constitution of 1971, the principles of the Shari'ah first appeared to be a main source of legislation. Less than a decade later, the wording was amended to stipulate they were the main source to affirm the religious credentials of the regime. And moreover, al-Sadat's adoption of the title of *al-ra'is al-mu'min* (the Believer-President) can be construed as a play on *amir al-mumineen* (Leader of the Believers) coined by Umar ibn al-Khattab to describe himself as the head of the Muslim community. Islam and the nation-state were by no means incompatible. However, the interpretation and scope of Islam could either narrow or widen its meaning to add secular and religious elements.

Nationalist politics created a context where the notion of citizenship brought a new dynamic expanding the possibility of a new political identity. For Tariq al-Bishri, according to Leonard Binder, the Egyptian nation-state is rooted in an Arab-Islamic turath (heritage) uniting both Muslims and Coptic Christian. [29] Nation and religion are thereby found to be indistinguishable. During the 1980s, the palpable presence of an Islamist trend expounded a vision of renewal and renaissance within the context of Egypt. A group of prominent figures emerged from within this trend including al-Bishri, Fahmi Huweidi, Muhammad Selim al-Awa, Muhammad al-Ghazali and Yusuf al-Qaradawi. The notion the palpable presence of an Islamist trend expounded a vision of renewal and renaissance within the context of Egypt.

A group of prominent figures emerged from within this trend including al-Bishri, Fahmi Huweidi, Muhammad Selim al-Awa, Muhammad al-Ghazali and Yusuf al-Qaradawi. The notion of the middle path in Islam was captured in the name of *wasatiyya* applied to this group of thinkers, writers and religious scholars. Nationalism is no conceived to be the antithesis of a religiously defined identity. To the contrary, the Shari'ah, Raymond William Baker notes, was invoked by this group, counting among its ranks Muhammad al-Ghazali and Yusuf al-Qaradawi, to support the position that Muslims could vote for non-Muslims to be their elected representative. [30] Recognition of other political frames of reference, seemingly non-Islamic, are accommodated and even sanctioned by Islamic authoritative discourses.

The establishment of al-Wasat Party in the mid-1990s was a harbinger for this trend in an explicitly political manifestation. Among its co-founders, were former Muslim Brotherhood members, Essam Sultan and Abul Ala Mady, and a Christian writer, Rafiq Habib, seeking to forge a new path in an authoritarian context. Islam as civilisation, not simply a religion, was a principal cornerstone of this party, not yet legally registered as such, with membership open to both non-Muslims and Muslims. [31] Political identities were self-consciously adapted to the changing times of Muslims. The Egyptian nation-state in the party's 2009 political programme was located in *al-hadara al-arabiyya al-islamiyya* (the Arabo-Islamic civilisation). [32]

In the same period, a directly secular reading of the Islamic heritage was being undertaken by a collection of Egyptian intellectuals. The *Jamiyyat al-Tanwir* (the Enlightenment Society), founded in 1992, invoked Ibn Rushd in its project to separate religion from politics. [33] References to symbolic figures from the Muslim past were intended to endow indigenous authority to new positions on the status of

Islam in state and society. Additional evidence from the past is marshalled by Fouad Zakariyya for the venture of secularism. The wide-ranging efforts of Muhammad Ali Pasha, the pioneering figure of *nahda* (renaissance), are perceived to be the first genuine move towards a comprehensive secularism in Egypt inspired by a model of European society. [34] Delving deeper into the past, Zakariyya argues that tradition is not rejected by secularists who, instead, subject it to criticism and selection in the same rationalist spirit of the medieval Mu'tazilites. [35]

The integration of al-Azhar into the state witnessed a political alignment between officials within the former and the latter's policies on a variety of matters. High ranking positions from the Shaykh al-Azhar to the Grand Mufti of Egypt were essentially appointees by the incumbent regime. *Fatawa* (legal edicts) from the widely respected institutions of al-Azhar played an indispensable role in endowing religious legitimacy on the nation-state. From Abdel Nasser's Islamic socialism to the peace treaty concluded with Israel by al-Sadat, the support of al-Azhar has been enlisted. Similarly, the battle with militant groups disputing the authority of the Egyptian state in the 1990s witnessed the involvement of the al-Azhar *ulema* for and against Mubarak. Legitimacy to the state was granted challenging these militants.

They were condemned and described as by the Shakyh al-Azhar as Khawarij, a puritan faction that rebelled against the Caliph Ali, by the Shakyh al-Azhar Jad al-Haqq. [36] Violence perpetrated the institutions of the Egyptian nation-state was in no uncertain terms an assault on the Muslim community. The Islamic Research Academy, headed by the Shaykh al-Azhar, is cited by Ali Gomaa, in 2007, to support the stance that women are qualified to be Egyptian judges according to Muslim jurisprudence. [37]

Within the judiciary, the secular form of Egyptian law has been coloured by cases of an Islamic import. Courtrooms had become the battleground for Islamic interpretations. Extensive reforms have removed the enforcement of Islamic law from its traditional juristic confines to the judicial courts of the modern state which have taken the initiative to interpret it. [38] Invocation of the *hisba* (regulation of public morality) by Egyptian citizens to file cases against individuals or actions supposedly contravening Islam took place in these courtrooms. Nasr Hamid Abou Zayd's involvement in a legal suit as a defendant, examined in detail by Hussein Ali Agrama in *QuestioningSecularism*, is perhaps one of the more infamous instances of the *hisba*. [39] 'Private' matters such as faith were brought to the attention of Egyptian judges to declare null and void the legality of a marriage if a defendant, in the cases of Abou Zayd and Nawal al-Saadawi, was deemed to be an apostate. Subsequent moves to curtail the initiation of *hisba* by individual citizens, allocating this authority exclusively to the Prosecutor General, were frustrated with the decision of a judge that all Muslims have an inherent stake on issues concerning Islam through it. [40]

Muslim jurisprudence and its key precepts exist in an ambiguous set of circumstances where their invoked authority can either empower Egyptians, including women, or intrude directly into their lives. State institutions were influenced by broader debates in society about the Egyptian nation-state's secular or religious nature. Regular assertions of the authority of the state over religious affairs culminated into direct control of Islamic law and its procedures. Boundaries between religion and politics were porous which was clearly evident in the final years of the Mubarak regime.

Egypt's Constitution between Shari'ah and the Army

The birth pangs of the Arab Spring appeared amid rising sentiments that the authoritarianism of Arab regimes failed to address the economic and political ills of society. Movements cutting across ideological lines were founded. Kifaya (Enough) emerged on to the Egyptian political scene in the decade prior to Mubarak's ousting. Senior members of this diverse social movement consisted of Islamists and secularists such as Abul Ala Mady, Ayman Nour and George Ishak who were united in heir determined opposition to Mubarak's regime. [41] Successive regimes, as previously observed, relied on both Islam and nationalism to bolster their claims of legitimacy. Democracy was a major bone of contention during the era of Mubarak for all political actors.

Although Mubarak neither possessed the nationalist charisma of Abdel Nasser nor al-Sadat's proclivity towards religious posturing, various organs of the state were deployed to obtain popular support. The Ministry of *Awqaf* (Religious Endowments) was integral in this process of furnishing a religious quality to the office of president. Mahmoud Hamdi Zaqzuq, Mubarak's longstanding Minister of *Awqaf*, was at the helm of a government department that generated its own interpretations of Islam. His administrative responsibility for thousands of mosques and religious preachers necessarily implied a great scale of authority on religious interpretations being taught and disseminated. Islamic texts supplied the justification for pursuing the agenda of reform that disseminates legitimate interpretations of Islam through the state's nationwide control of mosques. [42]

Inevitably, particular stands on politics were taken by Zaqzuq in the last years of Mubarak's reign in line with policies of the regime. In November 2010, *imams* (prayer leaders) were given orders to urge citizens to vote as a religious and national obligation in parliamentary elections against the background of mass-boycott threats by opposition groups. [43] On the eve of the popular protests that unseated Mubarak, the deed of Muhammad Bouaziz in Tunisia was being imitated in Egypt. Both the Ministry of *Awqaf* and Zaqzuq announced the *khutba* (Friday prayer sermon) in mosques would condemn suicide citing the sacred Islamic texts to stem the tide of copy-cat self-immolations as acts of civil disobedience. [44]

Events, however, overtook the state apparatus, particularly

its security organ, with millions taking to the streets and public squares of Egypt demanding the resignation of Mubarak. The mass protests that began on 25th January eventually forced Mubarak to step down on 11th February signalling the beginning of a convoluted transitional period with a greater public role for the Egyptian military. Concurrent to this phenomenon, the Muslim Brotherhood emerged as the dominant political force in the country through parliamentary and presidential elections. Islamist participation implicitly entailed recognition of the legitimacy of the nation-state.

Al-Wasat Party became Egypt's first formally registered political party shortly after Mubarak fell. Its ideological position can be ascertained from Mady's distinction between politics and religion. The party is committed exclusively to politics as a civil party with *marjiyya islamiyya* (an Islamic reference). [45] Primary focus on political participation sets aside the desire for religious missionary activity in society. In the Middle East, Turkish Islamists also demonstrated the compatibility of their time in the government with a widely accepted nationalist agenda. Abdullah Gul in the office of presidency and Tayyip Recep Erdogan as Prime Minister provided ample evidence that the religiously-oriented Adalet ve Kalkinma Partisi (Justice and Development Party), described to be 'conservatives', upheld the interests of the nation-state. A 'Turkish Model' for Islamists in the region to be emulated has acquired a certain amount of credence in political circles. Erdogan's statements while he was in Egypt urging his Islamist counterparts in Egypt to follow suit in the acceptance of secularism as the basis for the state was met with incredulity.

The Muslim Brotherhood, nonetheless, adopted one part of the Arabic equivalent of the name of Erdogan's party in its formation of Hizb al-Adala wa al-Huriyya (Justice and Freedom Party). The party's 2011 programme stressed the identity of *al-dawla al-islamiyya* (the Islamic state) and *al-dawla al-madaniyya* (the civil state) precluding the rise of a theocracy. [46] Further, the notion of the equality of citizenship defines the very essence of the state. [47] Islamic conceptions of identity did not necessitate the rejection of the Egyptian nation-state. Conversely, the political arm of the Muslim Brotherhood accepted and incorporated elements not overtly religious in origin. Rafiq Habib, a senior member of the party and a Christian writer, also advocated the idea of a civil state inspired by an Islamic reference: namely the Shari'ah. [48]

Disagreements, however, over the meaning of the Shari'ah in the Egyptian constitution and the civil nature of the state have acquired renewed importance since early 2011. The prospects of a supra-constitutional document materialised aimed at laying down the foundations for a future constitutional committee drafting Egypt's post-Mubarak constitution. To this end, Essam Sharif's interim government, under the auspices of Supreme Council of the Armed Forces then headed by Muhammad Hussein Tantawi, composed such a document. Ali al-Selmi, a Wafd Party member who was a Deputy Prime Minister, spearheaded this effort giving the army the role of the guarantor of *al- shariyah al-dustouriyya* (the constitutional legitimacy) in Article 9 alongside wide extensive powers in Article 10. [49]

These two articles were interpreted to be a move to formally codify the idea of the Egyptian army as the custodian of the nation-state. Furthermore, the national unity of Egypt is accorded primary importance facing the putative threat of the establishment of a theocracy. Rigorous opposition to the document's challenged both the possibility of its binding nature and substance. [50] The established idea of the military intervening in politics was received ambivalently by Egyptians. Conflation of the nation-state with the country's armed forces certainly found a quintessential ideal in the person of Jamal Abdel Nasser, and its ubiquitous role in society and the economy. Despite the numerous precedents affirming the military's privileged position in politics, the newly drafted 2012 constitution eschewed completely Article

9 and reworded Article 10 from al-Selmi's proposed supra-constitutional principles.

Although Article 2's stipulation of the principles of the Shari'ah to be the main source of legislation was accepted, statements from the current Shaykh al-Azhar have emphasised its central function in defining Egypt. Ahmed al-Tayyib has argued that Article 2 illustrates succinctly the identity of the country with the contribution of the Shari'ah to legislation not excluding other sources of law. [51] The authoritative voices of al-Azhar and its senior scholars have asserted the Islamic characteristics and overwhelming legitimacy of the nation-state. The Shari'ah's legal implications in Article 2 were elaborated further in Article 219.

This insertion into the constitution referred to the body of rules and principles produced by the Sunni *madhahib* (rites of jurisprudence). And moreover, the acknowledgement of Christianity and Judaism in Article 3 enshrined the legal import of these two religions in Egypt. [52] Laws relating to the Shari'ah by the legislature required, according to Article 4, the consulting of the revived group of the Senior Scholars of al-Azhar. Formal enshrinement of a religious body to oversee legal and Islamic matters highlighted the religious dimension of the nation-state and the high esteem al-Azhar enjoyed among sections of the Egyptian population—particularly Islamists.

The constitution drafted during Mursi's term in power was eventually suspended when he was prematurely unseated as president in a coup d'etat after mass protests for and against his rule. Egypt's Defence Minister, Abdel Fattah al-Sisi, executed this coup in response to calls for Mursi to resign to make way for new presidential elections. Opponents to the ousted regime such as the Tamarod (Rebel) movement demanded the intervention of the military, bypassing the democratic process, to bring down an elected president. Fears of an impending Islamist takeover of the state needed to be confronted by the custodian of the Egyptian nation-state. Against this backdrop, the ideological mantle of the army was illustrated in stark terms. Islamism was perceived to threaten national unity.

A new constitutional drafting process to rectify the putative flaws in the suspended constitution set about rolling back the overtly religious articles contained therein. Deliberations by a committee composed of 50 members, based on recommendations by a 10-member committee, arrived at the near unanimous positions of removing al-Azhar's consultative role in Article 4 and deleting Article 219 completely. [53]

Egypt's army has emerged, once again, to be one of the principal arbiters of Egyptian nationalism. Eschewal of a purely military function has created opportunities for intervention in politics. Despite vehement rejection of this overtly political role, the marriage between the nation-state and the army has acquired greater ideological meaning. The notion of being the guardian of the nation also includes the protection of the institutions of the state. In a recently published article, Hugh Roberts has astutely illustrated the army's actions on 3 July to be a recovery of its place as the chief source of power in Egypt. [54]

Notwithstanding the seeming identity of the army and the nation-state, critics have emerged of any formal codification of a link between the former's intrusion into the domestic politics of the latter. Significantly, Abdel Moneim Abu al-Fotouh, a former senior Brotherhood member, has declared that the stipulation of the non-interference of the army in politics must not be changed in the new constitution being drafted. [55] Celebration of the army's participation in the overthrowing Mursi has rekindled, in some quarters, the importance of this institution of the state.

A decree in late August by the new interim president, Adly Mansour, changed the wording to the oath of fealty sworn by Egyptian military officers from the president to the country. [56] Civilian political offices, singling out that of president, no longer form the official point of loyalty for the army. Rather, the nation-state is elevated to occupy this position with no intervening institutions.

Self-conscious parallels have been drawn between al-Sisi and Abdel Nasser in the role of the heroic leader of the Egyptian people. Threats, whether internal or external, are confronted in an existential struggle. Al-Sisi is perceived to be the embodiment of the nation-state manifesting its wishes and desires against those who would divide the country. The sacrosanct nature of Egypt is interchangeable with the will of the army. Domestic politics enters the scope of action for the custodian of the nation-state—not merely protecting its borders. A direct military presence in political office has certainly been a core part of Egypt's presidential tradition. The daughter of Jamal Abdel Nasser, Hoda Abdel Nasser, wrote an open letter in the Egyptian press calling al-Sisi to run for president citing the precedent of her father. [57]

Pointed analogies between the recent past and the present occur in a context flattening the specificities of each to maintain the continuity of an ideological reading of the military's role as guardian of the nation-state in Egypt. Exclusion of Islamism in a post-coup scenario requires not merely a broadly secular conception of society and state but also the eliciting of religious authority. The highest ranking *ulema* of al-Azhar duly lent their backing to the coup. Yet again, the mosque pulpit permitted Ali Jumah, previous Grand Mufti of Egypt, to extol the Egyptian army to be *al-jund al-gharby* (the western army) mentioned in a *hadith* from the Prophet Muhammad. [58] The Muslim past was invoked to anticipate, more accurately affirming, its nationalist and martial credentials. Essentially, religion and politics were intertwined. No such separation existed to prevent the interdependence between the learned authority of a *shaykh* and the power of the predominant organ, the army, of the state.

Conclusion

Public discourses on the nation-state in Egypt emerged from the imposition of political reforms that changed its social fabric. Muhammad Ali Pasha's state-making project, including the creation of a standing army, gradually inculcated a greater awareness of national identity among Egyptians. Tribal and religious affinities were transformed to accommodate the new sense of belonging to a shared community based on a putative ancient heritage and revolving around state institutions. The impetus towards anti-colonialism was kindled by Yaqub Sanu in the slogan 'Egypt for the Egyptians' in his writings published in Egypt and France.

Similarly, erstwhile Muslim reformists such as Sa'd Zagloul adopted the idea of an Egyptian nation-state in opposition to both the British colonial protectorate of Egypt and the despotism of the descendants of Muhammad Ali Pasha. Further credence was added to the nationalist mythology of the living Zaghloul whereby his home became known to all Egyptians as *Bayt al-Ummah* (House of the People). Man, abode and his political career acquired the mantle of nation-ness. A secular flavour to Egyptian nationalism elevated the national unity of Christians and Muslims that de-emphasised the public role of Islam. This de-emphasis however, did not imply exclusion. Rather, the 1923 Constitution was drafted to specify Islam as the religion of the state. Religion was enshrined into the foundation of Egypt's political identity.

Presumptions of the incompatibility between the public position of Islam and the national state were firmly rebutted by Muhammad al-Ghazali in the early 1950s. Jamal Abdel Nasser and Anwar al-Sadat positioned al-Azhar and the Shari'ah respectively within the orbit of political life. Egypt, more so under a republican system rather than the monarchy, relied on religious institutions and symbols to strengthen the legitimacy of the nation-state as conceived by the incumbent regime. The pious title of *al-ra'is al-mu'min* adopted by al-Sadat sought to combine the republican spirit of the office of president with the aura of religious legitimacy. In this period, a shift among religiously- minded thinkers and scholars can be gleaned that has been ambivalently perceived to be both against and for the nation-state.

The rise of the *wasatiyya* trend brought together religious and national elements. Although a primary reference to Islam inspired their writings, the nation-state had a visible presence in the reinterpretation of the Shari'ah. A decade later, al-Wasat Party was formed explicitly singling out the leading luminaries of this trend in its advocacy of a civil state. The idea of the Egyptian nation-state did not contradict its existence against the backdrop of the Arabo-Islamic civilisation. Other voices, such as Fouad Zakariyya, expounded a secular position rejecting the arguments of their religious compatriots. The Egyptian nation-state was essentially secular in nature. Secularism in Egypt has its roots in the period of the *nahda* initiated by Muhammad Ali Pasha's reforms.

After February 2011, the debate surrounding the public role of Islam was resuscitated. The first political party to obtain formal registration was al-Wasat Party based on the proposition of a civil political identity inspired by, although not exclusive to, Islam. A plethora of different parties subscribing to different strands of the shared frame of reference of the nation-state competed against one another. Previously existing parties such as the Wafd, revived in 1978 after nearly three decades of proscription, and new parties like Abdel Moneim Abul Fotouh's Misr al-Qaweya (the Strong Egypt) filled the political scene. 'Post-Islamist' reverberations could be felt in Egypt.

State-making in the form of the drafting of new constitutions has introduced a polarised dimension to the status of the Shari'ah in the legislative process. Article 219 of the constitution passed in 2012 fleshed out the meaning of Article 2 in accordance with the classical corpus of Muslim jurisprudence. Following the ousting of Muhammad Mursi in the summer of 2012, however, the constitutional committees charged with the formation of a new constitution deleted this article and removed the consultation of al-Azhar in Shari'ah-related laws in Article 4. As a result, these actions have reallocated once again the authority to define the Shari'ah and national legislation in general to the country's Supreme Constitutional Court. The nation-state is a constitutional entity with the contribution of religion to its laws primarily interpreted by the judiciary.

More importantly, the intervention by the armed forces into politics, ousting both Mubarak and Mursi, has been complemented by a revival of nationalist sentiments. Certain variants of Egyptian nationalism are intertwined with the institution of the military. Projected images of its heroism capture the duty of being the custodian of the nation-state. Interpretations of the Muslim past, specifically produced by the officialdom of al-Azhar, have offered legitimacy to the political actions of the army. Nationalist and Islamic imageries are equally invoked to sanction the participation of the army in Egypt's domestic affairs. The transcendence of religion can readily assume more mundane and worldly forms pervading nationalism.

Seemingly incongruent elements are interpreted to bridge different periods in the past. Dominant interpretations of the past may acquire a hegemonic status seeking to marginalise other compelling or latent interpretations. Nationalist discourses construct a past that either assimilates alternative political identities or reduces the ability of these identities to galvanise citizens. Exclusive conceptions of the nation-state can be decentred whereupon the critique of the monopoly of defining their meanings by state institutions creates a vision of the nation-state that is inclusive.

Endnotes

1. Ashis Nandy, *The Intimate Enemy: Loss and Recovery of Self under Colonialism*, New Delhi: Oxford University Press, 2011, 59.
2. Ashis Nandy, "History's Forgotten Doubles", *History and Theory*, 34/2, May 1995, 64.
3. Serif Mardin, "Civil Society and Islam", in John R. Hall, *Civil*

Society: Theory, History, Comparison, Cambridge: Polity Press, 1995, 289.
4. Olivier Roy, Carol Volk (trans.), *The Failure of Political Islam*, Cambridge, Massachusetts: Harvard University Press, 1996, 22-23.
5. Fazlur Rahman, "Islam: Challenges and Opportunities", in Alford T. Welch and Pierre Cachia (eds.), *Islam: Past Influence and Present Challenge*, Edinburgh: Edinburgh University Press, 1979, 316-317.
6. Anthony Gorman, *Historians, State and Politics in Twentieth Century Egypt*, New York: Routledge, 2003, 3-4.
7. Elie Kedourie, *Politics in the Middle East*, Oxford and New York: Oxford University Press, 1992, 27-28.
8. Ibid., 29.
9. Yaqub Sanu, *The Egyptian Patriot*, 2, 17th November, 1983.
10. Kedourie, *Politics in the Middle East*, 82-83.
11. Marshall, G.S. Hodgson, The *Venture of Islam: Conscience and History in a World History*, Volume 3, Chicago and London: The University of Chicago Press, 1977, 288-289.
12. Albert Hourani, *Arabic Thought in the Liberal Age*, Cambridge: Cambridge University Press, 1983, 204-207.
13. Tamim al-Barghouti, *The Umma and the Dawla: The Nation State and the Arab Middle East*, London and Ann Arbor: Pluto Press, 2008, 139.
14. Kedourie, *Politics in the Middle East*, 164, 170.
15. Joseph A. Kechichian, *Power and Succession in Arab Monarchies*, Boulder and London: Lynne Rienner, 2008, 25-26.
16. Yunan Labib Rizk, "When they gathered", *Al-Ahram Weekly*, 705, 26th August-1st September, 2004, 5.
17. Enid Hill, "Al-Sanhuri and Islamic Law", *Arab Law Quarterly*, 3/1, February 1988, 48-49.
18. Barghouti, *The Umma and the Dawla*, 65-66.
19. Zafar Ishaq Ansari, "Contemporary Islam and Nationalism: A Case Study of Egypt", *Die Welt des Islams*, 7/1-4, 26.
20. Khalid Muhammad Khalid, *Min Huna Nabda* (From Here We Start), Cairo: Dar al-Nil lil-Tiba'ah, 1950, 195.
21. Ibid., 195.
22. Muhammad al-Ghazali, *From Here We Know*, Kuala Lumpur: Islamic Book Trust, 2011, 7-8.
23. Ibid., 39.

24. Hamid Enayat, *Modern Islamic Political Thought: The Response of the Shi'i and Sunni Muslims to the Twentieth Century*, London and New York: I.B. Tauris, 2005, 115.
25. Malika Zeghal, "Religion and Politics in Egypt: The Ulema of Al-Azhar, Radical Islam, and the State (1952-94)", *International Journal of Middle East Studies*, 31, 1999, 374-375.
26. Fouad Ajami, "The End of Pan-Arabism", *Foreign Affairs*, 57/2, Winter 1978, 365.
27. Fred Halliday, "The Nationalism Debate and the Middle East", in Martin Kramer (ed.), *Middle Eastern Lectures*, Tel Aviv: Tel Aviv University, 1999, 36.
28. Ibrahim M. Abu-Rabi, *Contemporary Arab Thought: Studies in Post-1967 Arab Intellectual History*, London and Sterling, VA: Pluto Press, 2004, 253-254.
29. Leonard Binder, *Islamic Liberalism: A Critique of Development Ideologies*, Chicago and London: The University of Chicago Press, 1988, 286-287.
30. Raymond William Baker, *Islam without Fear: Egypt and the New Islamists*, Cambridge, Massachusetts and London: Harvard University Press, 2003, 166-167.
31. Joshua A. Stacher, "Post-Islamist Rumblings in Egypt: The Emergence of the Wasat Party", *The Middle East Journal*, 56/3, Summer 2003, 427-428.
32. Al-Wasat Party, Birnamij Hizb al-Wasat al-Jadid (Programme of the New Wasat Party), May 2009, available at, http://kurzman.unc.edu/files/2011/06/Wasat_2009.pdf.
33. Fauzi M. Najjar, "The Debate on Islam and Secularism in Egypt", *Arab Studies Quarterly*, 18/2, Spring 1996, 12-16.
34. Fouad Zakariyya, Ibrahim M. Abu-Rabi (trans.), *Myth and Reality in the Contemporary Islamist Movement*, London and Ann Arbor, Pluto Press, 2005, 15-16.
35. Ibid., 41-42.
36. Steven Barraclough, "Al-Azhar: Between the Government and the Islamists", Middle East Journal, 52/2, Spring 1998, 238.
37. Muhammad Khalil, "Q&A with the Grand Mufti of Egypt", *Asharq Alawsat*, 14th July, 2007.
38. Noel J. Coulson, *Conflicts and Tensions in Islamic Jurisprudence*, Kuala Lumpur: The Other Press, 2006, 107-108.
39. Hussein Ali Agrama, *Questioning Secularism: Islam, Sovereignty and the Rule of Law in Modern Egypt* (Chicago and

London: The University of Chicago Press, 2012).

40. Steve Negus, “Female Circumcision on Trial”, *Middle East International*, 554, 11th July, 1997.
41. Manar Shorbagy, “The Egyptian Movement for Change-Kefaya: Redefining Politics in Egypt”, Dilip Parameshwar Gaonkar (ed.), *Cultures of Democracy*, 175-196.
42. Mustafa Khalid, “A Talk with Egypt’s Awqaf Minister Mahmud Zaqzuq”, *Asharq Alawsat*, 16th August, 2010.
43. Ahmed el-Beheri, “Minister Tells Imams to Encourage Citizens to Vote in Parliamentary Polls”, *Egypt Independent*, 24th November, 2010. Ahmed el-Beheri, “Friday Sermons to Discuss Religious Prohibition of Suicide”, *Egypt Independent*, 20th January, 2011.
44. Ahmed el-Beheri, “Friday Sermons to Discuss Religious Prohibition of Suicide”, *Egypt Independent*, 20th January, 2011.
45. Abu Ala Mady, “Tatwir al-Khitab al-Siyasi lil-Fikra al-Wasatiyya: Hizb al-Wasat Namozaja (Development of the Political Discourse to the Idea of Centrism: al-Wasat Party Model)”, *al-Wasat Party website*, 7th November, 2012), available at, http://www.alwasatparty.com/defult_inner.php?id=3&namefrm=2#.UksqqIa1ESN.
46. Freedom and Justice Party, *Birnamij Hizb al-Huriyya wa al-Adala* (Programme of the Freedom and Justice Party), 2011, 15.
47. Ibid., 11-12.
48. N.a., "Coptic Intellect: MB wants Civil State which offers Copts their Rights, Freedom and Justice," *Ikhwanweb*, 18 April 2011, http://www.ikhwanweb.com/article.php?id=28420.
49. “Masrawy Yanshur Nass wa Theqa al-Selmi howla al-Mabada’ al-Asasiyya lil-Dustour (Masrawy Publish al-Selmi’s Text and Document about the Fundamental Constitutional Principles)”, *Masrawy*, 2/11/2011, available at, http://www.masrawy.com/news/Egypt/Politics/2011/November/2/4559080.aspx%2F4559080.aspx.c.
50. Mohamed Mahmoud, “Debate Intensifies Over Egypt’s Constitutional Principles Document”, *al-Shorfa*, 8/11/2011, available at, http://al-shorfa.com/en_GB/articles/meii/features/main/2011/11/08/feature-02.

51. Ahmed el-Beheri, "Shaykh al-Azhar: Natamasik bil-Abqa ala al-Mada al-Thaniyya dun Ta'deel lil-Hefaz ala al-Hawiyya (Shaykh al-Azhar: Stick to Maintain Article 2 without Amendment for Preservation of the [Islamic] Identity)", *al-Masry al-Youm*, 11/7/2012, available at, http://today.almasryalyoum.com/article2.aspx?ArticleID=346012&IssueID=2559.
52. Nariman Youssef, "Egypt's Draft Constitution Translated", *Egypt Independent*, 2/12/2012, available at, http://www.egyptindependent.com/news/egypt-s-draft-constitution-translated.
53. Bassem Sabry, "22 Key Points in Egypt's New Draft Constitution", *Al-Monitor*, 23rd August, 2013, available at, http://www.al-monitor.com/pulse/originals/2013/08/egypt-draft-constitution-guide.html; Hugh Roberts, "The Revolution That Wasn't" *London Review of Books*, 35/17 (12th September, 2013), available at, http://www.lrb.co.uk/v35/n17/hugh-roberts/the-revolution-that-wasnt.
54. Hugh Roberts, "The Revolution That Wasn't", London Review of Books, 35/17, 12th September 2013, available at, http://www.lrb.co.uk/v35/n17/hugh-roberts/the-revolution-that-wasnt.
55. N.A., "Abul-Fotouh Warns Against Removal of Military Neutrality from Egypt Constitution", *Ahram Online*, 9/9/2013, available at, http://english.ahram.org.eg/NewsContent/1/64/81171/Egypt/Politics-/AbulFotouh-warns-against- removal-of-military-neutr.aspx.
56. N.A., "Pledge of allegiance to president removed from army oath", *Egypt Independent*, 28/8/2013, available at, http://www.egyptindependent.com/news/pledge-allegiance-president-removed-army-oath.
57. Hoda Abdel Nasser, "Open Letter to Lieutenant General Abdel Fattah al-Sisi", *Egypt Independent*, 7/8/2013, available at, http://www.egyptindependent.com/opinion/open-letter-lieutenant-general-abdel-fattah-al-sisi.
58. Ali Jumah, "Hadith Rasul Allah an Jaysh Misr (Saying of Messenger of God on Army of Egypt)", *YouTube*, 19th July, 2013, available at, http://www.youtube.com/watch?v=C8odslLsmrI.

13

Political Theology of Morsi's State (2012-2013) in Egypt

M.H. Ilias

The Arab Spring with its wide range imperatives brought a situation in which Islamist groups in West Asia and North Africa (mainly in Egypt and Tunisia) faced an acute dilemma: whether to establish an absolute 'theocratic' state or a completely 'secular' state,. Instead of that, they made an effort to create a civil state (*dawla madaneyya*) by giving appropriate space for the rights of minorities and other weaker sections in the society. [1] This does not mean that there was a complete departure from Islamic ideals. The role of religion was very visible and operative. In a more delicate act of pragmatic balancing, Muslim Brotherhood endorsed the components of both 'Islam' and 'democratic' tradition and an attempt was made by them to show that Islamist ideology and democratic governance were not poles apart. The demands for democratization of various kinds were attempted to address by the Islamists in Tunisia and Egypt through both religious and secular means and practices-a combination of the two. The attempt gathered sense in two ways; by seeing democracy both as a means of constituting the body politic and as a technique of governing. [2]

Though the constitutional debate initiated by Morsi led eventually to overthrow of the regime, the debate, in fact, was/is an open-ended one where a healthy street level public discussion on legalities of state have been taking place. Taking cues from the experiences of all Arab Spring states, Sadiki liked to see the whole debate as a part of an inevitable conflict between two competing but interchangeable sets of legitimacy; democratic and revolutionary. [3] The latter revolves mainly around a romantic politics in societies where the informal kind of politics was invalidated by fifty years of tyranny. [4] Asad substantiated this point further with his statement that the political imagination should not be limited by the matters of legality but by a different set of criteria to evaluate what we have been witnessing in Egypt. [5] The experiences in Egypt went beyond the procedural democratic legitimacy which often seeks formal structures, procedures and contracts that frame politics. [6] Rationalizing political debates in such cases always fail to understand the dynamics involved in the Arab Spring.

It is no less incorrect to say that the Muslim Brotherhood's conceptualization of civil state made a complete departure from both 'secular' and 'religious' states. This binary has been manifested in an apparent conflict between the colonially created 'modern' state and the local sense of identity that of belonging to umma along with the forms of political organization that stem from it such as Islamic *dawla*. The Islamic *dawla* represents a non-sovereign temporary political arrangement that is accountable to and responsible for the whole *umma*, not to a particular territory. In this context, the post-secular state does not entail the total rejection of the ongoing 'secularizing' process and also not a return to the medieval theological predominance. [7] Instead, this perspective assumes that there is the continued existence of religious ideals in a continually secularizing environment. Secular frameworks fail to explain religious determinants of the state; their normative presumption of the superiority of the 'secular' over 'religion' does not allow them to conduct an objective analysis.

Habermas defines the concept secularism as the continued existence of religious communities and movements in a continually secularizing environment. [8] Asad develops the thesis of post-secularism further by analyzing the failure of secularization theories in explaining religion in contemporary life. [9] The post-secular, according to Joas, does not mean a sudden increase in religiosity, after its epochal decrease with the rise of modernity, but rather a change in mindset of those who, previously, felt justified in considering the religious to be moribund. [10] It does not reflect an increase in the meaningfulness of religion or a renewed attention to it, but focuses on a changed attitude by the "secular public domain with respect to the continued existence of religious communities and the impulses that emerge from them", notes Joas. [11] Briefly put, post-secularism offers an alternative way of approaching the role of religion in conceptualizing the state and discusses the failure of secular efforts to analyze religious practices that determines a modern state with a predominance of scientific thought and rationality at the core. It also inculcates the need of reformulating the basic presumptions of religion and secularism in the light of emerging complexities in contemporary times.

This paper addresses the need of re-evaluating the basic presumptions of religion and secularism in the light of Muslim Brotherhood's experience in establishing a 'civil state' which reflects both an increase in the meaningfulness of religion and renewed attention to it and a focus on popular 'secular' ideals.

Modern Arab State and Secular Hangover

The significance of Morsi's state lies in its role to problematize the binary of the category of 'religion' and its presumed opposite, 'secular'. The experiences of the creation of civil state demonstrated a new complex relationship between religious and secular that cannot really be reduced to a conflict of 'universal democratic' principles against 'sectarian commitments' nor to one of reason versus belief. In terms of nature, composition and ideology, the body politic envisioned by the Muslim Brotherhood remained incongruent to European concept of nation-state. Drawing up on a pre-colonial Islamic perception of politics, it also rejected the political imaginations generated by Arab nationalism as the underlying ideology.

The idea of secular modern-state entered most of the Arab societies through the colonial connection. Within a short span of time the concept of modern nation-state which cannot easily be isolated from the nationalist and organizational developments that took place in Europe, marginalized all other concepts of the state in the region. The European experience was internalized further with the development of modern state structure with elaborate bureaucracies, policing strategies and mechanisms of control by which post-colonial Arab states could manage their own population in the 1950s and 60s. During this period, a deep transformation of polity affecting the relation between religion and state was taking place. The evolution of a 'secular' bureaucracy was closely paralleled even in countries like Saudi Arabia, where the *wahabi* inspired nation-building in the 1930s had followed a distinctive tribal mode. [12]

Most of the states in the Arab world, however, failed to develop into viable modern nation-states though they unsuccessfully tried to emulate the path of 'progress'. As what happened in Egypt, the state was increasingly envisioned in a more idealized form-as socialist and secular. But the reality was different as most of the states did not live up to the imaginations of political elites. The opposition to the failed state came mainly from the religious groups who were sidelined during the nation-building process. In order to overcome the situation, elites in the Arab states engaged in eliminating 'problematic' opposition.

Looking at the history, one can say that the Arab states emerged at a time when the intellectual discourses were mostly pre-occupied either with the *umma* (global Muslim community) defined in terms of Islamic politics or *watan* (national community) defined in terms of Arab nationalism. Because of the long historical preponderance of these two concepts, Arab scholars at the initial stage did not show much of enthusiasm to endorse the concept of the body-politic based on territory, territorial sovereignty as such. [13]

With a few exceptions, the state as a concept and as an institution appeared quite alien to most of the Arab countries. As the modernization and secularization [14] of the state did not occur at the open political domain, the role of Islamic *umma* and Arab *watan* remained operative with greater amount of social as well as religious legitimacy. The lack of social and cultural cohesion furthered the complex relations between the modern, 'secular' state and their 'religiously oriented' people. The prevalent concepts of state that Arabs tended to borrow from the West, therefore, were excessively formalistic at the initial state, though later on became instrumentalist. [15] The newly established states in West Asia and North Africa, in fact, functioned as a colonial tool to make people of the region to fit into a frame of reference familiar and useful to the colonial masters. [16]

The Egyptian political scientist Hamid Rabi's observations are particularly significant in this context. Rabi' was a staunch critic of basic conceptualization of modern Arab State. He did find futility in interpreting Islamic state in the framework of European enlightenment tradition. Nation-state emerged in the Arab world, according to him, was mainly an emulation of the Catholic model, seemingly with the mission of creating a direct unmediated relationship between the citizen and the state. [17] The European model in actuality, forcing the Church to be a mute spectator and thus purging out all religious agents ended up in the hegemony of a particular religion or sect. Modern Arab states with no inspiration from the Islamic model by way of revival of the *turath* or 'cultural heritage' and guided by a distinct 'political function' (*wazifa Siyasiyya*) exemplify this mismatch. [18]

Though not familiar with the vocabularies of 'voting', 'formal institutions' and 'organized opposition', the Islamic model was politically vital with an alternative set of concepts and ideas for political equilibrium.[19] These concepts, Rabi suggested, include moderation, control between the Caliph, the *ulama* and the judges. [20] So, Islamic polity, in that sense, can't translate to the state in European context with well defined territories and sovereignty. It rather connotes to an organized politico-religious community or *umma*. The libertarian aspects of European enlightenment tradition, therefore, seldom overpowered the idea of justice (*'adl*) in Islamic polity. [21] While the concepts of freedom and liberty were at the centre stage of statist discourse in the West, they carried slightly different connotative meanings in the Islamic political discourse that go transcend the limits of the state and nation.

Looking at the genealogy, one can see the state in traditional form in the Arab/Islamic world as the outcome of two processes; a natural evolution of the Sultanic state and a reform process. [22] Of which the latter was by and large a product of change in material aspects of society reflected mainly in administrative arrangements. The reformist tradition, though not completely, had borrowed substantially from the European experiences. This tradition did find its expression first in *tanzimat* which was introduced by the Turkish Sultan in order to consolidate his own authority internally and externally and later on carried forward by the European colonialists in order to expand their imperial market and weaken the local leadership. [23] Apart from extending the reach of imperial market, the modern state helped the colonialists to accommodate the then emerging social elites into their political constituency.

However, the modern state as an imported commodity came into being partly under colonial pressure and partly under the influence of imitating the West, [24] failed to capture the popular political imagination and to transform the attitude of Arabs towards it. The Arab political imagination during that period was hinging more around other overarching concepts of cultural unity and political integration than the concept of state. Pan-Islamism with religio-political orientation and Arab Nationalism with linguistic-cultural bond were the two major ideologies that contested each other to gain the edge over the Arab public sphere. [25] The former represented a comprehensive Islamic concept of *umma* while the latter was an embodiment of secular nationalism defined in terms of a more inclusive concept, *watan.* Both had lively spread as the Arabs thought of politics in terms of a non-territorial affair. The 'foreignness' of modern state prevented it from being identified by the people emotionally. [26]

Though there were a lot of ensembles to state in Egyptian history, the history of state in the modern sense with territorial integrity based on sovereignty externally and legal institutions internally traces back to the reign of Muhammad Ali who came to power in 1805. [27] He was the first to introduce the concept of citizenship and modern system of education, to build national army, compact bureaucracy and state-owned industrial networks and to create a class of political elites in Egypt. [28] Muhammad Ali's attempt to build a 'modern state' represents a balance borrowing components from both European experiences and the pattern which was prevalent with Ottoman rule. The state system continued even after his defeat in 1840s under successive regimes, but internal contradictions and threats led to the failure of the state system and eventually to the British occupation of Egypt in 1882.

What happened with the formation of modern state in the postcolonial period was the total abandonment of cultural function of the state in favour of 'purely secular' political functions. The romance of secular modern state continued to capture the imagination of political elites in the region even after the national liberation movements gained a clear hegemony in the political realm. The growth of modern nation-state system in West Asia and North Africa was directly linked to the 'secularization thesis' developed in the west keeping separation between religion and public space. [29] Cultural and religious specificities of each society were conveniently ignored in order to build 'modern' states.

Though at ideological front, they tried to undo the ill-effects of colonialism, offering an alternative to the colonial concept of state seemed impossible for national liberation movements. This inability led to a compromise between the populist ideology of Arab nationalism and the realpolitik of colonially created Arab states with repressive apparatuses. Jamal Abdul Nasser, for instance, looked for legitimacy from both Arab nationalist doctrine and strong colonial 'secular' modern state and contained Islam in order to build a 'modern' Egypt.

Nasserite state was a combination of a modern secular colonially-inspired and Arab socialist state; both of these mutually conflicting ideas existed in one synthesis. Although the socialistic component of it was appealing to many in the third world, the 'secular' 'modern' hangover of Nassarite State made it alien to Egyptian society. Though the state machine and apparatuses of it were very much influential in the daily life of people, the state failed to create an emotional bond with the society. Despite the rhetoric of Arab nationalism, Nasser could not offer an alternative to the modern state modelled on European experiences. His perceptions, therefore, remained surprisingly vague about the issues pertaining to the nature and form of an Arab nationalist state.

Though initially attempted in creating an alternative state with Arab socialistic background, Nasser's statist experiments ended up with an autocratic one taking modern liberal state as its frame of reference. Unable to move far from the hangover of secular modern state, Nasserite state, in effect, maintained a strange balance between the ideology of Arab nationalism and colonially created nation-state. This mismatch between the ideology of Arab nationalism and the secular modern nation state with coercive military, as happened elsewhere in the region, manifested in a brutal suppression of popular political movements. Communists and Muslim Brothers were the two major victims of such suppression.

Although the ideology of state changed from Arab

Socialism to neo-liberalism, Sadat's state exemplified how neo-liberalism and secularism are connected in a circuitous fashion, not just conceptually but practically through a mechanism of governance separating religion and state. It also illustrated the unique character of modern 'secular' Arab state in terms of its inherent commitment to the idea of authoritarianism. The neo-liberal state, adhered to the principles of separation of religion and state and control of popular religious groups, engaged in totalitarian exercise of power. The notion of 'secularism' was seen as a bid by the Sadat regime for centralization of power and consolidation of authoritarian state.

Secular state under Mubarak also carried a negative connotation of regime's consolidation of coercive and autocratic state subordination of its policy to that of the United States in exchange for financial and military aid. Military coercion was central to Mubarak's 'secular' governance. [30] On his part, Mubarak consolidated the political and economic dependence on the West re-configuring economy further, enforcing secularism and fighting Islam and traditional culture.

Secularization remained to be the basic task of the government with which Mubarak sought to transform Egypt an authoritarian state with tight control. Intellectuals from both liberal and left spectrum also sided with the regime tacitly and have long supported a thorough going secularization of Egypt and crystallization of Islamist groups in the name of secularism. Most of the left and liberal critics, according to Asad, simply saw the formal separation of 'politics' from 'religion' as the solution to threat of sectarianism in the Egyptian society. [31] Mubarak found excellent justification in authoritarianism for his attempt to crush Islamist organizations. The 'secular' state functioned as a guarantor of national security especially in the backdrop of American initiated 'war on terror'.

These elements in the ideology of 'secular' state came under criticism because of its justification for state-sponsored violence in the post-Arab Spring period. The idea of state as the chief secularizing agent from Nasser's period met a rejection and religious-based 'non-modern' or 'pre-colonial' concepts of state begun to emerge in response to it. The creation of the civil state by the Brotherhood offered a bid to unpack the heterogeneous elements involved in what we mean by religion and not to focus solely on abstract theological notions. Within the strict framework of 'civil', Morsi tried to offer an opposition to pro-western neo-liberal dictatorial regime. The Muslim Brotherhood, at the same time, did not hide that their goal was a state based on *Sharia* as the frame of reference. The biggest challenge to the creation of a civil state was the remnant forces [32] of 'secular' system that outlived the 25 January revolution and their supporting networks in the army, media, business, civil society and judiciary.

Digging a bit deeper, one would not surprise, why civil society movements which protested vehemently against SCAF's (Supreme Council of Arm Force) threat to the revolution tacitly allowed the army to sack the first popularly elected president. Even though a variety of important civil society groups emerged or survived, transformed for last six decades, the state either went to some lengths to accommodate many within its 'secular' constituency or to prevent, pre-empt or destroy others. The 'liberal' middle class content of civil society at times sought patronage of state in some way or the other, though they could easily break the relationship with the Mubarak state, when the revolution happened.

Muslim Brotherhood in power posited a tradition of challenge against the incommensurable divide between strong religious belief and a secular world view. The civil sate they conceptualized, on its part, tried to direct others' attention to how the religious and the secular [33] are not so much immutable essences or opposed ideologies.

Dialogic Aspects of *Dawla Madaneyya*

Arab Spring, at least for a short while, brought a situation in which people witnessed to the unpopularity of the states in the region created by the colonial powers and supported by the neo-colonial powers. The event also contributed to de-westernize the West Asian and North African politics through the embrace of non-western (mainly Islamic) ideals of democracy. Though Turkey ignited such a move making 'civil religion' more appealing as an alternate to 'secularism', Islamist parties in Tunisia and Egypt made it more popular world over.

The state envisioned in Islam, *dawla* shows the character of a doctrinal or ideological ('aqa'idiyya) state based on a practical merger of ethical principles with pragmatic political ideals and on a non-separation of private and public. [34] Culture remains to be an inextricable part of such a state and through *dawla* Islam presents certain cultural ideals if not a specific political model. [35] The Islamic state also rejects the concept of state autonomy and attempt to confine the state's function to a fixed territory and political domain. Barghouti defines it as a non-sovereign, non-territorial, temporary political arrangement that is accountable to and responsible for the whole *umma* or the whole community of Muslims, not only to a portion of it, regardless of borders and nationalities. [36]

The linguistic origins of the word state in European context and of the word *dawla* in Arab context actually imply two different things. [37] It is the concept of *umma* or the community, especially in its religious sense, is more important in the Islamic political tradition than any concept of the state or political system. [38] The history of Islam characterizes this basic binary-of *dawla* and the *umma*. The question which of the two has responsibility for the enforcement of Islamic law has been perpetuated throughout the history. *Dawla madaneyya*, in its traditional sense, is considered to be a departure from the religious state, as opposed to the reformation of such a state in a new guise, or an understanding of the state as open, secular and flexible. But in wider senses of the term, the idea contemporarily denotes to a response to the challenges posed by both theocracy and secularism.

Dawla madaneyya, in theory, implies a contrast with military state or theocratic state not governed by clergies or generals but by technocrats who comply with a written constitution to protect the civil liberties of both Muslims and non-Muslims alike. [39] By definition, it must be based on institutions and on consultation and the operative decision-making process should be civil in nature. Such a state rules recognizing the will of people through the categories of democratic or undemocratic, not through those of faith or of its rejection.

Dawala Madaneyya in the Egyptian context offers an alternative to the empire/caliphate and the differences are apparent in their use of *Sharia* or Islamic Law. The implementation of *Sharia* in the former context is done by the people's choice and free will. Unlike caliphate, civil state carries specific associations with democracy, constitutionalism and equality of citizens before the law. The stress here is not on the 'secular' aspects of the 'civil' but 'democratic' with strong sense of popular sovereignty. [40]

The contemporary relevance of this term, civil state, is not just associated with the political discourse induced by the Arab Spring. Though having roots to the pre-colonial debates of the state in West Asia and North Africa, it was Muslim Brotherhood which made the civil state with Islamic background popular in the 1950s. [41] Idea of 'civil state' has always been attracted the wrath of other Islamic organizations mainly, *Salafis* who see 'civil state' as identical to the 'secular state' and both for them are referred to Western, opposed to Islam and therefore, illegal under Islamic legal provisions. [42] But the Brotherhood literature inculcates that the civil state is fully compatible with Islam and Sharia. It is western-modelled secularism that, in fact, is something antithetical to Islamic jurisprudence hence not suitable for the Islamic world.

The 'secular' criticism of *dawla madaneyya* with Islamic reference revolves most importantly around the issue of *sharia* as the source of law and its inherent inability to sanction practices like the decentralization of power, plurality, and freedom of expression and public liberties. [43] The moderate Sunni objection to the concept of *dawla madaneyya* was its alleged attempt to make the idea of rulership a religious mandate. Sunni factions see 'civil state' with Islamic background as a revival of the old shibboleths of the Brotherhood, *Hukumat e-Ilahi* [44] considering the rulership as an organic part of religion. By insisting that rulership is fundamentally part of religion, the political process becomes an end in itself for the Brotherhood rather than a means to democratize Egyptian politics.

By re-interpreting the concept of 'civil', Muslim Brotherhood articulates that *madani* or civil in the Arab Islamic context is something that is not opposed to the role of religion in public life. In that sense 'civil' can not necessarily be often employed as a kind of euphemism for *almani* or 'secular'. The latter in the specific historical and political milieu of West Asia and North Africa shows a tendency to take on a more military anti-religious meaning, whereas, the concept of 'civil' does not dissociate completely from religion and indicates a more neutral and acceptable area of secular. [45] As articulated by the Muslim Brotherhood, there is an apparent difference in meaning between 'secular' and 'civil' here as *dawla madaneyya* is defined not in terms of its non-religious attributes but as something that stands sharply against the tyrannical rules of any sort. [46] Simultaneous to maintain aspirations for a non-military state, the term 'civil state' envisages an absence of complete hegemony of a single religion in the political affairs. With the use of 'civil' in opposition to military, what the leaders of Muslim Brothers had in mind was to create a united front of both 'religious' and 'secular' forces against the tradition of 'secular' state with repressive apparatuses.

The second related connotation of the 'civil state' according to Morsi was that of a 'democratic' or 'constitutional' state. While defining his vision of state, Morsi articulated that the state would be "the Egyptian national, democratic, constitutional, legal and modern state". [47] Such a state, he went on to say that "is ruled by the people through an elected parliament that represents the popular will". [48] In that sense, the state should be discussed in terms of its open and flexible structure that could ensure the political independence, plural religious identity and cultural specificities of the Arab world. [49]

The 'civil' in this sense does not insist on the separation of religion from the political sphere, but on accommodation of a multi-religious base for the polity. As Tariq Ramadan argued, the term has been adopted by the Islamist groups in the context of Arab Spring in part to distance from 'secularism' on the one hand and from Iranian-style 'theocracy' and their old call for a pure 'Islamic state' on the other. [50] President Morsi himself has expressed that the 'civil state' dissociates equally from 'secular' and 'theocratic-religious' government in principle and practice. [51] Brotherhood maintains the view that a civil state functions as an alternative to secularism and the hegemonic rule of one religion, both of which they argue, are the products of western political culture. [52] The civil state with Islamic references, in Tariq Ramadan's words comprised threefold response-religious, cultural and political and cultural- to the imposition of western models. [53]

What Brotherhood conceptualized was a civil state based on Islamic references, with three completely independent authorities: the parliament, judiciary and the government. [54] People regardless of religion and class are the paramount source of the power in such a state based not on theocratic concept. Islam, according to Morsi, confirms the independence of these authorities. [55] Although, the Islamic framework to a great extent controls the government and behaviour of the state, the notion of Islam cannot be imposed on the people from the top. To quote Morsi: Islam has to be initiated, created and agreed up on by the people. [56] Calling it a civil, democratic state guaranteeing equality and justice, Brotherhood stressed that Egypt is not following an Iranian model and has no intention of implementing, or attempting to implement, a theocratic state modelled on Iran. [57]

The re-conceptualization of the state and democracy in the new context had also echoed in the statements of many scholars who are subscribed to the ideology of *ikhwan* all over the world. Yusuf Al-Qardawi, a prominent Islamist ideologue associated closely with the movement, made it clear that it is incorrect and unjust to say that Brotherhood in Egypt is establishing a theocratic state. "The call of Brotherhood is for an Islamic civil state that by no means will end up in theocratic rule". [58] The same had resonated in the words of the leader of *Ennahada* in Tunisia, Rachid Ghannouchi interpreting religious texts in a way that is compatible with the idea of secularism and civil state. He objected the notion that Islamic principles and civil state are poles apart. Ghannouchi's only objection is to secularism as a philosophy of state. There is nothing essentially wrong with secularism as a 'procedural measure' that helps a nation with cross-cultural base to build a consensus. [59]

The concept *dawla madaneyya* in the Egyptian context involved a convergence of Islamism and secularism around the term civil. The secular/Islamic binary has already become meaningless with a complex set of reactions to the suppression and tyranny by the secularists. As discussed elsewhere in this paper, the term 'secular' in the Arab context was either quite synonymous with tyrannical rule or did not offer any alternative to the tyranny. In contrary to the general situation, it was actually the religious movements with its victimhood under the 'secular' rules of Nasser, Sadat and Mubarak, had contained space for resistance to the 'secular' politics. The ill-effects of globalization in the pre-Spring period had contributed further to the blurring of religious-left divide. There was a near-total absence of the state in mediating the conflict between ordinary people in the society without purchasing power and the market which made the regimes mute spectator in the neo-liberal context. It was again the Islamic organizations which had been very instrumental in the struggle against both tyrannical state and the imposition of American imperialism through neo-liberal politics in the Arab states.

In short, *Dawla Madaneyya* in its conceptualization recognized the public relevance of religion and religious ideas in conceiving statist discourse. But their recognition moved beyond the visibility of religion with affirming its symbolic values manifest in public rituals and rhetoric, made increased cultural influences of religion on government. It also represented a democracy that moved away from its general conceptualization as a technique of government. The dialogic aspect of it should be taken as an evidence of using democracy by the Islamists Egypt as a means of constituting the body politic. The Islamic model in this context boasted a political vitality that inspired contemporary politics and offered an alternative way of approaching the role of religion in conceptualizing the state. The entire debate led to exposing the failure of secular efforts to analyze religious practices that determines a modern state with a predominance of scientific thought and rationality.

Conclusion

The creation of civil state in Egypt and Tunisia, in a sense, marked a transition of Islamist politics from the principles of revealed religion to the experiences and patterns of living traditions. This slice in history also proved that Islam and civil are not opposite to each other, but with shared concerns against tyrannical rule. But from the line of traditional secularist thinking, the establishment of 'civil state' by Muslim Brotherhood was conceived as yet another cycle of events leading to the expansion of Islamist forces. Many left intellectuals from inside and outside the Arab world, focused on explaining what they saw as something anomalous to the 'democratic' rule. This perspective was based on a misconception being held by the liberals and leftists alike that the genuine democratic sense in the Arab world is limited to a narrow set of secular elites. Secular paradigm in its conventional form seemed to be not sufficient enough to make sense of the situation which needs to be understood within a multilayer of contexts. The experiences of Egypt realigned the debate away from the traditional binaries of religious versus secular. The new binaries emerged in its place were democratic versus anti-democratic and freedom versus tyranny.

Endnotes

1. See the Interview with Talal Asad by Nathan Schneider, The Suspicious Revolution: An Interview with Talal Asad, Immanent Frame, http://blogs.ssrc.org, accessed on 3rd March, 2011.
2. Democracy's use in the former sense in the contemporary political discourses, according to Agambern, seldom overpowers its apocryphal meaning as an 'administrative' practice with politico-managerial attributes. Giorgio Agemben, *Democracy in What State*, New York: Columbia University Press, 2011, p. 1.
3. Larbi Sadiki, "Egypt Back to Square One: Tahrir or Dictatorship", www.aljazeera.com accessed on 16th July, 2013.
4. Ibid.
5. See Asad (2011) the conversation by Talal Asad and Ayca Cubukcu, "Neither Heroes, Nor Villains: A Conversation with Talal Asad on Egypt after Morsi", www. Jadaliyya.com accessed on 23rd July, 2013.
6. Larbi Sadiki, "Egypt Back to Square One: Tahrir or Dictatorship".
7. Jurgen Habermas, "Religion in the Public Sphere", *European Journal of Philosophy*, 14:1, 2006, pp. 1-25.
8. Ibid.
9. See Asad (2011), the conversation by Talal Asad and Ayca Cubukcu, "Neither Heroes, Nor Villains: A Conversation with Talal Asad on Egypt After Morsi".
10. Hans Joas, *Braucht der Mensch Religion*? *Uber Erfahrungen der Selbstranszendenz* (Freiburg im Breisgau: Helder, 2004), p. 124, cited in Hent de Vries, "Introduction: Before, Around and Beyond the Theological-Political", in Hent de Vries and Lawrence E. Sullivan, *Political Theologies: Public Religions in*

a Post-Secular World (New Delhi: Orient Longman, 2007), pp. 1-34.

11. Ibid., pp. 124-125.
12. As McLachlan points out, two developments in Saudi Arabia worked towards the agenda of reducing the influence of religious and tribal institutions in the administration. The process of centralization of power and the introduction of modern institutions deliberately attempted to enhance the positions of ruling dynasty at the direct expense of *Ikhwan*. Keith McLachlan, "Saudi Arabia: Political and Social Evolution", in Ian Richard Neton (ed.), *Arabia and the Gulf: From Traditional Society to Modern States*, London: Croom Helm, 1986, pp. 92-95.
13. Nazih Ayubi, *Over-stating the Arab State: Politics and Society in the Middle East*, London: IB Tauris, 2006, pp. 4 and 135.
14. Secularization in the Arab world's context means to nothing but the partial displacement of tribal or religious-based perception of how the state should be organized by the bureaucratic and economic perceptions.
15. Nazih Ayubi, *Over-stating the Arab State: Politics and Society in the Middle East*, p.9.
16. Tamim Al-Bargouti, *The Umma and The Dawla: The Nation State and the Arab Middle East*, London: Pluto Press, 2008, p. 3.
17. Hamid Rabi, Suluk al-Malik fi Tadbir al-Mamalik: Ta'lif al-'Allamma Shihab al-Din ibn Abi al-Rubayyi, Vol. 1, Cairo: Dar al-Sha'b, 1980, pp. 15-16.
18. Ibid.
19. Hamid Rabi, Suluk al-Malik fi Tadbir al-Mamalik, pp. 46-51 and 133-49.
20. Ibid., pp.144-149.
21. Except few, the Arab Scholars were not much inclined towards the idea of freedom, which was a cornerstone of modern European politics. Khair al-Din of Tunisia and Tahtawi of Egypt preferred justice to freedom. Ahmad Lufi al-Sayyid held a belief in the emancipator potential of the State to bring freedom, was an exception. For further details of this debate, see Albert Hourani, *Arabic Thought in the Liberal Age 1798-1939*, London: Oxford University Press, 1970.
22. Albert Hourani, *Arabic Thought in the Liberal Age 1798-1939* and Nazih Ayubi, *Over-stating the Arab State: Politics and*

Society in the Middle East, p. 23.

23. Nazih Ayubi, *Over-stating the Arab State: Politics and Society in the Middle East,* p. 23 and Abdullah Laroui, The Crisis of the Arab Intellectual, trns., Berkely, CA: California University Press, 1976, pp. 129-133.
24. Yadh Ben Achour, L'Elat Nouveau et la Philosophie et Juridique Occidentale, Tunis: Imp. De la Republique, 1980 quoted in Nazih Ayubi, *Over-stating the Arab State: Politics and Society in the Middle East*, pp. 22-23.
25. While Afghani and Abdu advocated for Islamic unity, the proponents of Arab nationalism stood for the unity of Arabs on the basis of language and culture. Anyway, both undervalued the importance of secular state with clearly defined borders and populations as artificial political construct. See Nazih Ayubi, *Over-stating the Arab State: Politics and Society in the Middle East*, p. 21.
26. Ibid., p. 23.
27. Ibid., p. 99.
28. Ibid.
29. Lailufar Yasmin, "Crisis of Modernity and Secularism: The Cases of Egypt, Turkey and Bangladesh", *Open Democracy*, 17th August, 2013.
30. Talal Asad. Fear and the Ruptured State: Reflections on Egypt after Mubarak, *Social Research*, Vol. 79, No. 2, Summer 2012, p. 279.
31. Ibid.
32. The opposition, according to Asad, consisted a diverse spectrum of elites; the rich businessmen who established themselves during Mubarak's neo-liberal regime; high court judges that maintained close links with the army; ambitions politicians and ex-politicians; left and liberals; army officers and journalists. The left politicians disliked Brotherhood for its ideology as well as its country-wide grassroots organizational set up. See Asad (2011) the conversation by Talal Asad and Ayca Cubukcu, *Neither Heroes, Nor Villains: A Conversation with Talal Asad on Egypt After Morsi*, www.Jadaliyya.com accessed on 23rd July, 2013.
33. Secular in this context is understood not simply as the doctrine of separation of church from state, but the re-articulation of religion in a manner that is commensurate with modern

sensibilities and modes of governance. See Mahmood (2013) "Is Critique Secular", *The Immanent Frame*, blogs.ssrc.org accessed on 8th July, 2013.

34. Nazih Ayubi, *Over-stating the Arab State: Politics and Society in the Middle East,* p. 18.
35. Hamid Rabi, Suluk al-Malik fi Tadbir al-Mamalik, pp. 289-293.
36. Tamim Al-Bargouti, *The Umma and The Dawla: The Nation State and the Arab Middle East,* p. 2.
37. Nazih Ayubi, *Over-stating the Arab State: Politics and Society in the Middle East*, p. 15.
38. Ibid.
39. Hassan Hassan, "Muslim Brotherhood Still Fails to Offer a 'Civil State' Solution", *The National*, June 18, 2012, www.thenational.ae., accessed on 10th August, 2013.
40. www.ikhwanweb.com/print.php?id=28368.
41. Peter Hill, *The "Civil" and the "Secular" in Contemporary Arab Politics,* www.muftah.org, accessed on 8th July, 2013.
42. Ibid.
43. Hassan Hassan, "Muslim Brotherhood Still Fails to Offer a 'Civil State' Solution".
44. Al-hakimiyya refers to the idea that sovereignty and governance are the prerogative of God alone. Though it had a set of other contextual meanings given by the Islamic scholars like Maulana Mawdudi and Sayed Qutub, Hukumat e-Ilahi is seen by many as the inverse of the concept of sovereignty within the modern nation-state and will of the people. Almost a similar sort of idea, *wilayet al-fqaih* or guardianship of the Jurist was held by Ayathollah Khomeini and was used to justify clerical rule in Iran.
45. Peter Hill, *The "Civil" and the "Secular" in Contemporary Arab Politics.*
46. www.ikhwanweb.com/print.php?id=28368.
47. See Interview with Mohamed Morsi; "What to Expect from the Muslim Brotherhood", available at, www.policymic.com/articles/380/exclusive-Interview-with-mohamed-morsi-what-to-expect-from-the-muslim-brotherhood.Morsi, September, 2012.
48. Ibid.
49. Tariq Ramadan, "Not an Islamic State, but a Civil State", *ABC Religion and Ethics*, 30th January, 2012.

50. Ibid.
51. See Interview with Mohamed Morsi.
52. Hassan Hassan, "Muslim Brotherhood Still Fails to Offer a 'Civil State' Solution".
53. Tariq Ramadan, "Not an Islamic State, but a Civil State".
54. See Interview with Mohamed Morsi.
55. Ibid.
56. Ibid.
57. El-Arain: MB wants a civil state; Egypt will not become another Iran, www.ikhwanweb.com/print.php?id=28368.
58. Yusuf Al-Qardawi as quoted in Hassan Hassan, "Muslim Brotherhood Still Fails to Offer a 'Civil State' Solution".
59. Ibid.

14

Arab Spring and the Changing Dynamics of Political Islam in Egypt

Fazzur Rahman

All praise be to Allah, today I can see those faces in Parliament about whom in past even an utterance was a legal crime": Egyptian Prime Minister, Kamal Ganzouri in his address to the National Assembly. [1]

The Arab Spring has sent a shock wave across the Arab world and came out to be the biggest moment of the 21st century so far. The turmoil, simply triggered by the self immolation of a Tunisian Youngman on 17th December, 2010 has put to rest the entire stereotype notion about Arab and Islam. This individual act was a collective expression of the grievance against the prevailing socio-economic and political system that created a reverberation in other parts of the world too. This Arab tumult has so far forced the Egyptian President to resign, Tunisian President to flee the country, the Libyan regime has been overthrown and Colonel Gaddafi himself has been killed and Yemeni president has conceded power to his deputy. In addition to that, an intense turmoil is in full sway in Syria along with the protests in Bahrain, Iran, Saudi Arabia, Kuwait, Iraq, Oman and Morocco.

This protest of millions around the Arab presents a call for social justice, equality and national sovereignty and dignity. It predominantly reflects people's flight from culture of authoritarianism and urge for democratic participation. It is a call for shift from policy of surrender to politics of assertion. This has provided an open space to all kinds of political voices to compete with each other's irrespective of ideological leaning and political inclination.

This Arab Spring has debunked many of the culturalist

assumption like; democracy and Arab/Islam cannot co-exist and political Islam is the real perpetrator of violence, brutality, and disorder. For the first time in history, these assumptions have been contested and successfully discredited by the people themselves through this movement.

If one notices the trajectory of these protest movement, he or she will find that the responses of Islamist forces have been very positive, though well-guarded and very strategic. Many of the political observers have named this spring an Islamic Spring too, being well aware of the fact that Islamists would be the real beneficiary of this turmoil.

This paper will first analyze the ongoing phenomena called Arab Spring and will deal at length the changing nature of political Islam. It will focus on the response and role of Islamist in Egypt and analyse its prospect in near future.

Introduction

A great wave of anger, frustration, defiance and democratic demand has swept across the Arab world from the Atlantic shore to the Gulf of Aden and from Amman to Khartoum. Since the early days of 2011, the notion of the Arab Spring has become a household one across the globe. Not a single month has passed with some leading stores capturing the imagination and thoughts about the Arab spring and its possible repercussion.

This is the single biggest uprising in modern Arab history being termed by western media as Arab Spring and what Professor Aijaz Ahmad, a renowned scholar has termed it an "autumn of the patriarchs". [2] One can gauge the level of fury of the common people by the report in Egyptian media which calls Mubarak the biggest traitor of the history who helped assassinate Sadat and kissed Israel to please US.

Popular power and non-violent resistance put the old regimes to rest that are unprecedented in history. The protests spread from village to city, region to region, from one country to another, and eventually became an overall pan-Arab uprising bearing all the hallmarks of the Information Age. The great weapon of this uprising has been the Internet and the electronic media. Much has happened because of the immediacy with which visual images of the latest events can circulate around the world through 24x7 news channels, YouTube, *Al Jazeera* and even cell phones. Similarly, there is a breathtaking rapidity with which millions can be brought into overlapping networks of communication through e-mail, SMS, Facebook, Twitter, and so on.

This was the self-immolation attempt by an unemployed graduate, Mohamed Bouazizi from a small town, Sidi Bouzid in central Tunisia that detonated the Arab revolution in the last month of 2010. Once triggered, it became impossible for Arab dictators to contain the marches of million in different parts of the Arab world. This upsurge forced many regimes to change in the region and before this tide could touch the palace of the monarchs in the gulf, they themselves initiated several political reforms.

This uprising has already laid to rest the "Westocentric" myth that Muslim masses can only be mobilised through religious exhortation, and it has also refuted the claim of American-sponsored dictators that they are the great bulwark against a rising tide of "Islamo-fascism" (a word of American coinage) that is sweeping the Arab lands.

This carries good old values of the French Revolution as the marching army is demanding democracy, freedom, equality, justice, dignity and national sovereignty. This is an autonomous and universal in nature and a cry for transformation of political self- power of the Arab people.

The present development has brought the region at the crossroads of political and social transformation. Great uncertainties have enveloped the region and processes of transitions are still unfolding which are not resorting to identical routes everywhere.

One of the most prominent features of this movement is its non-ideological orientation, its homogeneity and non-ethnicity in some countries like Egypt, Tunisia, Morocco while others like Libya, Yemen and Syria are fraught with religious sectarianism and ethnicity. [3] Arab Spring brought a new era of politics in the region and has sown the new seeds of democracy and constitutionalism.

Genesis of the Arab Spring

The origin of Arab Spring can be traced into the womb of the autocratic character of regime in post colonial Arab world. One can decipher its genealogy in colonial and post-colonial background and it is an outcome of a prolonged turbulence and turmoil in the region. This is an expression of collective anger against the sense of deprivation of dignity, freedom, social justice and national sovereignty by the masses. This upheaval is a response to utter despondence against the dictatorship and it is a passionate desire for independence of oneself and the nation. This is a triumph impelled by shared vision of responsibility and accountability. Ziauddeen Sirdar calls it a post normal world and a tiger-wounded reaction.

All forms of political opposition and mobilisation known to modern societies—political parties, trades unions, the independent press, and liberal liberties of various sorts—were so thoroughly and successfully suppressed, or at least compromised, by all the dictatorial regimes that any sort of political dissent was unfeasible.

This is a response to political status quo seeking political pluralism and legitimacy to political activities. Arab system and society has become so status quoits that one of the French Magazine wrote reacting to the revolt in the Arab world that "Even Arab can have a revolution". [4] It was wail against securitized nationalism where denial of all freedom was the key political philosophy.

A surveillance-Police state had given rise to a state calling for fundamental change but the dictators had imprisoned, killed or driven into exile those who could plausibly lead a successful and coherent revolution. All Arab states had become a police state where each and every individual act was not only observed but closely monitored. In Egypt only, there are 1.5 million security person employed to watch the common men's activities. There was every abuse of human right by the state in the name of national security and emergency law was in practice for last thirty years in Egypt that was nothing but a licence for the police to arrest, torture anybody.

This rebellion was a refusal of the obedience to the autocratic and foreign-dictated regime. The system had become external and the role of indigenous state had become an implementing agency. They were taking dictation from their foreign masters and, in turn, dictated to the people of their countries. Collusion between the agent of external hegemony and perpetuators of internal tyranny sabotaged the purpose of the entire freedom and liberation from the colonial masters.

The youths were motivated by three rhetorical fetishes of American-style promotion of democracy: human rights, democracy and corruption. Democracy was denied in all these countries, human rights were suppressed and corruption had reached gigantic proportions. These are perfectly legitimate issues as the structural origins and sources of power of these dictators form no part of the consciousness of the majority of what one might call the Twitter revolutionaries. [5]

The economies of countries such as Tunisia and Egypt have been devastated by unbridled liberalism and the diktats of the International Monetary Fund (IMF), which were happily carried out by same dictators. Liberalised economy had led to concentration of wealth in few hands and creation of nexus between capitalist and government bureaucrats that deprived million of their opportunity of livelihood. For example, only in Egypt, more than 50 percent people live below poverty line or earning only US$ 2 a day. [6]

Most of the Arab rulers had surrendered the national sovereignty to the dictate of foreign powers. Egypt in particular has abandoned its regional role and its centrality in the regional affairs. The memory of Camp David was still fresh in the mind of the people causing the exit of Egypt from Arab-Israel conflict. Egypt had stopped supporting Arab cause and very often acted indifferently towards most of the Arab issue caused a sense of humiliation for the Egyptian masses leading to the revolt.

Hussein Kaykal, a well known political commentator of Egypt has put it very truly that "Arab Spring is the outcome of what we have done to ourselves, what the regime has done to us and what Israel has done to us". [7]

Egypt's sole reliance on United State further angered the people (one could read the anti-US slogan during the protest). US failed to promote democracy in the Egypt and the Arab World because its only concern in the region was secure root of oil, security of Israel and stability and status quo in the region.

What is Political Islam?

Before I proceed further, I would like to deal briefly with the phenomena called political Islam. Over the past few decades, the "Political Islam" as an ideology has acquired an apocalyptic implication for both western academia and the media. Political Islam as a comprehensive ideology has invaded both the scholar's lexicon and popular imaginations across the world. This concept has recently navigated from its narrow religious reference to other domains as well. It has become a key feature in modern day Arab-Islamic world and has found an expression in number of Islamic revivalist movements. There is lot of debate regarding its appropriation, its rejection or its transformation.

Political Islam is a form of political and religious utopia acts as an ideological alternative to the invasion of modern doctrine of secularism, communism, socialism and liberalism. It is a form of instrumentalization of Islam by an individual, group, or organization that pursue political objective. It provides political response to today's societal challenges by imagining a future, the foundation for which rest on re-appropriated, invented concept borrowed from the Islamic tradition. [8]

It is treated as an ideology couched in language of descent, opposition and resistance to modern global order opposing the existing socio-political ideology and acts as a quest for freedom, dignity and sovereignty and stands against authoritarian secular modernity of west. This is battle between ideologization of religion and idealization of secularism. Political Islam as a philosophy attempts to synthesize the traditional Islamic thoughts to the modern concept of an accountability and pluralism and rule of law.

This is a political ideology rather than religion or theology. Its adherents believe that Islam as a body of faith has something important to say about how politics and society should be ordered. Islamists are distinguished from other Muslim fundamentalist by their insistence on engagement with political structure and state apparatus as a mean of establishing Islamic society. It is about primacy of religious authority over directorial authority. It has a belief in different epistemological order where west represent different sets of knowledge for them and the Muslims are the inheritor of different set of knowledge and tradition.

This is a modern phenomenon and its roots lies in the socio-political condition of 19th and 20th century of Muslims World. It is a product of interaction with the west in economic, political, social, cultural and intellectual arena when Muslim became object rather than subject of the history.

Unlike Marxist's overemphasise on socio-economic aspects of social order, the adherents of political Islam is an ardent believer in moral and cultural transformation. The integration of Islam as a primary agent of identity formation is a major component of this discourse. The colonial entrenchment may have acted as a force behind the ideologization of Islam and confrontationist ideology but it was the failure of the Arab regime too to deliver wealth, dignity and power to expectant population that popularised it further. The departure of colonial master and the advantage of change never ticked down to the common men in the Arab world. Oppressive nature of regime has played a great role in according the status and legitimacy to this phenomenon.

This entire phenomenon can be seen in social and political context. The quest for political Islam is not driven by religious concern but more it has been a cry in the crisis. It has always arisen as an attempt to provide a definitive answer for the existing political and religious predicament. It has been more a reaction rather than an action and stands for an ideological contestation with the far enemy and the near enemy, far enemy connoting the colonial master and near enemy representing the remnants groups of political and military elite of the Arab world.

All political Islamic movement in Arab world has arisen as a reaction to the western socio-political and cultural assault that provided a context for the text of political Islam. The early and mid 20th century witnessed the emergence of a number of Islamic political groups in Asia and Africa carrying its indigenous attributes but not without commonality among themselves.

For instance, Muslim Brotherhood (henceforth MBH) MBH in Egyptian has come into existence in its own imperial context while the rise of Jamaat-e-islami in South Asia can be interpreted in the colonial context. Similarly, the rise of An-Nahda in Tunisia and Nahdatul Ulema of Indonesia has their own contextual specificity. Likewise, Shiite Amal in Lebanon and Sunni Algerian FIS has different histories, background and philosophies but both are known as bone of global political Islam.

In the following pages I will deal at some length with political Islam in pre-Arab Spring phase, its assertion and transformation in post Arab Spring phase and future scenario in Egypt with particular reference to MBH.

Changing Dynamics of Political Islam

If one needs to decipher the true nature and dynamic political Islam, or the core of today's Islamic polity, he or she should examine the *Al-Ikhwan al-Muslimeen* (Muslim

Brotherhood) founded in Egypt in 1928 by Hasan Al-Banna. This is MBH which truly represents the spirit and attributes of political Islam in contemporary Arab World.

One of the major objective of the MBH since its commencement has been to fulfil the core objective of Islam by reshaping the society in the light of Quranic teaching. The ideology of the MBH was driven by spiritual and religious state of masses and political and economic deprivation of the people at large. Islam for Brotherhood is simultaneously a civilization, a way of life, an ideology and in final culmination a state in itself. [9]

MBH is considered to be the fountainhead of all Islamic movements around the world and its several outfits are operating in different parts of the Arab countries with variant names like in Kuwait, it is known as *Constitutional Movement*, in Jordan it carries the name of *Islamic Working Front*, in Palestine it is called *Hamas* and Yemeni branch carries the name of *Reform Movement* and in Algeria it is *Peace Movement*. [10]

MBH in its initial days had concentrated more and more on building the organization and showed no inclination towards playing a substantial political role in national politics and the role of MBH did not go beyond occasional suggestion to the king. In 1936, Al-Banna wrote a letter to President Farouk pursuing him to establish an Islamic order and advocated for more and more power to local political bodies and again in 1938, he is reported to have asked King Farouk to dissolve all the political parties since all had gone corrupt and proving very catalyst in dividing the society on ideological lines. [11]

In late 1940s, MBH altered its tactical relationship with the regime and they sought altogether different mechanism to facilitate the change in the regime. This sudden change in MBH policy introduced a new era of relation between King and MBH when both were at path of confrontation.

The relationship between MBH and regime touched the

lowest ebb during Nasser. Nasser tried to silence all the voices of opposition in the name of making Egypt a modern, independent and progressive state. Showing his secular Pan-Arab nationalist posture, in no lesser time Nasser made it categorical that he had neither desire to introduce an Islamic order in Egypt nor was ready to tolerate the powerful dissent to his authoritarian rule. This was the beginning of war of attrition between the Nasser and MBH when undermining the legitimacy of each other became main components of their political plank.

According to one political analyst, Osama Ghazali, Nasser had skilfully exploited existing regional and global political situation in his favour and was able to marginalize the other canters of power too including like MBH. [12] This political behaviour of Nasser played a critical role in shaping the future political and intellectual outlook of MBH leadership towards the regime and the newly established political institutions.

In February, 1954, large number of members and followers of MBH were sent to jail. The legislative council of 1957, a large number of nominations was rejected and main objective of rejection was to prevent MBH sympathizers form joining the fray. [13] Between1954 and 1969, no one suspected of having any kind of affiliation with MBH was allowed to contest the election of any political body. But the defeat of Egypt led Arab world in 1967 caused a different course of relationship between religion, state and the society. This particular moment was blessing in disguise for MBH. [14]

MBH joined the mainstream street political movement and the March Declaration of 1968 by Nasser he introduced some major changes in his policy aiming to provide political spaces for opposition. [15] Large numbers of MBH cadres were set free from jail and according to a contemporary repot, there were only 140 members left in jail in 1970 when Sadat came to power after departure of Nasser. [16]

To leave the legacy of Nasser behind, Sadat opted to get

rid of Communists within Egyptian political system adopting the policy of co-existence with MBH. He adopted the policy of accommodation vis-à-vis religious forces with the notion that his Islam-driven policy will accord him a political legitimacy that he required urgently to consolidate himself in power.

MBH members were allowed to come back to Egypt. Sadat had announcing that he would seek all cooperation and coordination of MBH but would not change the official rank of MBH. Only between 1977 and 1990, for more than forty times, the issue of revoking the ban against MBH was raised with several Egyptian courts but in vain. [17] Given the soft policy of Sadat vis-à-vis MBH, they had hoped that he would allow them to enter in the Parliament but Sadat showed no inclination of this sort. He suggested them to merge with three existing major block.

In the first election of 1976 under Sadat, MBH fought the election under the banner of Arab Socialist Party and six of its members made to the Egyptian parliament and refused third consecutive offer by President Sadat to accord MBH a status of charitable organization. [18]

The most impulsive phase of relation between state and MBH came when President Sadat landed in Israeli Knesset leading to singeing of the Camp David Agreement in 1979. This had angered all the Islamic forces who termed it an un-Islamic act. Sadat responded to the rejection of MBH of his new policy with the large scale crackdown and hundreds of MBH members were arrested.

Mubarak's era can be said to be an era of open confrontation between the sate and MBH. The main objective of State's overarching power was to oppress all sort of Islamic voices. At first, Mubarak had softened his policy towards MBH like he set free thousands of Islamist thrown in prison during last days of Sadat. This was to contain the extremist element. Unlike 1970s, now MBH was in favour of political participation as an independent and organized body in alliance with one of the existing legal party. In the election of 1984,

MBH entered into parliament for the first time as an opposition block with alliance of Wafd Party which had 58 seats and the share of MBH was eight.

One of the member commented saying that "We are not worried about the size of our number here but what is important for us at this moment is to make our presence realized by both people and the state". [19] Now MBH has no apprehension in forging political alliance with its ideological and political adversaries and extending all cooperation to communist and Nasserite as well.

By late 1980s, MBH had emerged as a force which can't be any more pushed aside since it had established itself as major political force, if not in national politics, at least among student Unions and other professional trade unions. Their voice was no more confined to seek the recognition for itself alone but they were determined to play an important role in shaping the structure of the national politics. [20]

In the fresh election of 1987, MBH made alliance with Labour party and Ahrar Party and enhanced its performance by gaining 36 seats and emerging as the single largest opposition party. [21] End of 1980s had witnessed lot of extremist activities in Egypt and only in 1988, more than nine incident of fighting took place between member of extremist Jama-al-Islamiyah and Security Forces. [22]

In its attempt to counter the extremist voices, state itself adopted the policy of islamisation of its institution. It started Islamic daily and weekly like *Lawau-al-Islam* and *Aqeedati* and extended the hours of TV and Radio program devoted to religious teaching. The beginning of 1990 witnessed a fundamental change in relation between MBH and President Mubarak which can be well described as a shift from cooperation and coexistence to open contestation and confrontation. The victory of Islamist in Algeria and growing popularity of Hamas had given new fervour to MBH.

MBH decided to boycott the election of 1990 on the ground of apathetic attitude of the government in last parliament and new discriminatory election MBH participated in the election of 1995 under its own banner but Security forces entered to prevent them from entering into political fray and as a result only one member could make it to parliament who himself later was ousted allegedly because of his association with some illegal party. [23] Hundreds of MBH activists thrown in jail and several were tried in military court which had its only precedent during Nasser's regime.

The election of 2000 was judicially administered where member of MBH also participated as an independent. The slogan of "Islam is the only solution" was completely absent and despite the absent of free and friendly environment, MBH was able to secure 18 seats and had emerged once again as single largest opposition party.

The election of 2005 proved to be a catalyst for MBH as 88 members won out of total 161 MBH had filed. To check the growing popularity of MBH, a comprehensive constitutional amendment was introduced in 2007 granting sweeping power to security forces and banning all political parties with religious or any particular ideological leaning. [24]

We have seen above that how political institutions with Islamic orientation were suppressed and their voices were scuttled and members were tortured and such experiences gave rise to profound bitterness. The political space for Islamic forces was shrunken during the successive autocratic regimes in Egypt and no scope was left for expression of Islamic voices. The impressive political performance of MBH in successive election in a given limited free space pushed the state further to tighten the grip over the stretching root of political Islam.

For decades, MBH has been banking on politics of hope to attract the supports and broaden their influences. When politics of fist iron fist was in place their suggestion of remedy was attractive to various sections and the arrival of Arab spring has brought this opportunity for them. The movement has pushed the region towards redefining its political landscape where political Islam has emerged as an inevitable force to negotiate its space in the new emerging socio-political order. The change in the region has triggered a new debate on the future role of Islam inviting various interpretations on the mode of its operation and politics of accommodation and adaptation in the newly created political vacuum. This uncertainty has brought a change in the traditional vocabulary and conduct of the political Islam that it is already visible. The absence of religious rhetoric in the demonstration and protest in Egypt is a case in point.

Islamist has got an independent place and new public space for the first time. All ideologies suppressed so far have come out in an open sky to compete with each other. It has given an opportunity to the Islamists to exploit the political maturity they have accumulated in last five decade of the struggle with the regime and lesson they have learnt through the revolution of Iran, victory of Hamas in Palestine and FIS in Algeria.

Islamist forces have captured the centre stage in Egypt, Tunisia, Morocco and Kuwait. There has been mounting tension between Islamist and the secularist and many warn that Arab Spring will lead to Islamic winter. [25] Political Islam as an ideology has swept across the region and it can be seen as a reaction to half century of its suppression by autocratic and so called secular regimes. One member of MBH (Syria) Mr. Bayamon has put it very rightly when he remarked that, "For every success there is context and that must be respected". [26] Arab Spring has created a situation where no longer it is possible to denounce the Islamist.

The Arab spring has brought a radical transformation into political ideology of Islam itself. There is a new search for Islam in post revolutionary period. It has opened a new chapter of enlightened and moderate Islamic democracy where is no scope for intra ideological confrontation among different Islamist organizations one hand and western liberal democratic model on other hand. This has brought departure from ideological debate to political debate, from confrontation to conformation, from exclusion to inclusion. Now they are learning to work within the political process as they have learnt bitter lesson from their past when they were crushed everywhere.

With the fall of third republic in Egypt after the January revolution, Islamist forces have been spurred into action in search of the role and gains in the fourth republic. [27] MBH which struggles for almost six decades to get political recognition has come out as the most popular and acceptable voice in the aftermath of Arab Spring. This is the manifestation of political and ideological current running through the entire the Arab world. It is not the Islamic rhetoric but the question of democracy that is nearer to their heart. The real concern for believer in political Islam is to highlight the democratic element of Islamic polity and opt for political alliance with even liberal forces. Freedom and Justice Party which include Christian Copts has gone out of its way to say that it seeks a constitution that respects both Muslims and non-Muslims and committed to pluralistic and democratic Egypt. [28] Freedom and Justice Party sent its representative to attend the Coptic festival of Cairo and it also entered into intense dialogue with the Christian Coptic youth movement and three Christian organizations and first political alliance comprising both MBH and Coptic member came out. [29]

It is the democratic wave that has compelled the Islamist to abandon its exclusive and narrow Islamic character of politics and join the mainstream national polity. The legitimacy and authenticity accorded to the Islamist forces have brought modesty in their mode of political engagement. The Islamists are making all efforts to project their moderate face by entering into dialogue with Coptic Christian.

The uprising in the Arab world has pushed the Islamist forces on a protective mode and they are striding a cautious path. During the heyday of revolution in Egypt, MBH did not create its own rhetoric to convey its message. According to one of the official members of MBH, they had opted not to play remarkable role in the revolt just to preserve the national and secular identity of the revolt. [30] The compulsion of politics of negotiation has also brought some fundamental changes in political approach of the Islamists.

A sense of pragmatism has prevailed over the Islamists in the aftermath of this upsurge and they are no more acting regressive in their orientation but acting in more progressive manner. Their political manifesto does not highlight the issue of Palestine but like all other political forces in Egypt talked of employment, social justice and poverty. [31] The formation of FJP places the MBH on equal electoral footing in terms of having to draft a national party platform and specific policies which, no doubt, in longer term will impact it Islamic ideology.

Arab Spring brought benefit to many but the real beneficiary is Islamist forces. For the first time in modern Egypt, a large number of religious parties have been permitted to participate in the election. Freedom and Justice Party, Political wings of MBH and ultra conservative Al Nour party, political wing of Salafist have captured nearly three quarter of seats in lower house of parliament. Salfists who constantly condemned political participation for its non religiosity but given the changing environment, it joined the fray and fared well. The most shocking and surprising was the emergence of Salafists in this election that have remained so far, a non-entity in political sphere. There has been no convergence on ideological and political level between MBH and Salafist but in near future both will have to come closer to project a united Islamic front and to remain in the power structure of Egypt. There is lot of buzz going around regarding the future relationship between two major Islamic blocks of the country.

Their vote was the vote of protest and vote to do away not with the regime alone but to do away with the system itself. There are other smaller parties like Construction and Development Party, Fadhila Party, Salafist al-Asala (Authenticity), Al Haya al-

Sharia lil Islah who have also appeared on the national political horizon. Liberals also entered the fry and did not lag behind in asserting their religiosity and that shows the grasp of Islamist over political landscape of the country.

Some have already expressed their apprehension over the impressive victory of Islamists in Egyptian and calling Egypt in advance an Islamic republic of Egypt under Qarzavi. [32] One of the political commentators described the development in following words, "The people who have paid high price will not ripe the fruit because of its Islamic character. [33]

The response of Islamist to social upheaval is one of the key reasons for their success" [34] and Islamist take over cannot be attributed to its ideological appeal alone but it was also because other voices too were suppressed in last 60 years

Emergence of new leadership in MBH (between the age group of 40-45) are moderate and do not believe in the rhetoric of ideological Islamic state or Islamic caliphate and global Ummah. They believe more in democratic ballot box and receptive to external political ideas too. There is no more debate over the intricacy, nuances and origin of western liberal democracy and its comparison with Islamic model of polity. The participation of conservative party like Salafist in the election of Egypt is itself suggestive of this radical transformation within political Islam.

The demographic character of Egypt also has some impact on transforming the ideology of political Islam. More than 70 percent of Egyptian population are below the age of 30 whose primary objective only is to remove the corruption, nepotism. They are Islamic in practice but do not comprehend any ideological element in Islamic oriented political parties. This is the generation of post-Islamist ideology and people are more bothered about national prosperity and sovereignty.

Conclusion

In the preceding pages, we have seen how the Arab Spring has opened a new political vista for Islamist forces across the

Arab world. This has opened a new prospect for so far suppressed ideology, scuttled voices and a banned action to come out and lay down a fresh blue print for the masses. Arab Spring has not touched the shore of the Red Sea and Mediterranean Sea merely to oust the regime but to transform the entire system itself. Vocabulary of this Arab spring has remained same and syntax might differ across the Arab world guided by local condition.

It has accorder legitimacy and authenticity to several ideological players to experiment their political model. Like many other ideologies, Islamic political narrative flourished more in opposition. From the mid twentieth century, repressive government, dire economic situation and corruption have created a breeding ground for Islamic political movement across the Arab world Now, after many years of being in opposition, they are finally reaching to the corridor of power Islamists for the first time have been put to both legitimacy and accountability and these two are the hallmark of democracy.

The recipe for MBH was Islam, a religion which majority of people adhered in Egypt and their motto "Islam is the solution". MBH was successful in constituting the sharp binaries of religious versus secular where former promise of social justice while latter represents corruption.

There are apprehensions that given the fundamental and economic problem in Egypt might discredit the Islamist since they cannot resolve the matter any faster than any other forces. This short term lack of success in delivering what they have promised historically might harm their reputation. Many observers have spoken about the paradigm shift and the return of Islamic control in the region but irresistibility of political Islam will be seriously challenged.

Political Islam has reached to a stage where one has a feeling that it is not Islam which will shape the politics but it is the politics that will shape the Islamism. The shift in the slogan from 'Islam is the Solution' to Freedom is the suggestive of conceptual shift in the political ideology of Islamist.

Islam as a political ideology will have to face several internal and external constraints and challenges and it is time for the Islamist to project its new democratic and moderate images. For the first time MBH has entered into a party system which they had looked down upon in the past condemning the culture of party system but now they have been forces to be larger political groups. Islamist will have to balance between people's aspiration and their ideological commitment. This is an experimental phase for Islamist and uphill task is ahead for them to get integrated in mainstream national politics. Once they have been democratically elected, exponent of Islamic parties will have no more alibis. The best consequence that the Arab spring has so far produced is to bring Islam out in the air. Coming to power through ballot box may mainstream political Islam and the nitty gritty and the tedious dynamics of governing will moderate the tenor of political Islam.

Meanwhile, this is a unique opportunity for the West too to demonstrate that it will no longer support despotic regimes and support instead the democratic process in the Arab world. This wave of political Islam is an opportunity to create a democratic, moderate and despot free Arab world.

The ascendancy of Islamist in Egypt has manifested that people want the democracy of their own choice unlike Iraq and Afghanistan. Things will not settle in months or year and will take time to settle down and take the true political direction. The trust-deficit will have to be bridged with others and give a new shape to old Egypt. Mr. Heikal, a well known commentator speaking on Egypt said that, "no party has clear blueprint for the future of Egypt and Egypt particularly being a religious country cannot be ruled religiously. [35]

Endnotes

1. Al-Ahram Newspaper, Cairo, January 31, 2012.
2. Frontline, February 25, 2011.
3. Thomas. L. Friedman, New York Times, April 13, 2011.
4. Al-Mustaqbal Al-Arabi, March, 2011, Issue No. 358, p. 101.

5. Aijaz, Ahmad, Frontline, February 25, 2011.
6. Ziyad, Hafiz, *Sauratu Yanayir Fi Misr: Tasaulatal-Hazir wal-Mustaqbil*, Al-Mustaqbal Al-Arabi, March, 2011, Issue No. 358, p. 71.
7. Akhbaralaalam, November 14, 2011.
8. Guilain, Denoeux, "The Forgotten Swamp: Navigating Political Islam", Middle East Policy, June 2002, p. 61.
9. Ibrahim, Abu M., "Contemporary Arab Thought Rabi, London: Pluto Press, 2004, p. 65.
10. Hisham Al-Auzi, Siraa ala-Al-Shariah Al-Ikhwanul-Muslimun wa Mubarak 1984-2007, Beirut: Mrkaz-Dirasatyl Wahdatul Wataniyah, pp. 52-53.
11. Mir Zohair Hussain, Global Islamic Politics, New York: Harper Collins Publisher, 1995, pp. 53-54.
12. Hisham Al-Auzi, Siraa ala-Al-Shariah Al-Ikhwanul-Muslimun wa Mubarak 1984-2007, Beirut: Mrkaz-Dirasatyl Wahdatul Wataniyah, p. 69.
13. Hisham Al-Auzi, Siraa ala-Al-Shariah Al-Ikhwanul-Muslimun wa Mubarak 1984-2007, Beirut: Mrkaz-Dirasatyl Wahdatul Wataniyah, p. 71.
14. Ibrahim Abu Rabi, *Contemporary Arab Thought*, p. 61.
15. Hisham Al-Auzi, Siraa ala-Al-Shariah Al-Ikhwanul-Muslimun wa Mubarak 1984-2007, Beirut: Mrkaz-Dirasatyl Wahdatul Wataniyah, p. 73.
16. Sami Sharf, *Abdul Nasser: Kaifa Hakama Misr*, Cairo: MAdbuli-al-Saghir, 1996.
17. Hisham Al-Auzi, Siraa ala-Al-Shariah Al-Ikhwanul-Muslimun wa Mubarak 1984-2007, Beirut: Mrkaz-Dirasatyl Wahdatul Wataniyah, p. 79.
18. Hisham Al-Auzi, Siraa ala-Al-Shariah Al-Ikhwanul-Muslimun wa Mubarak 1984-2007, Beirut: Mrkaz-Dirasatyl Wahdatul Wataniyah, p. 83.
19. Hisham Al-Auzi, Siraa ala-Al-Shariah Al-Ikhwanul-Muslimun wa Mubarak 1984-2007, Beirut: Mrkaz-Dirasatyl Wahdatul Wataniyah, p. 129.
20. Salwa Ismail, *Rethinking Islamic politics: Culture, the state and Islam*, London: I.B. Tauris, 2003, p. 33.
21. Hisham Al-Auzi, Siraa ala-Al-Shariah Al-Ikhwanul-Muslimun wa Mubarak 1984-2007, Beirut: Mrkaz-Dirasatyl Wahdatul Wataniyah, p. 168.

22. Hisham Al-Auzi, Siraa ala-Al-Shariah Al-Ikhwanul-Muslimun wa Mubarak 1984-2007, Beirut: Mrkaz-Dirasatyl Wahdatul Wataniyah, p. 174.
23. Hisham Al-Auzi, Siraa ala-Al-Shariah Al-Ikhwanul-Muslimun wa Mubarak 1984-2007, Beirut: Mrkaz-Dirasatyl Wahdatul Wataniyah, p. 239.
24. Hisham Al-Auzi, Siraa ala-Al-Shariah Al-Ikhwanul-Muslimun wa Mubarak 1984-2007, Beirut: Mrkaz-Dirasatyl Wahdatul Wataniyah, p. 272.
25. Guardian, November 27, 2011.
26. Akhbaralaalam, November 25, 2011.
27. Mohammad Hafez, Al-Ahram (Weekly), November 16, 2011.
28. Guardian, December 3, 2011.
29. Mohammad Hafez, Al-Ahram (Weekly), November 16, 2011.
30. Ziyad Hafiz, *Sauratu Yanayir Fi Misr: Tasaulatal-Hazir wal-Mustaqbil*, Al-Mustaqbal Al-Arabi, March 2011, Issue No. 358, p. 79.
31. *Munaqashaat*, Al-Mustaqbal Al-Arabi, March 2011, Issue No. 358, p. 101.
32. Al-quds-Al-Arabi, November 25, 2011.
33. Qantara Dialogue, Egypt is Not Tunis! Or is it, November 11, 2011.
34. Noah Feldman, *The Fall and Rise of Islam,* Princeton: Princeton University, Press, 2008, p. 3.
35. Akhbaralaalam, November 14, 2011.

Part V: Arab Spring: Global Responses and Regional Implications

15

American Response to the Arab Spring: Foreign Policy in Quandary

Chintamani Mahapatra and Obja Borah Hazarika

United States' foreign policy towards the developments in the Middle East and the North African (MENA) region was characterized by frustrating ambivalence. A conflict between American values and its interests was primarily responsible for the contradictory approach of the US. On generating a historical discourse, it becomes amply clear that the US had hitherto maintained a dichotomous relationship with the polities of the MENA region which led to its varied response to these states. While on the one hand the US was acerbic in its criticism about Syria, and until 2003 about Libya; on the other, it shored up the equally, if not copiously worse, unsavoury regimes in Bahrain, Egypt, and Saudi Arabia. Keeping these antecedents of the US's policy in mind, this article attempts to capture the US response to the phenomena that seared the MENA, popularly dubbed, the 'Arab Spring'.

Introduction

Spread of democracy in various parts of the world has been a signature development in world politics in the last several decades. However, the 'success of authoritarianism' [1] in the Middle East and North African region (MENA) until the 'Arab Uprising' of 2010 was an anomaly in the general direction of evolution of world polities elsewhere in the world. The 'Third Wave' [2] of democracy which swept Eastern Europe in the aftermath of the Soviet collapse failed to resonate in the MENA region. This region which continued to be governed by regimes anachronistic in the 21st century suddenly awoke on 17th December 2010 with the self-immolation of Mohammed Bouazizi of Tunisia, [3] to usher in long overdue changes, catching much of the world by surprise. The so-called 'Jasmine Revolution' in Tunisia soon infected the neighbourhood. The region, which was largely devoid of any democratic experience, was seared by social protests against the authoritarian structures which had seemed impregnable only a couple of years ago. It was optimistically emphasized by some observers that the 'Arab Spring' would lead to democracy, fair economic opportunities, and reduction in corruption. [4]

The optimism sprang out of the deposition of four Heads of State in a row: Zine El Abidine Ben Ali of Tunisia, Hosni Mubarak of Egypt, Muammar al-Gaddafi of Libya and Ali Abdullah Saleh of Yemen. Elections took place in Tunisia and Egypt, where the populace largely voted in favour of the Islamist parties. The transition in Libya nonetheless was marked by lawlessness, disorder, violence and protests, which illustrated the competing visions racing to fill the political vacuum in the country. Bahrain in the meantime witnessed popular protests that warned of a probable regime transformation. Syria subsequently was subjected to anti-regime demonstrations that spiralled out of control and turned violent with ferocious attacks by the anti-government forces and brutal counter-attack by the military.

Apart from changes in Tunisia, Egypt, Libya, and protests in Syria and Bahrain there were major uprisings in Algeria, Djibouti, Iraq, Jordan, Oman and Yemen; and comparatively minor protests in Kuwait, Lebanon, Mauritania, Morocco, Saudi Arabia, Sudan and Western Sahara. This gamut of protests invoked impressions of an approaching change, what some analysts dubbed, Arab Spring.

What happened in the MENA region immediately grabbed world attention, since its strategic and geo-economic importance to the world is formidable. [5] Apart from being a hydrocarbon powerhouse; significant trade routes straddle the Arab world rendering it a geo-strategic region of opportunity and concerns. Any transition from the status-quo hitherto maintained in the region could unfavourably affect the flow of oil to the world and spike off an astronomical growth in petroleum prices breaking the back of many economies already reeling under the current global economic crisis. Fears of prolonged civil war and spiralling of terrorism added to the apprehensions of the global community. However, intervention was not an easy option as internal matters remained beyond the legal jurisdiction of external powers. Besides the question of legality, the rising cost and unpopularity of US military interventions in Iraq and Afghanistan and the prevailing economic downturn were additional factors that prevented direct foreign intervention in the political upheavals unfolding in the region.

The domino effect of the 'Jasmine Revolution' in Tunisia on other Arab countries was particularly noticed in the US in view of the strategic importance of this region to American global interests. After World War II, control of this region has for long been considered indispensable by the US policy makers to sustain and nourish global American hegemony. [6]

While the US role in the oil economics and politics of this region has been substantive in the post-Second World War era, the health of the American economy has not been determined directly by the events in this region. Significantly, the US is not directly and excessively dependent on the hydrocarbon resources of this region, whereas Washington's potential rivals (such as China) and allies (such as the EU and Japan) draw large amount of their energy resources from the Middle East (please see the graphs below). The military control of this region gives the US the lever to sway decision making in Asia and Europe on critical areas.

It is important to note that the US administrations have never invoked their democratic ideals and political values while dealing with the governments in this region. While traditionally playing a substantial role in the political and security affairs of the Arab world, successive US governments maintained cordial ties and alliance relationship with several of the Arab dictators for generations.

The dictatorial rulers, mainly in Egypt, Saudi Arabia, and Bahrain, found straightforward support from Washington as they served US interests in return for unquestioned authoritarianism which they had unleashed and sought to perpetuate on their populace for decades. [7] However, the US has had cacophonous relations with a few of the rulers of this region, especially with the Syrian regime and until 2003, with the Gaddafi regime in Libya. The dichotomy in the customary US approach to the dictators of this region, cradling some while opposing others; emanate from the exigency to perpetuate interests yet appear to remain on the 'right side of history'. This explains to certain extent a complicated and mystified reaction from the US to the recent political developments in the Arab world. The US responded to recent popular uprisings unfolding in the MENA in a manner that varied from state to state and shifted from time to time. [8]

There is little doubt that the cultural, political and economic landscape of the MENA region is marked by complex diversities. Islam and authoritarian governing structure were common to many, but were not sufficient for the US policy makers to craft one single policy that would fit the entire region. At the same time, democratic ideals hardly drove US decision-making on issues related to this region!

Prior to delving into the analysis of the Washington's confounding approach to Arab revolts; it is imperative to take stock of the general US response to anti-regime demonstrations in some of the nations where the political turbulence has been the strongest. This article will examine the US response to protests in some of the Arab countries, namely Tunisia, Egypt, Libya, Bahrain, Yemen and Syria in order to assess the impact of these uprising on US hegemony in the region in particular and the world in general.

Tunisian Jasmine Revolution

It was in tiny Tunisia that the first in the series of Arab

anti-government protests began in December 2010. Promptly dubbed as 'Jasmine Revolution', it ended with the overthrow of President Ben Ali who was in power for over two decades.

The Obama Administration's initial response to Ben Ali's handling of the protesters marked a muted response in view of friendly relations between the US and the Tunisian regime and likelihood of the success of the regime in suppressing the uprising. Washington first vowed neutrality. Secretary of State Hillary Clinton said on 11th January 2011 that Americans 'are worried, in general, about the unrest and the instability, and what seems to be the underlying concerns of the people who are protesting', but '...we are not taking sides'. [9] A couple of days later, as the demonstrators had the upper hand and as President Ben Ali fled the country, President Barack Obama changed tack and 'applauded the courage and dignity of the Tunisian people' and called for 'free and fair elections'. [10] More dramatic was President Obama's statement in his State of the Union Address: 'The United States of America stands with the people of Tunisia and supports the democratic aspirations of all people'. [11]

By February 2012, Hillary Clinton was already in Tunisia where she described herself as 'a very strong champion for Tunisian democracy'. [12] Despite the uncertainties clouding the political atmosphere in Tunisia, one certainty was well known: Ben Ali would not be able to stage a political come-back. The US had to establish ties with whoever came to power to continue friendly ties with Tunisia. About three thousand US soldiers had laid their lives during the Second World War to liberate this country. Moreover, Tunisia was a friendly country throughout the Cold War and a cooperative ally against terrorism.

Nine months after the overthrow of the Ben Ali regime, national elections were held in Tunisia in October 2011. The Islamist Ennahda Party, won more than 40 percent of the votes and formed a coalition government with two secular parties. Hillary Clinton flew to Tunisia to strengthen relations with the new government, pledging expanded trade relations, US economic assistance and even bearing some costs of the transition.

However, protests in Tunisia cropped up in 2012 yet again. Salafi Islamic extremists clashed with security forces. In August 2012, thousands of demonstrators protested in Tunisia against moves by the government to reduce women's rights. In February 2013 Prime Minister Jebali resigned after his ruling Ennahda party rejected his proposals to form a government of technocrats. In July 2013, the assassination of opposition politician Mohamed Brahmi prompted mass demonstrations, a general strike and calls for the government to resign. In October 2013 the governing Islamist party, Ennahda, agreed to hand over power to a caretaker government of independent figures tasked with organising fresh elections in 2014. In December 2013, Ennahda and the mainly secular opposition agreed on appointment of Mehdi Jomaa as head of interim government. [13]

On 26 January 2014, it was reported that Tunisian President Moncef Marzouki and the head of the National Assembly had signed the country's new constitution. US President Barack Obama called interim Tunisian Prime Minister Mehdi Jomaa and congratulated him on the new constitution. [14]

In Tunisia, the vanguard nation of developments related to 'Arab Spring', initially, the US was caught unaware about the tumult; and at the onset of the development refrained from 'taking sides'. [15] However, as the rebellious ranks continued to swell and people's participation persisted, President Obama abandoned Ben Ali in time. Without delay, efforts were soon afoot to carve a new relationship with the post-Ben Ali dispensation.

Tahrir Square Movement and Fall of Mubarak

The popular uprising in Tunisia was truly contagious. The first country to get affected was Egypt—a long standing American ally. The US has always regarded Egypt as a strategically vital ally not only because of its hydrocarbon resources but also because of its size, history and its influence in the Arab world. Washington's strategy of making Israel politically acceptable to the Arab world began with an American sponsored peace treaty between Egypt and Israel in 1978. In order to buy Cairo's support, the US played ball with dictatorial regimes in that country, including that of Hosni Mubarak for long and also consistently made huge economic assistance on annual basis to such regimes.

The biggest challenge from the Arab Spring to US interests in the region came from the domino effect of the Jasmine Revolution on Egypt. As huge number of Egyptians in early 2011 gathered at the famous Tahrir Square in Cairo demanding regime change, the Obama Administration grew anxious in view of the anti-American overtone of the demonstrations. Washington was mostly able to buy the Mubarak regime's support to its regional policy, but the Egyptian people had viewed the US as a perpetrator of authoritarianism in their country. It has been reported that some demonstrators sought to play down anti-American rhetoric for fear of pushing the US to back the regime. However, anti-American sentiments were very much in the air. [16]

More worrisome was the democracy promotion policy that the new Obama Administration had inherited from the previous administration of George W. Bush. When the Egyptian masses started demanding democracy, the Obama Administration was in a fix. Choice had to be made between an ally and democratic values which the US champions.

When the Tahrir Square uprising began, Secretary Clinton, initially remarked that, the Egyptian 'government is stable.' [17] Hosni Mubarak had been a staunch supporter of the US policy in the region which made it difficult for the US to embrace the protestors in Cairo. Mubarak had served several interests of the US, ranging from aiding the US in the struggle against international terrorism to enhancing lucrative commercial relations with the West. Additionally, the US was pressurized by Israel, Saudi Arabia, Jordan and the United Arab Emirates to maintain a benign posture towards Mubarak as his ouster could 'further destabilize the region'. [18]

Three weeks of intense pressure by pro-democracy demonstrators left little chance for the Mubarak regime to survive. The US position on Egypt changed when the protests intensified. The US dilly-dallied for some time, but finally deserted its long time ally and switched sides by championing the cause of the protestors. The tone was cautious, as President Obama declared that 'orderly transition must be meaningful, it must be peaceful, and it must begin now.' [19] The US's volte-face could have been due to fear that prolonged instability could adversely affect vital US interests in the region, primarily continuation of Egypt's peace accord with Israel. Abandoning the protesters on the streets of Cairo would have amounted to turning a blind-eye to the US's values and goals and would have smacked of hypocrisy given the ideals President Barack Obama extolled in his Cairo speech. It would have been a bad public relations exercise in the era of instant messaging and widespread social networking.

Mubarak was ousted on 11th February 2011; elections were held in the country, but the new democratic government in Egypt did not inspire the US. Liberal and secular elements in Egypt failed to win the election and form the government; instead the Muslim Brotherhood gained the most number of votes. It was not easy for the US leadership to embrace the Morsi government, but there was no alterative available. Washington did try to reach out to the new leadership in Cairo by promising assistance to tackle economic crisis, but uncertainty over new directions in the country's foreign policy continued to cause concern in Washington.

The Obama administration tried hard to reverse decades of its mistrust of the Muslim Brotherhood, as it sought to forge closer ties with the organisation that was irreconcilably opposed to the US policy towards Egypt and the region. [20]

However, stability of the Morsi government was illusive and before long political fractions and social unrest began to disrupt post-Mubarak Egypt. By June 2013, the Morsi-led Islamist government was overthrown and an interim government backed by the military began running the country which took up the task of planning the political transition of the country. It was for all practical purposes a military coup which met with defiance from the other political parties as well as the citizenry. The Egyptian population was polarized with some supporting the Muslim Brotherhood Party because of their faith in democracy and elections and others the military for purposes of restoring stability to the country. While Egypt grappled with its polarized politics, the US attempted to articulate its responses according to its interests.

The Obama Administration found it difficult to characterize Morsi's ouster as a coup as that would have led to imposition of sanctions on Egypt further worsening the economic situation in that country. There was also fear of losing existing leverage in Cairo. Egypt remains the second largest recipient of about 1.5 billion dollars in annual US aid, ever since the Camp David Accords were signed in 1979, which in turn had helped maintain peace between Egypt and Israel.

The actions of the Egyptian military, which has been handling the situation with highhandedness and massive use of force, induced President Barack Obama to condemn the interim government's actions. While hedging its bets by slowing down military aid and cancelling military exercises with Egypt, Washington has allowed humanitarian aid to continue unremittingly. The Egyptian military and the Islamists are both incensed with this response from the US and the former has shown signs of reaching out to Russia. Congress and the Obama Administration are currently engaged in a debate regarding the extent to which the US military and economic assistance to Egypt '...should continue and/or be subject to various conditions and/or existing legal restrictions'. [21] The rapidly deteriorating security scenario in Egypt has become one of the most formidable challenges for US policy in the region.

Upheaval in Libya and Brutal End of Gaddafi

Unlike Tunisia and Egypt, anti-regime protests in Libya appeared to have brought new opportunities for the US to facilitate deposition of the Libyan Strongman Muammer al-Gaddafi. Gaddafi had been a constant headache for the United States and its allies for decades and he was even designated a "mad man" by President Ronald Reagan at a point of time.

The US-Libya relationship, which was marked with constant consternation for decades, had suddenly improved in 2003 when Muammer al-Gaddafi, under Washington's pressure, decided to end his pursuit of nuclear weapons and even agreed to pay reparations for Libya's involvement in the Lockerbie incident. American intervention in Iraq leading to the removal of Saddam Hussain from power was also responsible for the change of mind of Gaddafi when he did not challenge the Western intelligence findings about his pursuit of nuclear weapons. As he agreed to behave at the instance of Washington and aspired to ensure a smooth succession of power to his son, western sanctions were removed, diplomatic relations restored and some military cooperation began.

The improvement in the US-Libya relations was halted when the 'Arab Spring' reached Libya. The battle for Tripoli launched by anti-regime militias drew support from the US and some of its NATO allies. The UN was roped in to back the Western position leading to the imposition of an UN-sponsored no-fly zone over Libya. [22] The goal was to prevent Gaddafi from using his air power against his opponents.

Neither Tunisia nor Egypt in the wake of their respective political upheavals invited American military intervention. The fierce fighting in Tripoli between Gaddafi's army and several militia groups, however, made it appear that Gaddafi would survive the Arab Spring. The US, France, Britain and a few other countries could not remain silent. While the Obama

Administration did not come forward with direct military action, the White House fully backed the French and British military efforts against Gaddafi. Many American critics and foreign policy analysts in other countries initially viewed Obama's policy as an example of the loss of US leadership. But others characterized it as 'leading from behind'! In fact, the Obama Administration in response to the fierce fighting in Libya declared a 'state of national emergency' in February 2011 and has continued to extend it every year since then. Significantly, the latest declaration considers events in Libya as posing 'extraordinary threat' to American foreign policy interests. [23]

President Obama defended the American-led military assault in Libya, saying it was in the national interest of the United States to stop a potential massacre that would have '…stained the conscience of the world.' [24] American trade with Libya, Libyan oil trade with the US allies, and Libya's strategic geographic position at the confluence of Asia, Europe and Africa could have influenced the US decision to put a quick end to the tumult in Libya.

In the aftermath of Gaddafi's overthrow and his assassination, there were marked changes in the social and political life of Libya. National Transitional Council (NTC) began the process to form a new government. They also started to prosecute former Gaddafi officials. Armed militias began to assert their role as 'guardians of the revolution'. But when clashes between rival militias continued to threaten stability in the country, it was feared that militant Islamists may hijack the political space in post-Gaddafi Libya.

Elections were held in July 2012 to a General National Congress (GNC). In November 2012, Ali Zeidan was sworn in as Prime Minister. Zeidan listed his government's priorities as security, defence, health, public services, the economy, and starting the process of national reconciliation. The GNC is concerned with organising a constituent assembly, which will write Libya's new constitution. US officials applauded the conduct of the July 2012 election, and welcomed the newly elected GNC. [25]

More recently it has been reported that Government authority in Libya has been disintegrating in all parts of the country and that Libyans are increasingly at the mercy of militias which act outside the law. Popular protests against militiamen have been met with gunfire. Several high-profile assassinations have tainted the political scene in the country. The oil rich areas of the country are seeking more autonomy which is putting further pressure on the near-moribund Libyan economy.

The security circumstance in Libya poses yet another serious challenge for the US in the region especially since the September 11, 2012, attacks on the US diplomatic mission compounded. Even the US Ambassador to Libya, Christopher Stevens, was killed during this attack which raised the political temperature in Washington. In the wake of the attack, the US military repositioned its troops in southern Europe and reoriented its plans to be able to ensure speedy response to such attacks on US personnel in North Africa.

In addition, the proliferation of military weaponry from unsecured stockpiles—including small arms, explosives, and shoulder-fired anti-aircraft missiles (MANPADs)—has remained a serious concern for the US. The Obama Administration has been implementing a program with Libyan authorities to retrieve and disable weapons, including MANPADs. US officials 'believe that nuclear materials and chemical weapons components are secure (including previously undeclared chemical weapons), and Libyan leaders have recommitted to destroying the remnants of Qadhafi's chemical arsenal'. [26]

In terms of aid, the US government allocated more than $200 million in assistance for Libya since the start of the uprising in 2011. The attacks on US personnel and facilities disrupted US aid programs temporarily. However, despite the attacks, the US proposed expanded security cooperation to Libyan officials.

The US is mindful of the fact that the chaos that is ensuing in Libya could lead to the proliferation of weapons, continuing unrests, and unceasing bloodshed. As the kidnapping and release of the head of the transitional government, Ali Zeidan on October 10, 2013 shows, the situation in Libya is terse and precarious. The situation shows signs of spiralling out of control leading to grave policy related challenges for the US.

The US and its allies have witnessed the bitter truth that removal of dictators in certain areas may be easy, but maintaining stability after the regime change is difficult. Big hopes of doing business in Libya after Gaddafi's ouster still appear to be a pipe dream. Despite the precarious law and order situation, the Obama Administration has pinned hopes on the democratically elected government and has begun to relax sanctions. However, three years after Gaddafi's assassination, the turmoil in Libya has compelled President Obama to extend the 'national emergency' in February 2014.

Managing Popular Uprising in Bahrain

The US handling of anti-regime protests in Bahrain and Yemen was markedly different. Bahrain has been a close strategic ally and hosts the US Fifth Fleet and Yemen has been close ally in America's war against Al Qaeda.

The uprising against Bahrain's Al Khalifa royal family that began on February 14, 2011 failed to topple Bahrain's regime or bring down the royal powers by making the country a constitutional monarchy. The main goal of the majority Shia population in Bahrain was to end minority Sunni rule making way for democratic governance. The Sunni minority in Iraq headed by Saddam Hussain was Washington's adversary. The Saddam regime was brought down by the US much before the Arab Spring by military means. But the Sunni minority rule in Bahrain was important for American security interests.

Washington appears to have put its weight behind Al Khalifa to ensure that the popular unrest would not cause a regime fall. However, unrest continued in that country as the

Shiites sought 'to bring outside pressure to bear on the Sunni-dominated government to increase Shiite political influence and rights'. [27]

A 'national dialogue' held in July 2011 managed to reach consensus on a few modest political reforms. A report by a government-appointed 'Independent Commission of Inquiry' (BICI) was released on November 23, 2011 making critical remarks on the government's actions against the unrest and recommending several changes in the governing structure. However, expanding political polarization in the country became responsible for the dialogue to break down. Political dialogue among important factions was again resumed in February 2013, but little concrete progress could be made and the opposition groups withdrew from the dialogue process after months of trial and error in October 2013'. [28]

In a direct contrast to the US prompt response to anti-regime efforts in Libya, the US reaction to the crackdown by the rulers of Bahrain on pro-democracy forces was rather mellow. The Obama Administration made no calls for an end to the Al Khalifa regime, although it made formal criticisms against its use of repressive measures to suppress the anti-government movement and urged a negotiated compromise. The Obama Administration came under fire from the Bahraini anti-government groups for being overly protective of its security interests and ignoring the democratic aspirations of the people. But it fell on deaf ears.

Bahrain, the headquarters of the US Fifth Fleet which patrols the Persian Gulf, the Red Sea, the Arabian Sea, and the east coast of Africa to ensure the freedom of trade routes, is of utmost importance to the US strategic interests in the region. Furthermore, Bahrain provides quick access to the gulf's sea lanes and protects the disgorging oil pipelines of Iraq, Kuwait, Saudi Arabia and, further south, the United Arab Emirates and Oman. [29] The Defence Cooperation Agreement (DCA) signed by the US with Bahrain in 1991, designated Bahrain as a 'major non-NATO ally'.

The designation qualified Bahrain for sales of sophisticated US weapons systems. But when anti-regime demonstrations were held and Bahrain got caught in the Arab Spring, Washington was careful in halting some of the announced sale of weapons. As a palliative to pro-democracy forces, it was argued that sales were being halted to prevent use of such weapons against the protesters. But then the regime could not be isolated. In May 2012 the US announced that it would 'proceed with the sale to Bahrain of other arms that can be used only for external defence despite calls by some outside experts to consider relocating U.S. military personnel from Bahrain entirely'. [30]

Non-violent Departure of a Dictator in Yemen

Spread of the Arab Spring to Yemen posed another similar security challenge for the US. The Obama Administration had to walk the tight rope for fear of quickly losing a crucial ally in the midst of a war against Al-Qaeda and other terrorist groups. In addition, Yemen lies adjacent to strategic shipping lanes into the Red Sea and the Suez Canal. Political upheavals in strategic spots could be counterproductive to US interests. Thus the US response to the popular uprising against the dictatorial regime was quite muted.

After nine months of mass protests, Ali Abdullah Saleh signed an agreement transferring his powers to the vice president in return for immunity from prosecution. US President Obama hailed the historic transition, and congratulated the Yemeni people who had '…set their country on a path for a more stable, secure, and democratic future'. [31]

In February 2012, Abdrabbuh Mansour Hadi was inaugurated as president after uncontested elections. In May 2012, international donors pledged more than US$ 4 bn in aid to Yemen to help improve infrastructure and security. In March 2013 the delayed National Dialogue Conference began with the aim of drafting a new constitution. In July 2013, the US intensified drone strikes against Al-Qaeda. In August

2013, several foreign embassies shut temporarily over fears of attacks by Al-Qaeda. [32]

On 25 January 2014, the National Dialogue Conference, finally released a peace plan. The peace plan aimed for stability and gradual change rather than rapid, potentially destabilising shifts. Its backers point to the unrest in other post-Arab Spring states as evidence that transitions that move too quickly are often derailed equally quickly. But critics of the plan argue that political participation has been limited to the conference, which was made up of 565 delegates from the country's many political factions. These include the GPC, the JMP, southern separatists, youth activists, and the Houthis, a Zaydi Shia group that fought an on-and-off civil war against Saleh between 2004 and 2010. [33]

The US has been closely assessing the turmoil in Yemen. The US cultivated close ties with the new leadership in Yemen and in May 2012 issued an executive order threatening sanctions on those who disrupted political transition under President Hadi. The US closed over two dozen diplomatic facilities and escalated the drone campaign in Yemen against a possible Al-Qaeda plot by the AQAP. Critics have challenged the drone strikes by arguing 'they engender anti-Americanism, alienate populations from the Yemeni government' and make the AQAP popular among locals. [34] Drone strikes are increasingly becoming unpopular with the locals as several civilian deaths have been reported. The Al-Qaeda threat emanating from Yemen continues to be the most significant issue for the US and the drone strikes are seen as crucial for dismantling any networks or plots of the Al-Qaeda.

The US succeeded in managing regime transition in Yemen and ensuring a cooperative successor. Although drone attacks have been unpopular, the US faces little hurdle in continuing its war against Al-Qaeda. Will the Yemeni people turn against the current regime and the US? The question remains open-ended.

Messy Approach to Syrian Civil War

As in the case of Libya, the ruling establishment in Syria was not a very savoury and friendly one with the United States. As the wave of Arab Spring spread to Syria and intense anti-regime demonstrations were staged, Washington remained undisturbed. Its stakes were different. Change of regime in Syria could lead to a relatively cooperative regime coming to power. In fact, the US would greatly benefit if the Assad regime collapsed as it provided support to anti-American forces in the region, such as Iran, Lebanon, Hamas and Hezbollah.

But as the Assad regime reportedly used brutal force to suppress anti-government movements, the opposition groups turned violent too. The situation in Syria turned into an escalating civil war and posed a serious challenge for the international community. However, as in the case of Libya, Washington refrained from taking any hasty decision to use any direct military means and had reservations on initiating a no-fly zone in Syria. Syria's relatively strong air defence system, its chemical and biological weapons, and close friendship with Russia encouraged the US to go slow. Yet another complicating factor was a lack of a centralized opposition group coordinating the fight against the Syrian military. Any thoughtless or improper plan to arm the Syrian rebels could empower Al-Qaeda elements in Syria. The situation in Syria continued to be terse. Since March 2011, the conflict has generated 2.3 million Syrian refugees and millions of internally displaced populace along with several thousands killed.

As the civil war ravaged on, efforts were made by external powers to unite the anti-government factions in Syria. In November 2012 in Qatar, several major opposition forces held negotiations and formed the National Coalition for Syrian Revolutionary and Opposition Forces and the Syrian National Council'. [35]

But even then the Obama Administration did not offer any

open military assistance to opposition forces. While American help did come to the Syrian opposition, it was characterized as humanitarian aid, which was more than one billion US dollars. Even this US assistance to anti-government forces was placed on hold in December 2013, as the civil war like situation made monitoring of funds 'impossible'.

The Syrian situation turned more serious with evidence of use of chemical weapons during the civil war. Washington accused the Assad regime and President Assad accused the opposition groups for the use of chemical weapons.

President Obama faced enormous difficulty to act on his stated intention to punish Syrian President Bashar al Assad for use of chemical weapons by his troops. Majority of American people had developed war fatigue and resisted any further military involvement by the US at a time when preparations are in the full swing to pull out of the Afghan quagmire. The US Congressmen and Senators were divided on the issue of military intervention in a civil war that hardly impinged on core American interests.

Obama's predicament was no less in enlisting the support of America's influential allies in Europe and Asia. Germany was opposed to use of military means for tackling the Syrian situation. The British Prime Minister obliged, but his Parliament refused to come on board. Obama decided not to go ahead with the plan to punish Assad for crossing the 'Red Line' only with the backing of France and Turkey and silent acquiescence of Japan and South Korea.

More problematic was the stiff resistance to any military intervention in Syria by Russia and China—two veto yielding members of the UN Security Council. Russia confronted the Obama Administration's assertion that the Assad regime used chemical weapons against his own people. It voiced the opposite scenario that rebels used chemical weapons to draw Western intervention against Assad regime. Significantly, the UN Secretary General Ban Ki Moon's and the Pope joined the Russian chorus against military strikes on Syria. BRICS members, including India, demanded UN, and not US action.

Previously, when the George Bush Administration presented evidence about Saddam Hussein's nuclear arsenal, it went on unchallenged in the Security Council, but the administration was later shamed, as the military intervention could not find any nuclear weapons in Iraq. President Obama knew that even if the US intelligence reports could be presented as evidence of use of chemical weapons by the Assad government, there would not be many takers.

Furthermore, US military strike could tilt the balance in the Syrian battle ground against Assad and could even lead to his fall. But at what cost? American people had begun to question the Obama Administration's lacklustre pressure on the Egyptian military that ended democracy in the country and now they could question the rationale behind use of force to remove the Syrian dictator!

Finally, Russia's proposal to diplomatically handle the issue of Syrian chemical weapons carried the day. The Obama Administration found this to be acceptable in the absence of any other credible alternative.

As things stand today, the stated US preferences seem to be contrary to the outcomes being sought by the most powerful anti-Assad armed forces. Islamist militias seeking to impose varying degrees of Sunni Islamic law on Syrian society, including the newly formed Islamic Front and Al-Qaeda affiliates such as ISIL and Jabhat al Nusra, have been able to flex their muscles against fellow groups, 'including some who had received U.S. assistance.' [36]

Analyzing American Approach to Arab Spring

Overall, the US response to the occurrences in the Arab world have been crafted according to the dynamics of the movements in particular Arab states and have also been hinged on the nature of relationship which the US had had with these nations at an individual level prior to these uprisings.

The primary rhetoric that emanated from Washington was

supportive of the movements that seared the MENA region. President Obama, in May 2011, remarked that the US would stand by the protesters, even as 'change will come differently in different countries.' [37]

The G8 was supportive about the movements in the Arab world and remarked that: 'The changes under way in the Middle East and North Africa (MENA) are historic and have the potential to open the door to the kind of transformation that occurred in Central and Eastern Europe after the fall of the Berlin Wall. The aspiration of people for freedom, human rights, democracy, job opportunities, empowerment and dignity, has led them to take control of their own destinies in a growing number of countries in the region. It resonates with and reinforces our common values'. [38]

Regardless of the positive Western pronouncements with regard to the developments in the Arab world, Washington was unprepared for the foreign policy dilemma it faced. [39] It has been observed that the reaction of the US to the Arab Spring 'has been primarily verbal and indirect. Washington has deliberately shunned a visible leadership role'. [40]

First, the US refused to employ hard power, military deployment was limited to Libya and there were no other special alerts, ship, troop or aircraft movements. Additionally, the amount of funding released by the US to the protestors was paltry. Thirdly, there were no US efforts to harness the Arab upheavals to gain diplomatic leverage by the US. Finally, 'the Arab Spring elicited no overall statement of strategy by the president...By not declaring a new doctrine for the region, President Obama has foregone an agenda setting opportunity and left all stakeholders wondering where this vital region is headed and how the United States will respond'. [41]

Several reasons underlay the reticent response of the US to the changes which were unleashed by the 'Arab Spring'. First, the 'Arab Spring' led to a conundrum for US foreign policy as its interests and values were at once in conflict. Although the US's values were in conformity with the ideals of those of the protestors, the interests of the US lay in resisting the ouster of long-standing friends and allies in the Arab world, despite their unsavoury styles of leadership. Thus, in an attempt to juggle interests and values, the initial US reaction to these movements, was at best cautious and wary; almost as if scared of promoting the revisionist tendencies that marked the region.

The US had dissimilar relationships with the nations of the Arab world. There were acquiescent authoritarians who were its allies—mainly Egypt, Tunisia, Jordan, Yemen, and Saudi Arabia. With regard to these nations, the US was less determined to pursue the ouster of the rulers as they could be counted on to support key American interests. Then there were adversarial or unreliable authoritarians like the Asad regime in Syria and the Gaddafi regime in Libya, in whose cases, the US was more than happy to be on the 'right side of history'. [42]

Furthermore, the US's apprehensions about change in the region could have been compounded by the fact that free elections in Iraq, Lebanon and the Palestinian territories did not yield democracies of the kind the US expected. This outcome made the US wary of any sudden change in the region. The US had misgivings about the eventual result of the protests in the region as it could provide fodder to the simmering anti-Americanism already prevalent in the region. [43]

As a result, the US tended to treat events in the Arab world with caution. In their eyes, further democratization in the region could destabilize traditional US allies, like Egypt and Saudi Arabia, at a time when Washington needed their help to root out Al-Qaeda and contain Iran. [44] Islamists had swept the polls in Egypt and Tunisia which ratcheted fears that 'Islamist parties will inevitably advocate policies less aligned with Western interests and values'. [45] During the Cold War, communists and nationalists in developing countries were not acceptable to the successive American administrations. Now the US policymakers find it hard to co-habit a world with myriad Islamist groups at the helm of affairs.

Moreover, throughout the Cold War, the US had built alliance relationships with autocracies as part of the wider cause of anti-communist containment, to ensure that oil supplies would not be 'disrupted for political ends, threatening not only the American economy but the system of industrial capitalism itself'. [46] Although the US is not a major importer of Arab oil, its allies continue to be heavily dependent on hydrocarbons from this region, which could have led to apprehensions in the US with regard to extending support to the popular forces in motion in the MENA region as it could have resulted in the establishment of unfriendly regimes, which would have affected oil supply to the US allies, especially in West Europe and Japan. If the upheavals of the Arab Spring were to spread to the Eastern Province of Saudi Arabia, the consequences could be globally catastrophic. [47]

Besides, President Obama's late overtures to the protesters in the Arab world could have been a reflection of America's unchallengeable commitment to Israel which generated immediate interests in the survival of the Saudi regime and the containment of Iran. [48] Israel's apprehensions about the consequences of the Arab Spring '...for its own security translate directly into political pressure in Washington. [49]

Additionally, concrete support from the US for the uprisings could have even been withheld as a result of it being constrained domestically by economic recession and fatigue with the extensive international engagement and military adventures of Afghanistan and Iraq. [50] Moreover, the US's cautious approach could have been influenced by the unpopularity of the Freedom Agenda perpetuated by George Bush. Concerns that over-enthusiastic American support might actually undermine the revolutions' authenticity could have led to the US's mitigated support for the movement. [51]

Wariness of military over-stretch could have lead to the muted response of the US as the US is already overextended in the Arab region. There are more than 100,000 US troops in the region and the US 'is the primary military partner of numerous other Arab countries…The Middle East has for some thirty years consumed about half of all US foreign assistance...the Middle East continues to breed terrorism and political violence…new US intervention could have other negative, unforeseen consequences'. [52]

Overall, the US response to the sweeping changes that marked the Arab region was inconsistent and characterized by multiple standards. Lending support to the acquiescent Arab dictators was rendered an illegitimate and immoral act by the social forces in action. The US eventually threw its weight behind the popular forces in Tunisia, Egypt, Libya, and Yemen. On the other hand, Washington was accused of surreptitiously ensuring the continuance of the unpopular regimes in Saudi Arabia, Bahrain and others. Thus, the US policy was led by circumstances beyond its control which spiked off intense debate about an imminent decline of the US. Although, the US detested any change in the status-quo in the Arab world which it had painstakingly created to ensure the fulfilment of its interests, when the popular risings seemed irrevocable, Washington was forced to abandon the potentates in the Arab world and stand on the 'right side of history'.

Endnotes

1. Albrecht, H. and O. Schlumberger, (2004), 'Waiting for Godot: Regime Change without Democratization in the Middle East', *International Political Science Review*, 25(4), 371-392.
2. Huntington, S. (1991), 'The Third Wave: Democratization in the Late Twentieth Century', USA: University of Oklahoma Press.
3. Rose, G. (2011), 'The New Arab Revolt; What Happened, What it Means, and What Comes Next', New York: Council on Foreign Relations.
4. Ramadan, T. and A.H. Ali, (2011), 'The Arab Spring after Osama', *New Perspectives Quarterly*; Green; Shelley, Fred M. (2011), 'Orientalism, Idealism, and Realism: The United States and the 'Arab Spring', *The Arab World Geographer*, 12(2), 169-173.
5. Lesch, W.D. and Mark L. Haas, (2013), 'The Arab Spring: Change and Resistance', Colorado, Westview Press.

6. Until World War II, the United States had little political or economic interest in the Middle East. This region was fundamentally dominated by the British and the French. By 1945, however, "the American consortium of oil companies, the Arabian-American Oil Company (Aramco), was the largest single private American investment overseas". The first significant political interest of the US in the region began with the creation of Israel in 1948. As the British hegemony ended, the US hegemony took root in the region. For details, See Ferrell, H.R. (1975), 'American Diplomacy: A History', New York: W.W. Norton and Company, 737.
7. Bresheet, H. (2012), 'The Arab Spring: A View from Israel', *Middle East Journal of Culture and Communication*, 5, 42-57.
8. Kahl. H.C. and Marc Lynch, (2013), 'U.S. Strategy after the Arab Uprisings: Toward Progressive Engagement', *The Washington Quarterly*, 36(2), 39-60.
9. Tran, M. (2011), 'Tunisian Police Clash with Protesters as Unrest Spreads', *The Guardian,* available at, http://www.theguardian.com/world/2011/jan/12/tunisia-protest-spreads, accessed on February 2, 2014.
10. Obama, B. (2011), Statement by the President on Events in Tunisia, The White House, January 14, 2011, available at, http://www.whitehouse.gov/the-press-office/2011/01/14/statement-president-events-tunisia, accessed on February 2, 2014.
11. Obama, B. (2011), Remarks by the President in State of Union Address, The White House, January 25, 2011, available at, http://www.whitehouse.gov/the-press-office/2011/01/14/statement-president-events-tunisia, accessed on February 2, 2014.
12. Clinton, H. (2012), Clinton Remarks After Meeting with Tunisian President Marzouki, U.S. Department of State, February 25, 2012, available at, http://iipdigital.usembassy.gov/st/english/texttrans/2012/02/20120225151619su5.215961e-02.html#axzz2sR1UrGES, accessed on February 2, 2014.
13. Tunisia profile, BBC News, December 12, 2013, available at, http://www.bbc.co.uk/news/world-africa-14107720, accessed on February 11, 2014.
14. Tunisia signs new constitution into law, Aljazeera, January 27,

2014, available at, http://www.aljazeera.com/news/africa/2014/01/tunisia-assembly-approves-new-constitution-201412622480531861.html, accessed on February 12, 2014.

15. Ghattas, K. (2011), How does the US view Tunisia's revolt?, BBC News, available at, http://www.bbc.co.uk/news/mobile/world-us-canada-12200851, accessed on January 16, 2011.
16. See, Zunes, S. (2014), Egyptian Junta Claims US Conspiracy While Accepting US Support, Epoch Times, February 22, 2014. available at, http://www.theepochtimes.com/n3/524409-egyptian-junta-claims-u-s-conspiracy-while-accepting-u-s-support/, accessed on February 24, 2014.
17. Sanger, E.D. (2011), As Mubarak Digs In, U.S. Policy in Egypt Is Complicated, New York Times, New York, available at, http://www.nytimes.com/2011/02/06/world/middleeast/06policy.html?scp=10&sq=US%20and%20egypt&st=cse, accessed on February 11, 2014.
18. Landler, M. and H. Cooper, (2011), Allies Press U.S. to Go Slow on Egypt, New York Times, available at, http://www.nytimes.com/2011/02/09/world/middleeast/09diplomacy.html?scp=16&sq=US%20and%20egypt&st=cse, accessed on February 11, 2014.
19. Obama, B. (2011), Remarks by the President on the Situation in Egypt, Speech made on 1[sst] February 2011 in Washington, D.C., USA, available at, http://www.whitehouse.gov/the-press-office/2011/02/01/remarks-president-situation-egypt, accessed on February 11, 2014.
20. Kirkpatrick, D.D. and S.L. Myers, (2012), Overtures to Egypt's Islamists Reverse Long time U.S. Policy, New York Times, available at, http://www.nytimes.com/2012/01/04/world/middleeast/us-reverses-policy-in-reaching-out-to-muslim-brotherhood.html?pagewanted=1&_r=1&sq=US%20and%20Egypt&st=cse&scp=11, accessed on January 3, 2012.
21. Sharp, M.J. (2014), Egypt: Background and U.S. Relations, Congressional Research Service, Government of USA.

22. Terrill, A.W. (2011), The Arab Spring and the Future of U.S. Interests and Cooperative Security in the Arab World, available at, http://www.strategicstudiesinstitute.army.mil/index.cfm/articles/The-Arab-Spring-and-the-Future-of-US-Interests/2011/8/2, accessed on February 11, 2014.
23. Ditz, J. (2014), Obama Order: Libya an 'Extraordinary Threat' to US Foreign Policy, available at, http://news.antiwar.com/2014/02/21/obama-order-libya-an-extraordinary-threat-to-us-foreign-policy/, accessed on February 24, 2014.
24. Obama, B. (2011), 'Address at the National Defence University in Washington', Speech made on 28th March 2011 in National Defence University, Washington, D.C., USA, available at, http://www.huffingtonpost.com/2011/03/28/obama-libya-speech-_n_841311.html#text, accessed on February 11, 2014.
25. Blanchard, M.C. (2012), Libya: Transition and U.S. Policy, Congressional Research Service, Government of USA.
26. Blanchard, M.C. (2012), Libya: Transition and U.S. Policy, Congressional Research Service, Government of USA.
27. Katzman, K. (2014), Bahrain: Reform, Security, and U.S. Policy, Congressional Research Service, Government of USA.
28. Katzman, K. (2014), Bahrain: Reform, Security, and U.S. Policy, Congressional Research Service, Government of USA.
29. Tristam, P. American Interests in Bahrain, available at, http://middleeast.about.com/od/bahrain/a/American-Interests-In-Bahrain.htm, accessed on February 11, 2014.
30. Katzman, K. (2014), Bahrain: Reform, Security, and U.S. Policy, Congressional Research Service, Government of USA.
31. Obama, B. (2011), 'Obama Statement on Presidential Transition in Yemen, Speech made on 25th February 2012 in Washington, D.C., USA, available at, http://iipdigital.usembassy.gov/st/english/texttrans/2012/02/20120225162653su0.8365071.html#axzz21iVKYJDS, accessed on February 11, 2014.
32. Yemen Timeline, BBC News, December 21, 2013, available at, http://www.bbc.co.uk/news/world-middle-east-14704951, accessed on February 11, 2014.
33. Salisbury, P. (2014), Yemen: Ready for Change?, Aljazeera, February 3, 2014, available at,

http://www.aljazeera.com/indepth/features/2014/02/yemen-ready-change-20142264830304367.html, accessed on February 11, 2014.

34. Masters, J. and Z. Laub, (2013), Al-Qaeda in the Arabian Peninsula(AQAP), available at, http://www.cfr.org/yemen/al-qaeda-arabian-peninsula-aqap/p9369#p7, accessed on February 11, 2014.
35. Syria Profile, BBC News, December 12, 2013, available at, http://www.bbc.co.uk/news/world-middle-east-14703995, accessed on February 11, 2014.
36. Blanchard, M.C., Humud, E.C. and M.B.D. Nikitin, (2014), Armed Conflict in Syria: Overview and U.S. Response, Congressional Research Service, Government of USA.
37. Obama, B. (2011), 'Remarks by the President on the Middle East and North Africa', Speech made on 19th May 2011 in Washington, D.C., USA, available at, http://www.whitehouse.gov/thepress-office/2011/05/19/remarks-president-middle-east-and-north-africa. accessed on February 11, 2014.
38. G8 Declaration, (2011) 'Declaration of the G8 on the Arab Spring', Made on 27th May 2011 in Deauville, France, available at, http://www.g20-g8.com/g8-g20/g8/english/live/news/declaration-of-the-g8-on-the-arabsprings.1316.html, accessed on February 11, 2014.
39. Dabashi, H. (2012), 'The Arab Spring: The End of Post-Colonialism', London, Zed Books Limited.
40. Springborg, R. (2012), 'The US Response to the Arab Uprising: Leadership Missing', in Riccardo Alcaro and Miguel Haubrich-Seco, (eds.), 'Re-thinking Western Policies in Light of the Arab Uprising', Edizioni Nuova Cultura, Roma, p. 34.
41. Springborg, R. (2012), 'The US Response to the Arab Uprising: Leadership Missing', in Riccardo Alcaro and Miguel Haubrich-Seco, (eds.), 'Re-thinking Western Policies in Light of the Arab Uprising', Edizioni Nuova Cultura, Roma, p. 41.
42. Miller, D.A. (2011), 'For America, An Arab Winter', *Wilson Quarterly,* 35 (3), pp. 36-42.
43. Mahapatra, C. (2009), 'The US Approach to the Islamic World in Post-9/11 Era: Implications for India', New Delhi, Academic Foundation.

44. Ratnesar, R. (2011), 'Why U.S. Should Cheer Tunisia's Risky Revolution', National Interest, available at, http://www.time.com/time/world/article/0,8599,2042817,00.html, accessed on February 11, 2014.
45. McInerney, S. (2011), 'Islamist Victory in Tunisia Presents Opportunity for U.S. Engagement', available at, http://fikraforum.org/?p=1685, accessed on February 11, 2014.
46. Kitchen, N. (2012), The Contradictions of Hegemony: The United States and the Arab Spring, available at, http://www2.lse.ac.uk/IDEAS/publications/reports/pdf/SR011/FINAL_LSE_IDEAS__UnitedStatesAndTheArabSpring_Kitchen.pdf, accessed on February 11, 2014.
47. Springborg, R. (2012), 'The US Response to the Arab Uprising: Leadership Missing', in Riccardo Alcaro and Miguel Haubrich-Seco, (eds.), 'Re-thinking Western Policies in Light of the Arab Uprising', Edizioni Nuova Cultura, Roma, p. 44.
48. Kitchen, N. (2012), 'The Contradictions of Hegemony: The United States and the Arab Spring', available at, http://www2.lse.ac.uk/IDEAS/publications/reports/pdf/SR011/FINAL_LSE_IDEAS__UnitedStatesAndTheArabSpring_Kitchen.pdf, accessed on February 11, 2014.
49. Springborg, R. (2012), 'The US Response to the Arab Uprising: Leadership Missing', in Riccardo Alcaro and Miguel Haubrich-Seco (eds.), 'Re-thinking Western Policies in Light of the Arab Uprising', Edizioni Nuova Cultura, Roma, p. 45.
50. Dadush, U. and M. Dunne, (2011), 'American and European Responses to the Arab Spring: What's the Big Idea?', *The Washington Quarterly*, 34 (4), 131-145.
51. Kitchen, N. (2012), 'The Contradictions of Hegemony: The United States and the Arab Spring', available at, http://www2.lse.ac.uk/IDEAS/publications/reports/pdf/SR011/FINAL_LSE_IDEAS__UnitedStatesAndTheArabSpring_Kitchen.pdf, accessed on February 11, 2014.
52. Springborg, R. (2012), 'The US Response to the Arab Uprising: Leadership Missing', in Riccardo Alcaro and Miguel Haubrich-Seco, (eds.), 'Re-thinking Western Policies in Light of the Arab Uprising', Edizioni Nuova Cultura, Roma, p. 42.

16

China and the Arab Spring: Perception and Policy Responses

Srikanth Kondapalli

Since the tumultuous events of December 2010 in North Africa and West Asia, the Chinese media, intellectuals and policy makers were seized of the phenomenon of Arab Spring, terming the events either as "social and political turbulence", or "social and political upheaval" or "revolution" or even as disruptive in nature. These perceptions are reflective of China's standpoint, interests and policy orientation towards the region with implications domestically, as the authoritarian leadership faced mounting pressures from the people. China views these events as widely shaped by the western governments, even as it wants to protect its citizens abroad, economic and energy interests in the region. China's policies vis-à-vis the Arab Spring are mainly two-fold, viz., containing its influence domestically and stall any political opposition to the Chinese Communist Party (CCP) rule and secondly in shaping the international environment conducive for the rise of China, specifically in the economic and strategic domain. In the process, several inconsistencies and contradictions, or even opportunistic postures are visible in China's foreign policies specifically towards the Arab states.

China had been watching carefully the events in North Africa and West Asia, cumulatively dubbed as "Arab Spring". The participation of wide sections of the society in the Arab states, the extent of media coverage and reach and the tumultuous nature of the political protests against the authoritarian regimes in this region have attracted China's attention for a number of reasons, viz., stability and continuity in policy regarding China's interests and stakes in the region, specifically in the economic and energy fields, human security of the Chinese citizens in the region, contain the impact of the ideas of Arab Spring domestically in China as political transition is expected to take place in October 2012 with the 18th Chinese Communist Party (CCP) Congress, shaping the international/regional discourse away from the United States/Western domination and in favour of China and the like.

As the global financial crisis intensifies in the western countries, decline in economic growth rates combined by layoffs and rising social and political protests in China have underlined for the CCP that stability and social harmony are paramount. [1] The leadership frequently brushes the public memory about the chaotic situation in the 19th century that led to the disintegration of the Qing Empire a century ago. They cite *neiluan, waihuan* [internal chaos (leading to) foreign intervention] as justification for authoritarian rule. That was also the pretext for the crackdown at Tiananmen Square in 1989.

Popular responses in China are limited in nature, even during the Arab Spring period, given the Chinese government's control over the media and curbs imposed on public assembly, etc. Calls by several political activists to conduct public agitation in major cities such as Beijing, Shanghai and others were quickly restricted and several were arrested. In Hong Kong, however, over 10,000 people marched leading to police action. Chinese vice president Xi Jinping warned Hong Kong delegates to Beijing to restore order and emphasis on "one country" rather than "two systems". [2] Collective leadership, economic reforms, strengthening of the security apparatus all are said to have resulted in avoiding Arab Spring in China. [3] According to Kevin Rudd, the foreign minister of Australia, Arab Spring will have hardly any effect on the political system of China and that the rising middle class of China would not be able to displace the CCP rule. [4]

However, Harry Harding argued that the current phase of China's political developments could offer scope for wider participation of the people, including the ill-effects of inflation, political succession in the CCP in October 2012 and the widespread application of media that connected the local with the provincial and the central regions of China. [5] On the other hand, Thomas L. Friedman in an open letter to president Hu Jintao on the subject of the Arab Spring argued that the central idea of the protestors in Syria, Egypt and elsewhere is to gain dignity through the use of widespread information exchange and that top down approaches to curb the networking cites would only prove to be "dumb". [6]

Assessing the Spring Thunder

China has a different perspective than the above western assessments. China's leadership indeed had been attentive to the unrest in the North African and West Asian states for their potential impact on its national interests in these countries as well as for internal stability in China. [7] This is reflected in the number of quiet diplomatic visits that the Chinese officials have undertaken in the region as well as carefully, if uneven, crafted manoeuvres. However, overall, China's press had been relatively silent in any extensive coverage of the protests in the Arab states, given their potential backlash domestically in China. Nevertheless, the Chinese press had cautioned the Chinese public extensively on the pitfalls of intervention by the western powers and the chaos that it could generate domestically.

To cite a few examples, the Chinese reportage from Cairo and other capitals overwhelmingly emphasized on "chaotic scenes" in the streets leading to instability in the region. These reporters suggested that energy and food prices are expected to rise due to the popular unrest, while their economies are set to decline, with immediate impact on tourism. This has been the general theme in the Chinese press since reform programme was initiated in 1978.

According to An Huihou, writing in People's Daily, the phenomenon of the Arab Spring is uneven throughout the region, with only five of the 22 Arab states severely affected by the mass movements, viz., Tunisia, Egypt, Libya, Yemen and Syria, while two states witnessing no impact and the rest managing to put down the uprisings. An also suggests that the region was subjected to diverse interests ranging from the Islamic forces, diplomatic forces, tribal forces, elites, political parties, and Western powers acting according to their interests.

However, these events cannot be depicted as revolutions. Great unrests and transformations will likely become the main themes of the Arab world for a long period of time. Real revolutions are likely to take place in some countries during the course of history. People expect that a new Arab world of prosperity, strength, civilization, progress, independence and dynamics will emerge in the world in the aftermath of such unrests and transformations. The goal cannot be fulfilled in the near future. It is still early to assert the emergence of the "Arab War" or the "Arab Revolution". It remains to be seen that whether newly established regimes in the countries have democratic, Islamic or nationalistic characteristics, as well as what policy directions they will take. The signs of revolutionary institutional transformations have yet to emerge in the regimes. [8]

Other assessments are equally critical. For instance, the large-scale renewal of protests in Egypt on November 18, 2011 was termed by Shih Chun-yu in a pro-Beijing newspaper as "the travesty and disappointment of revolutions". Shih argued that these "waves of revolutionary protests will only disrupt a country and harm its people". [9]

Li Hongmei, the editor of the communist party's mouth piece People's Daily writing on February 1, 2011, predicted that the US is "playing with fire" in Egypt and the larger region with its policies of promoting Jeffersonian democracy that could only lead to the rise of "radical and even extremist forces". Li observed, "if Uncle Sam's cleverness overreaches itself, he will be hoisted with his own petard."

Nevertheless, the recent dynamics in the Arab world should be treated as "Great Arab changes" [*alabo da bianjun*] according to Li Shaoxian, vice president of China Institute of Contemporary International Relations, due to their "deep endogenous quality". Li suggested that such protests in the Arab world are inevitable as the region exhibited "rigid political systems, distorted economic structures, extremely high birth rates, large numbers of unemployed youths, tremendous gaps between the rich and the poor, and serious corruption". Li suggested that Arab world today reflects to political decentralisation, political Islamisation and rising national awareness against Israel and the US. [10]

China's Interests

The Chinese assessments above are closely linked to the Chinese interests in the region as well as domestically. Last three decades of reform and opening up of China had resulted in China becoming the second largest economy in the world, with its attendant linkages to import of raw materials, hydrocarbon resources, export of finished manufactured goods, capital, etc. In many of the countries in North Africa and West Asia, China's rise resulted in participation of Chinese in the economic activities of the region, burgeoning bilateral trade, import of energy resources and investments. Overall, China's trade with the Arab world amounts to US$ 145 billion in 2010 and is poised to increase. For instance, in the last decade, China's trade with Egypt nearly tripled from the US$ 3 billion figure in 2006.

Significant business opportunities provided by the automobile assembly plants of Chinese companies Chery and Brilliance in Egypt or the Suez economic and trade cooperation zone project or the Port Said container terminal project built with Chinese assistance could be in jeopardy with the current unrest, although soon after taking over the reins in

Cairo the Egyptian military said it will abide by all international agreements signed previously. [11] China had also assiduously built other stakes as well in Egypt, including the party-to-party relations with the then ruling National Democratic Party. Two Confucius Institutes began operations in 2004 at Cairo University and in 2008 at Suez Canal University. A week before Mubarak resigned, China's foreign minister Yang Jiechi suggested that his country hopes for stability in Egypt. His ministry spokesman Ma Zhaoxu stated that China is critical of any "foreign interference in the internal affairs" of that country even as he hoped for continuity in the "strategic cooperation" between the two countries evolved since 1999. A similar approach was followed by China with Libya and Syria as well.

The rise of China resulted in its "go out" strategy of investing abroad. While China became one of the largest attractive destinations for foreign investments, in the last few years, China is also investing abroad, thanks to its foreign exchange reserves of more than US$ 3 trillion. However, most of this investment initially went into the energy sector abroad, including in North Africa and West Asia. Some of the investment is also in the related infrastructure projects. For instance, an estimated 70 Chinese companies have invested in 50 large-scale projects in Libya including railway, telecom, oil etc worth about US$ 18.8 billion. Libya exports 10 percent of its oil to China which accounts for nearly 3 percent of China's oil imports a year. Overall, West Asia contributes to nearly 56 percent of oil imports for China, with Saudi Arabia, Kuwait, and Iran topping the list. With political unrest in the region, it appeared to the Chinese leadership that its investments will be threatened.

According to Wen Zhongliang, deputy director of China's commerce ministry's foreign trade department, "Due to the changes in the Libyan situation recently, our investment activities in Libya have been impacted. China's investments in Libya, particularly our oil investments, reflect mutually beneficial economic cooperation between the two countries. We hope to continue to develop economic and trade cooperation with Libya in every aspect". [12] Indeed, due to the political instability in the region, China's oil companies have shut down nearly six major energy projects in the region, including one in Libya.

Another factor uppermost in the Chinese interests is its citizens living in the region. An estimated 45 million Chinese live abroad, excluding those in Macao and Hong Kong. Of these there are over one million workers in construction and other projects, while 1.5 million Chinese students study abroad. [13] The safety of the Chinese living abroad has become a major foreign policy objective recently. This is reflected in the sharp diplomatic response of China when Chinese workers and others were killed in Pakistan and Afghanistan. China is also concerned about the safety of the Chinese workers living in West Asia and North Africa. Soon after the Chinese crack down of Uighur separatists on July 5, 2009 (which killed 189 people in a span of two hours), the Maghreb Al-Qaeda threatened to target nearly 50,000 Chinese workers in the region. However, no casualties were reported. During the civil war between the pro-Gaddafi forces and rebels, China evacuated nearly 36,000 Chinese citizens from Libya through major air, land and sea evacuation measures. [14] About 1800 Chinese citizens, likewise, were evacuated from Egypt.

Again, the Chinese model of development could be threatened with the popular uprisings as China had cultivated the ruling elites in several authoritarian regimes across the world and specifically in Africa and West Asia with assistance in lieu of control over strategic resources and international collaboration. It is not without reason that the Egypt-China Friendship Association defends China or that several of these countries obeyed the Chinese call to boycott the Noble Peace Prize ceremony at Oslo for dissident Liu Xiaobo.

More significantly, China had stated in its foreign policy goals that the United Nations should be treated as sacrosanct and that there should be no violation of state sovereignty and interference in the internal affairs of member states. In the light of the Rose revolution in Georgia, Orange revolution in Ukraine, Tulip revolution in Kyrgyzstan, aborted purple revolution in Iraq and saffron revolution in Myanmar, the Chinese concerns appeared to be reactive in nature with its efforts to ward off such a fall out in China. Following this principle, China had opposed the US intervention in Iraq in 2003. On the Libyan developments, since February 2011 when the popular movement erupted against the Gaddafi's government, China's above position was tested with many inconsistencies coming to the fore, but with an overall cautious approach. [15]

Some have interpreted this as "ruthlessly pragmatic opportunism". [16] The UNSC passed two major resolutions—1970 and 1973—on the Libyan developments. The 1970 resolution called for arms embargo, freezing the assets of Gaddafi and his family members and ban on travel. Later, the 1973 resolution called for establishing a no fly zone. China had supported the first resolution, but abstained on the second. [17] China was also critical of the NATO strikes on Libya terming them as interference in the internal affairs of the country. [18] A pro-Beijing newspaper in Hong Kong, for instance, noted that "the Western countries cannot wait to take the opportunity of the wave of Jasmine revolution across Africa to get of rid the "thorn in their flesh"—Libyan leader Muammar al-Gaddafi". [19]

Nevertheless, as the Arab League consented for a no fly zone in Libya, China (and Russia) has acquiesced to this move. This was followed by quiet diplomatic moves by Beijing to protect its interests in the affected states. For instance, it was reported that the Chinese Ambassador to Qatar Zhang Zhiliang met Mustafa Abdel Jalil, the chairman of the transitional national council—a move that can be interpreted by Libya as intervening in its internal affairs. Later, China's foreign minister Yang Jiechi invited senior rebel leader Mahmud Jibril in June 2011 to Beijing for talks and termed the Libyan leader as an "important dialogue partner".

When Libyan foreign minister Abdul-Ati al-Obeidi visited China, he was told that while China respects Libyan sovereignty and territorial integrity, it also is concerned with the Libyan people's choices. Nevertheless, by the second week of September 2011, Beijing finally recognised the transitional council. In May 2011, the Syrian deputy foreign minister Mekdad visited Beijing. [20] While China acceded to the early 2011 UNSC resolution 1970 on arms embargo on Libya, nevertheless, it was reported that in July 2011 when a Libyan official delegation visited Beijing, the latter reportedly agreed to sell US$ 200 million worth of arms to the Gaddafi government. [21]

While China wriggled out of the Libyan situation after the downfall of Gaddafi, its position on Syria is leading to concerns in the region. When the UNSC discussed the clamp down of Syria's ruler Assad over the protestors, China and Russia expressed reservations by suggesting that the global community should not interfere in the domestic issues of Syria. However, in a quick turn-around, later in October 2011 Beijing called for reforms in Syria. According to the Chinese foreign ministry spokesman, "We believe the Syrian government should move faster to honour its reform pledges and swiftly start to push forward the inclusive political process with the broad participation of all parties in Syria". [22] Nevertheless, when a majority of the UNSC members supported a resolution critical of Assad's government handling of domestic unrest, China (and Russia) opposed the move on February 4, 2012. [23] Ruan Zongze argued that China's actions are consistent with its position of no regime change. [24]

Later, China sent its former envoy to Syria Li Huaxin to propose a six-point agenda on overcoming the Syrian crisis, which reiterated no regime change, political negotiations, not to use humanitarian aid to interfere in Syrian affairs, etc. [25] China is also of the view that Kofi Annan's proposals are the most viable suggestions for ending the Syruan crisis. Reflective of the influence of Beijing, Syrian government representative Bouthaina Shaaban visited China in August 2012. [26]

Impact on Domestic Politics

While the external dimension of the Arab Spring saw inconsistencies in China's policies with the North African and West Asian region, on its domestic front, it is more concerted in its positions and actions. Domestically, the Chinese government made it a point to puncture the influence and spread of the Arab Spring. Even though China had been witnessing a number of political protests and socio-economic unrest for more than a decade after the suppression of the 1989 Tiananmen Square incident, the government was able to crack down on dissent. Some of termed this as "contained contention" in China. [27]

According to some estimates, China witnessed 5,000 protests in 1991, while these figures galloped to 74,000 protests in 2005, 87,000 in 2006, 120,000 in 2007 and 140,000 in 2008. [28] According to other estimates, in 2007, 80,000 mass incidents were reported across China, while about 60,000 incidents occurred in 2006 according to a study conducted by the Chinese Academy of Social Sciences. In 2009, it was reported that there were as many as 90,000 "mass incidents" according to a study conducted by Nankai University researchers. [29] Subsequently, in a survey conducted by the Qinghua University, China witnessed 120,000 such incidents across the country in 2010. According to Chen Chih-jou Jay, of the Institute of Sociology of Academia Sinica in Taiwan, more than 50 percent of these protests are against privatization of public assets, loss of social welfare benefits and/or against cadre corruption.

A few events in the last one year indicate to the widespread political unrest in China. In early 2011, the north-eastern city of Dalian residents forced the government to shift a polluting chemical plant. [30] In May, riots broke out in Inner Mongolia after a herder was over-run by a truck. [31] This resulted in mass protests resulting in Premier Wen Jiabao making a hurried visit to the region. [32] In June 2011, clashes between migrant workers and the police took place in Guangdong at a ceramics factory. In July 2011, at Dadun in Zengcheng city in southern China unrest broke out when a migrant pregnant woman hawker was manhandled. [33]

In November 2011, 7,000 workers at a shoe factory in Guangdong Province clashed with the police on the issues of layoffs and wage cuts. [34] In December 2011, Wukan villagers of Guangdong province drove away the CCP cadres riled as they were about the land grab and increasing economic woes. The movement, started in September by over 15,000 residents, protested en masse after Xue Jinbo was allegedly tortured by the local police. They erected road-blocks and elected their own leaders. On December 22, the Guangdong Party officials negotiated a deal with the newly elected village chief Lin Zuluan, that was termed as "conciliatory approach" by the CCP. [35]

Specifically, looking at the impact of the Arab Spring, it did have its resonances in China, although due to the clampdown of the state, these have not evoked much publicity in the media. In early 2011, several appeals were made to the people to gather at designated places in 23 cities from 1400 hours every Sunday. On February 20, people gathered at Beijing and Shanghai, but soon due to the intervention of the public security agencies, these activities were physically curbed. [36] Journalists and others, likewise were prevented from reporting at these places. [37]

Counter Measures

To overcome the influence of the Arab Spring on China, the Chinese authorities have undertaken a number of counter-measures, including arrests, [38] curbing media reportage of the Jasmine revolution, "enhancement of social management".

[39] etc. To enhance internal security mechanisms, in 2011, the budget for the People's Armed Police Force was raised to over US$ 95 billion, a figure higher than the allocations for the defence of the country. A number of political activists were arrested and incarcerated across China since February 2011. One of the foremost critics of the CCP, whom he labelled as a bunch of "gangsters", Ai Weiwei, the architect of Birds Nest during the Beijing Olympics was arrested and released after more than three months in jail. [40]

Other rights activists, critics of the government and lawyers who were arrested include Hu Jia, Teng Biao, Jiang Tianyong, Li Tiantian, Zhu Yufu, Ding Mao, Chen Wei, Wang Lihong, Guo Weidong, Zheng Chuangtian and Li Fangping. [41] By mid-2011, it was speculated, however, that in the backdrop of the 90th anniversary celebrations of the CCP, China had assessed that the Jasmine revolution had withered away, leading to release of some activists like Sichuan's Ran Yunfei and Guangzhou's Tang Jinling for "lack of evidence" in their alleged "subversion of state power". [42] However, this remained only transitory as further clampdown on the activists continued recently.

China had imposed subtle censorship in its media coverage on the events related to Arab Spring with President Hu Jintao calling for "guide online public opinion". [43] With more than half a billion internet users in China, it is easier for the netizens to spread their message quickly. Indeed, in the last decade the Chinese cyberspace had seen unprecedented activity through the social networking sites. These have created space for a number of discussion fora—with some venturing into criticism of the authoritarian rule as well. After the popular unrest spread in West Asia and northern Africa, Chinese government imposed media curbs and several micro-blogging cites content has been "regulated", while mass text messaging discontinued. [44]

However, blogs which praised the communist party rule, stability or those critical of "paid protestors" in Iran allegedly by the US—all were allowed to flourish. Nevertheless, with social unrest increasing year-by-year and across China, these sites have become the places for fastest spread of information and ideas, much like in North Africa and West Asia. The governmental curbs on the social networks also increased substantially in the recent period. [45] In April 2011, NetEase portal was shut down. In October 2011, the propaganda department of the CCP held an annual meeting to reform the cultural system and tighten control over the media. Major internet portals like Baidu, Sina, Muzi, Youku, etc were instructed to censor "rumours" in the cyberspace domain. [46] A 15 day "administrative detention" of those who spread rumours on the internet was ordered. [47] The Chinese government had in December 2011instructed millions of "weibo" (launched in August 2009) micro bloggers of one of the largest internet portals, Sina to register their real names. Further, to curb protests, China had redeployed the 128th Division of the People's Armed Police Force unit from Xinjiang to Henan in April 2011. [48]

Conclusions

China's responses to the Arab Spring indicate to a domestic curtailment of the message and resonances of the Jasmine Revolution and carving out a furrow internationally with the message of non-interventionism. With the Chinese leadership and public security forces' actions, eventually the Arab Spring ended with a whimper in China with hardly any major protests on the scale witnessed in the Tehrir Square. Externally, China's stance tested its principles of non-interference, sanctity of the UN Charter and more significantly international isolation as China pursued its interests and stakes in the North African and West Asian region. While China had exhibited pragmatism of following the leads of the Arab League and African Union, the vote of China (and Russia) on Syrian developments have surprised many in the region. For sure the veto of China indicates to the recent trend of assertiveness in the international areas as reflected in such positions on Saffron Revolution in Myanmar and the civil strife in Zimbabwe. China's position on the Libyan developments indicated to the inconsistencies in its non-intervention policy. Overall, then the Arab Spring came as a shock to China—with reverberations in the external and domestic spheres in years to come.

Endnotes

1. It is not lost on the Chinese leadership that within a month after the self-immolation of Mohamed Bouazizi that the Tunisian president Ben Ali had to resign. Although the Chinese context is structurally different from that of the Arab state and the CCP is stronger with over 83 million cadres, with an ever-vigilant security apparatus, the Arab Spring does pose a challenge to the Chinese leadership internally.
2. In 1997, Hong Kong reverted back to China after the UK-China 1984 agreement. China agreed to set up Hong Kong Special Administrative Region under the one country, two systems policy of autonomy for Hong Kong. See Bill Schiller, "China fears a Jasmine Revolution", May 13, 2011, accessed at, http://www.star.com.
3. Peter Rutland and Orion Lewis, "Why It Won't Happen in China", International Herald Tribune, March 10, 2011, accessed at, http://www.nytimes.com/2011/03/11/opinion/11iht-edrutland11.html.
4. Rudd made the comments speaking to Asia Society in New York in January 2012. See "No Arab Spring will halt China, says Rudd", The Age, January 15, 2012, accessed at, http://www.theage.com.au/world/no-arab-spring-will-halt-china-says-rudd-20120114-1q0fp.html#ixzz1jWS9njnD.
5. Harry Harding, "China: Political Stability amid Jasmine Revolution?", May 4, 2011, accessed at, http://asiafoundation.org/in-asia/2011/05/04/china-political-stability-amid-jasmine-revolutions.
6. Thomas L. Friedman, "Advice for China", The New York Times, June 4, 2011.
7. Jonas Parello-Plesner and Raffaelo Pantucci, "China's Janus-

Faced Response To The Arab Revolutions", European Council on Foreign Relations, June 2011, accessed at, http://www.ecfr.eu/page/-/ECFR34_CHINA_ARAB_REVOLUTIONS_AW.pdf.

8. An Huihou, "Arab Spring: Turbulence or Revolution?", People's Daily, October 26, 2011, NewsEdge Document Number: 201110261477.1_90b300a7ba11eb8c, Accession Number 325400435.
9. "Current Egyptian Unrest: Proof That Revolution is Harmful to Nations", Ta Kung Pao, Online November 25, 2011, NewsEdge Document Number: 201111251477.1_da870b5c8d07dc55, Accession Number 326900359.
10. Li cited at Luo Chaowen and Li Xueyong, "Perspective on Great Arab Changes", December 19, 2011, *Jiefangjun Bao Online* December 22, 2011, NewsEdge Document Number: 201112221477.1_2b8705b3bbe91f8d, Accession Number 328250247.
11. Srikanth Kondapalli, "Why China is Wary of Middle-East Uprisings", Rediff.com, March 9, 2011, accessed at, http://www.rediff.com/news/column/why-china-is-wary-of-middle-east-uprisings/20110309.htm.
12. See "China Seeks To Protect Libya Trade Ties", AFP, August 23, 2011, NewsEdge Document Number: 201108231477.1_d30c0064388a0ce0, Accession Number 322200443.
13. Wu Zhong, "China Sees Bright Side of Elite Exodus", The Asian Times, May 5, 2011.
14. See Ni Eryan, "The Point of the Military is to Prevent Violence: The Far-Reaching Significance of the First-Time Participation of a Chinese Military Vessel in an Overseas Evacuation", Wen Wei Po Online, March 11, 2011, NewsEdge Document Number: 201103111477.1_519a0744b69609b8, Accession Number 313951319; and Yan Xuetong, "The Sources of Chinese Conduct", Project Syndicate, March 28, 2011, accessed at, http://www.project-syndicate.org/commentary/xyan1/English.
15. Jonas Parello-Plesner, "China and the Arab Spring: External and Internal Consequences and Implications for EU-China Cooperation", accessed at, http://www.ispionline.it/it/documents/Analysis_53_2011.pdf. and Yuan Jing-dong, "The Arab Spring and China's Evolving

Middle East Policy", December 20, 2011, accessed at, http://www.worldpoliticsreview.com/articles/10992/the-arab-spring-and-chinas-evolving-middle-east-policy.

16. Kelley Currie, "China and the Arab Spring", The Daily News, January 8, 2012, accessed at, http://www.thedailynewsegypt.com/china-and-the-arab-spring.html.
17. For these inconsistencies of China see Jonas Parello-Plesner, "China's Desert Dance around Libya", October 27, 2011, accessed at, http://chinausfocus.com/slider/china%e2%80%99s-desert-dance-around-libya.
18. According to a Chinese military assessment of the situation in Libya, the NATO forces succeeded in Libya because they organized a coalition of "many fighting against one". Secondly, the NATO forces also "compet[ed] with its opponent for supporters [through internet, psychological warfare, etc] and put forth efforts to internally disintegrate the other side." Thirdly, the NATO units successfully intruded into Libya's military systems and networks. See, for this assessment, Li Lin and Li Zezhong, "Perspectives on NATO's Use of Its Military Strength in Libya", October 31, 2011, *Jiefangjun Bao Online,* November 1, 2011, NewsEdge Document Number: 201111011477.1_9f1e04ebbec3bf61, Accession Number 325700146.
19. See, "TKP Editorial Criticizes US, European Air Strikes on Libya" Ta Kung Pao Online, March 24, 2011, NewsEdge Document Number: 201103241477.1_04a702d985f5069d, Accession Number 314600386.
20. See, Mu Chunshan, "China's Middle East Diplomacy", The Diplomat, June 20, 2011.
21. China's foreign ministry clarified that while such discussions took place with state owned enterprises, Beijing government neither had the knowledge nor did they sell weapons to Libya. See Frank Ching, "Beijing's awkward moment with Gadhafi group", The Japan Times, September 29, 2011, accessed at, http://www.japantimes.co.jp/text/eo20110929fc.html.
22. "Assad Must Listen as Beijing Leaves Syria Veto Row Behind", Gulf Times Online, October 12, 2011, NewsEdge Document Number: 201110121477.1_6898009e379a587c, Accession

Number 324700874.

23. Yang suggested that Syrian developments could lead to more humanitarian disasters. Yang Liming, "Syria becomes focus of struggle among great powers", China Daily, February 8, 2012, accessed at, http://english.peopledaily.com.cn/90780/7723446.html; Willy Lam, "Beijing Joins Team Anti-America", Wall Street Journal, February 10, 2012, accessed at, http://online.wsj.com/article/SB10001424052970203646004577212522050195282.html; "China and Russia to counter Western influence", February 2, 2012, accessed at, http://www.thechinatimes.com/online/2012/02/2130.html; On inconsistencies in China's policies, see Ian Bremmer, "China's Fast growing Middle East Problem", Foreign Policy, March 13, 2012, accessed at, http://eurasia.foreignpolicy.com/posts/2012/03/13/chinas_fast_growing_middle_east_problem.
24. Ruan Zongze, "China, Russia open window of opportunity for solving Syria issue", People's Daily, February 8, 2012, accessed at, http://english.peopledaily.com.cn/90883/7723514.html.
25. Chris Buckley, "China to send envoy in bid to ease Syria crisis", Reuters, March 5, 2012, accessed at, http://www.reuters.com.
26. "China seeking to coax compromise in Syria: state paper", Reuters, August 15, 2012, accessed at, http://www.reuters.com/article/2012/08/15/us-syria-crisis-china-idUSBRE87E03F20120815.
27. James Reilly, "Not the next Arab Spring: The China method for managing popular unrest", East Asia Forum, September 20, 2011, accessed at, http://www.eastasiaforum.org/2011/09/20/not-the-next-arab-spring-the-china-method-for-managing-popular-unrest.
28. Murray Scot Tanner, "China Rethinks Unrest" The Washington Quarterly, Vol.27, No. 3, Summer 2004, pp. 137-156.
29. James Pomfret and Chris Buckley, "China Migrant Unrest Exposes Generational Faultline", Taipei Times Online, July 5, 2011, NewsEdge Document Number: 201107051477.1_b74a0394923fcd20, Accession Number 319750051.
30. Shi Jiangtao, "Anger over toxic plant reopening", South China Morning Post, December 31, 2011.

31. "China Mongols protest in Xilinhot over shepherd's death", BBC, May 25, 2011, accessed at, http://www.bbc.co.uk/news/world-asia-pacific-13547933; Brian Spegele, "China Makes Effort to Cool Unrest in Inner Mongolia", Wall Street Journal, May 31, 2011, and B. Raman, "China's Inner Mongolia: A Jasmine Revolution with a Difference" South Asia Analysis Group June 2, 2011.
32. While the Moody's Investors Service suggested that the social unrest could have a bearing on the social stability, it also stated that the Chinese government's response so far had been balanced and swift. See Kim Young-gyo, "Recent Unrest in China Adds Challenges For Chinese Leaders: Moody's" Yonhap, June 21, 2011, NewsEdge Document Number: 201106211477.1_b063004dceb5cac5, Accession Number 319050950.
33. James Pomfret and Chris Buckley argued that this incident is much like the maltreatment of the vegetable seller in Tunisia that triggered the Arab Spring movement in the region. However, they argue that "The CCP is armed with fast economic growth, a powerful security apparatus and an aura of public authority to shield it from such risks". See "China Migrant Unrest Exposes Generational Faultline", Taipei Times Online, July 5, 2011, NewsEdge Document Number 201107051477.1_b74a0394923fcd20, Accession Number 319750051.
34. "Unrest Challenging China Before Leadership Change", AFP, December 18, 2011, NewsEdge Document Number: 201112181477.1_c26900e3e2732962, Accession Number 328050180.
35. See Willy Wo Lap Lam, "The Grim Future of the Wukan Model for Managing Dissent", China Brief, Vol.12, Issue 1, January 6, 2012.
36. Kim Young-gyo, "China warns Hong Kong media over 'Jasmine Revolution" reports Yonhap, March 2, 2011, NewsEdge Document Number: 201103021477.1_818e004f9bbf838b, Accession Number 313500107. See also Frank Ching, "China hopes to avoid fresh revolts", China Post, April 27, 2011.
37. "Further on PRC FM Spokesman Saying Media Must 'Cooperate' After Clampdown", AFP, March 1, 2011, NewsEdge Document Number:

201103011477.1_fbee009daabe8c60, Accession Number 313452207.

38. Donald C. Clarke had argued that the Chinese effort in arresting scores of activists here is not about the rule of law but how efficiently governance is to be enforced. According to him, "In China, the difference between detention according to law and detention not according to law is one of policy and convenience. If activists are 'disappeared', it is not because some fragile and immature rule of law has broken down in the face of overwhelming political pressures. It is because the authorities have decided that the message sent by disappearing someone is preferable to the message sent by detaining them in accordance with legal procedures, or because the detention was considered too urgent to allow time for proper procedures". See "China's jasmine crackdown and the legal system", East Asia Forum, May 26, 2011.
39. Sun Chia-Yeh, "PRC Authorities Simultaneously Crack Down, Stress Livelihood", Ming Pao, March 4, 2011, NewsEdge Document Number: 201103041477.1_290501d0243f7a15, Accession Number 313600713 and "Rights Groups Criticizes PRC's 'Repression' on Calls for 'Jasmine Revolution' AFP, March 3, 2011, NewsEdge Document Number: 201103031477.1_d8920068c3dbcc34, Accession Number 313550651.
40. Joshua E. Keating, "Cultural Revolutionaries", Foreign Policy Magazine, May 10, 2011.
41. "Rights Groups Say Ai Wei Wei Case Indicates New China Tack To Quiet Critics", AFP, June 23, 2011, NewsEdge Document Number: 201106231477.1_fd3700b6c5c8a92e, Accession Number 319151748; "Veteran China Rights Activist Jailed for 9 Months", AFP, September 9, 2011, NewsEdge Document Number: 201109091477.1_baa200563ff59982, Accession Number 323050455; "Pro-Democracy Activist Zhu Yufu of Hangzhou 'Democracy Wall' Officially Arrested for Issuing Article in Support of the 'Jasmine Revolution' and on Charges of 'Inciting To Subvert State Power', Hong Kong Information Centre for Human Rights and Democracy, April 13, 2011, NewsEdge Document Number: 201104131477.1_2d3b00582ef7b110, Accession Number 315601710.

42. "PRC Lifts Restrictions on Rights Activists Following Withering of Jasmine Revolution", Ming Pao, August 25, 2011, NewsEdge Document Number: 201108251477.1_f3ad020cab149c5f, Accession Number 322300140.
43. Wee Sui-Lee, "Chinese government fights to win over country's microbloggers", Reuters, March 9, 2011, accessed at, http://www.theglobeandmail.com/news/technology/tech-news/chinese-government-fights-to-win-over-countrys-microbloggers/article1935047.
44. "China to step up web monitoring to fend off 'Arab Spring' influences", Taiwan News, February 7, 2002, accessed at, http://www.taiwannews.com.tw/etn/news_content.php?id=1834403.
45. Kathrin Hille, "China's love affair with blogging wanes", The Financial Times, December 9, 2011.
46. "PRC Propaganda Authorities Seek To Tighten Controls Over Internet", AFP, October 15, 2011, NewsEdge Document Number: 201110151477.1_3c3500d2509b4265, Accession Number 324850207.
47. Malcolm Moore, "China fights to silence the social network", The Telegraph, October 26, 2011.
48. "Situation in the Mainland Tense, Armed Police Mobile Division Assisting Xinjiang Recalled", Hong Kong Information Center for Human Rights and Democracy, April 14, 2011, NewsEdge Document Number: 201104141477.1_4ff700a059ad34ae, Accession Number 315651234.

17

Persian Gulf and the Arab Spring: Implications for India

Monish Tourangbam

Long time dictators have been falling like dominoes in the Arab World, starting from Tunisia to Egypt, to Libya where erstwhile strongman Gaddafi fell to rebel forces, the latter supported by heavy NATO airpower, and to Yemen where Ali Abdullah Saleh resigned lately. The Arab Spring has outlived succeeding seasons and continues to rattle the regional balance with international repercussions, with the spotlight now on Syria, where Assad's regime hangs on amidst widespread condemnation. Winds of change is sweeping through the Arab streets, challenging the long-held status quo, and the advent of new technologies and the speed with which information are shared through social networking sites have been a potent tool for the protestors.

West Asian and North African countries hold approximately 61 percent of oil reserves and 45 percent of natural gas reserves. The region's exports account for roughly 40 percent of oil and 20 percent of natural gas traded internationally. [1] As such, unrest in these countries and potential conflicts in the horizon are major issues of concern to energy importers around the world, of which India is one. Though, Arab states in the Persian Gulf have not faced the magnitude of upheaval, till now, seen in other more volatile states of West Asia and North Africa, the burning tensions there assume equal or even more importance practically for Indian foreign policy. Arab states in the Persian Gulf hosts a large number of Indian expatriates working there, and who have become a major source of the huge influx of remittances to India every year.

In the event of any major upheaval, India has to brace itself up for one of the biggest evacuation programme for Indians there (a glimpse of which was seen in the case of Libya as well and during the Gulf Crisis in the early 1990s). Moreover, this oil-rich region is the main energy exporter to India and hence any major disturbance to the fragile situation there will have unsettling repercussions for India. The Persian Gulf presents more geopolitical challenges as the perennial Shia-Sunni divide threatens to intensify. Allegations of Iran's interferences in Bahrain, a Shia majority country ruled by a Sunni minority (where Saudi Arabia sent troops to quell protests) is testament to this tension that might become hot anytime and will then change the whole dynamics of the region, with major international implications.

This paper is an attempt to understand the trajectory of the Arab Spring in the Persian Gulf, in the context of the existing regional balance of power and identity-based tensions in the region; and to assess India's vital interests in the region. The turmoil in other countries of the West Asian and North African region have been a major eye opener to the kind of geopolitical challenges that India will face in the Persian Gulf, if and when the events turn out of hand.

Persian Gulf and the Arab Spring

In December 2003, Al Jazeera talk show host Faisal al-Qassem opened a programme, asking, "Why does every nation on Earth move to change their conditions except for us? Why do we always submit to the batons of the rulers and their repression? How long will Arabs wait for foreign saviours?" [2] Well, it seems his question has been partly answered with the Arab movements, although it is too early to predict the sustainability of the monumental changes that the region has seen in this past one year.

The common language of Arabic has accentuated the

emotional chords across the Arab states of the region, and has played a big factor in the protests spreading in the region. The paper essentially looks at developments in the politics of revolution in the Arab States of the Persian Gulf, which are also incidentally members of the Gulf Cooperation Council (GCC), which again are monarchies, viz. Saudi Arabia, Kuwait, Bahrain, Qatar, United Arab Emirates (UAE) and Oman. So, the narrative has been that of popular participation vs. dynastic rule. The movement in large part seems targeted against any form of guardianship, whether male as seen by women or whether by a strong ruler or monarch as seen by the people, and that rights are not privileges but basic and fundamental to human lives.

The preservation of human dignity has been seen as a prominent argument for the protestors, starting with the self-immolation of the Tunisian street vendor Mohamed Bouazizi against the confiscation of his wares and the reported harassment and humiliation meted to him by officials. There is no denying that people took the streets generally for the same reasons, namely rampant corruption, cronyism, high unemployment, lack of justice and transparency and a sense of relative deprivation, accentuated through greater exposure. A young population fed with web-based instant information and opinion has been a potent tool for the current uprising in many parts of the Arab world.

The monarchies of the Arab States of the Persian Gulf have largely been able to stem unrest in their countries, except that of Bahrain where the Al Khalifa rulers, belonging to the Sunni sect have been grappling with means to tackle the uprising. Given the Shia majority in this country, the protests and the standoff with the government have largely taken a sectarian face, which has complicated matters further. Moreover, the Sunni-Shia tension in the region, represented at the strategic level by the Saudi-Iranian rivalry, is most clearly reflected in tensions enveloping the island kingdom of Bahrain.

Protests against the ruling governments have not gone passed other kingdoms in the region, but the tensions in these places have not yet gone over the brim, although given the volatility of politics in the region post the Arab spring, no one will dare predict the future course of events. The events in the past year have been redrawing the political map of the region, also impacting the sectarian tensions in the region, most clearly amplified by the tussle of regional supremacy between a Sunni-Saudi Arabia and a Shia-Iran. The deficit of oil can only be replaced only by oil, at least in the foreseeable future, thus increasing global implications of the crisis in this oil-rich region and also giving a premium to the Iranian threats to close the Strait of Hormuz, as a result of the continuing sanctions from the West.

Arab Spring versus Gulf Monarchies

Excepting Bahrain, protestors in other Gulf monarchies have not rattled rulers to the extent to which they become fearful of losing their hereditary powers. The awakening that has already overthrown four long time dictators and threatens to dethrone another one in Syria, definitely has had its impact on all the rulers of these states, forcing them to listen to the public rant, or whispers of discontentment if for no other reason, to offer ad-hoc concessions and monetary hand-outs to calm down any simmering signs of tension. Even Qatar, which has not seen protests or petitions as in some other neighbouring states, sought to pre-empt rather than wait for a bottoms-up demand, by announcing it would hold elections for its legislative authority—the Shura Council—in 2013. Qatar has been largely successful in putting itself ahead in the regional scheme of things, seeking to adopt an independent and pragmatic foreign policy, engaging countries like the United States and Iran simultaneously, and taking the initiative to support pro-democracy movements in the region. *Al Jazeera*—the Doha-based voice of the Arab revolutions—has risen in stature, so too have its Qatari sponsors. Qatar's GDP per capita, which is the highest in the world, has also helped to a large extent in putting off the anti-monarchy movements there. [3]

Protests also broke out in Oman, but the protestors in that country have not risen to the point of threatening to dethrone the monarch. In fact, it is reported that most of the protests while calling for changes, pointed out that they did not want their monarch to go. The protests in Sohar, 200 km. northwest of Muscat, prompted Oman's leader, Sultan Qaboos bin Said, to introduce swift appeasing measures—giving orders for the provision of 50,000 jobs and unemployment benefits worth nearly US$ 400 a month; to establish a committee to examine bestowing some legislative powers on the 84-member Shura council, an elected body which currently acts in a purely advisory capacity, to boost social benefits for students and to create a consumer protection bureau, and look into opening cooperatives. A protestor taking part in a sit-in in Muscat, said: "Omanis are calling for [the government to] combat corruption and fight the rising cost of living, in addition to many other issues, [such as] raising salaries and [greater] media freedoms". Sultan Qaboos, who has ruled Oman for the past 40 years, had tried to ease tensions by reshuffling his cabinet after a small protest in the capital Muscat. Oman also reportedly raised minimum wages for an estimated 150,000 private sector employees to US$ 520 from US$ 364 a month. [4]

Kuwait also announced parliamentary elections to be held in early February 2012, the fourth poll in under six years for the Gulf state seeking political stability. The move came only days after Emir Sheikh Sabah al-Ahmad Al-Sabah swore in a new cabinet with only minor changes to the government that resigned in November 2011 over allegations of corruption. The government has reportedly agreed to allow Kuwait Transparency Society to monitor the elections and also decided to establish hotlines in various areas for people to report violations. It is the first time that Kuwait, which introduced parliamentary elections in 1962, will allow anybody to monitor the elections which are supervised and managed entirely by the ministries of interior and justice. [5] Wealth in the Gulf monarchies, and many of them being major business destinations, have largely been instrumental in keeping off the Arab Spring from sweeping with all its force in these countries, and United Arab Emirates has been no exception.

Quite early, reports predicted that large scale protests were quite unlikely in UAE, a small state with huge oil reserves. It has one of the highest per capita incomes in the world and a huge trade surplus. Notwithstanding their overseas investments, the domestic spending of some of these states, including UAE might be instrumental in keeping off large scale protests. Sheik Mohammed bin Zayed al-Nahyan, crown prince of Abu Dhabi, toured the country early 2011 and held talks with residents in various places to determine its needs; and ordered a US$ 1.5 billion investment in electricity and water projects in the northern emirates. The government also decided to cut food prices, according to experts, to pre-empt any dissent that may develop in the northern regions of the UAE, such as Ras Al Khaimah and Sharjah, which are home to about 40 percent of the country's population.

The high standard of living among the workers compared to Tunisia, Yemen and Egypt might also be a factor in the calm. Nationals enjoy many advantages and profit from social security and housing benefits. Unemployment is high, but it is a matter of choice, according to an expert who said, "Quite a few Emiratis are unwilling to perform certain jobs in the private sector. They generally come from families that can provide them with a safety net, so they choose to turn to entrepreneurship in the form of business sponsoring". [6]

Saudi Arabia, which at present, is being dubbed the leader of the "counter-revolution" has seen its own share of protests, with fears and concerns ,mainly being raised by movements and clashes with security personnel at the eastern region of the country, home to a large Shia-minority, and also home to its oil industry. The Shia community accounts for somewhere between 10 to 15 percent of the total population. They complain of marginalization in the Sunni-dominated kingdom. Demonstrations have been held in the eastern region to call for the "release of political detainees, reform and an end to sectarian discrimination".

Saudi Arabia accused those detained of serving the agenda of a foreign power, usually a reference to Iran, thus underlining the larger strategic tussle playing out in the country based on Sunni-Shia divide and Arab-Persian tensions. [7] Taking inspiration from the movements in Tunisia and Egypt, women activism has raised its head in Saudi Arabia, demanding equal treatment and greater say in electoral politics through the "Baladi" or "My Country" campaign. Activists among Saudi Arabia's women, who can't drive or vote and need male approval to work and travel, started turning to online organizing. [8] Saudi royal adopted a ban on public demonstrations and acts of civil disobedience. On March 11, 2011—the so-called Day of Rage on a Facebook page—the Saudi rulers deployed massive numbers of security forces in the streets. They also played the Shia card, arguing that public protests throughout the region were being orchestrated by Shia Iran, and were anti-Sunni and sectarian. [9]

As Saudi authorities feared the unrest, Saudi Arabia's King Abdullah announced unprecedented economic benefits worth tens of billions of dollars, on housing facilities and medical facilities, employee benefits and student benefits. The unemployed were to be given monthly payments of around US$ 260. But, at the same breadth, King Abdullah also warned that security forces will "hit" whoever undermines the kingdom's security and stability, in a speech aired on state-run television. He thanked residents and security forces for being "the hands" of the country's stability. [10] According to Tim Niblock, professor of Gulf Studies at the University of Exeter, Britain, the regimes in the Gulf countries face no immediate threat though they will continue to feel the effect of the Arab Spring. [11]

But, conditions in the island kingdom of Bahrain, although not growing to the level of uncertainty seen in other more volatile states, mirror all things that is feared from a strategically more potent force of the Sunni-Shia divide, with Saudi Arabia and Iran standing on opposite sides as custodians of Islamic power, impacting upon regional dynamics, almost forcing countries that have stakes in the region to take sides. This is of particular importance to a country like India that has maintained pragmatic working relationships with both Iran and Saudi Arabia. The tiny island kingdom produces little oil but is of vital strategic importance in the Persian Gulf, a seaway that carries 18 percent of the world's oil. [12] The threats that Iran has faced over the years and continues to face from the United States and others regarding its suspicious nuclear programme and Iranian threats of reprisal make things all the more complicated.

There are disturbing accounts from major human rights organizations about abuses in Bahrain and the systematic state violence that has been unleashed on the opposition movement against the monarchy of the Al Khalifa family. While Cairo's Tahrir Square has become a symbol of the Arab Spring, Bahrain's Pearl Roundabout, by contrast, has ceased to even exist. The government brought in bulldozers to demolish it. There have been reports of large scale arrests and torture to clamp down on the protestors in the country. The Sunni-led government and private employers reportedly fired thousands of workers, nearly all of them Shiite Muslims. In Bahrain, the government and its media allies have been accused of stoking sectarian conflict, stirring fears among the country's Sunni elite of an Iranian-controlled Shiite takeover.

The demographic realties of the country, where a Sunni minority rules over about 70 percent Shias has become all the more stark with the current round of protests and repressions by the monarchy, with assistance from its other Gulf neighbouring monarchies. There were reports of medics being tortured in custody, with military courts sentencing some to 15 years in prison. An investigation by an international panel of jurists verified the accounts of torture and indiscriminate arrests. Organizers of the uprising said that they may be Shiite but that they are committed to pluralism, secular rule and even the ruling family—if it grants the people a bigger voice. [13]

But, the strategic plot involving Bahrain has the potential to escalate tensions within the region that might have deep-felt repercussions for actors beyond the region. For one, the United States has been accused of resorting to acute selectivity as it provided only a guarded rebuke on the Bahrain's monarchy decision to call in Saudi troops to quell protests. Washington urged Bahrain (home to the US Navy's Fifth Fleet) to use restraint and repeated the call to other Gulf nations but said it did not consider the entry into Bahrain of Saudi security forces an invasion. And, the United States' ties with its ally in the region and a strategic bulwark against Shiite Iran, Saudi Arabia need no further elaboration. Towards the end of 2011, Obama administration announced an arms deal with Saudi Arabia valued at nearly US$ 30 billion, an agreement that will send 84 F-15 fighter jets and assorted weaponry to the kingdom. [14]

Sunni-Shia Divide: Race for Regional Dominance

The involvement of Saudi Arabia has taken the events in Bahrain (connected by a 16-mile causeway to Saudi Arabia's oil-rich eastern province) to a different level with deep ramifications for the strategic contest in the region between a Sunni-Saudi Arabia and Shiite-Iran. Saudi Arabia sees the uprisings as an unprecedented threat to regional security and sought unity among the GCC monarchies. The GCC put together a $20 billion (Dh73.4billion) aid package for Oman and Bahrain. In March 2011, the GCC's Peninsula Shield Force, with troops from Saudi Arabia and police from the UAE, entered Bahrain to help quell the protests there. Saudi Arabia and the UAE have repeatedly accused Iran of fomenting instability in the region, particularly in Bahrain, which has a majority Shiite population. A statement issued by GCC foreign ministers had charged Iran with meddling and "violating the sovereignty" of member states. [15]

The fear of a possible Iranian encroachment taking advantage of the Arab awakening drove the Gulf States, towards adopting the Saudi King's recommendation to move the GCC toward "unity". Expressing their fears of "attempts by foreign entities trying to export their internal crises through the effects of discord and division, and inciting sectarianism", they outlined a strategy "to fortify the home front" to counter these attempts through their "determination to achieve the highest degree of economic integration and development of defence cooperation and security", [16] The Al-Saud monarchy in Saudi Arabia, for pragmatic reasons, is highly concerned of the situation in Bahrain. Besides the perceived Iranian shadow hanging over the Shia population in the country, the Saudis fear that the Al Khalifa family losing their grip on the power, might trigger a domino effect in the region, thus impacting the fate of the Gulf monarchies.

Demonstrations in Bahrain as well as in parts of Saudi Arabia have made it amply clear that people desire political power to be shared, and that normal people should have proper say in the management of the resources of the country, rather than the fate of the country being decided by a single family. Although, Iran, due to strategic reasons, has been blamed for the unrests in Bahrain and parts of Saudi Arabia, commentators argued that Iran did not have a direct role in the protests, despite Iran having a vested interest in what is happening in Bahrain, and having a degree of cultural and political influence throughout the wider Persian Gulf area. The contention is that the protests are "primarily about government accountability, social justice and human rights" and that the demands cut across "religious, ethnic, tribal and class lines".

The Al Khalifa ruling family in Bahrain has been blamed for playing the sectarian card "in order to divert attention away from the demands of the people by blaming Iran for the uprising". [17] Reflecting on the Saudi's approach to the Arab Spring in the neighbourhood and their major concerns, former CIA official and a prominent analyst Bruce Riedel observed: "One of the last absolute monarchies, the Saudi family seems to represent all that the Arab Spring is fighting against: closed societies with unequal distribution; repressed minorities living within manufactured boundaries; strong Islamist sympathies across its lands; a latent Sunni-Shia power struggle embedded in the country's fabric-not to mention a string of surrounding states struggling to stave off revolutions that could easily have a contagion effect". [18]

Riedel contended that "Riyadh has become the de facto leader of the counterrevolution" in West Asia, which is "shoring up its borders and tampering down neighbouring unrest". Riyadh has created an alliance to "quell any revolutionary movement" in six monarchies belonging to the GCC. [19] Frederick Wehrey of the *Rand Corporation*, giving a slightly different opinion on the same issue, argued that, "The Saudi and Iranian approaches to the Arab uprisings cannot broadly be labeled revolutionary or counter-revolutionary; instead realpolitik considerations carry the day. Thus, both states buttress friendly regimes that face protest movements but they also find themselves in uncomfortable position of fanning opposition when it threatens their adversaries". [20]

To prove his point, Wherey added, "In Bahrain, Iran is on the side of political change as a path to Shiite empowerment and a blow to its Saudi rival, while in Syria, Tehran stands firmly against change. In Riyadh's case, the reverse is true. Saudi Arabia sent troops to Bahrain to quash the revolt there, but in Syria it has called for the fall of Bashar al-Assad's regime". [21] Adding fuel to fire, the US government recently charged Mansoor Arbabsiar, a dual U.S.-Iranian citizen, and Gholam Shakuri, an alleged member of the Iranian Quds Force (a division of the Revolutionary Guards), with conspiracy to assassinate the Saudi Arabian ambassador to the United States,

Adel Al-Jubeir, and to attack both the Saudi and Israeli embassies in Washington, D.C.

The nature of Iranian government involvement remained to be seen, but the indictment added another chapter to the long-held cold confrontation between Saudi Arabia and Iran. Iran and Saudi Arabia have long been at loggerheads with each other, competing as major exporters of energy and as leaders of their competing versions of the Islamic faith, more specifically since the Islamic Revolution of 1979. While Saudi Arabia remained an ally of the United States; Iran became a relentless foe.b The 2003 US intervention in Iraq that empowered the Shiites there, at the cost of the Saddam-led Sunni regime has only intensified the rivalry between Saudi Arabia and Iran. [22] And, in the wake of US withdrawal from Iraq, and increasing sectarian tensions in the country, a potential return to a civil-war like situation, looms large over Iraq.

Moreover, the continuing escalation of tensions between the United States and Iran over the latter's nuclear programme, might negatively impact the downward spiral seen in Saudi-Iranian rivalry in the region, in the wake of the Arab Spring. As a response, to western sanctions against Iranian financial activities, Iran announced a nuclear fuel breakthrough, carried out naval exercises and test-fired a new radar-evading medium-range missile in the Persian Gulf. Iran threatened to close the Strait of Hormuz, a narrow gulf shipping lane through which 40 percent of world oil flows, if sanctions hit its oil exports. The United States and Israel say they have not ruled out military action against Iran if diplomacy fails to resolve the dispute over its nuclear program. Western analysts say that Iran sometimes exaggerates its nuclear advances to try to gain leverage in its standoff with the West. [23]

Persian Gulf and India's Interests

The statistics of India's engagement with the Gulf countries speak much louder than thousand words of rhetoric. India's economic liberalization and its sustained growth provides a major energy market for the oil and gas rich countries of the Gulf and the economic investments in the GCC countries provide a fertile ground for a huge number of Indian expatriate workers to earn for themselves and their family back home. According to defence studies expert Harsh V. Pant, "India wants to secure energy supplies and consolidate economic and trade relations" with members of the GCC while these states have adopted a "Look East" policy allowing them "to carve out a much more substantive relationship with India than in the past". [24]

India's energy demand continues to rise despite a slowing global economy. According to the International Energy Agency (IEA), hydrocarbons account for the majority of India's energy use. The country consumed 3.2 million barrels per day (bbl/d) in 2010. The combination of rising oil consumption and relatively flat production has left India increasingly dependent on imports to meet its petroleum demand.

In 2010, India was the world's fifth largest net importer of oil, importing more than 2.2 million bbl/d, or about 70 percent of consumption. A majority of India's crude oil imports come from West Asia, with Saudi Arabia and Iran supplying the largest shares. Iranian oil's share of Indian imports has decreased in recent years, largely due to issues with processing payments. As of 2010, Saudi Arabia accounted for about 18 percent, Iran for about 11 percent, with other West Asian countries together accounting for another 34 percent of India's oil imports. In 2010, India consumed roughly 2.3 trillion cubic feet (Tcf) of natural gas. Natural gas demand is expected to grow considerably, largely driven by demand in the power sector. Despite the steady increase in India's natural gas production, demand has outstripped supply and the country has been a net importer of natural gas since 2004. India's net imports reached an estimated 429 billion cubic feet (Bcf) in 2010. [25]

Economic Linkages

Saudi Arabia is the 4th largest trading partner for India.

The value of the two-way trade between the two countries in 2010-11 exceeded US$ 25 billion. Saudi Arabia is the largest supplier of crude oil to India. It provides around a quarter of India's crude imports. 2.0 million Indians are at present working in Saudi Arabia; over 70 percent in the blue-collar category. According to Saudi Arabian General Investment Authority (SAGIA), as of 31.12.2009 it has issued 357 licenses to Indian companies for joint ventures/100 percent owned entities, which are expected to bring total investment of US$ 1619.66 million in Saudi Arabia, covering diverse sectors including management and consultancy services, construction projects, telecommunications, information technology, pharmaceuticals, etc.

Moreover, several Indian companies have established collaborations with Saudi companies and are working in the Kingdom in the areas of designing, consultancy, financial services and software development. [26]

United Arab Emirates (UAE) is home to more than 1.75 million Indian expatriate community, making it the largest expatriate community in the UAE. 15-20 percent of the community is made up of professionally qualified personnel, 20 percent belong to the white collar non-professionals (clerical staff, shop assistants, sales men, accountants, etc.) and rest (about 65 percent) belongs to the blue-collar workers. There is also a significant business community from India. India-UAE trade was valued at US$ 43.4 billion in 2009-2010 and was projected to exceed US$ 50 billion during 2010-2011. UAE was the fifth largest import source of crude oil for India in 2009-10 with an import of 11.60 mmt crude oil. Total FDI from UAE to India is estimated to be US$ 1.8 billion making it the tenth biggest investor in India in terms of FDI. Several prominent private and public sector Indian companies and banks are also operating in the UAE. [27]

India's bilateral trade with Qatar increased from US$ 1.2 billion in 2005 to US$ 3.7 billion in 2009. India is the fourth largest export market for Qatar after Japan, South Korea and

Singapore. India has signed an agreement to purchase 7.5 million tonnes of LNG every year from Qatar for a period of 25 years. Negotiations have continued for about a year now for additional quantities (India's demand now stands revised to 15 million tones). A large number of Indian companies such as L&T, Dodsal, Punj Lloyd, Voltas, Simplex, Wipro, Aptech, Satyam Mahendra, NIIT etc. have set up offices in Qatar and have secured major contracts/business. The Indian community is estimated to be in the range of 500,000. Indian professionals constitute an important component. Major Indian IT firms have been engaged in high profile projects in Qatar. Qatar is proposing to set up a smart city and is looking at Indian companies for possible collaboration. [28]

According to April 2009-March 2010 estimates, India-Bahrain non-oil bilateral trade stands at US$ 753.07 millions. The number of Indian expatriates in Bahrain is now estimated at under 400,000 out of a total of 1.3 million residents in Bahrain, constituting more than one third of Bahrain's population. Bahrain has expressed interest in the Indian manpower expertise in the oil and gas sector and India is keen in on substantially increasing its US$ 518 million (BD196m) crude and other oil products' imports from Bahrain and discussions have been held regarding cooperation between Bahrain's National Oil and Gas Authority and India's Oil Ministry. [29]

India-Kuwait trade was US$ 9.03 billion in 2009-2010, of which non-oil trade accounted for approximately US$ 1.1 billion while petroleum exports from Kuwait to India were approximately US$ 7.9 billion. Kuwait is the largest supplier of crude oil to India from the Gulf region after Saudi Arabia. [30] According to the Kuwaiti Ministry of Interior, there are approximately 640,000 Indians, who constitute the largest expatriate community in Kuwait. A large proportion of the Indian expatriates are unskilled and semi-skilled workers. Professionals like engineers, doctors, chartered accountants, scientists, software experts, management consultants, architects; skilled workers like technicians and nurses; semi-skilled workers; retail traders and businessmen are also present in the Indian community. [31]

In year 2010, India ranked 2nd as the destination of Omani non-oil exports after UAE and 3rd as the top destination of Omani crude oil exports. There are around 140 Indian companies in Oman, not yet listed on Muscat Securities Market (MSM). Regarding foreign direct investment in Oman from India, as of July 2010, there were around 1527 Indian-Omani Joint Ventures, covering almost 13 socio-economic sectors with a total investment of US$ 7.53 billion in which Indian participation was estimated around US$ 4.52 billion. In 2009-2010, bilateral trade jumped to US$ 4.5 billion from almost US$ 2 billion in 2008-09. There are 573,000 legally registered Indian workers in Oman. It is estimated that some 2,000 Indian doctors work in Oman in Government hospitals and in clinics in the private sector and some 30 Indian academics work in the Sultan Qaboos University. There is prominent Indian presence in various sectors like oil and gas, mining, manufacturing, IT and telecom, power and water, construction, real estate and consultancy, healthcare, warehousing and logistics, railway sector and steel etc. [32]

India is seeking additional volumes of oil and natural gas from the Gulf suppliers, Saudi Arabia is planning to increase its supply of crude oil to major Indian refineries and these demand for supplies may increase all the more if the sanctions against Iran become more stringent, curbing the ability of other countries' commercial activities with Iran. [33] Moreover, Gulf hydrocarbon producers will likely remain heavily reliant on expatriate labour given the relatively high growth in their economies and the shortage of skilled manpower in their native population, according to experts. [34] And despite the political turmoil in the Arab world, the talks for a free trade agreement (FTA) between India and the GCC seemed to be still on track. India and GCC signed a Framework Agreement for enhancing and developing economic cooperation between the two sides in August 2004. Two rounds of talks for finalizing aspects like tariff rules, rules of origin etc. have been held and further rounds are awaiting finalization of GCC stance on the issue. [35]

Major Source of Remittance

Migrant remittances have come to occupy a prominent place of importance in a nation's balance of payments, especially for developing countries like India, more so with the liberalization of the Indian economy. Overseas Indians have come to put a lot of faith in the Indian economy, given the phenomenal growth that India has experienced and the fact that India has stood its ground during the global financial crisis has sustained this faith. Add to this increasing incentives and tax exemptions coupled with liberalized foreign exchange controls. [36] India is the largest recipient country in terms of both global and GCC remittances , accounting for roughly 50 per cent of money transferred from the Gulf according to sources. According to Sudhir Kumar Shetty, the Chief Operating Officer of the UAE Exchange Centre, the sum remitted during 2010 was estimated to be between $25 billion to US$ 30 billion. According to the World Bank's Migration and Remittances Factbook 2011, India continued to be the largest recipient of remittances in 2010, with remittances rising from US$ 49.6 billion in 2009 to US$ 55 billion in 2010. [37] Moreover, the World Bank Factbook 2011 says that remittances flow has remained more resilient compared with private debt and equity flows and foreign direct investment during the global financial crisis. [38]

Reflecting Indian concerns regarding the safety and security of Indian expatriates in the Gulf States, Prime Minister Manmohan Singh addressing the 10th Pravasi Bharatiya Divas at Jaipur early 2012, said, "We are acutely conscious of the safety and security of Indians living abroad, particularly in regions characterized by instability. There are over six million Indians living in the Gulf and West Asia. We need to be alert to the unfolding developments in this part of the world. We have conveyed to the countries of the region that we have a stake in the peace and stability of this region, and that we expect that they would appropriately look after the interests of Indian communities in their countries". [39]

According to the Indian PM, following the upheaval in Libya, evacuations plans were carried out under the Operation Safe Homecoming to evacuate more than 16,000 people from the strife torn areas through special flights, passenger and naval vessels. Similar evacuations were carried out in Egypt and Yemen on a lower scale. Moreover, the government, according to him, has constituted an Inter-Ministerial Committee under the Cabinet Secretary to make recommendations on issues relating to repatriation, ıelief and rehabilitation of Indian nationals affected by recent developments in West Asia, with the Ministry of Overseas Indian Affairs having prepared an Action Plan to implement its recommendations. [40] The Operation Safe Homecoming reportedly cost ` 115 crore (US$ 25 million), as per government data. [41] India has seen this scenario before. The Indian economy was adversely affected during 1990-91 as a result of the Gulf Crisis. The direct impact that year was much more than ` 4,000 crore (over US$ 2.2 billion) and the direct and indirect costs combined to add to the worsening balance of payment crisis. India had to single-handedly launch the biggest airlift since the Berlin Airlift to evacuate from Iraq/Kuwait (through Jordan) 117,000 Indian citizens who had suddenly become hostage to the Iraq-Kuwait War. [42]

Indian foreign policy analyst C. Rajamohan asserted that, "...any sensible Indian policy towards the Middle East must be rooted in an unflinching defence of its expansive interests on the Arab side of the Persian Gulf. India's trade with the GCC countries is touching US$ 100 billion and the near six million Indian workers there send home US$ 30 billion dollars every year. Above all, the GCC supplies more than 40 percent of India's rapidly expanding crude oil imports. None of the other Indian interests in the Middle East are comparable to these high stakes in the GCC". [43]

Conclusion

The Saudi Arabia-Iran rivalry is a major subplot, that has the potential to become the leading plot of the whole scenario there, and an Iran increasingly threatened by western sanctions, will, all the more, look for greater leverage in the region, prompting Saudi Arabia to up its own ante. India has good diplomatic and economic ties with both these energy-rich countries, and in the event of an open jostling for power in the region, India will have to walk a tightrope. Many have criticized India for failing to take hard decisions towards the Arab Spring. True, India cannot be a benchwarmer given its great power aspirations and being an important player at the UN Security Council. But, India needs to preserve its own manifold interests in the region, and for that it has to monitor events closely before acting or making statements. The fall of dictators is a welcome development anywhere, but the harder part is what comes after. The lack of proper institutionalization often hinders the process of democratization and one sees the uncertainties that prevail. India needs to find its own feet in the new changing Arab world, and use its democratic credentials and offer its assistance towards the reconstruction of conflict-torn countries, and in institution and capacity building, in agreement with concerned countries.

India's links with the Arab states have been largely on secular, pragmatic grounds of policymaking where the countries have come together at a very practical globalized business-interconnections regarding selling and consumption of energy or the migration of Indian working population, to these Arab monarchies, resulting in high amount of remittances flowing back into India. It has become almost a cliché to say that India needs a pro-active foreign policy, but unfortunately in many issues, regional and international, India has often found to be reactive. The Arab monarchies of the Persian Gulf have not seen the level of upheaval seen in other countries of North Africa and West Asia. The wealth in these countries and the measures adopted by the ruling families to calm the restive parts of the population and buy consent at many times, with huge domestic spending have put things under control, but hardly anyone would dare predict the course of events in this region.

As such, India needs to be prepared, but concerning the vital interests that India needs to preserve in these countries, foreign policymakers in this country needs to wait and watch and be silent at times, rather than make diplomatic steps that would jeopardize the safety and security of Indian workers there and the economic interests that India needs to sustain in its relationship with the Gulf countries. India's influence in this region is largely restricted at the commercial and trade levels and do not have the resources to effectively influence internal dynamics in these countries. At the most, India needs to develop its own narrative, of the regional developments, commensurate with its foreign policy objectives and our vital interests in the region. The expatriate's issue which is a secondary plot for policymakers there and other extra-regional powers is a main plot for Indian policymakers. In one to-one discussions, India can, with diplomatic caution, raise the issue of the future of West Asia in the face of changing political landscape, but not at the expense of being accused as an external power seeking to interfere in their internal affairs.

Endnotes

1. For details see "Middle East and North African Unrest: Implications for Oil and Natural Gas Markets", *CRS Report for Congress*, March 10, 2011, available at, http://www.fas.org/sgp/crs/mideast/R41683.pdf.
2. Quoted in March Lynch, "The Big Think Behind the Arab Spring?," *Foreign Policy*, December 2011, available at, http://www.foreignpolicy.com/articles/2011/11/28/the_big_think ?page=full.
3. Shadi Hamid, "There Aren't Protests in Qatar: So Why Did The Emir Just Announce Elections?" *The Atlantic*, November 1, 2011, available at, http://www.theatlantic.com/international/archive/2011/11/there-arent-protests-in-qatar-so-why-did-the-emir-just-announce-

elections/247661.

4. "Oman benefits Student Benefits," *AFP*, February 26, 2011, available at, http://www.google.com/hostednews/afp/article/ALeqM5ie73NUpvWHkuIAFKwLnqmyl0paLw?docId=CNG.29a2ebdaf178435a5e82e857cf4725de.ac1; and "Deaths in Oman protests", *Al Jazeera*, February 27, 2011, available at, http://www.aljazeera.com/news/middleeast/2011/02/2011227112850852905.html.
5. "Kuwait to hold early general election on February 2", *AFP*, December 18, 2011, available at, http://www.google.com/hostednews/afp/article/ALeqM5j3iEoEHineaoOiXnAXfxH2KFXTHg?docId=CNG.fad80dffc69b5105a37f43fbbaedadfd.261.
6. Mona Alami, "Protests unlikely in 'oasis' of United Arab Emirates", *USA Today*, March 17, 2011, available at, http://www.usatoday.com/news/world/2011-03-17-uae17_ST_N.htm.
7. "Saudi forces clash with protesters in Qatif", *Al Jazeera*, January 13, 2012, available at, http://www.aljazeera.com/news/middleeast/2012/01/2012113143917567124.html.
8. "Donna Abu-Nasr Saudi Women Inspired by Fall of Mubarak Step Up Equality Demand", *Bloomberg*, March 29, 2011, available at, http://www.bloomberg.com/news/2011-03-28/saudi-women-inspired-by-revolt-against-mubarak-go-online-to-seek-equality.html.
9. "Bernard Haykel, Saudi Arabia vs. the Arab Spring", *Project Syndicate*, August 16, 2011, available at, http://www.project-syndicate.org/commentary/haykel4/English.
10. "Saudi monarch announces billions in handouts," *Al Jazeera*, March 18, 2011, available at, http://www.aljazeera.com/news/middleeast/2011/03/2011318174117916648.html. Also see "Saudi king announces benefits, warns against sedition," *Gulfnews.com*, March 18, 2011, available at, http://gulfnews.com/news/gulf/saudi-arabia/saudi-king-announces-benefits-warns-against-sedition-1.778928.
11. "No threat to Gulf states from Arab Spring, says expert", *The*

Economic Times, November 3, 2011, available at, http://articles.economictimes.indiatimes.com/2011-11-03/news/30354879_1_arab-spring-gulf-countries-north-african-countries.

12. "Oil Pressure Rising", *The Economist*, February 24, 2011, available at, http://www.economist.com/node/18233452.
13. Marc Fisher, "Arab Spring yields different outcomes in Bahrain, Egypt and Libya", *The Washington Post*, December 21, 2011, available at, http://www.washingtonpost.com/world/arab-spring-yields-different-outcomes-in-bahrain-egypt-and-libya/2011/12/15/gIQAY6h57O_story.html.
14. Jason Ukman, "U.S., Saudi Arabia strike $30 billion arms deal", *The Washington Post*, December 29, 2011, available at, http://www.washingtonpost.com/blogs/checkpoint-washington/post/us-saudi-arabia-strike-30-billion-arms-deal/2011/12/29/gIQAjZmhOP_blog.html.
15. Shadi Hamid, "From the Arab Spring comes a more unified GC", *The National*, April 15, 2011, available at, http://www.thenational.ae/thenationalconversation/comment/from-the-arab-spring-comes-a-more-unified-gcc?pageCount=0.
16. Ahmed Souaiaia, "The Gulf Cooperative Council and the Arab Spring", December 26, 2011, available at, http://www.fpif.org/articles/the_gulf_cooperative_council_and_the_arab_spring.
17. "Arshin Adib-Moghaddam, "Bahrain in the shadow of Iran, Saudi Arabia and the United States," *CNN*, April 25, 2011, available at, http://articles.cnn.com/2011-04-25/opinion/bahrain.saudi.iran.arshin_1_bahrain-al-khalifa-family-saudi-arabia?_s=PM:OPINION.
18. Bruce Riedel, "Brezhnev in the Hejaz", *The National Interest*, September/October 2011, No. 115, p. 27.
19. Ibid.
20. Frederick Wehrey, "Uprising Jolt the Saudi-Iranian Rivalry", *Current History*, December 2011, Vol. 110, No.740, p. 352.
21. Ibid.
22. Mohsen M. Milani, "Iran and Saudi Arabia Square Off: The Growing Rivalry between Tehran and Riyadh", *Foreign Affairs*,

11 October 2011, available at, http://www.foreignaffairs.com/articles/136409/mohsen-m-milani/iran-and-saudi-arabia-square-off?page=show#. Also see Karen Leigh, "The Saudi-Iran Cold War: Will the Assassination Plot Heat It Up?", *Time*, October 13, 2011, available at, http://www.time.com/time/world/article/0,8599,2096764,00.htm

23. Parisa Hafezi, "Iran claims nuclear fuel advance, test-fires missile in Gulf, *The Washington Post*, January 2, 2012, available at, http://www.washingtonpost.com/world/middle_east/iran-claims-nuclear-fuel-advance-test-fires-missile-in-gulf/2012/01/01/gIQAbrXpUP_story.html.
The contending views regarding American response to the Iranian nuclear programme has been one of the most persistent agenda of US foreign policy in recent times, and the sabre-rattling has only continued complicating developments in West Asia. For more on the issue, see Chintamani Mahapatra and Monish Tourangbam, "Iran's Quest for Nuclear Weapons Status: American Debate on Pre-emptive Strike", *India Quarterly*, Vol. 67, No. 3, September 2011, pp. 229-244.
24. Harsh V. Pant, "India's Relations with Iran: Much Ado about Nothing," *The Washington Quarterly* , Winter 2011, Vol. 34, No.1, pp. 65-66.
25. For details, see US Energy Information Administration, http://205.254.135.7/countries/cab.cfm?fips=IN. Also see, "The International Energy Outlook 2011", *US Energy Information Administration*, September 2011, available at, http://www.eia.gov/forecasts/ieo/pdf/0484(2011).pdf.
26. "India-Saudi Arabia Business Relations," *Embassy of India, Riyadh*, available at, http://www.indianembassy.org.sa/Content.aspx?ID=784&PID=6
27. "India-UAE Relations," *Embassy of India, Abu Dhabi*, available at, http://www.indembassyuae.org/drupal/IndiaUAEPolitical
28. "India-Qatar Bilateral Economic Relations," *Embassy of India,* available at, http://www.indianembassyqatar.org/bilateraleconomic.html
29. "India-Bahrain Bilateral Relations," *Embassy of India, Kingdom of Bahrain*, available at,
30. http://www.indianembassybahrain.com/india_bahrain_bilateral_

relations.html; and "Bahrain to Bolster India Energy Links," *Gulf Daily News*, 29 December 2011, available at, http://www.gulfinthemedia.com/index.php?m=economics&id=585044&lang=en&tblpost=2011_12&lim=60.

31. "India-Kuwait Bilateral Trade and Economic Cooperation", *Embassy of India, Kuwait*, available at, http://indembkwt.org/pendind/indokuwaiteconomic.php.
32. "India and Oman Relations," *Ministry of External Affairs, India*, available at, http://www.mea.gov.in/mystart.php?id=50044507.
33. Anthony DiPaola, "India Seeks Crude, Gas From Persian Gulf, Oil Minister Says", *Bloomberg*, December 5, 2011, available at, http://www.bloomberg.com/news/2011-12-05/india-seeks-crude-gas-from-persian-gulf-oil-minister-says.html; and Anthony DiPaola, "Saudi Arabia Raises 2012 Crude Sales to India: Persian Gulf Oil", *Bloomberg*, November 21, 2011, available at, http://www.bloomberg.com/news/2011-11-21/saudi-arabia-raises-2012-crude-sales-to-india-persian-gulf-oil.html. Also see Nidhi Verma, "HPCL Says to Buy Less oil from Iran in FY13", *Reuters*, January 25, 2012, available at, http://www.reuters.com/article/2012/01/25/india-iran-hpcl-idUSL4E8CP5US20120125.
34. Nadim Kawach, "GCC Set to Remain Reliant on Expatriate Labour, *Emirates 24/7 News*, June 1, 2011, available at, http://www.emirates247.com/news/gcc-set-to-remain-reliant-on-expatriate-labour-2011-06-01-1.399810.
35. Huma Siddiqui, "India, GCC Discuss FTA," *The Financial Express*, 16 August 2011, available at, http://www.financialexpress.com/news/India--GCC-discuss-FTA/832318/; and "India-GCC Relations," *Embassy of India, Riyadh*, available at, http://www.indianembassy.org.sa/Content.aspx?ID=708&PID=6
36. "Remittances from Indian Diaspora: A Report," *Overseas Indian Facilitation Centre*, August 2009, available at, http://www.oifc.in/Uploads/MediaTypes/Documents/ReportonRemittancesFromTheDiaspora.pdf.
37. 'Gulf Remittances Rise, India Top Recipient, *Business Today*, June 15, 2011, available at, http://businesstoday.intoday.in/story/gulf-remittances-uae-exchange-centre-world-bank/1/16310.html.

38. Migration and Remittances Factbook 2011, *World Bank*, p. 17, available at, http://siteresources.worldbank.org/INTLAC/Resources/Factbook 2011-Ebook.pdf.
39. "PM's address at the tenth Pravasi Bharatiya Divas", *Prime Minister's Office*, January 8, 2012, available at, http://pmindia.nic.in/speech-details.php?nodeid=1124.
40. Ibid.
41. Rohan Joshi, "Opportunities Post Arab Spring", *Pragati*, October 2011, p. 19.
42. Jasjit Singh, "Growing South Asian Interests in the Persian Gulf Region; Problems and Opportunities", *Strategic Analysis*, December 1999, Vol. XXIII, No. 9, www.idsa-india.org/an-dec9-1.html.
43. C. Rajamohan, "The Widening Gulf, *Indian Express*", December 23, 2011, available at, www.indianexpress.com/news/the-widening-gulf/891024.

18

The Israeli Dilemma: Winds of Change or More of the Same?

Mushtaq Hussain

The Arab Spring is one of the very few pan-regional events/movements in recent history that does not depict Israel as the instigator or target. When Mohamed Bouazizi set himself on fire in the Tunisian provincial town of Sidi Bouzid he was not protesting against the 'atrocities committed by Israel' or highlighting the 'plight of the Palestinian people'. The same holds true for the millions protesting in Tahrir Square, in Pearl Square or fighting in Homs. These uprisings have essentially been targeted at the misrule, exploitation, harassment and violence of the ruling regimes, and aimed at throwing away the yoke of despotic rule in their respective countries.

Regardless of the final outcome of the Arab Spring, Israel has been anxious at the fast-paced changes that are taking place in the Arab world and the resultant instability in the region. [1] The majority of Israeli political spectrum, whether in the government or the opposition, have been concerned that a change towards democratic rule would bring in Islamists, the only organized opposition group in almost all affected countries, to power. This has already happened in Tunisia where the En-Nahda [2] won an overwhelming majority in the parliamentary elections held in October 2011. In Egypt, the political wing of the Muslim Brotherhood, the Freedom and Justice Party, and the Salafist Islamist Al-Nour Party together won 67 percent of the seats in the parliament that would frame the new constitution for the country. [3] In the Kuwait elections, held in February 2012, the Islamists secured a majority and there is a consensus that in a free and fair election the Islamic Action Front could secure a majority in Jordanian parliament as well. The unfolding crisis in Syria may also result in strengthening the position of the Muslim Brotherhood and other Islamist groups.

By and large, the popular protests in North Africa and the Persian Gulf have only had limited direct and strong bearings upon the political and strategic considerations of Israel so as to warrant an anxiety at the overthrowing of the old regimes. There are three major exceptions, Egypt, Syria and Jordan; and Israel is seriously concerned about the political stability in these countries with which it shares common borders.

Israel and turmoil

For much of Israel's early history Egypt was the most dangerous enemy. [4] This situation changed when President Anwar Sadat and Prime Minister Menachem Begin signed the peace treaty in 1979. Since coming to power in 1982, President Hosni Mubarak maintained that peace. He was definitely not an ally of Israel and consciously kept the bilateral relations as 'cold peace'. Despite playing a significant role in the peace process, especially on the Israeli-Palestinian track, Mubarak had kept the relations to the barest minimum. On a number of issues such as non-proliferation [5] and Israel's normalization with the wider West Asian region, he clashed with Israel. While prepared to host Israeli leaders from different political parties and factions, President Mubarak deliberately avoided visiting Israel. His few hours' of stay during the funeral of slain Prime Minister Yitzhak Rabin in November 1995 was the sole exception.

Yet, for Israel President Mubarak was preferable to other leaders of the region who chose to maintain the traditional distance with it. Moreover, Israel's prolonged siege of the Gaza Strip would not have been possible without an understanding, if not cooperation, of the Mubarak regime. Although Egypt's compliance in the Israeli siege of the Gaza

Strip had been widely denounced by the other Arab countries as well as Turkey, the threat of a domestic political backlash was never allowed by the Mubarak regime to materialize. This was, to a great extent, because the Mubarak government had successfully persuaded much of its citizenry that the 'blame for Egyptian-Gazan tension lies with Hamas and Israel, even mobilizing state-funded religious authorities to criticize Hamas and give their blessing to Egyptian security measures on the Gaza border'. [6]

Hence, the prospect of Mubarak's removal through popular uprising sounded alarming and senior Israeli leaders were quick to seek the continuation of the status quo. Indeed, they were not alone. While the Tahrir Square was teeming with protesters, even a few Arab heads of states expressed support for the embattled Egyptian President. For Example, King Abdullah of Saudi Arabia criticized the protestors, terming them 'infiltrators'. [7] With the Islamists being the only organized opposition political force in Egypt, Israeli leaders feared that post-Mubarak Egypt would not usher in liberal democracy but an Islamist regime. That spectre was especially undesirable as it prompted comparisons to Iran. Indeed, in recent times, there had been speculations in Israel that the eventual succession of Mubarak could turn Egypt into an "Iran next door". [8] These fears were suddenly heightened by the swift changes brought about by the uprising. Talking to the *Washington Post*, an Israeli official captured this sentiment succinctly when he said: "When some people in the West see what's happening in Egypt they see Europe 1989. We see it as Tehran 1979". [9]

In view of the strategic importance accorded by Israel to Mubarak's regime, his forced departure is a huge strategic challenge. Having a peaceful southern border and being able to pursue other interests in the region without a fear of backlash from Egypt had a huge impact on its strategic policy. Having to spend less on defence on account of peace with Egypt has had a tremendous impact on Israeli economy. Though its economic ties were minimal, Israel was getting significant quantities of natural gas from Sinai through a pipeline. Since the fall of Mubarak, there were as many as 12 sabotage attacks on the pipelines in as many months. [10]

Primarily, Israel is concerned with fate of the peace treaty under a post-Mubarak authority. Such fears seemed justified with some Islamists initially calling for a review of the 1979 treaty. [11] Overwhelmed by such sentiments, even Nabil El-Araby, who succeeded Amr Musa as Secretary General of the Arab League, observed that the peace treaty is 'not sacred as the Quran.' [12] The killing of six Egyptian soldiers by Israel following a terror attack in Eilat in Southern Israel on 18 August 2011 [13] resulted in massive public protests in front of the building housing the Israeli embassy in Cairo. [14] This led to members of the Israeli embassy being rescued and evacuated to safety. However, a new ambassador was sent to Cairo within three months of the attack on the embassy. [15]

At the same time, the Supreme Council of the Armed Forces vowed to honour all international peace agreements including the treaty with Israel. [16] Despite the public animosity towards Israel, the Egyptian military does not want to assume a belligerent attitude towards Israel. Peaceful relations with Israel are important for Egypt, and critical to its military, because of the US largesse it receives as a result. [17] Further, the Salafists also committed to honour the country's peace treaty with Israel and expressed support for negotiations with the Jewish State. [18] For his part, Israel's ambassador to Egypt said his country would try to open communications with Islamic groups in Egypt, including the Muslim Brotherhood and the Salafi movement's Al-Nour party. [19] Thus, Israel came around to the idea of dealing with a post-Mubarak Egypt and there is belief, not unrealistic, that the peace with Egypt would endure.

In view of these tumultuous developments in the region, following the departure of Mubarak, Israeli leaders have remained cautious towards upheavals elsewhere. Prime

Minister Benjamin Netanyahu has frequently expressed his apprehensions regarding the 'direction of the Arab Spring'. [20]

With regard to Jordan, despite occasional calls in support of the argument that *Jordan is Palestine*, for the mainstream Israelis the survival and stability of the Hashemite Kingdom serves their long-term interest. Jordan has been a close ally of Israel, cooperating on intelligence matters, stopping infiltration into the West Bank and assisting Israel in counterterrorism. However, King Abdullah-II rules over a Palestinian-majority population and his openly pro-Western and pro-Israeli stances are not domestically popular. [21] Any strong and violent change in Amman, or worst the ouster of the Hashemite rule, would mean more troubles for Israel.

Two instances highlight the Israeli caution more vividly. The Hashemite Kingdom has not appointed an ambassador to Israel since the previous one ended his tenure in mid-2010. [22] Israel has decided to pursue this without undue public statements. Secondly, the renewed unity efforts between Fatah and Hamas resulted in the Doha Declaration signed in February 2012 under the mediation of the Qatari Crown Prince. Under this, President Mahmoud Abbas agreed to head the interim government. Naturally, Israeli leaders have reacted angrily to this development. At the same time, the rapprochement between Jordan and the external leadership of Hamas headed by Khaled Mashal did not evoke any public criticisms from Israel. The meeting between King Abdullah and Mashal in Amman on 29th January, 2012 [23] is viewed by many as a prelude to the return of Hamas to Jordan after its expulsions in 1999. The Jordanian regime feels threatened by the changes in the region and by the rising demands of their own public, particularly Islamists. The regime feels the need to appease their Islamists and this appeasement is pushing the Jordanians to bring Hamas back into Jordan and normalize relations. [24] Israel has maintained a studied silence in public on this issue.

Syria is the third country that causes anxiety in Israel. Continued unrest could ultimately threaten Syria's integrity and this, in turn, could result in a sectarian conflict and domestic instability. The political uncertainty in Syria and refusal of Hamas to rally around the Assad regime has led to signs of the movement's departure from Damascus. The willingness of Hezbollah to rally behind Assad has politically weakened that organization in Lebanon. At the same time, the al-Assad regime has guaranteed a stable border for nearly 40 years despite the recurrent rhetoric. As one Israeli official put it, Syria is 'the devil you know'. [25] If Egypt is historically important, Syria is geo-strategically crucial. Changes in Syria could bring to power a new government that might not follow the same rules of engagement and might play to populism disregarding strategic reality. These considerations have led Israel to maintain a studied silence on the situation in Syria and follow a 'wait and watch' strategy.

There are a few disturbing developments for Israel. One, the political unrest in Syria has resulted in Hamas moving out of Damascus and a number of senior members and their families have left Syria. Jordan is often suggested as the possible new location for Mashal. Second, for the first time since 1967, there was violence along the Israeli-Syrian border, on 15th May, 2011, when thousands of Palestinian refugees in Syria marched towards the de-militarized border in Majdal Shams in the Golan Heights. Some of them broke through the barriers resulting in a violent confrontation leading to the deaths of thirteen people. [26] This indicated the fragility of the ceasefire line in case of a violent overthrow of the Assad regime.

Impact upon Israel

On a cursory appraisal, it would appear that the Arab Spring has led to Israel's isolation, and damaged its regional position and strategic calculus. There were anti-Israeli slogans among the Tahrir Square protests against Mubarak. Many, both within and outside Egypt, denounced him for his proximity with and friendship towards Israel. In the absence of a strong leadership in Cairo and the Egyptian army's pre-occupations with domestic governance, Israel had to shore up its defences along its border with Egypt. The opening of the Rafah border by Egypt without any coordination [27] also unnerved Israel. Elsewhere in the region, President Assad indirectly blamed Israel for the unrest in Syria. [28] Indeed, with the growing influence of Islamists across the region, to many Israelis it seemed that the Arab world would now be less receptive to any future peace overtures. This, along with the deteriorating status of the United States in the region was construed as potentially detrimental to the prospects of peace between Israel and its neighbouring states. [29] Even the most stable peace treaties, like the one signed with Jordan in 1994, seemed under stress. [30]

In the light of these developments some fear that the Israeli response to the Arab Spring was one of 'winter hibernation'.[31] In their view, Israel has retreated from the regional limelight to its own shell and would be waiting until the mass outbreak of rage passes over. Others feel that the Arab Spring provides an opportunity for Israel to connect with the people who have taken control of their destiny or would soon be in control of their countries. [32] For example, in an article published in *The Guardian* in April 2011, Israeli President Shimon Peres wrote that, "We in Israel welcome the Arab Spring…Israel welcomes the wind of change, and sees a window of opportunity". [33] Similarly, Natan Sharansky, chairman of the Jewish Agency, wrote in *The Washington Post* in December 2011, "The West should bet on freedom in Egypt". [34] Reflecting this mood, Foreign Ministry Director-General Rafael Barak established several working groups to explore possibilities of people-to-people contact with some Arab countries, including Egypt, Jordan and Syria. [35] But these responses have not had a major affect on public policy.

In reality, the Arab Spring has not significantly changed Israel's regional position or its strategic calculus; at most, it has augmented existing trends. Israel has intermittently faced similar challenges since its formation in 1948. Since the start of the Arab Spring many Israeli, as well as other observers, have claimed and assured that it had nothing to do with Israel. However, in the wake of the attack on the embassy in Cairo on 9th September, 2011, [36] some in Israel and the West came to see it as another element in the 'siege' of Israel. This situation is quite similar to that faced by Israel in the years of advent and spread of Arab Nationalism in the region in the aftermath of the 1948 War. [37]

Further, there is nothing new even in the way Israel is targeted in demonstrations across the region. This is a continuing phenomenon wherein embattled rulers have tried to stir up anti-Israel passions in order to create some breathing space for themselves. Although the Arab-Israeli hostility originally centered on the establishment of a Jewish state in Palestine, and the subsequent dispossession of the Palestinian Arab population, over the years the dynamics of the conflict have resulted in a character often far removed from the original issue. [38] Traditionally, many Arab leaders have used Israel as a convenient scapegoat, turning public wrath against it and blaming it for their problems. The faint hope in the present scenario is that a freer West Asia might move away from such anti-Israel hostility because the overthrow of dictators would open up the public debate in these countries. But as the Arab Spring has progressed, some fear that Israel might again become a scapegoat, this time for unfulfilled revolutionary promises. [39]

The argument that the Arab Spring is isolating Israel is neither new nor unprecedented. Even before the Arab Spring, the Turkish-Israeli relations were growing cold and the peace process with the Palestinians has been in constant crisis, especially since the al-Aqsa Intifada. The regional isolation is not different form the one that Israel experienced since 1948 or after the 1967 War, when African, Eastern European, and Asian states began severing ties with Israel. [40] Fears of increased Arab hostilities can also be viewed as a re-enactment of the situation that prevailed after the Fourth Arab Summit of August 1967 where a resolution, known as the *three no's of Khartoum*, calling for 'no peace with Israel, no recognition of Israel, and no negotiation with Israel, was accepted. At that time, Henry Kissinger had described it as a sign of increasing Arab extremism. [41] However, within a little over a decade, Israel had signed a landmark peace treaty with Egypt.

Finally, discussions of how Israel must respond to these conditions are also recycled. Suggestions that Israel is searching for new friends [42] (for example, South Sudan, whose President Salva Kiir made his first overseas trip to Israel, [43] and Cyprus with which Israel is renewing its ties through a gas exploration deal) are no different from David Ben-Gurion's 'periphery strategy', which envisioned cultivating relations with countries beyond its immediate neighbourhood. [44] Since the early 1990s, Israel has been reaching out to countries such as Azerbaijan, India, Greece, Bulgaria, Romania and (Greek) Cyprus partly to overcome the situation in its immediate neighbourhood.

This is not to say that there are no strategic and diplomatic issues challenging Israel on account on the uprisings in Arab countries. Among the biggest challenges is the fact that Israel will no longer be able to enjoy the strategic benefit of a secured border and dependable neighbour on its southern front. This could soon be true for the northern front along the Golan Heights as well, accompanied by its fallout on the Israel-Lebanon front. Though it is not unfamiliar, the cost of growing security risks and, consequently, a larger defense budget, would be prohibitive. The fear of post-Assad Syria turning into another Iraq [45] already frightens many Israelis.

In short, for now ordinary Israelis are not feeling the consequences of this fast changing environment. In the words of Amos Gilad, senior official in the Ministry of Defence, despite the diplomatic and political uncertainty Israel is "living in the best security conditions ever," noting that the number of terror attacks was low and those tensions notwithstanding the peace with Egypt "is still stable". [46]

Conclusion

The Arab Spring is of course a historically important development in West Asia, with its potential, which has already been partially realized in Tunisia, Egypt and Libya, for restructuring and indeed bringing an end to the autocratic regimes of Arab politics. But both its duration and outcome remain uncertain, even in the medium-term. It is not clear how the moderate Islamist parties which have won in Tunisia and Egypt would govern and live up to popular expectations. Will they be better than the despotic regimes that they replaced? The current status quo in the Persian Gulf region, especially in Bahrain and Oman, has also demonstrated that the Arab Spring could be contained. [47]

There is no doubt that initially Israel was nervous about the Arab Spring. The fact that, despite a sophisticated intelligence apparatus, no one could warn of, let alone predict, such a tectonic shift in regional politics, came as a rude shock [48] to the Israeli establishment. But it has not been affected in a major way because it has already dealt with similar circumstances. What the current situation demands from Israel are clear country specific responses and broad regional tactics to meet the challenge of changed political dynamics. This is in part due to the new changes that are taking place in the region, primarily because they are popular and are directed primarily, often exclusively, at domestic authoritarianism rulers.

On a wider level, the Arab Spring has diverted the attention from the general Arab focus on Israel. The Jewish State is not the principal focus of or cause for the Arab Spring. Contrary to opinions in some sections, the Arab masses are more concerned about governance, corruption, rule of law, political rights, democracy and self-empowerment than Israel.

The latter could afford to maintain its calculated indifference vis-à-vis the Arab Spring. An overly-assertive strategy is not warranted under the current circumstances. Rather, a wait-and-see posture allows Israel to gauge where these dynamics are going, and to respond accordingly to specific changes and issues.

Arab democracy would open up the debate not only about Israel but also policies that the Arab regimes have pursued since Israel's establishment in 1948. As things stand, the process looks long, arduous and might even only be partially successful. Meanwhile, Israel can do almost nothing to affect the Arab Spring, especially when the negative consequences are limited and manageable. It does not have to do anything special or stupid. Even this is not new. Yitzhak Shamir followed it in early 1991 when Iraqi scuds were raining over Israel. Its current strategy vis-à-vis Arab Spring thus, is one of "No strategy" and will be so until more serious and systemic changes emerge in the region.

Endnotes

1. Efarim Inbar (2012), "The 2011 Arab Uprisings and Israel's National Security", *Mideast Security and Policy Studies*, No. 95, February 2012, p. 1., available at, http://www.biu.ac.il/Besa/MSPS95.pdf, accessed on February 29, 2012.
2. 'Tunisia's Ennahda wins poll,' *Arab News*, October 24, 2011, available at, http://arabnews.com/middleeast/article523841.ece, accessed on February 7, 2012.
3. 'Egypt election: Results show Islamists taking two-thirds of seats,' *The Telegraph*, January 21, 2012, available at, http://www.telegraph.co.uk/news/worldnews/africaandindianocean/egypt/9030179/Egypt-election-results-show-Islamists-taking-two-thirds-of-seats.html, accessed on February 4, 2012.
4. For detailed treatment of the subject see: Dowek, Ephraim (2001), *Israeli-Egypt Relations: 1980-2000*, London: Frank Cass; Cohen, Raymond (1990), *Culture and Conflict in Egyptian-Israeli Relations*, Bloomington: Indiana University

Press; Sachar, Howard (1981), *Egypt and Israel*, New York: R. Marck.

5. In the past, Mubarak had threatened to withdraw from the Nuclear Nonproliferation Treaty if Israel did not sign it. Later, though, some official statements had indicated that Egypt settle for an Israeli "statement of intent", provided that it contain a commitment to sign the NPT within a specific and reasonable timetable. For Details see, Shai Feldman (1995), 'President Mubarak's Visit and the Middle East Nuclear Debate', *The Washington Institute Policy Analysis No. 146*, April 5, 1995, available at, http://www.washingtoninstitute.org/policy-analysis/view/president-mubaraks-visit-and-the-middle-east-nuclear-debate, accessed on February 2, 2012.
6. Abigail Haulsoner, 'In the Siege of Gaza, Egypt Walks a Delicate Line', *Time*, January 11, 2010, available at, http://www.time.com/time/world/article/0,8599,1953015,00.html, accessed on January 29, 2012.
7. Chip Cummins, 'Saudi Arabia voices support for Mubarak', *The Wall Street Journal*, January 29, 2011, available at, http://online.wsj.com/article/SB10001424052748704653204576111780673298292.html, accessed on February 1, 2012.
8. Efraim Inbar, *op cit.*, p. 8.
9. Janine Zacharia, 'Israel wary of transition in Egypt, concerned about regional stability', *The Washington Post*, February 2, 2011, available at, http://www.washingtonpost.com/national/israel-worries-about-peace-amid-regional-tumult/2011/02/01/ABZtFbE_story.html, accessed on February 3, 2012.
10. 'Pipeline Supplying Israel is attacked', *The New York Times*, February 4, 2012, available at, http://www.nytimes.com/2012/02/05/world/middleeast/egyptian-pipeline-supplying-israel-is-attacked.html?_r=0, accessed on February 6, 2012.
11. 'Muslim Brotherhood: Egypt-Israel peace treaty needs to be reviewed', *Ha'aretz*, December 9, 2011, available at, http://www.haaretz.com/news/middle-east/muslim-brotherhood-egypt-israel-peace-treaty-needs-to-be-reviewed-1.400541, accessed on February 1, 2012.

12. 'Arab League Chief: Egypt-Israel peace treaty not as sacred as the Koran', *Ha'aretz*, August 26, 2011, available at, http://www.haaretz.com/news/diplomacy-defense/arab-league-chief-egypt-israel-peace-treaty-not-as-sacred-as-the-koran-1.380876, accessed on February 1, 2012.
13. 'Sixth Egyptian soldier shot by Israel dies in hospital as a result of injuries', *Ahram Online*, September 10, 2011, available at, http://english.ahram.org.eg/NewsContent/1/64/20843/Egypt/Politics-/Sixth-Egyptian-soldier-shot-by-Israel-dies-in-hosp.aspx, accessed on February 1, 2012.
14. 'Egyptians Protest against Israel in front of Israeli Embassy in Cairo', *Xinhua*, August 20, 2011, available at, http://news.xinhuanet.com/english2010/photo/2011-08/20/c_131063274.htm, accessed on February 7, 2012.
15. 'New Israeli Ambassador arrives in Cairo Months after Embassy was Attacked', *Guardian*, December 12, 2011, available at, http://www.guardian.co.uk/world/2011/dec/12/israeli-ambassador-cairo-embassy-ransacked, accessed on February 7, 2012.
16. 'Egypt tells Israel it is committed to peace treaty', *Ha'aretz*, March 24, 2011, available at, http://www.haaretz.com/news/international/egypt-tells-israel-it-is-committed-to-peace-treaty-1.351643, accessed on February 2, 2012.
17. Ahmed Hashim (2011), "The Egyptian Military, Part Two: From Mubarak Onward", *Middle East Policy*, December 8, 2011, available at, http://www.mepc.org/journal/middle-east-policy-archives/egyptian-military-part-two-mubarak-onward, accessed on February 11, 2012.
18. 'Egypt Salafi Party to honor Israel Treaty', *United Press International*, December 20, 2011, available at, http://www.upi.com/Top_News/World-News/2011/12/20/Egypt-Salafi-party-to-honor-Israel-treaty/UPI-21421324390812/, accessed on February 7, 2012.
19. Avi Issacharoff, 'Israel envoy seeks talks with Islamist groups in Egypt', *Ha'aretz*, December 18, 2011, available at, http://www.haaretz.com/print-edition/news/israel-envoy-seeks-talks-with-islamist-groups-in-egypt-

1.402025?localLinksEnabled=false&asid=d956437e, accessed on February 7, 2012.

20. Efraim Inbar, *op cit.*, p. 7.
21. Daniel Byman (2011), "Israel's pessimistic view of the Arab Spring", *The Washington Quarterly*, 34:3, Summer 2011, pp. 123-136, available at, http://twq.com/11summer/docs/11summer_byman.pdf, accessed on January 29, 2012.
22. Walid Obediat, former consultant to Jordan's foreign ministry, was appointed Ambassador to Israel in October 2012. Herb Keinon, 'Jordan Appoints New Ambassador to Israel', *The Jerusalem Post*, September 30, 2012, available at, http://www.jpost.com/Diplomacy-and-Politics/Jordan-appoints-new-ambassador-to-Israel, accessed on October 14, 2012.
23. 'Jordan's Kind Abdullah meets Hamas's Mashaal in Amman', *The Jerusalem Post*, January 29, 2011, available at, http://www.jpost.com/Headlines/Article.aspx?id=255598, accessed on January 29, 2012.
24. Charles A. Radin (2011), "Arab Spring Overshadowing Israeli-Palestinian Conflict", December 19, 2011, available at, http://www.brandeis.edu/now/2011/december/shikaki.html, accessed on February 9, 2012.
25. Tim Lister and Kevin Flower, 'Israel faces 'Regional Tsunami' set off by Arab Spring', *CNN*, September 22, 2011, available at, http://articles.cnn.com/2011-09-22/middleeast/world_meast_israel-arab-spring_1_defense-minister-ehud-barak-mavi-marmara-israeli-government?_s=PM:MIDDLEEAST, accessed on January 30, 2012.
26. Harriet Sherwood, 'Thirteen Killed as Israeli Troops Open Fire on Nakba Day Border Protests', *The Guardian*, May 15, 2011, available at, http://www.guardian.co.uk/world/2011/may/15/israeli-troops-kill-eight-nakba-protests, accessed on February 3, 2012.
27. 'Egypt Opens Rafah Crossing after Four Years', *Jerusalem Post*, May 28, 2011, available at, http://www.jpost.com/Middle-East/Egypt-opens-Rafah-crossing-after-four-years, accessed on February 9, 2012.

28. Jack Khoury and Avi Issacharoff, 'In First Public Statement since Riots began, Assad Blames U.S.-Israeli Plot', *Ha'aretz*, March 31, 2011, available at, http://www.haaretz.com/print-edition/news/in-first-public-statement-since-riots-began-assad-blames-u-s-israeli-plot-1.353175, accessed on February 2, 2012.
29. Efraim Inbar, *op cit.*, p. 8.
30. Herb Keinon, 'Anti-Normalization Forces Gaining Strength in Jordan', *The Jerusalem Post*, August 9, 2011, available at, http://www.jpost.com/Diplomacy-and-Politics/Anti-normalization-forces-gaining-strength-in-Jordan, accessed on October 14, 2012.
31. Barak Ravid, 'The Arab Spring and Israel's winter hibernation', *Ha'aretz*, December 8, 2011, available at, http://www.haaretz.com/opinion/the-arab-spring-and-israel-s-winter-hibernation-1.400345, accessed on January 29, 2012.
32. Carlo Strenger, 'Mideast can accept Israel if Netanyahu will let it', *Ha'aretz*, December 14, 2011, available at, http://www.haaretz.com/blogs/strenger-than-fiction/mideast-can-accept-israel-if-netanyahu-will-let-it-1.401403, accessed on January 29, 2012.
33. Shimon Peres, 'We in Israel Welcome the Arab Spring', *The Guardian*, April 1, 2011, available at, http://www.guardian.co.uk/commentisfree/2011/apr/01/palestinians-science-soil-arab-uprisings, accessed on February 2, 2012.
34. Natan Sharansky, 'The West should Bet on Freedom in Egypt', *The Washington Post*, December 16, 2011, available at, http://articles.washingtonpost.com/2011-12-16/opinions/35287425_1_muslim-brotherhood-tahrir-square-stability, accessed on February 3, 2012.
35. Barak Ravid, *op cit.*
36. 'Cairo's Israeli embassy attacked', *BBC*, September 10, 2011, available at, http://www.bbc.co.uk/news/world-middle-east-14863758, accessed on January 28, 2012.
37. Brent E Sasley, 'Israel and the Arab Spring: But the season doesn't matter', *Huffington Post*, December 28, 2011, available at, http://www.huffingtonpost.com/brent-sasley/israel-arab-spring_b_1171821.html, accessed on October 14, 2012.

38. Beverly Milton-Edwards (2011), *Contemporary Politics in the Middle East*, Cambridge: Polity Press, p. 114.
39. Ethan Bronner, 'Beyond Cairo, Israel sensing a wider siege', *The New York Times*, September 10, 2011, available at, http://www.nytimes.com/2011/09/11/world/middleeast/11israel.html?_r=1&pagewanted=all, accessed on January 29, 2012.
40. Brent E Sasley, *op cit.*
41. Quoted in Yoram Meital (2000), "The Khartoum Conference and Egyptian Policy after the 1967 War: A Reexamination", *Middle East Journal*, 54(1), p. 64.
42. 'Amid Arab Spring, Israel seeks new friends', *United Press International*, December 6, 2011, available at, http://www.upi.com/Top_News/Special/2011/12/06/Amid-Arab-Spring-Israel-seeks-new-friends/UPI-85151323196753/, accessed on February 4, 2012.
43. 'South Sudan Leader visits Israel, Ties Deepen', *Al Akhbar English*, December 20, 2011, available at, http://english.al-akhbar.com/node/2677, accessed on February 4, 2012.
44. Benny Morris, 'Israel's New Allies', *The National Interest*, February 2, 2012, available at, http://nationalinterest.org/commentary/israels-new-allies-6441, accessed on February 5, 2012.
45. Andrew Arsan, 'Assad the Orientalist', *Foreign Policy Blogs*, November 1, 2011, available at, http://foreignpolicyblogs.com/2011/11/01/assad-the-orientalist/, accessed on February 7, 2012.
46. Tim Lister and Kevin Flower, *op cit.*
47. Brent E. Sasley, *op cit.*
48. Efraim Inbar, *op cit.*, p. 7.

19

Reading of the Arab Spring: Implications for Palestine

Abdulkhalek Al-Zamli

Introduction

The birth of the Arab freedom movement had first seen the light at the beginning of the last century. That era witnessed a political instability during the Ottoman ruling of the Arab World. Many Arab nationalists engaged in revolutionary acts against the Ottomans for the freedom of their region. Unfortunately, the collapse of the Ottoman Empire after the WWI did not bring independence for their people, rather another type of colonization by the victorious powers. Although the Arab nationalists were promised of freedom and independence, the secret Sykes-Picot Agreement [1] between Britain and France provided for the territorial division of West Asia between these two powers. The Arab nationalists, felt betrayed, had no other choice but to continue their anti-colonial opposition to the new European rule.

After several revolts against the post World War colonialism, some Arab countries were granted relative independence. This relative independence encouraged Arab nationalists to put forward programs of action against colonial powers in the region, including in Palestine especially after the increasing growth of Jewish immigration and "Belfour Declaration".

All Arab countries had achieved their independence after the WWII, except one: Palestine. It was remained the core issue in the political, social and even psychological life of the Arabs in the Middle East since then.

The nationalist regimes that came to power after independence in the fifties of the last century had derived its legitimacy from "false slogans" such as, liberating Palestine and bringing social and political justice to their own people. For decades, the Arab masses, aware of these unfounded agendas, have lived under the rule of doctorial regimes and corrupt leaders. A number of factors may have contributed to Arab masses' uprising against their dictator regimes, *inter alia*: (a) the financial wealth has not been justly distributed with only a few incurring all profits at the expense of the many who are increasingly impoverished; (b) Arab middle class has been ailing and starting to disappear as a result of this unjust distribution of wealth; (c) the police suppression of people and the absence of almost all types of freedoms and the minimum democracy. While the police actions have to be confined only within the application of the role of law, the situation in the Arab Word has been completely the opposite: the main task of the police is protecting the ruling regime without any minimum consideration of the basic right of people; and (d) the inappropriate expenditure on development, community infrastructure, creating jobs, education and health.

After more than six decades, neither Palestine is liberated nor social or economic justice has been accomplished in the Arab World. The Arab Spring, therefore, was an inevitable result of decades of injustice, suppression and dictatorship. A variety of factors have contributed to the revolution of the suppressed Arab People.

Unjust Allocation of Wealth

One of the main factors that has the negative impact on the welfare and development of the Arab World is the huge expenditure on the military establishment on the expense of the development of health, education, and infrastructure. At a time when rates of unemployment in Arab countries is 30 percent and illiteracy number is 70 millions, estimates of military shows that the Arab countries assumed the first position globally in terms of military and security spending. Reports indicate that the total military spending in the Arab countries has reached an average of $75 billion annually. In addition, according to a report issued by the "Arab Institution for Investment", most Arab countries defence spending is more than 7 percent of their GDP during the past ten years, which is one of the highest rates in the world.

Three years after the eruption of the Arab Spring, the unjust distribution of wealth is still eliminating the success achieved. International reports say that military establishments in the countries of the Arab Spring are still suffering from large financial corruption. According to the report issued by Transparency International, the military services in the countries of the Arab Spring spend money in secret, and awarded contracts to those who are close and affiliated with some of its officials, and hampering efforts to transition to democracy. The report added that the main reason for the spread of corruption within the military establishment is the lack of scrutiny by regulators on the budgets of security and military institutions.

The significance of this report is that it is shedding the light on sensitive aspects in the countries of the Arab Spring, which is supposed to have benefited from the change in order to move towards a better future for the people yearning for freedom and salvation from the domination rule of dictatorships and militarism.

Dignity

What is happening throughout the Arab World today is *"The genie that came out of the bottle"*. It is nothing less than the awakening of several phenomena that are critical for a stable society, dignity, social justice, democracy, and the rule of law.

The word *"Dignity"* has captured every important dimension of the Arab Spring. It explains why the Arab region is revolting. The typical Arab citizens have felt humiliated in recent decades by their governments who treat their people as without rights and beneath contempt. Many feel they have been denied their basic human rights and their citizenship rights, the result of decades of socioeconomic stress and political deprivation. As Professor Rashid Khalidi [2] explains: the term *'Dignity'* involves a dual demand: dignity of the individual in the face of rulers who humiliated their people and the collective dignity of the whole Arab nation. This was the demand that nationalist leaders rode to power in the 1950s, as they targeted neo-colonialism. After that generation's failures, they were replaced by dictators who provided the "stability" so prized by the West—stability purchased at the price of the dignity of the individual and the collective.

Although the Arab Spring was not, in most cases, really peaceful rather accompanied by violence and bloodshed initiated by the regimes that the masses wanted to change. But one should recognize its positive aspects. People are not anymore afraid or intimidated. They have the courage now to stand up, protest and overthrow ant tyrant regime. The wall of fear has been brought down, and people will stay on the alert. The struggle for democracy, good governance, social justice, human rights and the elimination of corruption will continue.

Freedom and social justice have never been easy or covered with roses. We have always to consider paying heavy price to achieve these goals. The countries of the Arab Spring are not all at the same stage of progress. Some have gone very far ahead; others are still in the midst of the struggle against their brutal regimes; and others are awaiting the genie that may come out of the bottle.

It is worth mentioning the tremendous role played by the social electronic media which became the major vehicle carrying information across borders in spite of the most restrictive measures of censorship and oppression of freedom of press.

Arab Spring: Unforgettable Palestine

The first half of the last century had witnessed the loss of Palestine and the creation of the long lasting suffering of the whole nation of the Holy Land. By 1948, Palestine had become not only a part of Arab politics on the official level, but also an essential element in the political and psychological consciousness of the Arab and Muslim masses and the freedom-lovers worldwide. It has also acted as a focus for Arab political solidarity. Since then, demands and protests have never stopped in support for the Palestinians legitimate rights.

The question of Palestine, subsequently, has had a central role in shaping the political dynamics in the Arab World and is used, by the Arab regimes, as an end to control the Arab street under the excuse of preparing for the *"battle of destiny" i.e., liberation of Palestine*. At the same time, the question has been manipulated and served a powerful tool of legitimating those regimes, who, in reality, have brutally suppressed Palestinians, in several occasions, in order to bring the Palestinian issue under control.

While Arab regimes have used a lip-service sympathy for the Palestinian struggle for self-determination as a way of gaining legitimacy and justifying their dictatorship ruling, that struggle has also served as a tool to deflect their own populations' aspiration for political freedom and deprive them of the basic means for a decent standard of living.

The Arab Spring proves that Palestine question is no longer serves as a tool of legitimating the Arab regimes, and while there is widespread sympathy with the just cause of Palestine, the false slogan of *"the battle of destiny or liberating Palestine"* long promoted by Arab regimes is not being allowed to be used as an excuse for putting democratic rights and social justice on hold. This was nothing but an attempt to run away from the political dues of the reform process.

Arab Spring and Palestine: Same aspirations

For many years now, Palestinians are fighting for their dignity and legitimate rights. Their struggle for liberation has inflamed and inspired Arab peoples around a common goal.

The issue of Palestine has always been present; an integral part of the way Arab regimes failed the people and failed the Arab nation. Every single Arab cries for the Palestinian *Nakba* and their dispossession in 1948. It is there in their hearts and minds generation after generation. Given these sentiments, it is reasonable to ask whether the Palestinian struggle has influenced today's Arab Awakening—-and whether the Arab Awakening has, in turn, energized the Palestinian struggle. The answer to both questions is yes; inspiration has flowed in both directions. [3]

The Palestinian case does not differ much from that of other Arab countries, despite the fact that it has been defined by their major confrontation with the Israeli occupation. This does not mean that the experiences of the neighbouring Arab people will pass without affecting Palestine, entailing demands for more freedoms, democracy and fighting against corruption. It is worth noting that the Arab Spring uprisings are mainly concerned with internal affairs, arranging their priorities according to the national agenda and not the external policy of the state. Despite, the just cause of Palestine was largely existent among the crowds particularly in Egypt.

The large public demonstrations, especially at Tahrir Square in Cairo, represented a historical phenomenon and a lesson for all people, including the Palestinians, on the viability of perseverance and peaceful resistance against injustices and tyrannies and the refusal of provocation by the regime or the occupation. Unity among different sectors in Egypt has achieved results. Palestinians should learn from Egyptian model the importance of ending their internal division and start working together for building their institutions and fighting the barbarian occupation. This will, hopefully, get the Palestinian cause beyond the present dilemma of the closed horizons of the peace talks.

The Palestinians' rights and interests enjoy worldwide support on the peoples' level, in contradiction with policies, interests and alliances that govern international positions. The big query here is about these popular positions and their relative weight in contrast with international interests and policies. The continued Palestinian struggle for freedom, justice and independence has become a symbol for all people, and the Palestinian *Kofiyyeh* has become a symbol for protest and resistance against injustice throughout the world.

This introduces the perception of "soft power" that is based on ethics and values of political position rather than only on military "hard power" or on state interests. Self-determination and freedom from occupation are two ethical and human rights-based positions that the Palestinians can build upon. Consequently, Palestinians should present their great gratitude to all people of the world who support their just struggle, based on ethical commitments to human rights and justice.

Palestinians shouldn't expect much from the American position, despite America's role as a broker of the peace process and as the only superpower at the Security Council and most international institutions. United States Secretary of State John Kerry's recent plan shows how much fragile is the Middle East's US offers. Palestinians should reconstitute their alliances, relationships and long-term strategies to get more international support for their bid of freedom. It is important to closely work with Arab states, friendly states, and regional and international organisations to take serious stands utilizing all available pressures, whether diplomatic, political, economic or legal, to bring the freedom of Palestinian people into existence. The Palestinian diplomatic endeavour has gained political, economic, and academic grounds worldwide. Many countries have given recognition to the independent Palestine and raised the diplomatic representation of Palestinian delegations to the level of missions, particularly in Europe and Latin America.

The peaceful marches against settlements and confiscating land, undertaken by Palestinians and their supporters, were clearly inspired by the model in the Arab World, and they marked the first time the Nakba has been commemorated in this way since Israel dispossessed and exiled the Palestinians in 1948. They have not only given visible public expression to the refugees' demand to exercise their right of return but are also reclaiming the vision of a Palestinian people united by a struggle that goes beyond the so-far fruitless quest for a sovereign, independent state.

Palestinians are now implementing aspects of popular mobilization away from political parties. According to Palestinian human rights attorney Noura Erakat, [4] in the wake of the Arab uprisings young Palestinian citizens of Israel decided to organize Land Day demonstrations independently, limiting the role of traditional Arab political parties. Rami Zurayk noted a similar dramatic change among Palestinians in Lebanon during preparations for the May 15th "Return to Palestine March", where Independents played as great role in organizing and leading that March as the traditional parties.

For their part, Egyptian activists squarely situated the roots of their revolution in the second Palestinian intifada, which erupted in September 2000. In his interview with Professor Mark LeVine, [5] the Egyptian blogger and activist Hossam El-Hamalawy said: "The outbreak of the al-Aqsa intifada was especially important because in the 1980s-90s, street activism had been effectively shut down by the government as part of the fight against Islamist insurgents. It only continued to exist inside university campuses or party headquarters. But when the 2000 intifada erupted and Al- Jazeera started airing images of it, it inspired our youth to take to the streets, in the same way we've been inspired by Tunisia today". [6]

The greatest promise of the Arab Spring is that Arabs will reclaim the vision of a larger body within which they can operate, an Arab region built not on ethnic or religious purity but bound by a common striving for human rights and fundamental freedoms. For Palestinians, perhaps the most significant inspiration of the Spring has been the way in which it has restored hope and their vision that through struggle they can win self-determination and human rights; and if the revolutions bring about democratically elected governments in some Arab countries, this will energize the Palestinian cause, given the strength of popular Arab support for it.

What is Accomplished?

The fundamental change and development, on the Palestinian level, was shaping their political consciousness. Inspired by the Arab Spring, Palestinians are trying to reconcile between the two main parties—Fatah and Hamas. Another important development is that the Arab Spring was one of the key factors contributed to the Palestinian decision to pursue recognition at the United Nations. The Palestinian President responded to growing public expectations despite all pressures to give up or postpone this United Nations bid. These developments also give the Palestinians a new set of diplomatic options, and a potential source of pressure that can be intensified or relaxed with changing circumstances.

The diplomatic success Palestinians has achieved was at the UNISCO with an overwhelming majority (107 for, 14 against, 52 abstentions) voting in favour of admitting Palestine as a full privileged member at this United Nations agency. Other achievements for the Palestinians are the prisoners' release.

Conclusion

The Arab Spring was an inevitable result of year of injustice. It has achieved much positive changes on the political, economic, and social levels. The era of tyranny and dictatorship in the Arab World is now part of the ugly past. *The main message of the Arab Spring to the Palestinian people is that the quest for freedom, democracy, and social justice is intertwined.* Their aspirations remain unfulfilled unless they can restore their national unity. On the other hand, as the Spring continues, more and more Palestinians are expanding their vision beyond the search for statehood and finding ways to re-establish core principles of the struggle such as self-determination, the right of return, freedom and equality. Israel, which through its steady settlement expansion in the West Bank has made the creation of an independent Palestinian state impossible, may see this as a mortal threat, but the consequences are clear: as the two-state solution recedes, a federal single state in which all citizens have equal rights and duties looms ever larger.

Endnotes

1. Fromkin, David (1989), "A Peace to End All Peace: The Fall of the Ottoman Empire and the Creation of the Modern Middle East", New York: Owl, pp. 286-288.
2. Rashid Khalidi, Edward Said Professor of Arab Studies at Columbia University, is the author, most recently, of *The Iron Cage: The Story of the Palestinian Struggle for Statehood.* For more information, please see:
http://www.campus-watch.org/article/id/11638,and,
http://www.intifada-palestine.com/2011/03/rashid-khalidithe-arab-spring.
3. Rami Zurayk, *Food, Farming, and Freedom: Sowing the Arab Spring,* Virginia: Just World Books, 2011.
4. Noura Erakat is a Palestinian human rights attorney and activist. She is currently an adjunct professor of international human rights law in the Middle East at Georgetown University and the Legal Advocacy Coordinator for the Badil Centre for Palestinian Refugee and Residency Rights. Please see:
http://uspcn.org/2011/05/04/palestinian-youth-new-movement-new-borders-by-noura-erekat.
5. Mark LeVine is a professor of history at UC Irvine and senior visiting researcher at the Centre for Middle Eastern Studies at Lund University in Sweden. His most recent books are Heavy Metal Islam (Random House) and Impossible Peace: Israel/Palestine Since 1989 (Zed Books).
6. Hossam El-Hamalawy, is an Egyptian journalist and blogger for the website 3arabawy. Please see:
http://www.aljazeera.com/indepth/features/2011/01/201112792728200271.html.

Index

Index